THE
ENTREPRENEUR'S
≣ MANUAL

THE ENTREPRENEUR'S MANUAL

Business Start-Ups, Spin-Offs, and Innovative Management

RICHARD M. WHITE, Jr.

CHILTON BOOK COMPANY

Radnor, Pennsylvania

8 9 0 1 2 3   6 5 4 3 2 1

TO THE READER. . . .

I hope you have at least half as much fun
in the reading as I've had in the writing.

Contents

THE
ENTREPRENEUR'S
MANUAL

Before We Start

This book has four primary purposes. They are:

(1)   To give you a workbook which explains, in everyday English, the simple and straightforward machinery to convert your ideas into a viable business.

(2)   To give you a manual which shows the techniques involved in uncovering market gaps (those which will support a company) and to translate these gaps into real products and services.

(3)   To give you the control tools which maximize profits. As a management consultant, I see "work hard . . . not smart" control systems continually enforced. The companies which enforce these wasteful methods pay a very high price through reduced personnel efficiencies, profits, sales, and missed opportunities. This manual will show the very practical "work smart" controls: Management-By-Objective, Management-By-Exception, and Management-By-Motivation systems that not only translate into profits but address the primary failure modes of business.

(4)   To eliminate the excess of misinformation, rumors, and bad counsel that exists in abundance concerning business start-ups.

ABOUT THE FORMAT

At the beginning of each major paragraph, you'll find a heading followed by the letters "M," "IS," "RS," or "F." These letters stand for "Manufacturing" (nationwide distribution) "Industrial Services" (nationwide), "Retail Sales" or "Retail Services" (local only), and

"Franchise" (local only). These keys allow you to swiftly identify those areas which apply to your interests and to ignore those sections which aren't particularly relevant to you.

You'll also see that the main text is amplified with indicated minor points, examples, and "cameos" that are miniature case histories. These are all identified by headings, and the cameos are printed differently. These features should allow you to:

(1) Read the primary text undistracted by its support information until you wish to dwell on a specific subject, and

(2) Give the book to your spouse just to read the cameos. Most of them are extremely interesting true stories which highlight what you are going through in your business start-up. You'll find that they can be read in an evening, winning you greater empathy and understanding for your needs as you address each milestone.

ABOUT THE CAMEOS   M, IS, RS, F

As a management and marketing consultant, I must remain silent about my clients' confidential and proprietary information in the same way a lawyer must remain silent about privileged information. Though this confidentiality is essential for obvious reasons, it certainly handicaps the consultant/author who wishes to use true examples to illustrate the reasons for certain actions.

I have therefore disguised the individuals in the cameos to protect my clients' proprietary plans and strategies. All cameos about my clients have been read by them and approved by them before this book was published. If we accidentally hit upon any non-client's plans, please realize that it was totally unintentional.

In some cases, we have written about non-clients whose case histories are in the public domain. There are a few of these cases that our researchers couldn't verify but they were of such value, that we wrote them anyway. As an example, there is the story about ITEK, an extremely successful conglomerate whose name originally stood for "I Took Eastman Kodak." Though several Rochester old timers swear that this case history is true, it is denied by present Eastman and ITEK management. True or false, the rumor certainly helped ITEK in its formative stages and therefore is included in this book to illustrate the value of your company's name.

THE RELIABILITY OF THE TECHNIQUES, SYSTEMS, FORMULAS, AND RECOMMENDATIONS OF THIS BOOK   M, IS, RS, F

Most of the strategies described in this book have been used by over 600 of our firm's clients for the past five years with an over 80% success rate. We define a success as a company which has made it through our fourth significant milestone (market penetration).

The techniques, systems, formulas, and strategies of our book have the following strengths and weaknesses:

STRENGTHS

(1) The majority of our clients have generated cash flows prior to approaching the venture capitalists. Not only did these cash flows significantly lower these companies' investment needs, they allowed our clients to give the image of an ongoing venture instead of just another risky start-up. The founders therefore maintained great equity and management controls over their companies.

(2) This book's control systems keep a management team (founders and employees) on track throughout the complete process.

(3) The speed with which these companies reached their fourth milestone (market penetration) was considerably faster than those start-ups which utilized the old classical techniques. We "guestimate" that most did it in one-half of the time on one-half of the dollars.

WEAKNESSES

(1) Since my company (Business Solutions—a consortium of 20 consultants who spend their non-prime hours working with founders) is always pretty close to saturation, we select only those clients who are addressing a growth industry and who are mature (mature meaning not age but those who accept things as they are instead of how they wished they were). Therefore, the techniques of our book have been tested only with a tiny sample and this sample size is far from representative of all who practice entrepreneurship.

(2) These techniques work as well or as badly as the capabilities of those who practice them.

(3) Since we have only worked with start-ups for 5 years now, we have no feel for how our clients will prosper after 10 years—after 20 years. The long range prospects look excellent with well over 95% of those clients who made it through the fourth milestone (80% of our clients) in excellent shape, however the proof is in the pudding and we'll not know how this pudding tastes for another decade.

HOW THIS BOOK WAS WRITTEN   M, IS, RS, F

Twice monthly, we hold a "murderers' row" session among our 20 consultants. Each consultant must stand before his 19 devil's advocates and give a progress report on each client. Then each consultant critiques the client's progress with respect to his specific discipline (i.e., manufacturing, marketing, sales, administration, finance, quality assurance or QA, etc.). These sessions are rarely dull and the cross-brain fertilization keeps us all broad and young. Frequently there's blood on the carpet after these sessions.

We treated this book as if it were a client, and each session I was forced to defend it before these killers. If you ever want an experience, try to float a book past 19 other consultants, each more knowledgeable about his specific discipline than you are. Torpedoes come from every conceivable angle.

Though I am claiming sole authorship (I have the scars to prove it), in truth there are 19 not-so-silent "silent co-authors." Please refer to the addendum for these people's contributions.

GIVE ME A FOUNDER WHO ISN'T WEALTHY
M, IS, RS, F

This book is written to the person who isn't wealthy and who must make every dollar do 10 dollars worth of work. In fact, being wealthy is a significant handicap in a start-up situation. Almost all of our largest and best-run companies were begun by people who couldn't afford failure. Since they couldn't afford it they didn't tolerate it—and therefore succeeded. The hungrier you are, the less you will allow half-hearted attempts.

EVERYTHING MUST MAKE SENSE FOR YOUR COMPANY
OR IT'S PROBABLY WRONG   M, IS, RS, F

Every strategy, every tactic, every system, every step, every component, and every formula that you get from this book or from any other source must make complete sense to you for your specific goals or it's probably wrong for your situation. Since there is a ton of mis-information, bad counsel, false rumors, and lousy advice available to everyone who is trying to pioneer new territories, be on guard. If something appears illogical to you and you have the normal allotment of brains and common sense, then it is probably part of that ton of mis-information.

CAMEO: THE ACCIDENTAL START-UP, OUR OKIE
MECHANIC, PART 1   M, IS, RS, F

This is my favorite case study because an uneducated "Okie" who had a lot of common sense, innovation, and drive really built a company of value under horrible handicaps.

It was at the height of the great depression (the early 1930s) when an out-of-work oil field mechanic decided that it was ridiculous for oil companies to install permanent drilling derricks over each drill sight. He conceived the concept of a portable drilling rig which revolutionized the oil industry.

Now this out-of-work mechanic had a few handicaps that might lead you to believe that he would never make a successful entrepreneur. He could barely read and couldn't write. He had absolutely no experience in either management or finance and therefore developed some unique opinions that should have killed his company's chances. For example, he believed, "No man who wears a necktie can be trusted." And, "Never put your money in a bank or do business with a banker or you'll lose it all." And "Never plan beyond today. The Lord will take care of tomorrow regardless of how much you fret."

He was a frugal man so that when he was laid-off, he had over $400 hidden in a sock (a small fortune in that era). He watched his savings dwindle to $325 in three months while he searched for "respectable" work and then he decided to risk $200 on his portable drilling rig concept. At this point the mechanic sold the International Harvester Truck dealer of Tulsa on his concept and borrowed a ten ton truck to demonstrate (the dealer couldn't move his inventory and agreed to the loan if he received payment-in-full when the mechanic sold his rig). He rented (at $10/month) a 50-ton draw-works from a hoist manufacturer (balance to be paid when the rig was sold). He purchased usable scrap steel ($30 down and $70 when the rig was sold) and spent all of his spare time (the hours when he wasn't standing in long lines looking for work) building his rig. It took him three months.

On his first demonstration, the drilling manager immediately saw the advantages of the concept and immediately bought the demonstrator. Oddly enough, the mechanic was thinking of asking for $7,500 (taking price he hoped would be at least $5,000) but when the manager seemed so enthused, the mechanic raised his price to $10,000. When the manager didn't balk, he then added $3,500 for the truck. He left the demonstration rig at the sight and hitchhiked home to await his $13,500 payment. He felt that the $8,500 profits would hold his sock in order until he found "respectable" work. However, when the check came, it was accompanied by an order for 10 more units at $13,500 each.

This caused our mechanic a very real personal problem. One cannot build 10 drilling rigs in his spare time and still search for proper work. If he accepted the order, he might miss out on a safe job. While he debated as to whether to return the order or not, another oil company (whom he had never demonstrated to) sent him a purchase order for 15 rigs, and so the mechanic's company was born.

Now $8,500 doesn't go too far when you want to build 25 drilling rigs unless you use some sound money-leveraging principles. Here's how our Okie made money stretch:

He put an advertisement in the local paper requesting the cream of mechanics for top wages (75¢ an hour) provided that the candidates accept the following terms: (a) they would have to work 50 hours/week in a farmer's barn (which he rented for $5/month); (b) they would be given only rent money and groceries until the rigs were delivered and payments were made; and (c) no interest would be paid on back wages. Five applicants for every opening showed up and he selected the cream.

Since this was a sizable order for both the truck and hoist dealers, they agreed to supply him with 5% down and the balance when he was paid. Of course no interest was charged.

He found several grocery stores which agreed to sell him all of the food his employees needed at 50% down, the balance when he got paid. Thereafter, every worker received a large sack of groceries each evening after work.

The scrap steel dealers drove a harder bargain. They received 25% down, 25% after two months, and the balance when he got paid.

Since excess inventories of paint, cables, chains, etc. existed, he rarely paid over 5% down and the balance when payments were received.

When the twenty-fifth drilling rig was delivered, his sock had dwindled down to $2,300. When he was finally paid, the company was in a cash-rich posture, a position which never changed until it was sold in the 1950s.

There were some problems which might amuse you. The management organization consisted of just the mechanic for the first 15 months. When government auditors came in to inspect the books, they were unhappy to learn that there were no books. The record keeping system was very simple. In the top right hand drawer of the company's only desk, all unfilled orders were kept. In the upper left hand drawer, all unpaid bills were kept. When an order was filled or a bill paid, it was pulled from the drawer and thrown in the wastebasket. "That way, we could always open a drawer and know what was coming in and what was going out." All other records were kept in the mechanic's head.

The auditors didn't feel that this was an acceptable accounting system and gave our Okie 30 days to develop proper records. He hired his first staff man, a cousin of one of his mechanics who was an educated man (he had finished high school and had once had a bookkeeping course). When the auditors returned 30 days later, they found a single sheet of paper which was a combined balance sheet, income statement, and miscellaneous additional items. They were extremely unhappy and when they started to padlock the door, the president pulled out a dozen socks (filled with about $650,000 in cash) and told them to "take what you think is fair."

When they took more than what the president felt was fair, he hired a qualified accountant, told him to leave his neckties at home, and to protect him the "next time those bandits come." The new controller was also given the following instructions: "Don't put a penny in the banks. Put 10% of all cash into dimes so that we can melt them down for silver if we have to. Don't keep any bills larger than a $5 bill because counterfeiters never work that low."

For months, this controller was developing ulcers concerning himself about the vast amounts of unprotected cash he had to carry. Then he started cutting out newspaper stories of holdups and left them on the president's desk. After several months and dozens of stories of how people had lost everything in holdups, the controller asked his president about the high risks they were taking with their bundles of cash. It was then that he learned that his president hadn't read the newspaper clippings because he could hardly read. So the controller read him the clippings aloud, scared the president, and was allowed to place half of the company's cash in five different banks. The other half had to remain in reachable cash. When the controller retired 20 years later, he handed his replacement in excess of $4,000,000 in dimes, ones, and fives. The company had never been robbed.

From a production and service standpoint, this company also had unique problems. For the first 250 units produced, the company never used anything but scrap steel. This forced unique production practices. Each rig was completely built by one master mechanic and three apprentices. Since the materials were scrap, each rig had to be engineered and built from supplies on hand. No records were ever kept and since serial number 131 was completely different from serial numbers 130 and 132, the field service people had to be extremely flexible and innovative. However, since he only hired the cream, this was never a real problem. When the Japanese government started buying all of the scrap steel that they could get their hands on, the prices rose so the Okie was finally forced to use new steel.

In the late thirties, the oil companies' demands finally exceeded his master mechanics' engineering abilities and he was forced to hire a real engineer. When the poor man first showed up to work, there wasn't one blueprint or one written production instruction in the entire company (it now employed over 500 people: 1 accountant, 1 engineer, 1 woman who handled all clerical jobs, 1 president, and 496 production mechanics). It took this engineer four years to convert the company to sound engineering control systems.

The company continued to be unique in many operating modes. When the Second World War hit, the government asked them to quote on building barrage balloon launchers. They quoted $12,000 while the next lowest bidder quoted $62,000. The company made $8,000 per launcher in profits while their competitors made less than $6,000 per launcher.

These uneducated people pioneered many of the innovative and sophisticated techniques used by today's most progressive companies. Let's come back to our Okie mechanic in later cameos to illustrate common sense solutions.

1 · An Overview of Your Start-up's Hurdles

PROLOGUE   M, IS, RS, F

If you had to boil this book down to a few pages, you would probably derive this first chapter's worksheet outlines. Use these worksheets as checklists to determine your company's status and progress. Make certain that you aren't unintentionally overlooking any important point.

Minor Point 1-1: Your Probabilities of Success   M, IS, RS, F

The saying, "figures never lie but liars figure" probably applies to this section because the data varies extremely according to whose statistics you use.

According to the Small Business Administration, approximately 50,000 new business start-ups open their doors every year. Eighty percent of these are doomed to failure within three years. However, if you dig a little deeper, you'll discover that 90% of these failures were due to bad management, inadequate financing, or dependence upon a stagnant or decaying market. Also, SBA considers every firm that is sold, merges, changes its name, or moves away from its start-up address a failure because their detection system doesn't cope with these variables.

The Bank of America's investment company has almost opposite data. The Small Business Investment Co. (SBIC) developed the following table:

8

Investment Growth	*Probabilities*
Greater than 10 to 1 growth in 5 years	17%
Greater than 5 to 1 growth in 5 years	42%
Greater than 3 to 1 growth in 5 years	33%
Failures within 5 years	8%

However, realize that the Bank of America's figures are just as biased as the government's figures because the bank will only invest in a start-up which: (1) has a strong management team, (2) addresses a growth industry or defines an easily capturable market segment, (3) requests adequate financing, and (4) has well-defined company objectives, philosophies, operating procedures, and projections. Since the bank only tracked those companies in which they invested and since they only invested in start-ups which met the four above requirements, you would expect their probabilities of success to be considerably higher than the government's.

Business Solutions' projections are even more biased than the bank's.

Therefore, your probability of success is totally dependent upon the techniques that you use. If you do things right, you stand a better than 80% probability of success. Otherwise, you stand a great chance of failing.

OVERVIEW WORKSHEET OF YOUR START-UP   M, IS, RS, F

The following table attempts to give you the components involved in a typical start-up and the relative importance (weightings) of each component as it applies to Manufacturing, Industrial Services, Retail Sales (or Services), and Franchises.

Be aware that we usually tailor these index points to each specific client but were forced to set arbitrary values for this book. In setting these values, we made assumptions which may or may not be true for your company. As an example, the value of a patent for most of our start-ups isn't too significant because very few have significant patentable breakthroughs, have the ability to police, protect, or enforce their patents, and have sufficient funds to properly get international protections (and therefore by just getting U.S. patents, they disclose to foreign manufacturers how to produce and import their products). As another example, we assume that you aren't wealthy and therefore must attract significant venture capital from sophisticated money sources (99% of the capital available to start-ups). We therefore weigh more heavily venture capital appetite-whetting techniques, your business plan, your business plan presentations, and your capital negotiations—more heavily than if you are financially independent, are not interested in retaining maximum management and ownership controls, or have assured non-sophisticated investors. See pages 10–13 for the worksheets.

I. THE SELECTION OF YOUR PRODUCT OR SERVICE

<table>
<tr><th></th><th colspan="4">Business Solutions Index</th></tr>
<tr><th></th><th>M</th><th>IS</th><th>RS</th><th>F</th></tr>
<tr><td>A. Define your personal requirements.</td><td>25</td><td>25</td><td>25</td><td>25</td></tr>
<tr><td>B. Define your company's broad-brush objectives and requirements.</td><td>25</td><td>25</td><td>25</td><td>25</td></tr>
<tr><td>C. Determine if A and B above are in harmony.</td><td>25</td><td>25</td><td>25</td><td>25</td></tr>
<tr><td>D. Determine the growth industries.</td><td>100</td><td>100</td><td>10</td><td>20</td></tr>
<tr><td>E. Segment these growth industries into their component parts.</td><td>50</td><td>50</td><td>25</td><td>5</td></tr>
<tr><td>F. Perform a market gap analysis of these segments.</td><td>100</td><td>100</td><td>25</td><td>5</td></tr>
<tr><td>G. Evaluate the gaps uncovered with respect to A and B above and select those which are in harmony with your needs.</td><td>25</td><td>25</td><td>25</td><td>25</td></tr>
<tr><td>H. Perform disguised and independent market tests on G's results.</td><td>75</td><td>50</td><td>25</td><td>10</td></tr>
<tr><td>I. Verify that the independent tests of I correlate with each other.</td><td>25</td><td>25</td><td>15</td><td>10</td></tr>
<tr><td>J. Make an unemotional decision as to which gap you'll address first.</td><td>100</td><td>100</td><td>10</td><td>20</td></tr>
</table>

II. MANAGEMENT AND PERSONNEL DEVELOPMENT

<table>
<tr><td>A. Determine the disciplines, personalities, experiences, and other qualifications that your founders and managers must have.</td><td>25</td><td>25</td><td>25</td><td>25</td></tr>
<tr><td>B. Determine the disciplines, personalities, experiences, and other qualifications that your key employees must have.</td><td>25</td><td>25</td><td>25</td><td>25</td></tr>
<tr><td>C. Develop, in broad strokes, your start-up's time base.</td><td>25</td><td>25</td><td>25</td><td>25</td></tr>
<tr><td>D. Determine the number of founders and employees that you'll need to meet C's conclusions.</td><td>10</td><td>10</td><td>10</td><td>10</td></tr>
<tr><td>E. Perform pre-screening techniques to select the strongest candidates defined in A, B, and D above.</td><td>150</td><td>200</td><td>50</td><td>25</td></tr>
</table>

F.	Test interactively your candidates and select those individuals who produce the best team "chemistry" and capabilities.	200	250	100	50
G.	Allow each candidate to play a major role in selecting his bosses, his peers, and his subordinates.	25	25	25	25
H.	Develop interactively your start-up's goals, objectives, philosophies, incentive systems, equity postures, organization, financial flexibilities, image, and priorities.	200	200	50	50
I.	Implement effective incentive systems.	250	350	100	100
J.	Implement effective management-by-objectives and management-by-exceptions systems.	200	200	200	200
K.	Develop short and long range time bases that are in harmony with H above.	100	100	100	100
L.	Continue to test, evaluate, and take corrective action on your team's capabilities.	50	75	50	25
M.	Begin to turn cash immediately.	250	250	100	100
N.	Develop your many images to capitalists, customers, fellow founders, and vendors.	75	100	75	100
O.	Meet your first objectives and priorities fast to establish a success momentum.	100	100	100	100
P.	Develop and maintain a stimulating and pleasant work atmosphere.	100	100	100	100

III. DEVELOP YOUR PRODUCTS AND SERVICES

A.	Develop your first products and services.	250	250	100	N/A
B.	Verify that A above continues to meet your market's demand and all of your company's objectives.	100	150	100	250
C.	Establish patent disclosures, copyrights, trademarks, and other protections.	50	50	N/A	N/A
D.	Determine optimum store locations.	N/A	50	1,000	1,000
E.	Develop your market profiles.	250	150	100	100
F.	Investigate and test your sales networks.	250	250	N/A	N/A
G.	Verify that your company's attributes developed in H of II above are still valid.	100	100	100	100

	M	IS	RS	F
IV. DEVELOP YOUR BUSINESS PLAN				
A. Develop your sales forecasting for five years.	250	150	100	100
B. Develop your projected budgets to meet these five years of sales forecasts.	100	100	100	100
C. Develop your proforma (projected) financial plans for five years.	200	200	200	200
D. Determine your cash flows for these five years.	200	200	200	200
E. Develop sound money-leveraging principles to lower your needs for cash injections.	100	100	150	100
F. Institute strong fiscal control systems.	100	100	150	150
G. Initiate profit center philosophies.	150	200	150	100
H. Prime your references for: yourself, your founders, your sales networks, your prime customers, and your vendors.	100	100	100	100
I. Develop your business plan so that it is both a sales document to attract capital and a blueprint on how you'll run your company.	150	150	150	100
J. Determine which of the venture capital avenues you will pursue and vector your plan to satisfy those avenues' requirements.	250	200	100	100
K. Determine the ideal mixes of these venture capital avenues and develop your asking and taking prices for the amounts of equity and management controls you'll surrender to attract your needed funds.	150	200	100	100
V. ATTRACT YOUR CAPITAL				
A. Perform appetite-whetting techniques prior to seeking capital.	300	300	150	100
B. Give the image of an ongoing company instead of just another start-up or spin-off.	500	500	100	100

	C	D	E	F
C. Give professional presentations to the venture capitalists.	150	150	250	100
D. Conduct yourself professionally in your preliminary negotiations.	100	100	100	100
E. Conduct yourself professionally in your final negotiations.	250	250	250	250

VI. RAPID MARKET PENETRATION

A. Set up, train, and motivate your sales networks.	250	150	N/A	N/A
B. Initiate the ongoing systems to maintain proper training and motivations of these networks.	350	250	N/A	N/A
C. Initiate the systems to sustain your sales networks and your customers.	350	300	N/A	N/A
D. Make all non-sales personnel sales oriented.	100	100	100	100
E. Keep your company the mirror image of your customers' needs.	500	500	500	500

VII. CONTINUING GROWTH AND HEALTH

A. Follow your business plan. When it becomes obsolete, update it and follow the update.	100	100	100	100
B. Follow your management-by-objectives and management-by-exceptions systems.	200	200	200	200
C. Remain lean, young, hungry, and innovative.	1,000	1,000	1,000	1,000
D. Become concerned when (a) your growth does not at least double your industry's growth; (b) when your systems do not flag pending problems long before they become actual problems; (c) your employees' incentives do not equal at least 50% of their salaries; and (d) your late shipments, your quality problems, and your customer returns equal 0.1% of your shipments.	200	200	200	200

THE USUAL PITFALLS OF A START-UP M, IS, RS, F

The following table was developed from Business Solutions' clients (whom we consider relatively sophisticated individuals). Percentages would probably increase significantly if the entire 50,000 per year start-up rate was available.

	Description	*Percentages of Occurrences*
1.	Premature Incorporation	32%
2.	Premature Product Releases	27%
3.	Premature Patents	41%
4.	Security Indiscretions	21%
5.	Improper Market Testing	73%
6.	Improper Market Segmentation	77%
7.	Improper Price Setting	81%
8.	Weak Marketing Tactics	47%
9.	Incorrect Sales Forecasting	73%
10.	Premature Approach of Venture Capital Avenues	61%
11.	Incomplete Homework of the Venture Capital Avenues	61%
12.	Poor Venture Capital Appetite-Whetting Techniques	84%
13.	Poor Market Gap Analysis	61%
14.	Management Weaknesses and Gaps	31%
15.	Addressed Stagnant or Decaying Markets	21%
16.	Poor Retail Locations	16%
17.	Weak Key Employees	41%
18.	Weak Money-Leveraging Methods	62%
19.	Lack of Realization of the Necessity to Turn Cash Immediately	76%
20.	Lack of Fiscal Responsibilities	28%
21.	Improper Control Systems	38%
22.	Weak Incentive Systems	93%
23.	Poor Self-Discipline	11%
24.	Weak Business Plans	73%
25.	Weak Motivation	8%
26.	Dishonesty With Self or Partners	11%
27.	Poor Financial Projections	41%
28.	Poor Communications	31%
29.	Personal Specifications in Conflict with Start-Up's Goals and Objectives	19%
30.	Lack of Understanding of Venture Capitalists' Goals	27%
31.	The Lack of That Zest for Life Which Sustains a Start-Up	14%
32.	Inability of Spouse to Accept the Entrepreneur's Drives and Values	29%

HOW VENTURE CAPITALISTS WEIGHT
A START-UP   M, IS, RS, F

This is probably the most important table of the first chapter because it graphically illustrates the importance of your management team. These weightings surprise most people because they show that if you simply attract top flight managers and address a growth industry you stand between a 70% and 90% chance of succeeding even before you develop your products and services. If you attract weak people, you have a 50% probability of failing regardless of how great the other factors are. This is why we will devote a significant portion of this book to showing the techniques of locating and welding a top grade founders' team.

THE MANUFACTURING START-UP

Category	Present Weighting
The Management Team	50–60
The Growth Industry Addressed	20–30
The Product	10–20
The Marketing and Finance Plans	5–10

THE NATIONWIDE INDUSTRIAL
SERVICE START-UP

Category	Percent Weighting
The Management Team	60–90
The Key Employees	10–30
The Growth Industry Addressed	10–20
The Service	10–15
The Marketing and Finance Plans	1–5

THE LOCAL RETAIL SALES OR RETAIL
SERVICE START-UP

Category	Percent Weighting
The Management Team	30–50
The Locations	40–50
The Products and Services	5–10
The Marketing and Finance Plans	1–5

THE LOCAL FRANCHISE START-UP

Category	Percent Weighting
The Management Team	20–50
The Franchisor	20–50
The Locations	10–50
The Growth Industry Addressed	10–30
The Products and Services	10–15
The Marketing and Finance Plans	5–10

THE MILESTONES OF A START-UP   M, IS, RS, F

Each successful start-up follows the same basic stages of development. We of Business Solutions define these stages as "Significant Milestones" and list them as follows:

(1)   The discovery of a viable market segment and the products (or services) which have enough demand in that segment to meet both your company's and your founders' goals and objectives.

(2)   The formation and development of an outstanding and well-oiled founders' team. (This includes the nucleus of your management team, the nuclei of your key employee teams, and the core of your board of directors).

(3)   The attraction of venture capital on your terms. (This includes the assurance of management controls, founders' ownerships, and ample options for future rounds of financing—provided that you perform).

(4)   Proper market penetration. (This includes the setting up, training, motivation, and sustaining of national distribution networks, gaining the purchasing loyalties of your industry's prime accounts, and the security of a guaranteed cash flow as divorced as possible from outside economic pressures).

(5)   The growth stages to industry leadership and the attainment of the rewards to both your company and your founders in direct proportion to your performances.

(6)   The freeing of the founders so that they may pursue their required life styles with both security and total control over their finances and time.

It is the intent of this book to discuss in depth the various tested techniques which will allow you to reach your fifth milestone reliably and in such a way that both the fifth and sixth stages follow naturally.

The book progresses as follows:

Spade Work: Chapters One through Three. There is a host of rumors, mis-information, and wishful thinking printed by "experts" that must be cleared before we can get into the meat of our subject. In the first three chapters, we'll cover those areas which are most frequently misunderstood so that you won't waste valuable dollars and time in false starts and wheel spinning.

Milestone One: Chapters Four and Five.
Milestone Two: Chapters Six through Nine.
Milestone Three: Chapters Nine through Thirteen.
Milestone Four: Chapters Fourteen through Eighteen.

The market penetration milestone is by far the most abused milestone. Since most founders neither understand sales nor the marketing machinery which makes sales work, their start-ups flounder.

CONTROL SYSTEMS   M, IS, RS, F

I am a firm believer in management-by-objectives systems, management-by-exceptions systems, and management-by-motivations systems, because of their outstanding track records with our clients. Throughout this book, you'll read of different control systems which fall into one or more of these three categories. Let's cover the definitions and philosophies of these essential systems now so that we don't have to break our train-of-thought when we implement them in the following chapters.

MANAGEMENT-BY-OBJECTIVES CONTROLS (MBO)

This is that family of control systems which force all employees, all groups, and all departments to strive to meet the company's goals first and their individual goals last.

Please observe that we mean operative systems . . . not just cheap lip service. The control systems must be workable and reliable to buy you their benefits.

The philosophies behind MBO control systems are obvious. They are:

(1) They force you and your co-founders to define your company's objectives, communicate these objectives down to the lowest employee, and to integrate them into all of your other controls.

(2) They force a singleness of purpose upon your complete founders' team. Briefly, if you and I are on the same management team and we have the same objectives, then we can function independently with a minimum of problems. However, if we both have different objectives, we cannot function even dependently. (As an example, let's say that you are profit-and-growth oriented and though I give these objectives lip service, in truth I am ego- and status-oriented. I can think of no decision or solution that I

could make that would satisfy you and none that you could make that would please me. On the other hand, if I were truly profit-and-growth directed, then we could be 3,000 miles apart and independently make decisions that would please each other.)

(3)   Not only does this singleness of purpose apply to individuals, it also applies to groups and departments. How many companies do you know of who have the attitude, "What's good for QA is good for the company" instead of, "What's good for the company is good for QA"? The primary cause of putting the cart before the horse is that top management does not communicate its company's directions and goals down to its middle management and it does not implement the working systems to enforce these objectives.

(4)   They force you to priority your company's objectives and address those objectives first which have the greatest benefits.

MANAGEMENT-BY-EXCEPTIONS CONTROLS (MBE)

This is a group of control systems which allow your people to ignore ongoing routine operations until these operations have a difficulty. Then a "flag" is raised calling your people's attention to the problem.

It is estimated that approximately 75% of top management's time and 95%–100% of middle and lower management's time is invested in making routine and predictable decisions. Not only is this lack of ongoing controls expensive in dollars, time, frustrations, and error modes, it forces your people to react instead of pro-act, it stifles innovations, and it causes a work-hard instead of work-smart atmosphere.

If any manager has to invest more than 25% of his time in routine decisions, if greater than 0.1% of your shipments are late, if your yield rates are less than 95%, if your rework requirements are greater than 2%, or if any of your people have to make the same decision more than X times each month, then it is a probability that your MBE control systems have problems.

MANAGEMENT-BY-MOTIVATIONS CONTROLS (MBM)

This is a relatively new field which appears to be extremely lucrative. Management-By-Motivations controls are simply those controls which reward or punish individuals, groups, and departments for their performances in meeting (or not meeting) their company's objectives.

MBM systems are usually tagged onto the MBO and MBE control systems and add the muscle to force everyone to want to meet these objectives. The average MBM system produces three times its costs in profits (if profits are an objective of your company). A combination of good MBM systems will allow your employees to make as much in rewards as they do in hourly pay. MBM systems not only reward (or punish) individual performances, they also reward (or punish) team efforts. The peer pressures of teammates turn out to be a far stronger control than any management controls yet devised. The surface of MBM systems has just been scratched and in coming years, this family of controls shows promise of being the most lucrative tool yet devised for management.

Minor Point 1-2: The Effects' Flags of Weak Management-By-Objectives Control Systems   M, IS

When a consultant goes into a new client's company, he has several dozen immediate flags which illuminate the likelihood of a problem. We all are familiar with the flags of weak Management-By-Objectives controls. Be very thankful that a significant number of American companies have fallen into this failure mode. It allows you to penetrate their industry and their customer base with a minimum of effort. The evolution always seems to follow this path:

First: The company's objectives become fuzzy in top management and therefore contrary and conflicting goals are passed down. Frustration in middle management occurs.

Second: Since the company's objectives are blurred, the control systems to assure their being met are either ignored or never set up.

Third: Empires begin to form and grow. Research and development (R&D) direction becomes out of phase with marketing, administration begins to follow many directions and becomes a scaler (force without direction) instead of a vector quantity. Sales is frustrated and directionless and its problems translate into production and quality problems. These departments attempt to follow sales' directionless lead.

Fourth: As frustrations begin to develop in all departments, buck passing and politics replace meaningful communications. Factions develop, the lines of differences are drawn and hardened, and soon politics is more important than profits.

Fifth: Overheads increase, flexibilities decrease, sales stagnate, profits plateau and begin to drop, protecting-of-flanks replaces constructive work, and filling in forms replaces thinking.

THE MAXIMS OF MANAGEMENT   M, IS, RS, F

The last thing that we want to do is invest your time in reading the obvious. These maxims are self-evident and therefore need no further discussions.

THE MANAGEMENT-BY-OBJECTIVES MAXIMS

(1)   Surround yourself with the highest caliber people. Remember that first rate people hire first rate people—while second rate people hire third rate people.

(2)   As a manager, you are the catalyst which interacts with your people and forces team accomplishments that are far superior to what you could expect from a group of individuals. The whole is far greater than the sum of its people in a well managed operation.

(3)   Enjoy the task of delegating authority. This creates a healthy climate for growth (both of your team and the individuals who make up the team).

(4)   Insist on planning for both yourself and your subordinates. Without planning, success is accidental. Be jealous of your time and budget it skillfully.

(5)   Order your priorities so that work done addresses the potentially largest yields.

(6)   Assume that as a manager, you will be judged by the work that gets done—not the work that you do.

(7)   Have the courage to make decisions. Also have the courage to reverse them.

(8)   Know your responsibilities in depth. Assume the corresponding authorities. If these two parameters (responsibility and authority) are out of balance, correcting this situation should be the first priority of the project.

(9)   Do not let the defeat of one battle alter your determination to win the war. However, do allow your course to victory to be altered.

THE MANAGEMENT-BY-EXCEPTIONS MAXIMS

(1)   Realize that your skill in recognizing problems is just as important as your ability to solve the problems once they surface and are illuminated. The key is to implement control systems which "flag" problem areas before they affect effects.

(2)   Look at each problem within the frame of reference of your company as a whole (its organization as a whole). If it doesn't fit, you may be solving the wrong problem. If you cannot see your company as a whole, you may be a significant part of the cause of the problem.

(3)   For every effect, there is a cause. Cure causes and the effects will be cured and remain cured. Cure only the effects and the cause will remain uncured, continue to fester, and generate new effects.

(4)   Base decisions on facts—not fiction. Accept things as they are—never as you wish they were. In a competitive environment, there is a tendency for managers to confuse facts with either opinions or wishes.

(5)   Have the courage to do the unpleasant aspects of your job.

(6)   Make every occasion on which you authorize dollars to be spent on man hours to be invested the soundest investment available to your company.

(7)   Successful managers are pro-active. Weak managers tend only to react.

THE MANAGEMENT-BY-MOTIVATIONS MAXIMS

(1)   Reward your people according to their accomplishments rather than their capabilities. Reward yourself as a manager according to the ratio of their accomplishments to their capabilities.

(2)   Know your people—their abilities and aspirations. Show them how your company needs their abilities and can meet their aspirations. If you cannot meet their reasonable aspirations, then consider yourself "flagged" to restructure your systems.

(3)   Let your people know you—what you stand for—and what you stand against. Have a short fuse for dishonesties, insincerities, and failure syndromes (in all of their many facets). Have a long fuse on innovations, experiments, and uniqueness (in all of their many facets).

(4)   Nothing breeds success like success. Recognize successes (small, medium, and large), compliment those who are responsible for them, and illuminate them for all team members to see and imitate.

(5)   Realize that managers think differently and have different goals from workers. Therefore, the most difficult and critical supervision task is supervising non-management people.

(6)   Recognize that people who do things make mistakes. The more a person attempts, the greater number of mistakes you should expect. When you have a longer memory for errors than you have for accomplishments, expect to see both action and innovativeness stifled.

(7)   Train, motivate, and sustain your people so that they continually achieve higher percentages of their potentials. When they stagnate, your company will peak and begin its long slide downwards.

(8)   Develop skilled replacements for yourself and each key person. No one can advance very far without a strong, knowledgeable, and experienced base to support his climb.

(9)   Most excellent managers believe that they must "sell—not tell" their department's goals and objectives. Continue to study salesmanship—because the best managers are outstanding salesmen. Only say things that you mean and can bring about.

(10)   Believe that success is comprised of both drive and ability. The function is multiplicative.

(11)   Think continuously about what you can do for your company. Your company will take care of the rest. (There are, of course, exceptions to this maxim.)

(12)   Be positive, constructive, and realistically optimistic.

(13)   Assume that your people are just as starved for constructive criticism as they are for praise. Provide both with discretion and justification.

(14)   Initiate communications bi-directionally. Feedback is an essential component of output and therefore the "communications loop" must always be closed. If work is fun for your people and for yourself, this attitude will transmit to those who are customers of your company.

(15)   Every Management-By-Motivations control system that your company implements should punish as well as reward all who are controlled. Ignore either rewards or punishments and your control system will become unbalanced and unreliable.

2 · Let's Screw Our Heads on Right

PROLOGUE   M, IS, RS, F

Before we start building your company, let's lay the foundations.

First, let's look at the usual misconceptions, errors, and things that founders never consider. Then, let's develop your own set of very personal specifications on what you want from this thing that we call life. Once we know what you want, we can intelligently develop our start-up's goals and objectives so that they meet your personal needs.

VENTURE CAPITAL   M, IS, RS, F

AXIOM ONE: IN A FREE ENTERPRISE ECONOMY, THERE ARE ALWAYS MORE DOLLARS SEARCHING FOR VIABLE AND DE-VELOPED IDEAS THAN THERE ARE IDEAS SEARCHING FOR DOLLARS.

We'll get into this in considerable depth later on, however right now realize that there are plenty of dollars searching for your business plan. The key words and your most difficult task is buried in the words "viable and developed ideas." No one is going to invest several million dollars in your venture until you make your venture sound.

Please keep an open mind on the many avenues of venture capital open to you, the techniques of properly mixing your venture capitalists and your venture capital avenues for management control, the proper techniques of whetting venture capital's appetites prior to requesting funds, and the ways of working with the capitalists, until after you finish this book. There is probably no group of people less understood and more feared than capitalists, and the blunders that this fear and misunderstanding precipitate are unforgivable.

THE MIRROR AXIOM　　　M, IS, RS, F

AXIOM TWO: YOUR COMPANY MUST BE THE IMAGE OF WHAT YOUR INDUSTRY NEEDS . . . THE INDUSTRY WILL NOT CONFORM AND BE THE IMAGE OF WHAT YOUR COMPANY NEEDS.

This is so obvious that I hate to waste your time with it, however you should know that many companies ignore it. Thank your lucky stars that they do ignore this axiom because in doing so, your competition gives you a red carpet pathway for penetrating their customer base.

CAMEO 2-1: THE MIRROR AXIOM　　　M, IS, RS, F

The founder stood before a group of potential investors and said, "Gentlemen, we propose to enter the construction equipment industry. Our competition is: (a) General Motors, (b) Ford Motors, (c) Chrysler Motors, (d) International Harvester, (e) Allis Chalmers, (f) J.I. Case and approximately 20 other lesser sized companies. Because of the quality of competition, it will take us 18 months to lead the industry in sales and another 5 years to sell more than all of our competitors combined."

If you were sitting in the audience, would you have walked out swearing the speaker was crazy or would you have stayed?

Many did walk out but enough stayed to listen, then invest, and the Caterpillar Tractor Company was born. I don't know if this story, found in the 1932 edition of D'Arlow's *Truth Is Stranger Than Fiction,* is correct but even if it didn't happen, it still makes sense.

The major automobile manufacturers knew automobiles but entered the construction industry as an accidental profit center. The farm equipment people looked on the construction industry as, at best, a secondary market. Therefore Caterpillar was alone in addressing the construction industry as it should be addressed and this is why they prospered. They pioneered construction service; they pioneered training equipment operators and gained their hearts by calling them "engineers"; they courted the construction workers' unions when others fought unions; they sent their engineers into the fields to work with construction firms while the others remained at their plants awaiting contractors to come to them to tell them what they wanted; they developed training programs, maintainance programs, and published booklets while others saw these as fringe expenses; and they set up one of the finest franchise organizations in the world. To qualify for a Caterpillar franchise, you must be between the ages of 25 and 45, have two million dollars, and prove that you earned it yourself. Therefore, all caterpillar franchise owners are pretty good businessmen in their own rights. Today, most of the other competitors operate like Caterpillar but they are the followers . . . not the leaders.

COMPETITION   M, IS, RS, F

You'll discover that the old bromide, "That company really hasn't been in business thirty years . . . it has been in business one year thirty times" will apply to much of your competition.

Very few companies know how to cope with the innovative person. Most executives (employees themselves) are primarily motivated to make their own personal positions secure, to realize promotions, and to realize the minor raises and incentives that they'll get if things go well. These men truly hate the untested and therefore insecure concept. They know that memories of failures are long, whereas memories for successes are extremely short. The bold idea that works has many fathers. The bold idea that fails is an orphan. When a bold idea fails, dozens of memos will be produced from middle and lower management files which free their authors of blame. So chances are that your competition will always be extremely predictable and therefore easily defeated by the lean, hungry, and innovative start-up.

The older and larger a competitor, the easier he is to compete against. Most men are fearful of taking on the giants in a competitive market. In all probability, it will take the giant's top management six months to a year to even learn that you exist, another six months to a year to become concerned about you, and one to two years to change their operating procedures to compete against you.

For your start-up's sake, I hope that you are blessed with at least one sharp competitor. A sharp competitor will keep you lean, hungry, and innovative, and therefore your firm will grow more rapidly and soundly.

EFFECTIVE OUTPUT EFFICIENCIES   M, IS, RS, F

Scientists and engineers have a way of measuring a machine's actual output against what that machine would do if there were no frictions, inefficiencies, or lost potentials. They call it effective output. If a machine's effective output is too low, the engineers redesign it to lower its frictions, improve its inefficiencies, and realize more of its lost potentials.

There is no "machine" with greater capabilities or more flexibilities than the people who will work with and for you. What percentage of output would you guess that most companies realize from their people with respect to what they could realize if everyone gave his fullest to his company? Would you believe that the average large company realizes between 1% and 3% effective output efficiencies. According to the Institute of American Business Consultants, the average bureaucracy realizes between 0.25%–0.50% employee effective efficiency, the average industrial firm with greater than 10,000 employees between 0.5%–1.5%; the average firm with greater than 500 employees, 1.0%–3.0%.

We'll discuss ways of rigging your company so that you'll incorporate the incentives and the systems to increase your team's output efficiencies to between 10% and 15% later, but for right now it is important that you realize that your start-up can work extremely well with from $^1/_4$ to $^1/_{10}$th the number of warm bodies that your competitors must carry.

SELF-DISCIPLINE   M, IS, RS, F

A great deal of self-discipline is required throughout all of the start-up phases. The hurdles that you must clear are very unforgiving to the disorganized or undisciplined individual.

Before you start each day, lay out the day's priorities and force yourself to stay on course. Doctor Richard Greene, an outstanding personnel consultant, was once asked what single attribute is the most important in a manager. Without hesitation, he replied, "Always being organized. If a man doesn't have the self-discipline to always remain organized, regardless of the circumstances, then he should be replaced immediately before he hurts your company."

ZEST FOR LIFE   M, IS, RS, F

You are going to be pleasantly surprised at the fun that is involved in entrepreneurship. If you have a zest for living, you'll have a ball in developing your company. You will enjoy interviewing candidates for your team, supervising their efforts, interviewing and negotiating with the many venture capital groups that you'll come into contact with, making your concepts mature into a viable plan, turning cash, etc.

If you are wise, you won't disguise your zest for living. Enjoy yourself openly. Those who work with you and for you will discover that your enthusiasms are contagious and your start-up will become a fun company to do business with.

CAMEO 2-2: LETTING YOUR LIFE STYLE SPILL OVER INTO YOUR COMPANY   M, IS, RS, F

They are a talented, childless couple. Liberal arts graduates, they had searched fruitlessly for meaningful jobs which would allow them to live with the arts. When they reached their forties, they hit upon the idea of renting art originals to plants, offices, and restaurants. They knew their arts, they knew their artists, and they had a flair of converting drab areas into a rich atmosphere by using original art pieces. The artists who supplied them of course realized incomes from the rentals and significant sales through the additional displays.

Now this type of company at best supplies a fringe service which is usually the first that customers' controllers cut when times get hard. However, rarely were this couple's services dropped because they allowed their life style to spill over into their business. Here is how they did it.

They live in a small cottage which overlooks San Francisco's bay. It will gracefully allow from 16 to 18 party guests to thoroughly enjoy themselves. The couple continuously hold small unique parties. One evening they will hold a poetry reading party in which all guests sip wine, watch the sunset's colors play on the bay, eat fondue before a roaring fire, and participate in reading poetry aloud. Only those who truly love and understand poetry are invited. The next evening might be a great books session, the next a Shakespeare evening, the next a Dixieland band session, the next a choral session, and so on through modern plays, Greek tragedies, chess tournaments, classical music, etc., etc.

Their parties are much more than a party . . . their parties are true events. If you are invited to one, you'll rearrange your schedule so that you can attend. It is an occasion that you'll never forget. From five to eight of the other guests will also be top executives of their firms. Not one of these executives will allow their controllers to cut this couple's fringe service because it might jeopardize their invitations to future outstanding parties.

ADVANTAGES OF ADDRESSING A GROWTH INDUSTRY
M, IS, F

This is such an important point that we are devoting a complete chapter to the advantages and techniques of determining and addressing a growth industry. However, for right now, let's state that you will increase your chances of getting venture capital on your terms by a factor of 10 if you address a growth industry. When the time comes to sell some of your stock to realize private gain, you'll observe that growth industry stocks command between 5–50 times the amount of money that firms, which are in stagnant industries, command.

EXPERIENCE   M, IS

Unfortunately, almost every author that I've read and almost every "expert" that I've heard, stresses the importance of addressing the industry in which you have the most experience.

Since growth industries are usually very young and very dynamic, rarely will you discover anyone with much experience in them. Though I certainly stress learning about the industry that you will service before taking the plunge, I certainly do not prescribe that you should not address the industry until you gain the experience that these experts lead you to believe that you need.

Well over half of Business Solutions' clients did not have appreciable experience in the industries that their start-ups addressed. They were successful because they either attracted the necessary experience in the co-founders they selected, saw their new industry with fresh eyes and were so unique and innovative in meeting their industry's needs that they penetrated with ease, or a combination of the above two. In all cases, the founders did their "homework" correctly before they opened their doors.

CAMEO 2-3: SELECTING A COMPANY IN HARMONY WITH YOUR NEEDS   M, IS, RS, F

We had a client (a CPA who is a recognized tax expert) who wanted to set up a computerized franchise tax service. He had developed an extensive set of computer programs which interrogated a taxpayer in such a way that he realized his maximum tax deductions. Well over 30 tax service companies had agreed to use this man's computer service. All he needed was $80,000 to set up his timesharing networks.

Now this man truly hated the IRS. He boiled at "their bureaucratic operations, their lack of employee professionalism, and their lack of ethics." He compared the IRS to an inefficient but all-powerful mafia and literally felt unclean after working with them. This hatred so drained his enthusiasm and energies that his business plan was progressing at a snail's pace. He devoted less than 20 hours a month on his start-up and its progress showed it.

We introduced this man to three engineers who were in the final development stages of their inexpensive non-pressurized submarine for recreational and professional skin divers. These engineers badly needed a controller.

In just three weeks, this accountant: (1) developed and initiated their fiscal operating procedures; (2) developed accurate production, administration, and marketing budgets; (3) developed their business plan's proforma (projected) financial reports; (4) increased their cash reserves significantly while lowering their initial funding needs through money-leveraging principles; and (5) was a major factor in attracting their venture capital. He meshed beautifully with the founders' team. The only problem that they ever had with him was trying to keep him out of their submarines until their shakedown tests were completed. This man wasn't a strong swimmer but he truly loved the ocean's depths.

This company was extremely successful and approximately nine months after it was started, they received an offer for over $6,000,000. The CPA realized over $125,000 for his share of the founders' stock. What is interesting is that this money was more than enough to allow him to finance his own tax service, but he decided not to pursue it.

Why did this man spend 60 hours a week as a minor co-founder of another start-up when he wouldn't invest even 20 hours a month on his own dream? Because he truly loved what he was doing with the submarines while he hated his tax service dream.

BROMIDES   M, IS, RS, F

Since childhood, we have all been bombed with "wise" sayings that we never questioned. For many people, these bromides or clichés have become cornerstones of their personal foundations. This is all right until you let these bromides become a major premise in your entrepreneur decisions. Then be aware that they may not be valid.

Perhaps the most damaging of the bromides is the saying, "Build a better mouse trap and the world will beat a path to your door." Engineers and scientists are particularly vulnerable to this notion. But we have seen many excellent new products and concepts that should have succeeded beyond their inventors' dreams fail miserably because they were never marketed. The founders waited for the world to beat a path to their doors and either failed or lost valuable time before they began marketing correctly.

Another damaging bromide is, "History always repeats itself." This is rubbish but too frequently you see otherwise sophisticated people state this saying and then try to copy the leader of their industry because by aping the leader, they'll become a leader. For every case that you can give me of history repeating itself, I'll give you two where it hasn't.

So, before you pull out a bromide to use in place of thinking . . . beware.

LOCKER ROOM LAWYERS   M, IS, RS, F

Every year, our local, state, and federal legislatures pass thousands of new laws and erase very few from the books. Though the new laws frequently update older laws each year, many obsolete laws remain on our books and are unenforced. This group of laws is lovingly called "the spittoon and sandbox laws" because many states still have unenforced laws requiring spittoons for hygiene and sandboxes for fire protection. Probably every day of your company's life you'll inadvertently break one of these laws and never know it.

However, one of the best ways to kill an untested and innovative idea is to say that it is against the law. The locker room lawyer defense will kill you if you do not follow a common sense approach in overriding it.

If something seems logical to you, if it appears ethical, and if your actions will benefit all parties (there is no damaged party because of your actions), you are probably safely within the law. In cases of doubt, see a qualified lawyer.

Minor Point 2-1: A Solution to the Spittoon and Sandbox Laws M, IS, RS, F

Frequently, dormant laws are unwrapped and enforced when it suits a government's purposes, for instance, to bar an out-of-state firm from doing business in a location.

Every management consultant and every manager of a multistate operation feels particularly vulnerable to these obsolete laws because they can block feasible plans. Therefore most campaign to have legislators place a life limit on each law that is passed. If every law had a fail-safe period (i.e., five years), then we would all be held accountable to only those laws which were reviewed and repassed every fifth year. We could all then be aware of the pertinent laws that apply to our operations and we would stop being a nation of law breakers. Consider mentioning this recommendation to your legislators and perhaps if we all request it frequently enough, our governments may listen and your job as an entrepreneur will be greatly simplified.

ESTABLISH YOUR PERSONAL MINI-INCOMES M, IS, RS, F

There is no alibi for any qualified individual in America not to realize a minimum of $2,000 a month (or $20 an hour) from his non-prime hours (evenings and weekends). If you are assured that you'll get $2,000 a month to live on while you establish your start-up, you can realize significant freedom from the worries of at least supplying your family with the minimum essentials while you plow your start-up's profits back into the firm.

Realize that it only takes ten $200/month mini-incomes to meet your $2,000/month goal. There are thousands of $200 a month opportunities.

We recommend to our clients the following guidelines as to whether or not they should take advantage of a mini-income opportunity:

(1) Each mini-income must be enjoyable and fall within the client's life style.

(2) Each mini-income should produce a minimum of $20 in profits for each hour the client invests in it.

(3) Once the initial spade work is completed, the mini-income is operating correctly, and the product (or service) appears reliable, our client should then pass on the day-to-day operations to others and just supervise the operation. This will free up enough time for him to address another mini-income.

(4) Each mini-income should be continuous in nature so that the client can lean on its profits when he quits his full-time job and begins his start-up.

(5) Each mini-income should supply our client with at least $500 per year in cash reserves which he can use as either "front" money for more mini-incomes or invest in his start-up on an as-needed basis.

Once you orient yourself to start looking for these mini-income opportunities, you'll be surprised at how easy they are to achieve. Eighty percent of our clients who attempted to practice this philosophy realized four mini-incomes within the first year which averaged $1,000/month additional income at the end of the first year. Very few average less than $2,000/month after the second year and $4,000/month after the third year.

CAMEO 2-4: THE 40-INCH CYLINDRICAL HARD BOILED EGG   M, IS, RS, F

A woman started about 10 years ago to develop her own personal profit centers (mini-incomes) so that her family could afford to live the life styles they wanted. She had three small children (ages two through five), so she was forced to develop centers which complemented her husband's (a design engineer) and her children's times and activities. Today, she has approximately 30 income-producing centers, two full-time employees, five part-time employees, and though she nets only $25,000 a year after taxes, she is still in total control of her time.

One of her more interesting mini-profit centers is her 40-inch cylindrical hard boiled egg. These eggs are used by restaurants for their salads. They have the showmanship that restaurants like (i.e., the egg slices are far wider and thinner than normal hard boiled egg slices, the yokes have interesting shapes, and slight amounts of white and golden food colorings make the whites whiter and the yokes more golden). The average restaurant consumes two cylinders a day and she realizes $5 in profits from each cylinder. Her operations are as follows.

Her three sons (now high school students) own their own chicken farm at the back of their estate. The boys collect the eggs and sell them to themselves and Mom for the restaurant profit center.

Every evening, the complete family spends an hour cracking eggs, separating the yokes from the whites, and pouring them into 40-inch molds.

While dinner cooks, approximately 60 molds are hard boiled. While the family eats and does dishes, the molds are cooled in water tanks. The molds are then refrigerated over night so that they will be chilled for delivery.

She comments, "Since the egg profits must pay for my children's private schools, special tutors, special lessons, and the bulk of their college education, I like to make this project as much their project as I can. Every morning, when I drive them to school, we pick a route which will allow us to deliver to at least two restaurants. After school, we deliver to at least three restaurants on our way home. The boys carry in all deliveries, have all customer contact, handle all complaints, and even occasionally have to collect overdue payments. When these children get into college, they will not only have a solid foundation in the academic and social areas, they will have a confidence in themselves and an understanding of business that few teenagers have."

CAMEO 2-5: OTHER MINI-INCOMES   M, IS, RS, F

Mini-profit centers are so easy and so lucrative that I am surprised that so few people attempt them. There are literally thousands of opportunities open to you. The following examples are not necessarily the best or the most lucrative—they are selected to stimulate your imagination and innovativeness in uncovering your own mini-incomes.

Keith C. Elliott is a well known mathematician and computer expert who dabbles continuously in interesting challenges. Some people relax watching television or reading a book. Keith relaxes by attempting to make his computer correlate religions, compose music, interpret languages, or anything else that is in the pioneering vein.

Several years ago, Keith discovered astrology. Though he didn't buy the logic behind astrology, it appeared an interesting exercise to utilize his computer to track the various planets and predict occurrences. When the predictions of this ancient discipline began to be accurate too frequently, he sought help from qualified astrologers. They started bringing him their problems and soon he was realizing approximately $250 a week in fees for a two-minute computer run. Then a tape casset house started using his program to personalize horoscope tapes for customers. Keith started netting over $600 a week and was pleased with his accidental mini-income until he discovered that people were taking his computer's predictions far too seriously. He has dropped his service to all but a few competent astrologers, however he still realizes approximately $400 a week.

The man in this second example is a top executive of a bank. He is a cactus buff and had a front and back yard filled with different species. He was concerned about his two sons' inability to find work after high school and during the summers so he decided to start a cactus farm and sell to the local nurseries. He and his sons developed unique and attractive pots and began a cactus breeder farm. Cactus is a particularly sturdy plant which lends itself to giving off hundreds of fast growing shoots if properly handled. Within a year, this front yard/back yard cactus farm was producing $800 a month in sales. In three years, this operation had moved to several vacant lots, employed eight high school students, and netted over $2,500 a month.

In a third case, a man worked his way up through the production department to general manager of a medium-sized electronic manufacturer. He truly missed the "hands-on" duties of a production manager. When he finally decided that he wanted to start up his own company, he swiftly realized that his family needed $2,500 a month to survive and that he couldn't last long without a salary. He would have to make himself financially independent before quitting his job.

He therefore decided to address, in his spare time, the production problems that most manufacturers have periodically. He decided to hire crews of swing shift and grave yard shift personnel and bring them into each customer's production facilities to lower their back orders. Very few firms will hire second and third shifts unless they are positive that their back orders will sustain those shifts for at least nine months. The costs of hiring, training, supervising, and firing are too prohibitive for short-termed back orders.

Within a year, he had 11 crews going and realized approximately $900 a month. Within the second year, he had 31 crews going, had hired three production engineers to supervise these crews and realized over $900 a week. Since many of his clients were small, he realized additional incomes from improving their operating procedures, utilizing central purchasing to lower their components' prices, and leasing or renting non-prime-time production space and equipment for his crews to produce other clients' products. These additional profit centers brought in approximately $400 a week.

The crowning feature is that he is now producing his own electronic products during non-prime hours, utilizing the best of equipment and components in rented facilities. His production costs, his overhead, and his operating expenses are a fraction of most manufacturers' expenses. He calculates that he can retain his full-time job, he can continue to use others' facilities and equipment, and that he can get along well with just three prime-time employees until he realizes 3% market penetration. Then he'll have to move into his own facilities. However, by then his cash reserves will allow him to do so without venture capital.

THE SICK COMPANY SYNDROME   M, IS, RS, F

There are probably as many *causes* for sick companies as there are sick companies. However, the *effects* stages always seem to basically repeat themselves. Let's take a look at these stages.

Stage One: The cause (or causes) for sickness are either ignored or improperly defined. Corrective actions therefore don't take place.

Stage Two: The first effects of the illness become observable. Your people begin making alibis, expedient actions attempt cosmetic cures of the effects (instead of getting to the heart of the causes), and wishful thinking that maybe the problem will go away on its own occurs.

Stage Three: Your sales and profits decrease. Top management's concern over this warning flag occurs and the first generation of effects are beginning to be the causes of the second generation of effects.

Stage Four: The effects of the effects now really begin to surface. Buck passing begins and your management-by-objectives atmosphere begins to suffer.

Stage Five: Your best people become gravely concerned about your inability to face and cure causes. The exodus of your cream begins at a trickle and increases as your work atmosphere deteriorates. Your best people are forced to begin reacting (instead of proacting) and innovation is stifled. The exodus of your best increases and you either cannot or do not replace them with equivalent talent, experience, or dedication.

Stage Six: The third generation of effects are born (the effects of the effects of the effects of the cause) and the process is becoming irreversible. The pyramid of effects now buries the original cause so deeply that you can't address it without first curing the effects. Your sales and profits begin their downward slide and your management-by-objectives systems degrade to only lip service instead of actual controls.

Stage Seven: Frustrations and emotions continue to increase as people start protecting their flanks. Communication becomes too strained and now your management-by-exceptions controls begin to fail. Politics flourishes as your one-team image splinters into factions and buck passing reaches its height. The classical corrective actions no longer even have a cosmetic effect as nothing seems to work and real surgery is essential.

Stage Eight: The fourth generation of effects is surfacing in continuous production slippages, quality problems, late shipments, lost sales, lost profits, cost overruns, and lost opportunities. Competition is having a field day with your decaying customer base. What talent that remains is now bogged down in fire fights and the excessive pressures cause stupid and expensive blunders. Your management-by-exceptions controls totally break down as the exceptions become the rule and everyone is forced to work hard instead of smart. Frustrations creep down to the lowest levels of production and labor grievances begin to consume far too much time and energy.

Stage Nine: Both sales and profits continue their downward plunge and nothing seems to work in reversing them. The pressures on top management by the investors are excessive and these pressures are transmitted downward to the lowest rungs. Both buck passing and politics decrease as despair sets in at all levels.

Stage Ten: The venture capitalists and investors have lost complete confidence in management and band together to replace you and your management team with a team that they hope can perform. Your company is then either turned around, sold, or forced into bankruptcy proceedings.

Note that once your company slips beyond stage three, the effects cloud the cause to such an extent that swift and inexpensive corrective actions become difficult. After the sixth stage, for all intents and purposes the cycle is irreversible without extreme surgery and years of curing.

THE IMPORTANCE OF THE SICK COMPANY SYNDROME TO A START-UP   M, IS, RS, F

It is important that you realize that the sick company syndrome exists in a major percentage of established companies—your competitors, your customers, your vendors, and even the bureaucracies (e.g., our postal service) on which we must depend. These companies' illnesses can hurt your efforts considerably if you do not leave options (escape paths such as secondary sources of supply, effective systems which flag problems before they effect your operations, etc.).

Realize that the sick company syndrome exists and can be a major threat to infest your young company. Recognize its symptoms so that you can take effective action fast.

If you select founders, managers, and key employees who face your problems squarely, define them honestly, and solve them permanently, your company will rarely deteriorate beyond stage two. However, since there are so many companies which continually live and vascillate between stages four and nine, many of the founders that you attract have been brought up and trained in this environment and consider the sickness as a normal attribute of business. You'll have to monitor these individuals' performances much more closely because many of them can't distinguish a cause from an effect. Therefore, their corrective actions will attempt to cure the effects while the cause festers.

PROFITS   M, IS, RS, F

THEOREM ONE: THERE IS NO SUCH THING AS AN UNJUST PROFIT.

Profits are nothing more than the difference between your sales price (a price set on the value of your product or service to the customers) and the costs involved in producing your product (or service). There is certainly nothing unethical, illegal, or improper in attaining the highest difference (profits) possible. I hang-up on this point because so many who come through our doors seem to have a mental hang-up on profits.

Profits are the name of the game in private industry and venture capitalists like to discover founders who are profit maximizers. This theorem only applies to nongovernment or competitive situations in countries with the free enterprise system.

GREED   M, IS, RS, F

Greed takes place when, to capture a larger percentage of your industry or to hold your customer base, you damage your company and your industry. In most cases, greed takes place when you state that all you want is your fair share of the market and your fair share is 100%. Therefore, to attain this slice of the pie, you must permanently eliminate your competition. In killing your competition, you destroy your industry.

Actually, as you'll see later, sales penetration is easy without damaging your industry. When you "bomb" prices to gain a larger percentage of the market, all that you are doing is admitting that you do not understand either sales or business and in trying to "buy" sales, you spoil your nest. Your prime concern is not how to penetrate the market but rather how to keep your competition from ruining the industry by dropping its prices in reaction to your sales penetrations. There are legal techniques open to you to maintain price and profit structures which we'll discuss later. However, at this stage, do not even make it a minor objective to beat your competition in sales. Make it a major objective to realize sales and profits through giving the customer what he wants. If you are mature, you'll realize that you are starting-up your own company which will be a vehicle to allow you to meet your life's objectives . . . not a vehicle to destroy competitors. There is plenty of room for many profit-oriented companies in each industry.

PROFIT RULES-OF-THUMB   M, IS

There are two rules-of-thumb frequently used by the venture capitalists concerning a start-up's profits. They are:

THE 5-TO-1 RULE

If the management team does not have a "track record," a minimum markup of 5 to 1 (sales price to production costs) is necessary. Sales price is defined as the price the end user pays and production costs is the simple addition of materials and labor to produce the product.

THE 3-TO-1 RULE

If your management team has a track record (and it is a good one) a minimum markup of 3 to 1 is acceptable.

I hate these rules-of-thumb for the following reasons.

(1) They seem to stick in the founders' minds and they force their start-up to just meet them. There are too many opportunities where mark-ups of 25 to 1 and greater exist which the founders pass by for a 5 to 1 opportunity.

(2) Frequently founders, who do not understand how to test for their optimum sales prices, take their production costs and multiply them by 5

and thus establish their sales price. By doing this, they either undercut the market's demand (and therefore throw away profits) or they are over-priced and lose sales.

(3) The third reason that I dislike these "rules" is that they aren't really significant. Venture capitalists actually would be extremely happy with even a 2 to 1 markup, however they frequently insist upon high ratios in the business plan because they know that there are many surprises and hidden costs not anticipated during the business plan development. When we read a business plan, we search for significant reserves for contingencies instead of the phony profit to production ratios.

Do not disillusion yourself with the needs for high profits in a start-up. From an economic standpoint, your most efficient operating profits will probably be when your firm is very young. As the growth industry which you address matures, you'll experience competition, your firm will have grown significantly and you must carry larger overhead expenses, your costs of sales will multiply significantly, and therefore your profit ratios will decrease. During the initial stages, you must realize high profits to build adequate reserves and to attract venture capital on your terms. The following rules-of-thumb apply to start-ups:

Category	Minimum Ratio	Marginal Ratio	Optimum Ratio	Description of Ratio
Manufacturing	3 : 1	5 : 1	25 : 1	Sales price to manu-facturing costs.
Industrial Service	2 : 1	3 : 1	50 : 1	Service fee to cost of service.
Retail Sales	1.4 : 1	1.6 : 1	2.5 : 1	Sales price to pur-chase price.
Retail Service	2 : 1	3 : 1	10 : 1	Service fee to cost of service.

Franchises   There are such a wide variety of franchise packages offered that no rules-of-thumb can be drawn.

SALES PRICES   M, IS

AXIOM THREE: YOUR SALES PRICE IS TOTALLY A FUNCTION OF YOUR PRODUCT'S VALUE AS SEEN BY YOUR CUS-TOMERS. IN NO WAY IS YOUR SALES PRICE A FUNC-TION OF YOUR COSTS TO PRODUCE YOUR PRODUCT.

In other words, if your product is worth $1,000 to your customers, then that should be its sales price regardless if it costs you $1 or $10,000 to produce. If the profit margins are not satisfactory, then select another product to produce which has satsifactory profits.

This axiom is important because it forces you to be innovative in increasing your product's value in the eyes of the customer. You'll be forced to search for a *marketable difference* and once you have discovered this difference and developed it, your company is well on its way to success.

If in your price testing to determine your product's value, you discover that several prices have equal customer demand, select the highest price for your first price. Not only do the higher profits help your start-up attract capital and grow, the image in the consumers' minds of both your product and your company is improved. The bromide "You get what you pay for" works for you.

CAMEO 2-6: THE COLUMBUS PRICE   M, IS, RS, F

Two chemists who are still employees with one of the more prestigious laboratories in the San Francisco area, developed, as a joke, a product that is so funny that it evokes laughs from everyone. The chemicals cost them 3¢ per pint and the packaging cost them 25¢ per bottle. Everyone who saw the product stated that they ought to sell it, so they came to us for guidance.

After the best belly laugh that we had had in a year, we decided to price test the product first at $14.92 (Columbus price), then $10.66, and finally $4.98 to see which price was the most attractive. The Columbus advertisement was prepared and placed in just one issue of one magazine. The orders inundated the two chemists to the extent that they have been back ordered ever since.

This fad joke had the surprise of becoming a staple product for ladies in the oldest profession and for swingers. Repeat orders of from one to three pints are received each month from the original orderers.

The chemists are still producing their product on their wives' stoves every evening and weekends and packaging it in their garages. They average approximately $3,000/week in profits while they are trying to make up their minds if this is a fad/joke product which will have a short-term life or whether their product has real value to the market segment that they are addressing and therefore will be a long-enduring product which will support them if they quit their jobs.

Is their product's value $14.92? If we used the 5 to 1 rule-of-thumb, they would have sold their product at $1.40 to $1.50.

CAMEO 2-7: FORTUNE MAGAZINE'S PRICING   M, IS

Fortune magazine was born at the height of the depression when other magazines were folding. The founders were extremely concerned what price they could charge at the newstands. The debate was whether the magazine should sell for 15¢ or 20¢ and wasn't decided until the day the first issue was to go to the printers. Since the artwork had been completed prior to the price decision, the founders told the printer to add the price to their cover.

In the verbal communications to the printer, an error was made and the first issue had $1.00 printed on its cover. No one observed the error until after the issue was given to the newstands. Sales were much greater than the founders' wildest dreams and they had to reprint the first issue three times to meet the demand. The consumer logic seemed to be, "any magazine which sells for a dollar in these hard times must really be valuable."

Though the logic was nice from a profits standpoint, it forced the founders to strive for and achieve a level of excellence that no other journal sought in those days.

CAMEO 2-8: DIAL SOAP   M, IS

The Armour Meatpacking division had supplied the major soap companies with their raw materials for years before one of Armour's executives asked, "Why don't we go into the soap business?" Armour decided to test the market.

These people were unique and brilliant in their testing. Instead of producing a standard soap, they developed a rounded-shoulder soap with a pleasant scent. Instead of testing it in grocery stores, they tested it by packaging 12 bars in a large attractive box and selling them through the better mens' clothing stores. For well over a year, only stores which sold top men's suits sold Dial soap. Since they gave extremely high commissions and supplied extremely attractive displays to each store, their soap was always prominently displayed. A box of 12 bars of soap sold for $7.50. Every man who visited a suit store saw the display and a few even bought.

When the decision was made to fully address the soap industry, Armour of course decided to sell through the normal soap distribution networks at a competitive price. When the consumers saw a soap that sold for over 60¢ a bar going for 17¢, they bought the bargain. Armour realized an immediate 7% penetration, an unheard of success story for the soap industry.

Minor Point 2-2: Project Your Sense of Humor   M, IS, RS, F

One of the biggest problems that we observe with clients is that they too frequently lose their perspective and therefore their sense of humor in their start-ups. A little humor goes a long way, especially if you allow it to project out to your customers.

CAMEO 2-9: THE POLISH-ITALIAN BROTHERHOOD SOCIETY   M, IS, RS, F

Do you remember the ethnic jokes that swept our country several years ago? This man developed his own mail-order business (a spare time operation) which traded on those jokes.

Every product that he produced was designed to be used in the home bar. Though every product worked reliably, each contained a major flaw which in itself was a sight joke. (Examples: He sold 60,000 shot measures in which was cast, "The Polish-Italian Brotherhood's Super *Qaulity* Rum Measurer." How many companies mis-spell the word quality? He sold 35,000 liter flasks in which the word liter was spelled "litter." He sold over 200,000 parched scrolls which proved that Christopher Columbus was really Polish and the original founder of the Polish-Italian Brotherhood Society. Since the scroll was printed in extremely ornate old English and was extremely attractive, it probably hangs in thousands of bars throughout the country.

This man never deluded himself that the ethnic jokes were anything more than a short-termed "target-of-opportunity." When the ethnic jokes began to diminish, he folded his moonlighting operation with only $1,100 of inventory and $200 of equipment. However, in his heyday, he realized well over $50,000 a year in profits.

Minor Point 2-3: Taxes

It is beyond the scope of this book to discuss taxes, however it is a subject which you shouldn't ignore too long after you open your doors. Remember the bromide, "It's not what you make that is important . . . it's what you get to keep."

CAMEO 2-10: FORD'S FOLLY   M, IS

Back in the Model T era, Henry Ford primarily depended upon outside manufacturers to supply him the components essential for his cars. The Ford Motor Company was primarily a fabrication house and Henry wanted to keep it that way until he considered his funds large enough to address in-house capabilities.

Since Mr. Ford considered the Model T the ultimate in the working man's car, he froze both the design and production of this vehicle and year after year repeated his production. So all his vendors supplied the same components year after year.

One year, Henry decided that he wanted his engines supplied in a special crate. Each crate was to be a perfect cube made of prime wood with no flaws. Each crate was to contain six engine castings and he even tied the dimensions of each side to within $1/16$th of an inch. The engine vendors were notified that if one side was even slightly damaged in shipment, then the complete crate would be returned unopened and payments would not be made until the damaged side was corrected.

When the bids started coming in, the controller was extremely upset with Mr. Ford because of the extra costs involved in Henry's requirements. "Mr. Ford, do you realize that you must pay $3 a crate more because of these unnecessary requirements?" he complained. Mr. Ford ignored his complaints and signed contracts with several suppliers for a year's production. Then he went completely "crazy" and issued special instructions to all Ford workers that no one was to touch a crate except a special crew. This crew was to have special padded crowbars and was to dismantle each crate with care and stack each side in a special shed that Henry had built for them. The enormous shed was laughingly called "Ford's Folly" by his workers.

When the first engines shipped in their costly crates finally arrived, Mr. Ford personally supervised his crate dismantling crew. He warned each man that if he so much as marked any side, he would be fired. Finally, when the engines that had been shipped in these crates reached the production lines, Mr. Ford closed his expensive carpenters' shops. You see, for 50¢ a car, his engine suppliers also had unwittingly begun supplying him with the Model T's floor boards. Though these suppliers only allowed Henry to get by with this for the one year that they had agreed upon in their contracts, that year's savings played an important role in building the Ford Motor Company's cash reserves that were needed for expansion.

FRANCHISES   M, IS, F

Franchises are actually a very sound technique for a manufacturer or an international service start-up to raise second-round financing. Actually, entrepreneurs are paying you for the privilege of operating from your business plan.

The machinery of franchising is as good as your ability to implement it, service it, and police it. There are many hundreds of excellent franchise arrangements that range from the franchisor paying for the privilege of following your plan all the way to where you pay the franchisee to carry your line.

DEVELOP YOUR PERSONAL REQUIREMENTS
M, IS, RS, F

Before you can properly begin your start-up, you have to determine where you want to go. We strongly recommend to our clients that they tightly define what they want from this thing we call life for the following essential reasons:

(1)   Since your start-up is nothing more than a vehicle which will allow you to meet your life's requirements, your company must be in complete harmony with your personal life style needs.

(2)   If you are going to attract strong individuals to join your founders' team, these individuals will swiftly detect if you are directionless and will lose respect for you. Then they will walk all over you.

(3)   If you wish to be an officer and a leader in your own start-up, you'll require a solid personal foundation to cope with the many pithy problems that will arise.

(4)   When you go before the venture capitalists for funding, you'll discover that they are greatly interested in your motivations and will invest considerable time and efforts to determine what makes you "tick." These people become greatly disturbed if instead of clear, clean, and well-thought-out replies, you give them weak or fuzzy answers.

(5)   The biggest reason for understanding yourself is that if you select a start-up that is in total harmony with your inner self, then you'll consider your work as the high point of your day. If you select a start-up that is in friction with your real self (it's easy to do), then your personal goals and objectives will be in discord with your company's priorities and both you and your company will suffer.

So before you start, tightly define what you wish to achieve, what makes you happy, and what kind of life styles your inner self demands. Once you do this, the job is easy to select the right kind of start-up to complement your inner needs and you'll save yourself a lot of time, frustrations, and money.

AXIOM FOUR: YOUR COMPANY'S OBJECTIVES MUST BE IN HARMONY WITH YOUR INNER SELF.

DEVELOP BROAD-BRUSH COMPANY OBJECTIVES
M, IS, RS, F

Now that you have developed your own very personal and confidential requirements, you are equipped to develop a preliminary set of company objectives. Though you'll probably never show your personal requirements to anyone, your company objectives and goals will probably be readily shown to fellow founders, venture capitalists, and future employees. Your set of preliminary company goals will probably be a reference point (a starting point) for your co-founders to build upon. If you are wise, you'll make your initial objectives relatively broad so that your options will not be too limited. As your start-up progresses, you'll be pleasantly surprised at the hundreds of opportunities that will present themselves to you.

CAMEO 2-11   EXAMPLE OF TIGHTLY DEFINED
PERSONAL SPECIFICATIONS   M, IS, RS, F

When this man wrote these personal specifications, he was thirty-two years old, had worked for three companies since his graduation, and had the same pattern with each (fast promotions and then he either quit or was fired with fireworks). He finally decided that he would never make a good employee for anyone other than himself. He started his own high-technology manufacturing firm and today is probably worth $200,000. In two years, he'll be worth a million and in five years, worth 10 million.

The following are my personal specifications. I make no apologies nor do I feel a need to defend my reasons for demanding the following:

I. The possessions that I require are:

a.	Five bedroom home in Portolo Valley	$150,000
b.	Two bedroom apartment in New York City	$ 65,000
c.	Mountain cabin (Colorado Rockies)	$ 27,000
d.	Four automobiles for self and family	$ 14,500
e.	Cessna airplane	$ 9,500

II. In addition to the above fixed assets, I'll require the following:

a.	Children's college education	$12,000/year
b.	Taxes	$22,000/year
c.	Household expenses	$10,000/year
d.	Utilities	$ 1,000/year
e.	Furniture reserve	$ 3,000/year
f.	Vacation reserve	$ 1,500/year
g.	Club memberships	$ 3,200/year
h.	Entertainment allowance	$ 1,000/year
i.	Medical reserves	$ 500/year
j.	Insurance premiums	$ 2,500/year
k.	Church obligations	$ 2,500/year
l.	Savings	$ 5,000/year
m.	Investments	$ 5,000/year

III. · I require the following time allotments:

a.	Yearly vacation	two weeks/year
b.	Three day weekend	six per year
c.	Weekly church services	two hours/Sunday
d.	Weekly services to church	four hours/week
e.	Family evening	one evening/week
f.	Exercise sessions	three two-hour sessions/week
g.	Wife's allotment of private time	three two-hour sessions/week

IV. In addition, I'll budget the following time allotments:

a.	Sleep	6½ hours/day
b.	Inefficient times	1 hour/day
c.	Misc. time for body functions, showers, etc.	1 hour/day
d.	Commuting	1 hour/day
e.	Prayers and meditation	½ hour/day
f.	Self-organization and priority development	1 hour/day
g.	Eating	2 hours/day
h.	Start-up investment	balance of time

V. Support: To maximize my efficiencies and outputs, I require:

a.	One and one-half secretaries	$1,200/month
b.	One office and one conference room (They'll both be kept busy simultaneously)	$ 500/month
c.	Eight file cabinets	$1,200
d.	Complete dictation equipment	$2,500
e.	Essential furniture for above	$5,000
f.	Computer services	$ 500/month
g.	Printing and reproduction services	$ 200/month

VI. Fellow Founders and Key Employees. I require that all my teammates be:

a. Innovative
b. Profit maximizers
c. Self starters
d. Decision makers
e. Well organized at all times
f. Communicators
g. Honest
h. Knowledgeable
i. Experienced
j. Problem solvers
k. Flexible
l. Responsible
m. In harmony with my philosophies, goals, and objectives.

I find it impossible to place these essential ingredients in order of importance. They are all necessary and will be an integral part of each founder with the exception of the last. If I am wrong, then they damned sure had better not be in harmony with my wrongness but fight me until they win.

VII. I promise those who join me as managers and key employees that,

1. They will see our venture become profitable within 12 months.
2. They will see our sales exceed $200,000/month within nine months.
3. They will see us realize a market penetration of 5% within 48 months.
4. They will see their equity in our venture be worth $100,000 within three years, $250,000 within five years, and $1,000,000 within seven years.
5. We'll get a heck of a kick out of this effort from day one. There are going to be some surprised individuals and competitors within the first six months and they will be believers within a year.
6. Everything that we undertake will have real value to both our customers and ourselves.

These are my minimums. Actually, I expect and will be greatly disappointed if we do not achieve much greater accomplishments.

CAMEO 2-12: USING ENTREPRENEURISM TO LOCATE "THE" JOB   M, IS

This cameo is not unusual. I've seen it repeat itself dozens of times.

Bob was an extremely high-paid and talented design specialist for Lockheed when he was laid-off in 1968. For 18 months, he searched fruitlessly for a job and though he was willing to accept a significant salary cut, no one would touch him. He barely met expenses by teaching math at night school, by performing small consulting jobs, and by attempting to sell real estate.

Bob then joined a start-up which was developing a word processor for industry. To determine the design criteria for this machine, Bob started interviewing the top executives in the San Francisco bay area. One of these executives was a vice president of his old firm, Lockheed.

In the "give and take" of this interview, the vice president realized that Bob was just the man he needed as a project manager. He offered Bob the $45,000 a year job (approximately $15,000 more than Bob had previously made at Lockheed), a three year contract, and reasonable performance rewards. Bob accepted and the vice president forwarded Bob's contract to his personnel department.

Then the fireworks began. Lockheed's personnel people had Bob pigeonholed as a design specialist, not a manager. How could a man who had been out of work for 18 months be hired for upper middle management? When the vice president persisted, personnel then attempted to lower Bob's salary to his old pay scale and eliminate the performance benefits. When that failed, they attempted to have Bob waive his previous 14 years of longevity with Lockheed which would greatly affect Bob's retirement benefits. Finally the vice president made a trip to personnel to stop the harassment and Bob was hired per his agreement. Bob has now been a project manager with Lockheed for four years, recently had his contract extended for an additional three years, and both Lockheed and Bob have benefited from their relationship.

How could Bob visit Lockheed's personnel department twice monthly for 18 months and not locate a design position and in just one visit sell a vice president on hiring him for a more responsible position? Because when Bob visited Lockheed's personnel department, he was just a design engineer looking for a design engineer's job. When he visited the vice president, he was a co-founder and a vice president who thought and acted like a manager.

The reasons that this happens so frequently are: (1) as you mature in the entrepreneuring cycle, the disciplines that you acquire and the outlooks that you develop are of considerable value to any profit-oriented company; (2) since most founders assign themselves significant titles and others accept these titles at face value, most are offered jobs several management levels higher than the jobs that they left; and (3) companies look for top men with guts. If you have enough personal courage and confidence to start your own venture, you'll probably have the strength they need to run their operations.

Minor Point 2-4: The Slave Syndrome

I don't understand this syndrome but since it occurs so frequently, it should be mentioned. Briefly, there are people who are searching for a winner's coattails to ride. These individuals seem to be willing to pay any price for the ride upwards.

Since you, as an entrepreneur, appear to these people as a certain winner, they'll attempt to become quasi-slaves for a coattail ride. With almost no encouragement on your part, they'll chauffeur you, type for you, run errands for you, clean your house, attempt to satisfy your sex needs, or whatever they feel that you need. In the initial stages, verbal recognition and gratitude appear to be enough payment.

The temptation to allow this master-slave relationship to develop is great because it is flattering and you wish to unload your dull tasks. However, every client who has allowed the slave syndrome to develop has soon wished that he hadn't. In almost all cases, the slave degenerates into a mentally ill person and the relationship which began with almost no effort became almost impossible to terminate.

3 · Select a Growth or Glamour Industry

PROLOGUE   M, IS, RS, F

Your decision to address a growth or glamour industry is of such importance that we should devote a complete chapter to it. Though there are many opportunities which would support your company in stagnant or decaying industries, a non-growth industry greatly limits your options in attracting venture capital on your terms, establishing industry precedents, and the eventual selling price of your company.

> *AXIOM FIVE:* IF THE FINANCIAL COMMUNITIES FEEL THAT AN INDUSTRY IS A GROWTH INDUSTRY, THEY WILL INVEST IN IT HEAVILY ENOUGH IN YEARS TO COME TO MAKE IT A GROWTH INDUSTRY.
> *AXIOM SIX:* IF THE FINANCIAL COMMUNITIES FEEL THAT AN INDUSTRY WILL PLATEAU AND BECOME STAGNANT, THEY WILL WITHHOLD ESSENTIAL FUNDS AND STUNT THAT INDUSTRY'S GROWTH SO THAT IT WILL INDEED PLATEAU AND BECOME STAGNANT.

The advantages of selecting a growth industry are many.

Usually, it is a young industry in which competition hasn't had the opportunity to establish itself. Therefore, market penetration is far easier and less expensive.

Usually, profit margins are significantly higher. In stagnant industries, profit margins between 3% and 7% are the rule whereas in growth industries, profit margins of 10 times production costs are not rare.

46

Most venture capital firms want 10 times investment growths within five years. Since these goals are virtually impossible in non-growth industries, most venture capital firms rarely invest in firms which are not in growth industries.

The buying patterns of stagnant industries are usually pretty well established and therefore your company must conform to them. In growth areas, you can frequently shape buying patterns.

The following multipliers are rules-of-thumb of your company's value. Apply these multipliers to your projected net profits to determine your company's probable sales price.

Decaying industry	Net profits times 2.5 to 5.0
Stagnant industry	Net profits times 4.0 to 10.0
Older growth industries	Net profits times 7.5 to 25.0
Vigorous growth industry	Net profits times 25 to 75
Growth and glamour industries	Net profits times 50 to 1,000

Therefore, if your company's projected profits five years from now are $100,000, then your company's value would be between $400,000 and $1,000,000 if it is in a stagnant industry. It would sell for between $2,500,000 and $7,500,000 if it was in a vigorous growth industry.

CAMEO 3-1: THOSE LITTLE OLD WINE MAKERS   M, IS, F

Two electronic engineers who were laid off from Lockheed in 1967 wanted to start up a specialty power supply manufacturing facility. These men interviewed 82 financial houses to determine which would be interested in bankrolling them. Of the 82 interviewed, not one felt that power supplies was a lucrative area, however 69 considered the wine industry as one of the major growth industries through 1975.

These engineers began to do their homework in the wine industry. They attracted four key employees (who were experts in grapes and wine production) for 10% of their planned founders' stock. They solicited and received the support of a Northern California county's officials so that they were placed first on that county's Economic Development Agency (EDA) priorities list; whereupon they negotiated for $2,000,000 in low interest EDA loans. They invested their total savings of $20,000 in their venture and raised $3,000,000 from four different venture capital groups. These young men (their ages are 37 and 32) are now meeting every milestone of their business plan and should be successful.

Note that these men had the good sense to drop their preconceived opinions that what this world needs is another power supply manufacturer, that they had the personal courage to address an industry that they knew little about. They had the self honesty to realize that they needed expert key personnel and sought highly qualified individuals, they were generous in their stock distributions (the key employees receive 10%, the four venture capital groups split 45%, and they are to receive the balance as they meet their milestones), and finally they invested 14 months to properly do their homework and innovatively set up their company.

CAMEO 3-2: THE EFFECTS OF A GROWTH INDUSTRY ON YOUR SALES PRICE   M, IS

Two firms that we'll call Data Share Inc. and Wetsub Inc. were sold at approximately the same time. Let's look at them, what they sold for, and why they sold for the prices that they did.

Data Share Inc. was approximately eight years old and was run by a team of real professionals which had turned profits on all eight years of their operations. This firm worked primarily on large computer main frames and had developed a loyal customer following and a significant program library. In the last year, the founders turned $500,000 in profits and wanted to sell their company and retire. They located a much larger computer service company which bought their firm for $1,000,000 in cash and $1,500,000 in shares.

Wetsub Incorporated was a nine-month-old company which manufactured a unique non-pressurized submarine for recreational and professional skin divers (see cameo 2-3). This small manufacturing firm had developed several unique and valuable patents and appeared well on its way to becoming a major force when the founders were approached by a large conglomerate to sell out. In the first six months of their operations, they had built 83 submarines and were slightly in the black. At the end of the ninth month, they could produce 35 submarines a month and were back ordered 185 units. They projected a profit of slightly in excess of $75,000 for their first year and conservatively $400,000 at the end of their second year. The founders sold their company for $4,000,000 in cash and $2,000,000 in stock.

Why the differences in selling price?

Data Share was a service company whose management team wanted to retire. Main frame computer services is a stagnant industry and extremely vulnerable to mini-computers and microprocessors. Had the founders set up a microprocessor division and stayed in it long enough to develop a track record, they probably could have realized 10 times the selling price.

Wetsub was a product company addressing both a glamour and a vigorous growth industry. They sold their firm for considerably less than they could have realized if they had completed setting up their distribution (they only had 132 distributors when they sold), if they had built their production capabilities to meet their market demand, and if they had shopped for a buyer. However, as one of their engineers said, "The largest salary any of the major stockholders had ever made was $23,000 per year. When we started Wetsub, we paid ourselves $500 a month and when we were approached by the conglomerate with the $6,000,000 figure, it seemed like such an enormous amount. The dye was cast when we told our wives about the offer. Here they were sweating out food bills, our kids' clothing expenses, and our mortgage payments and wham . . . almost two million dollars each was waived in their eyes. When you show your wife the chance for the standard of living she always dreamed about, there is no turning back."

Minor Point 3-1: Tracking Growth Industries   M, IS, RS, F

Very few marketing departments "track" the financial communities' opinions of the industries to which they sell. Because of this oversight, many firms are frequently caught off guard when their customer base weakens and decays. If the financial communities decide that your customers are in a stagnant industry, they'll dry up your customers' cash flows and your sales will slacken.

If you are wise, you'll force your marketing group to continually track the financial communities' opinions so that you will not be caught off guard. You'll also discover that you'll learn about the new growth industries and have the opportunity to develop services and products for them long before your competitors learn about them through the journals and papers.

GROWTH VS. GLAMOUR   M, IS, RS, F

Until I started writing this book, I thought I understood the difference between growth and glamour industries. However, in interviewing venture capitalists, I swiftly learned that my definitions were different from others' definitions. In fact, if you ask 20 sophisticated sources for their definitions, I'll bet you get 20 different answers. Basically, let's say that glamour industries are growth industries with "pizzzazzz."

However, make no mistake, glamour adds significant value to your start-up as the multipliers above show. Even the most hardened venture capitalists are vulnerable to the desire to sit on the board of directors and associate with a Nobel prize winner, a leading author, or some show business celebrity.

I like to add from one to five prestige names to our clients' boards of directors or staff consultants so that the start-up acquires a glamour image. This ploy is surprisingly easy and inexpensive because most celebrities feel extremely vulnerable and are continuously searching for escape paths if their fame should falter and they lose their demand. Being on several boards and acting as part-time staff consultants gives them a more rounded image if they should have to go out and find employment in industry.

Since I am a strong advocate of using board members, you'll discover that your celebrities can help your firm in many ways. Frequently they will name drop you over national television; frequently they will use and demonstrate your product as a prop in a movie; and usually they'll endorse your products. I like to use celebrities for "buddy calls" to gain admittance to some executive who would never see me without the celebrity. Top executives are just as vulnerable as everyone else in name dropping and will grant you hours if afterwards he can say, "I had lunch with

Art Linkletter today and he said that Elizabeth Taylor said . . . ."
Thereafter, in that executive's eyes, you are a quasi-celebrity because of
your connections and you'll gain easier access to that man.

CAMEO 3-3: USING CELEBRITIES   M, IS, RS, F

This start-up originally attracted a well known author to its board and
through the author attracted two top box office stars. Since the start-up was
using laser technology in food processing inspection, it had little trouble
attracting its three million in venture capital.

Things went extremely well for this company; however it was not able to get
the largest food processor on the west coast to even evaluate its equipment.
After three years of fruitless efforts, the laser company decided to try and penetrate the potential customer from the president downwards as well as from the
buyers upwards. They did it as follows. They learned that both the board
chairman and the president of the food company were extremely active in
supporting the Boy Scouts, were avid tennis nuts, and abhorred salesmen.
Since one of the movie stars on the board of the laser technology company
was a tennis nut, the company asked him to lend his name to a celebrity
tennis tournament for the Boy Scouts and to attract other movie and television stars to participate in the tournament. They got their potential customer,
the food processor company, to co-host the tournament with their firm. In the
tournament work sessions, they never mentioned their product but worked
with the co-host's top management to make the tournament a success. They
made certain that the co-host's top executives got the major credit for the
tournament's success (it was a complete sell out and made significant profits
for the Boy Scouts).

However, they never learned for certain if the efforts paid off because three
weeks before the tournament, they received an order for an evaluation test
console. Five weeks after the tournament, they were invited to retrofit all of
that company's inspection equipment with their laser technology. Their sales
manager and salesmen swear that they would have gotten the orders without
the tournament ploy. However, the penetration from the top down certainly
did no harm.

HOW TO DETERMINE THE GROWTH INDUSTRIES   M, IS

As axioms five and six define, the financial investment groups determine which industries will be growth and which will decay. Therefore, the
safest and best sources for determining which industries your company
should address are these financial groups. You will find most of the following groups are rather free in giving anyone their evaluations of industries
and therefore it is easy to determine the status of your industry. Interro-
gate several investment groups in each of the following venture capital
avenues:

(a) Private venture capital groups
(b) SBICs (small business investment companies)
(c) Commercial bankers
(d) Investment bankers
(e) Mutual Funds
(f) Foundations
(g) MESBICs (Minority Enterprise Small Business Investment Companies), if you are a member of a minority
(h) Investment clubs

As true with all testing, you test each category two ways. First as a potential start-up and again as a potential investor. Keep good records on who said what. You may want to include this information in your business plan and, more important, you may want to come back to the man for funding.

Now that you have identified the growth industries, it's time to segment them, perform a market gap analysis on those segments which interest you, and determine which industry will best support your start-up.

4 · Market Gap Analysis

Now that we have completed the basic fundamentals, we can get started in the interesting part of this book—meeting your company's significant milestones. In the next three chapters we'll achieve your first milestone, uncovering a viable market which will support your company's profit objectives and therefore allow you to meet your personal goals.

Market gap analysis is an extremely powerful tool for uncovering those areas in the market in which demand far exceeds supply. This tool, coupled with the verification techniques of Chapter Five, will assure your company of a lucrative market.

Like a wheat harvester, a good gap analysis has a hopper effect in converting everyday information into bunches of lucrative product and service gaps which few have thought of before. A typical gap analysis uncovers between 25 and 50 viable long-range gaps, between 10 and 20 short-termed gaps (targets-of-opportunity), and 50 to 100 mirages. "Targets-of-opportunity" are those short-term markets which are lucrative today but will dry up tomorrow. Many of our clients have started generating their cash flows by addressing these targets first and phasing in their long-term products as soon as they are ready. However, you must realize that you are addressing a target from the onset.

The major problem with market gap analysis, as any marketing man worth his salt will tell you, is never the uncovering of lucrative options. "When you run a good analysis, your problem is that you uncover too many gaps. There you stand with a couple of dozen multi-million dollar opportunities and you act just like a kid in front of a candy counter. You never know which gap to pursue first."

Minor Point 4-1: A Warning   M, IS

Market gap analysis can be a very intoxicating experience. It is easy to become quite lightheaded when a lucrative gap is uncovered. You must run this analysis as objectively and dispassionately as you would in using determinates to solve a math problem or reference tables to determine a quantity. Market gap analysis is nothing more than a tool and it works properly only when the tool is used right. If you allow yourself to become emotionally involved (and it is extremely easy to do), you will miss obvious gaps and what is worse, build bias into your analysis and chase a mirage.

CAMEO 4-1: THE POWER OF GAP ANALYSIS   M, IS

When an individual runs a gap analysis by himself, the analysis is only as good as the individual. However, when you add two individuals to one analysis, their results are usually over twice as productive as they would have been if each had run an individual analysis and totaled their results. This multiplying effect continues as you add people until the group becomes uncontrollable. However, with people you add another variable, as this cameo illustrates.

When the machinery of gap analysis was first developed, we ran the first gap seminar session for a very progressive major corporation (a Fortune 500 company). They sent 35 of their top marketing men for this experimental three-day session. Since none of us knew the power of the tool, no attempts to harness and control it were made. Here are the results:

(a) Well over 300 viable market gaps with sales potentials in excess of $10,000,000 each were uncovered.

(b) Since the company neither expected nor had the capabilities to even address a minor percentage of these gaps, their total new product development efforts were completely stopped for two years while top management wrestled with which gap to address first.

(c) Of the 35 attendees, 22 quit within one year after the session to address some of the more lucrative gaps on their own. Today, 18 are millionaires.

(d) With the loss of over 60% of their top marketing people, the company had major problems with their sales department and had to invest years of efforts in attracting equal executive talents.

(e) The frictions and frustrations involved in selecting which gaps to address first were surprisingly strong and long lasting in the top levels of management.

(f) The company has yet to invite us back to run a second session.

To the best of my knowledge, this was the only time in history that this machinery was allowed to operate for a company without extreme limitations. After four years of calibrating the machinery's controls to protect the host company, we thought that we had finally tamed the beast so that it would spit out only three to five viable gaps (a quantity any company can handle). Then we made the mistake of allowing vertical talents to participate and all hell broke loose again.

Briefly, this session was performed for a computer manufacturer and the attendees were specialists in R&D, manufacturing, marketing, sales, administration, customers, and users. Instead of having just one discipline, we had almost totally vertical participation. After two hours we knew that we were in trouble and began to add every limiting factor that we knew, but the beast ran wild with the following results:

(a) Fourty-three viable gaps with sales potentials in excess of $10,000,000/year.

(b) Seventy-three viable gaps with sales potentials in excess of $5,000,000/year.

(c) Twenty-seven lucrative targets-of-opportunity which could immediately be addressed with negligible front money.

(d) Eighty-seven mirages.

(e) Top management gave the go-ahead to address 15 gaps simultaneously. Not only did this decision spread their talents too thin to do an adequate job in any area, two years later they began to make the Wall Street Journal for their $350,000,000 in development expenses. The Rook Theory had struck again (minor point 14-6).

(f) We have never been asked to hold a second session.

HOW TO PERFORM A GAP ANALYSIS   M, IS

For ease in understanding, let's describe the analysis tool and simultaneously illustrate its use to uncover viable gaps in the leisure industry.

STEP ONE: Lay out your company's objectives as your reference point.

Example: As we discussed in the second chapter, you can't go very far unless you know where you wish to go. Therefore, you laid out your personal goals and from these derived your broad-brush company objectives. For this illustration, let's say that your broad-brush objectives are:

(1)   We want to address a long-term growth industry (in this example the leisure industry).

(2)   We want to manufacture an electronic product for this industry.

(3)   We want a minimum of 20 : 1 markup.

(4)   We want a minimum market potential of 1,000,000 units per year.

(5)   We want no viable competition immediately.

(6)   We want a new product but do not want the pioneering efforts that many new products require. In other words, we want immediate customer acceptance.

(7)   We want to sell through already existing sales networks. We want these networks to stock enough (on their dollars) so that no front money is required for our company. We'll factor our purchase orders.

(8)   We want a minimum of six different venture capital avenues open to us. We want to give the image of both a growth company and a glamour company.

(9)   We want to produce a low technology product which can be produced by a minimum of 12 jobbers (manufacturers who produce for other firms) in our area. We'll develop in-house capabilities when sales and profits warrant it.

(10)   We want a product which will allow us to pirate the top talents in the U.S.

If you are new to gap analysis, you may feel that these specifications are almost impossible to meet. However, you'll soon find that they are low demands and probably have over a thousand gaps in the leisure industry which exceed them. If you really want to "blow your mind," attempt a gap analysis in the mini-computer and microprocesser industries. Regardless of how tough you make the initial objectives, gaps which exceed them come out of the hopper in batches.

Since it is our intent to show you the machinery of how market gap analysis works, we'll only follow one leg of this example analysis. If you are interested in the leisure industry, it will be a minor task to pursue the other legs.

STEP TWO: Segment your industry into its major components.
   Example: The leisure industry can be segmented several different ways. Let's look at a few:

(1) Adult-Children-Family	(5) Economic Levels
(2) Male-Female-Both	(6) Educational Levels
(3) Active-Passive-Combination of Both	(7) Ethnic Groups, etc.
(4) Spring-Summer-Winter-Fall	

We'll follow the first leg of the first segment and explore only Adults in this example.

STEP THREE: Segment each of the major components of step two into its major sub-segments.
   Example: The major sub-segments of the Leisure-Adult segment can be divided into:

(1) Workdays	(4) Retirement
(2) Weekends	(5) Holidays
(3) Vacation	(6) Others

STEP FOUR: Segment the major sub-segments of step three into their minor sub-segments.

Example: Following only the first leg in our illustration, the minor sub-segments of Leisure-Adult-Workdays are:

(1) Post-Work/Pre-Dinner	(5) Awake/Pre-Work
(2) Dinner	(6) Coffee Breaks
(3) Post-Dinner/Pre-Bed	(7) Lunch Periods
(4) Bed	(8) Others

You'll note that so far, all that we have done is focus, magnify, refocus, remagnify, refocus again, remagnify again, until the large growth industry is divided into handleable portions. An industry like the leisure industry is so large that you cannot begin to see it until you segment it down to its sub-sections. We are now just beginning to see the trees in the forest. The more complex an industry, the more you have to divide, redivide, and reredivide.

STEP FIVE: Eliminate those areas which do not meet our specifications outlined in step one.

Example: In our particular case, our initial specifications are so broad and so easy that we cannot yet eliminate any sub-segment. The beginner might want to eliminate (6) Coffee Breaks as an unpromising area but in the last gap analysis that I conducted, even this small sub-segment produced over 70 viable gaps, each of which would support a healthy company. So go lightly in eliminating areas until you have at least examined them a little more deeply.

STEP SIX: List the problems that exist in each area of step four.

Example: Since we are following only the first leg, the problem of Leisure-Adult-Workdays, Post-Work/Pre-Dinner are:

(1)   When work ends, I am tired
(2)   Traffic frustrations on the way home from work
(3)   Feet are tired and hot
(4)   Clothes are rumpled, seem to cling, and are uncomfortable.
(5)   Wife is tired and grouchy
(6)   I experience post-work blaaaas
(7)   Grocery stores seem crowded and slow
(8)   Must shout at children to get them in for their baths
(9)   Must walk the dog and curb her
(10) Dog is in heat and every stray mutt within a mile is making passes
(11) Need pre-dinner cocktails to just unwind
(12) TV news is depressing
(13) Lawn needs mowing, gardens weeding, roses clipped, etc.

(14) Kids are grouchy and hungry

(15) Dinner preparations are slow, noisy, and smelly

(16) Telephone solicitors are irritating

(17) You can probably list between 200 and 400 other items which are common to all Leisure-Adult-Workdays, Post-Work/Pre-Dinner.

Now list them along the left hand side of a worksheet leaving ample room on the right for evaluations.

STEP SEVEN: Eliminate those problem areas whose solutions do not conform to our specifications defined in step one.

Example: Usually the beginner gets too fast with the blue pencil here and eliminates problem areas before he really thinks them through. If you are wise, you'll eliminate only those points which are so minor that you know customers will not pay for a viable solution. Since this book's purpose is only to give you methods and techniques, we must eliminate all but a few. Let's retain only (2), (3), (8), and (10) for our example.

STEP EIGHT: Matrix Analysis. On the sheet of paper in which you listed the problem areas along the left hand side, along the top place the numbers of your specifications in step one. Place a check mark in each column where the solution to the problem would meet your requirements. Select those areas that are most promising for future steps.

Example: With our easy initial specifications of step one, we suspect that all four problem areas selected will probably easily exceed our requirements, but for right now, we can only intuitively guess that we can meet our specifications (1), (4), (7), (8), and (10).

STEP NINE: Along the far right hand side of your matrix, list probable solutions to each of the problems. Do not hesitate to list many possible solutions to each problem.

Example: Leisure-Adult-Workday, Post-Work/Pre-Dinner items (2), (3), (8), and (10).

(2) Traffic Frustrations. This is a major gap with real promise. Let's face it, our present traffic control systems are expensive, ineffective, inefficient, not really safe, and irritating. Each year we waste billions of man hours, billions of gallons of fuel, and spend a billion dollars to implement, police, and sustain our lousy traffic control system.

How viable would it be to develop a roadway sign which would sense traffic densities, traffic speeds, the surface of the roadways, the quality of the visabilities, and vary the speed limits to these factors? How viable would it be to allow each sign to "talk" with signs on roadways parallel to it and shunt traffic to other less filled roads? How viable would it be to have these signs "talk" to signs upstream and downstream to warn drivers of upcoming hazards? None of these things are very tough to do from a scientific standpoint. If you examine the savings realized in police salaries by having the signs photograph offenders and ticket them by mail, then the signs would cost our governments nothing. They would generate dollars instead of being an overhead expense.

This gap appears viable and should be researched further.

(3)   Tired and Hot Feet. Approximately every adult who must stand or walk on concrete complains of this problem As the adult reaches middle and elderly years and circulation decreases, the problem compounds. Consider a pair of comfortable slippers which contain a vibrator to massage the feet as a person relaxes after work. Each slipper of course would be battery operated so that the wearer could walk without electrical cords. This gap should be explored further.

(8)   Must Shout At Children. Have you ever noticed that even the most petite and feminine wife sounds like a baseball umpire when she tries to catch Junior's attention to come in for his evening bath? And how women hate this task! Consider an electrical chime (or whistle) whose volume can be varied to beckon Junior even five blocks away. You could allow each customer to program her own ten-bar tune so that her call is unique from all others. Junior now has no excuse and all his mother has to do is press a button. Would it sell?

(10)   Female Dog In Heat. Consider, if you will, an electronic chastity belt which will allow the female to perform her usual body functions but will apply an electrical pulse (a shock) if any foreign object should attempt to penetrate the lady's pubic area. Nothing dampens a male sex drive faster than an electrical shock applied at the right spot.

We'll use the dog chastity belt as an example throughout this book.

STEP TEN: Select the best gap (or gaps) and begin verifying them in testing.

Example: At this stage, you do not truly know whether the gaps uncovered are viable or mirages. They must be tested to determine the market's demand. However, the four gaps discussed in our example have been subjected to thorough testing with the following results:

(2)   Traffic Controls is obviously not a leisure industry product, however at the time of this writing over 30% of the venture capitalists consider this a growth or an interesting area in which to invest. The market potential is 20,000,000 units per year, the sales markup is only 12 to 1 (however this increases to considerably above 20 to 1 with lease practices), there is viable competition, there is a significant pioneering effort involved because governments do not like to change operations and the police departments (and their unions) will outlaw this concept because it replaces policemen, there are five existing and efficient sales networks which will sell this equipment, there are 14 venture capital avenues open to it, and specifications (9) and (10) are easily met.

The primary drawbacks are that it will take from 18 months to three years to sell even evaluation units and will require considerable lobbying expenses to override labor's and policemen's hurdles. If you like to work in the government sector and if you'll be innovative in your marketing (i.e., give unions involved a bonus for each variable sign installed like the railroads pay for every truck piggybacked), then it is an extremely viable gap.

(3) Vibrator Slippers meets or exceeds all specifications except markup (3 to 1 markup for 1,000,000 pairs per year at $10 each). I would consider this gap as not viable for this one reason.

(8) Electronic Child Caller. For the 20 to 1 markup, a minimum sales price of $20 is needed. The demand would then be only 10,000 units per year. To reach the 1,000,000 units, you must lower your price to $4.98 which gives you only a 5 to 1 markup. This gap is marginal.

(10) The Electronic Chastity Belt exceeds all specifications by a considerable margin. At a sales price of $10 the volume will be approximately 10,000,000 units and the markup 25 to 1. The competition is large but extremely stagnant so therefore it isn't considered viable. There are 11 various sales networks and the opening stocking inventories will be around 1,000,000 units (more than enough to start a viable company).

Now that you have seen how gap analysis works, let's look at some other examples of how you might use this tool.

CAMEO 4-2: REVERSE GAP ANALYSIS   M, IS

This man was a buyer for a major electronics manufacturer when he decided that he wanted to start his own company. As a buyer, he observed a real weakness in the young and brash electronics industry. Those old line firms which had dominated the industry through the 1930s, 40s, and early 50s lacked the flexibility and drive that was needed in the newer segments (the growth segment) of his industry. He therefore performed a reverse gap analysis and searched for components manufactured only by these firms. He wanted to enter the components industry where the demand was large and the competition was the worst.

He took approximately nine months to investigate all of the ultra-conservative areas and finally decided that the circuit breaker segment deserved new blood. Of over 600 electronic buyers surveyed, approximately 520 were extremely unhappy with all circuit breaker suppliers and over 300 promised to give any new entry all of their business. We don't need to dwell on the circuit breaker segment here except to state that its blunders truly invited new blood. The technology is relatively simple and inexpensive, there are very few patents of value, and in the last 30 years, there have been few new products. To show you the sluggishness, one of the big five has its sales manager in charge of both QA and production. Its president was board chairman for another competitor while his son was general manager of a third competitor. All seemed to own controlling stock of all others.

So our buyer, along with five engineers, moonlighted and developed a complete family of miniature circuit breakers demanded by most instrument manufacturers. After approximately 300 man hours and $1,150, they felt that they were ready to notify the unhappy buyers of the new entry. They received small evaluation orders from 425 firms and when these firms had tested their first order, production orders began to follow. These men had only a rented two-room office, some stationery, an answering service, and 11 production houses which could build high quality circuit breakers.

When word of the new circuit breaker company got out, the better manufacturers' reps, distributors, and mail order houses started contacting them for permission to sell their components. These firms had been stung too often by the competitions' blunders, and since circuit breakers are a critical component of all instrument manufacturers, the new entry looked like a natural.

When the tiny company was really beginning to roll and the founders were seriously considering quitting their jobs to pursue it full time, they received a tender offer from one of their competitors for $350,000.

This in the industry is called a bribe price. Three hundred and fifty thousand dollars is a pretty good price for a company with no manufacturing capabilities, an infant sales network, no new products, rented offices, and a skeleton crew. The founders accepted the offer, signed an agreement not to enter the circuit breaker industry for 10 years, and are now busy developing another family of components in another abused area. All are still full-time employees in their original jobs.

CAMEO 4-3: A GAP ANALYSIS ON CUSTOMERS   RS, F

A barber had really experienced a string of setbacks and was deeply in debt when he visited us. There was something about the man that made you realize that he was a winner but when he came through our doors, he had debts in excess of $60,000 and only 200 spendable dollars. Though he could have claimed voluntary bankruptcy with honor (most of the debts were accrued by his ex-wife), he visited every creditor and asked for time to make payments. Since he had nothing, involuntary bankruptcy was impractical.

We found a marginal location for his barber shop (a semi-deserted shopping center whose owner agreed to a year's lease on credit). The location offered a minimum of $1,000 per month in gross sales. Our barber spent $195 on obsolete equipment, moved into his shop, and started cutting hair. He slept in the back of his shop. In three months he had built his business up to $1,500/month and there it leveled off. Since he needed $3,500/month in net profits, he could never make it operating like a standard barber. So he performed a gap analysis on haircut customers and then became a very unconventional barber.

Now a customer gap analysis is identical to a product gap analysis except you look at customer profiles (instead of industry profiles). Our barber quickly realized that most customers are extremely bored while they wait for a haircut. Most consider it essential down time.

Our barber therefore decided to "give free drinks" to his customers and observed that his income almost doubled from his additional "tips." Not only did his income per customer increase significantly, he attracted drinking men from a 20-mile radius. He was forced to hire two additional barbers. Within four months, his profits had reached $3,000/month.

Now the drinking man's barber shop had a unique personality which conflicted with the children, mothers, and non-drinkers who needed service. Therefore, he opened a second shop in another vacant store, hired two college students to babysit the children while their fathers enjoyed his primary shop, and decorated this second shop like a child's fairytale. His shop realized significant sales from mothers who wanted free babysitting while they shopped. The second shop's profits plateaued at $1,500/month.

The barber and the shopping center owner then went into partnerships in establishing a beauty parlor and a laundromat. Beauty shop hair driers, hair rinses, etc., were offered to laundromat ladies. Within six months, these two profit centers were adding another $2,200/month in net profits.

The slight "bending of the liquor laws" began to concern the barber. It was a miracle that the state's alcohol control board hadn't discovered and outlawed his "free drink" practices. He therefore opened a legitimate pub and package store next door to his shops. He then bought drinks legitimately from his pub and "gave" them to his drinking customers. The pub also served tasty snacks (venison, veal, oysters, etc.) and became profitable in itself.

When the barber first came into the semi-deserted shopping center, there were 22 vacancies in 48 shops. The additional customers that he attracted made the center an attractive location for other shops and after he opened his pub, the center was completely occupied. Though the additional traffic increased his businesses, his growth was stunted and his profits plateaued at $25,000/month. Today, he is beginning to realize additional profits from a line of barber and beauty shop services that he supplies to other shops.

Where would this man be if he had insisted upon being just another conventional barber?

CAMEO 4-4: DISTRIBUTION GAP ANALYSIS   M

This start-up was a failure because of timing but since its concepts were valid, it should be presented.

Briefly, several marketing analysts evaluated all of the major distribution networks to determine which network showed the most promise of guaranteeing a start-up's success. It didn't take long for these men to realize that the major oil companies' distribution networks were by far the strongest for reaching the consumer. Briefly, there are approximately 400,000 service stations and the average car owner visits one at least twice weekly. While his car is being attended, the consumer has approximately five minutes of "impulse buy" time. This distribution network realizes 125,000,000 five-minute sales chances each week. Even with a 0.01% sales close average, this would mean more sales than they could realize from any other network in the U.S.

These men then performed an in-depth market gap study on service station operations and uncovered 53 viable gaps which were in harmony with the stations' operations and complemented the blue chip images of the major oil companies. All 53 gaps offered considerable profits to all involved (the oil companies, the warehouses, the service station owners, and the start-up).

Prospects looked exceptional when they contacted the oil companies, received excellent treatment from their corporate offices, received extremely large orders to "test" the gaps, and received ample front money from the customers to begin operations. The founders were still in the lightheaded stage when the energy crisis hit, gasoline appeared to dry up completely, and all customers cancelled their first orders "until things stabilized." Though the founders lost a little over $15,000 in their venture, the same individuals are now developing another family of products for another extremely viable sales network. They'll probably invest another $15,000 and if some crisis hits to wipe it out, they'll probably invest another $15,000 in another attempt. However, one day they are going to hit and these boys will hit big.

Minor Point 4-2: The Use of Gaps in This Book   M, IS, RS, F

As stated at the beginning of this book, I cannot disclose confidential information about my clients and therefore have had to substitute product and service gaps for their real equivalents. Therefore, if a gap mentioned in this book seems attractive to you, feel free to test it and use it. Since I have a library of notebooks filled with market gaps, I can assure you that if you run your own gap analysis, you'll uncover lucrative areas far greater than the few mentioned in this text.

5 · Disguised Market Testing

PROLOGUE   M, IS

Now that you have performed your market gap analysis (in a growth industry I hope), it is time to determine whether those gaps are valid or just mirages or short-term targets-of-opportunity. Remember that approximately 50%–70% of your gaps may be mirages, 10%–25% will probably be only targets-of-opportunity, and the balance, long-term viable gaps. It's better to learn early whether your primary gaps are real or just a hopeful wish. Guard against bias until this hurdle is cleared.

To make certain that your start-up is addressing a viable gap, you should run several independent tests and then check their results to make certain that they correlate. It is the intent of this chapter to show several inexpensive test techniques which will give you confidence that your start-up will be built on a solid demand foundation. Incidentally, if your testing is solid, you'll discover that your venture capitalists will just verify a few points and then accept the balance. If your testing is incomplete, then the capitalists are forced to run complete market tests and your fundings will be delayed until these tests are completed and their results studied. No one is going to invest major dollars in any venture without being certain that you have significant market demand.

THE NEED TO PERFORM DISGUISED MARKET TESTS
M, IS

Realize that to protect your company you must perform disguised tests. If you make the error of illuminating your gap and your plans prematurely, you may lose your gap to someone or some company which is in a better posture to penetrate your market more rapidly than you. The world is filled with pirates. You may have your concepts stolen and patented before you can move. You could receive harassment, nuisance lawsuits, attempts to block your credit lines, and attempts to damage your reputation. Your concepts could be thrown in the public domain by jealous individuals who will publish your secrets. You may get biased and therefore invalid test results.

I know of no case where open testing in a true gap area did not bring unwanted repercussions. Though usually you can overcome the problems that others throw in your way, who needs unwarranted problems due to premature disclosures? You and your fellow founders are going to be busy enough clearing the hurdles essential for success without inviting unnecessary hurdles.

A WARNING

Realize that 95% of the people that you must interview consider themselves permanently locked into the employee syndrome. Expect many to be extremely jealous of you and your freedoms. Remember that professional people (engineers, scientists, managers) can be very petty. Realize that purchasing agents and buyers are notorious for leaking information to your established competition. Recognize that these competitors like the status quo and that your new company is a threat to this status quo. Most feel that a minor swat or series of swats will help eliminate you, a disruptive force, in your formative stages.

CAMEO 5-1: THE EFFECTS OF A NON-DISGUISED MARKET TEST   M, IS, RS, F

Approximately two years ago, we decided to test the pet chastity belt openly to see the effects of open testing on an "explosive" product. We wanted to see if we could correlate the open tests with the tons of disguised data that we had accumulated. Realize that this product would have the following effects on the pet industry:

(1) It would jeopardize the lucrative veterinarian neutering operations. (The average vet realizes from $4,000–$12,000 a year on these operations).

(2) It would jeopardize six major pet products which realize over $10,000,000/year each in sales.

(3) It would jeopardize approximately 75 lesser products.

(4) It would introduce a major new company into the well established pet products industry.

(5)   There is a great deal of emotionalism in the pet industries concerning species population controls. The chastity belt hit at the heart of this emotionalism.

Certain precautions were taken so that other market researchers, in investigating the effects of this new threat, could not penetrate the ploy. We used an established dummy company with established lines of credit. The researchers who investigated this dummy company would discover that it had in excess of $1,000,000 in initial investments and approximately $5,000,000 in options that it could claim at a moment's notice (several venture capital firms were aware of the tests and agreed to lend us their names as our money sources). The name of the president of the firm was totally fictitious (Martin R. Robinson) and seven of the board members were partially fictionalized.

The following results were observed:

(1)   Where the disguised test results correlated within acceptable limits, there were absolutely no correlations in the open tests. Sales would be from 5,000 belts a year to 15,000,000 belts a year depending upon which test results you accepted. (All disguised tests indicated 10,000,000 plus-or-minus-10% sales per year).

(2)   The fictitious president, Mr. Robinson, developed quite a rumored past in a very short time. Several of the major pet distribution managers confided in us that they learned from informed and reliable sources that Mr. Robinson was a convicted felon who had served several terms for confidence crimes.

(3)   It was rumored that the electronic chastity belt was extremely unsafe and had killed several children, hundreds of female dogs, and thousands of male dogs. Since only four prototype belts had ever been built and never sold, this rumor was particularly vicious.

(4)   The venture capitalists, who knew about the ploy and agreed to lend their names to our lines of credit, received pressures to drop us.

(5)   The city and county animal shelters were extremely concerned about the effects of these belts on their operations. It was rumored that if the belt was not made illegal, they would experience 10% lay-offs.

(6)   We learned of several dozen attempts to make local, state, and federal governments outlaw this "killer" belt.

(7)   The SPCA, which had received numerous complaints concerning the torture belts, requested six samples for evaluation.

(8)   The dummy company received inquiries and orders from approximately 600 pet stores.

(9)   In the three months we conducted the open tests, the company's answering service received 211 abusive telephone calls. Had the company had more than just a post office address, we would probably have received abusive visitors.

Though we had intended to allow the tests to run for six months, it became so ugly that we stopped after three months. We were extremely thankful for the protective shell that we had placed around ourselves because some of the ugliness might have splattered on our families, our homes, and ourselves.

Minor Point 5-1: Open-Ended vs. Closed-Ended Questions in Testing   M, IS, RS

A start-up should use open-ended testing in its initial stages because the answers given frequently illuminate the most lucrative segments of the industry. Once your product design has stabilized, you can switch to closed-ended questions for fine-tuning your specifications, however until then, keep your view broad. An example of a closed-ended question is "Which color dresses will women wear next year—red, green, or blue?" An open-ended question is "What do you think women will wear in the future?"

DISGUISED TESTING TECHNIQUES   M, IS, RS

Usually researchers use two disguises in testing and run these disguises through identical testing techniques. They cross check these parallel tests against each other to make certain that the test results correlate and that they aren't introducing bias into their tests.

For ease of explanation, let's use the pet chastity belt as our example throughout the balance of this chapter.

The first disguise is to develop one or more cover stories which will make the people that you test want to give you accurate information. In the case of the chastity belt, three cover stories were used. To pet stores and veterinarians, the researchers acted like potential customers who had dogs and cats who were coming into heat. To pet supply manufacturers, the researchers were considering opening a very large kennel which would purchase their products direct. They then cross checked these tests by posing as a consortium of animal clinics banding together to realize quantity purchasing discounts. To the SPCA branches and several dozen dog pounds, they posed as authors who were researching animal population controls for articles and books. Frequently they had the local agencies cross check with both vets and manufacturers so that they could further verify their data. You would be surprised at how accurate manufacturers and vets will be with agencies and how distorted their stories may be to potential customers.

The second disguise is to let the public think that you are going to release a very similar product and openly test that product. In the case of the chastity belt, researchers posed as potential founders of an odorant product which would disguise the female's in-heat odors so that male dogs wouldn't make advances. There were several products already on the market with these odorants and they were realizing only marginal sales because their products are only marginally reliable. Therefore the parallel product wasn't much of a threat.

Most market researchers utilize an alias when performing disguised tests so that when they are called on the telephone, the alias forewarns them to slip into their cover story before talking.

INEXPENSIVE MARKETING TESTS   M, IS, RS

There are many expensive, sophisticated market testing techniques which will not be covered because they require experienced professionals to run them and correlate the data. The following methods are simple, effective, inexpensive, and you can readily run them yourself.

(1) PERSON-TO-PERSON INTERVIEWS WITH MAJOR CUSTOMERS

AXIOM SEVEN: EIGHTY PERCENT OF YOUR SALES WILL COME FROM TWENTY PERCENT OF YOUR CUSTOMERS.

Person-to-person interviews are probably the best and most reliable technique that you can use because you can not only hear voice inflections but see facial expressions. Perform these interviews with only the largest and most knowledgeable users because their technique of gathering information is the slowest and most expensive that you can use. Be aware of the open-ended possibilities and allow a portion of these interviews to develop into a brainstorming session where the expert tells you where he sees his industry going in the next five years. You'll frequently discover that the experts you are interviewing are extremely accurate in their forecasts of the future, and you can change your plans significantly.

(2) TELEPHONE INTERVIEWS

This technique is considerably faster and less expensive than personal interviews but it is less flexible and versatile. At best, you'll have 15 minutes (8 minutes is the norm) of effective interview time and since you can't see facial expressions, you can't be as effective in open-ended techniques. However, you can hear voice inflections and if you'll allow yourself a portion of your 8 minutes for your tested person to lead you, you'll find it quite revealing.

(3) DIRECT MAIL QUESTIONNAIRES

This is a limited test method because you are usually limited to close-ended questions, most respondents will not invest more than five minutes (approximately five simple questions) on your questionnaire, and rarely can you expect more than five percent to respond within three weeks.

(4) COMBINATION MAIL-TELEPHONE SURVEYS

One of the more effective ways of overcoming the problems involved in both mail and telephone interviews is to combine them. Consider first writing the person you wish to interview and tell him who you are, what you are doing, why you need the information, the questions that you need answered, and then tell him that you will telephone him at a specific time on a specific date.

If you use this technique, you will not have to waste precious telephone interview time in a preamble. When you phone, he knows all of the introductory information, has had ample time to read, digest, and think about your questions, and you'll discover that your answers are much more accurate than if you catch him cold.

(5) LIBRARY RESEARCH

It is easy and inexpensive to learn the basic statistics of the industry that you are addressing from the libraries of the Department of Commerce, the Small Business Administration, the larger stock brokers, investment bankers, and commercial banks, and college and public libraries.

If you live in a major city, use your central library's professional researchers. These expert library researchers are free and can gather in-depth information for you in one-tenth of the time that it will take you. The primary drawback to using these researchers is that they require tightly defined questions (e.g., How many female dogs are there in the United States, how many neutering operations were performed last year, how many veterinarians are there in the southeast, who are the primary pet supply manufacturers in the U.S. and what are their addresses, etc.). A list of 130 questions on the chastity belt were asked and it took them three weeks to get the answers. It took our researchers five weeks to dig out the same information. Realize that these library researchers use Department of Commerce information, university information, authors' research, brokers' research, other government agency data, etc., for their answers. Do not expect to think that data picked up from different library research is independent: chances are they've used the same government and industry sources.

(6) MAIL ORDER PRE-SELL

Place an advertisement in the proper journal and see who orders or shows interest. Return all checks and orders with a cover story but keep accurate records because you'll want to contact them when you have a product to sell.

(7) *TRADE SHOW PRE-SALES*

Rent a booth in a trade show and attempt to pre-sell from preliminary sales literature and prototype samples. Frequently the caliber of information gathered from the professionals who visit your booth and answer your questions is equivalent to years of personal interviews.

(8) *SEMINAR JAMMING*

You see this technique being used more and more at conventions and trade shows where large numbers of experts gather to attend seminars. Select the sessions that will attract those experts whose opinions you need and jam it in such a way that these experts volunteer their information without realizing what you are doing. This is usually accomplished by sending in a team of ringers to audience watch and lead the seminar into their topic. One man asks the speaker a question close to his subject, then another ringer asks a question further away from the assigned topic and then the third ringer asks a question in your topic area. In a short time, the session degrades into a brainstorming session with the audience contributing in your research area. Though this is a rotten trick to pull on the main speaker, in an hour's time you'll collect several years of research.

(9) *DISTRIBUTION TESTING*

While you are investigating the distribution networks open to you, ask several salesmen to allow you to pull "buddy calls" with them on their customers. If you know how to conduct yourself in front of their customers, they'll help you collect your needed information.

CORRELATE YOUR INDEPENDENT TEST RESULTS

When you have completed your tests, make certain that each independent test's results correlates with the other test results to within acceptable limits (usually to within 15%–20%). If the data doesn't correlate, then one of the following is probably true.

(1)   You used invalid test procedures (i.e., one of your researchers sold instead of gathered information, someone "dry-labbed" his tests, etc.).

(2)   The market that you are addressing is too explosive and your test data became obsolete too fast.

(3)   You are chasing a mirage instead of a valid gap.

In the case of the pet chastity belt, the test results from the disguised tests correlated to within 10% for all disguises and for all test techniques used. The market was a strong 10,000,000 units a year provided that excellent marketing and sales disciplines were followed. When the disguises were dropped (Cameo 5-1), no data correlated either with the disguised testing or with any of the undisguised testing.

Minor Point 5-2: Try a 10-Minute Price Test   M, IS, RS, F

Many unsophisticated people feel that an ethical company will quote the same prices to all prospective customers. Try the following telephone test to see how valid this assumption is.

Telephone a veterinarian and in an angry voice say, "My kids brought home a female mutt several months ago and now the darned dog is in heat. I'm phoning all of the vets in the yellow pages to see who will quote the lowest price to neuter this German Shepherd. What do you charge?"

After you get the price, wait 10 minutes and have your wife telephone the same vet and say, "My little baby, Fifi, is a German Shepherd and such a sweet dog. Now all kinds of horrible boy dogs are beginning to get interested in her. Is a neutering operation safe? Will it affect her sweet personality? Will it affect her figure? How much does it cost?"

CAMEO 5-2: MAIL ORDER PRE-SALES   M

The founders of Berkeley Laboratories developed a revolutionary technique for sealing the glass used in a laser. They had the technology to produce more efficient lasers at a fraction of the costs.

They invested $10,000 (half of their total capital) building non-operating photographable mock-ups and advertising in the correct journals. They didn't want to approach the venture capitalists until after their firm was running and they knew that they could factor all purchase orders received for their operating capital. The advertisements brought several dozen orders and a nuisance lawsuit from a competitor which saw the ad and wanted to delay the start-up. The law suit killed their ability to factor their orders, stopped venture capitalists from investing in them, and even made most of their vendors place them on a COD basis. Therefore, with their remaining $10,000, they built to the mail-order pre-sales and had to wait to fill other orders until they were finally paid.

This tiny company limped along underfinanced for approximately two and a half years. They spent a good deal of their profits in legal costs trying to get the nuisance lawsuits into court for a decision. When the delaying tactics finally ran their gauntlet and a court date was set, the competitor dropped all of his charges and the company could breathe. They then started going after capital so that they could make their essential expansions, when another competitor, who realized the value of their breakthrough, offered them $6,000,000 for their company. They took it.

CAMEO 5-3: TRADE SHOW PRE-SALES   M, IS

At the 1965 Wescon show, Mr. Tom O'Rourke started the Tymshare Corporation. In that era, computer timesharing was a very revolutionary concept and Mr. O'Rourke could not convince venture capitalists that his ideas were viable. So he rented a booth, had the telephone company string several temporary telephone lines, rented a computer for four days, and demonstrated his concept to all visitors.

When the show was over, he had over 11,000 inquiries from booth visitors and several dozen prospective customers. The venture capitalists listened and invested. Also, two of the booth visitors were from IBM and General Electric. Within months these two companies also entered the computer timesharing industry.

CAMEO 5-4: DIRECT MAIL QUESTIONNAIRES   IS, RS, F

A Lockheed project manager sent out one of the most ineptly worded mail questionnaires in history and because of it, The Great Atlantic Lobster Company was born.

Briefly, for an MBA homework assignment, a student wrote 100 restaurants in the San Francisco area and intended to ask them questions about their lobster purchases. Marketing men shudder because he selected his 100 restaurant names at random from the telephone yellow pages. What was worst, by answering the questions, the restaurant owners were signing a legal contract to purchase lobster from a non-existent company, an effect that the student didn't intend.

In a normal direct mail survey, a five percent response is considered excellent. This MBA student received 32 responses, many of which had checks for lobsters enclosed. As it turned out, he had hit a major gap because at that time, San Francisco restaurants couldn't buy Atlantic lobster. So the student checked to see what was involved in supplying them with Maine lobster, found it feasible, and did it. He contacted several Maine lobster suppliers on the East Coast, had them fly the lobster to San Francisco, and here he placed them in pens in the bay until they were ready for delivery. When other restaurants started contacting him and the repeat orders inundated him, he was forced to quit his job at Lockheed, drop out of night school, and run his multi-million dollar operation.

CAMEO 5-5: THE 80-20 RULE APPLIED
IN REVERSE   M, IS

This man sold mini-computers for one of the major computer manufacturers when he noticed that everyone was concentrating on the 20% of the customer base which supplied 80% of the sales and no one was even making a feeble attempt to sell to the 80% segment.

Therefore, he decided to set up a special sales organization to service the smaller customers nationwide. He approached every mini-computer manufacturer and asked for permission to sell their products (for a commission) to the market segments that they ignored. Several manufacturers went along with him as long as he remained a non-disruptive force to their usual sales outlets.

This man set up an intricate distribution network that called on the smallest customers. The network worked well and within 16 months after he opened his doors, his firm was purchased for $750,000 by one of the manufacturers.

MARKET SURVEY CHECKLIST FOR MANUFACTURING AND INDUSTRIAL SERVICE START-UPS

1. Customer segments involved.
2. Prices that can be commanded in each segment.
3. Sales machinery (networks) available to penetrate each segment.
4. Product (or service) requirements in each segment.
5. Size and density of each segment.
6. Existing competitive products (services) in each segment.
7. Probable competitive products (services) after our entry into the market.
8. Existing major competitors.
9. Competitors' strengths.
10. Competitors' weaknesses.
11. Probable future significant competitors within the next five years.
12. Probable number of sales calls for each sales close.
13. Probable number of direct salesmen who will be selling our products (services) in each market segment.
14. Probable percent of their effective sales time that we can command from these salesmen.
15. The major customers in each market segment.
16. What are these customers' profiles?
17. What is each market segment's personality profile?
18. Areas that competitors are presently serving well.
19. Areas that competitors are presently serving poorly.
20. The "image" necessary to effectively penetrate each specific market segment.
21. Effective ways to "end run" competition and/or sales hurdles.
22. What products (services) will each segment want next year . . . five years from now?
23. What customer education programs are essential for our market penetrations?
24. What distribution education programs are necessary to realize greater coverage?
25. What are the best advertising medias for us?

MARKET SURVEY CHECKLIST FOR RETAIL SALES, RETAIL SERVICES, AND FRANCHISES

1. What are the optimum traffic patterns for the location I select?
2. What economic levels will patronize me the most?

3. Are my products (services) ethnic oriented?
4. What sex will be my prime customers?
5. What ages will be my prime customers?
6. Select the location options open which are in harmony with 1–5 above.
7. How far will the average buyer (user) travel for my products (services)?
8. What are the personalities of the different segments?
9. Do they have or want to have special buying patterns?
10. Who are my competitors?
11. What are their strengths and weaknesses?
12. What kind of walk-in traffic do they receive?
13. What are the optimum customer densities for my products (services)?
14. What locations in these densities are presently uncovered by competitors?
15. What is the personality of these areas?
16. What will these neighborhoods be like in 3 years . . . 5 years . . . 10 years?
17. What techniques are open to attract competitors' customers?
18. What ways are best to penetrate the immediate neighborhood . . . the surrounding neighborhood?
19. What images should I project for each market segment?
20. What additional profit centers are available to me which complement my services?
21. What are their profit potentials?
22. Are there any vacancies that meet all of my needs?
23. How can I be a different, interesting, and fun place for my customers?

6 · Develop Your Founders' Team

PROLOGUE   M, IS, RS, F

Now that you have: prepared yourself as a person for entrepreneurship, developed broad-brush objectives and goals for both yourself and your company, uncovered the gap (or gaps) which meet these goals (in a growth industry I hope), and verified that these gaps are viable, you are now ready to attract the caliber of people essential to attract venture capital and make your concepts work.

This is by far the most important step you will take because as the venture capitalists state, 50 to 60 percent of your probability of success depends upon the caliber of your management team.

Remember that Christ made a one-in-twelve error in attracting his founders' team. You may not do as well. Therefore, you should implement the fail-safe features of the next chapter (Rig Your Company's Incentives) with the techniques of this chapter. Then if a co-founder doesn't work out, he can be replaced with a minimal effect upon you.

It is the intent of this chapter to first eliminate the primary errors made by most start-ups and then to give you some techniques for attracting and testing qualified candidates.

SECTION ONE: THOSE FACTORS COMMONLY OVERLOOKED BY SOPHISTICATED MANAGERS

AXIOM EIGHT: FIRST RATE MEN HIRE FIRST RATE MEN . . . SECOND RATE MEN HIRE THIRD RATE MEN . . . THESE THIRD RATE MEN WILL THEN EMPLOY THE BULK OF YOUR COMPANY'S EMPLOYEES AND THEY TEND TO SELECT FOURTH RATE PEOPLE.

I won't insult your intelligence by explaining the ramifications of this axiom on your company, however attempt a 30-minute test to see how many effects this axiom will have on your company. If in 30 minutes you cannot name at least 45 illnesses that this will impose upon your start-up, then give yourself an "F" grade. The chain reaction starts when you select your co-founders.[1]

AXIOM NINE: YOU NEED TO ATTRACT TALENTS, DISCI-PLINES, AND PERSONALITIES WHICH COMPLEMENT . . . NOT DUPLICATE . . . EACH OTHER.

Most engineers feel comfortable only with other engineers and there-fore their founders' teams tend to be lopsided with technical types. These teams tend to be so narrow in scope that they frequently miss golden opportunities.

It is human nature to wish to associate with people your own age. Therefore, too frequently you will not find three years age difference in even very large founders' teams. Instead of looking at ages, consider looking for youth in innovation, in flexibility, and in attitudes. How many old men do you know who are 25? How many young men who are over 50?

Optimists tend to select other optimists instead of a few "show me" types. These teams tend to be like an electrical circuit that isn't grounded (or a kite attempting to fly with no one holding the string). Conversely, if everyone is a "show me" type, the start-up is like a circuit with nothing but grounds and no one applying the juice or the voltage (or like a kite for which everyone holds the string while no one attempts to launch it into the air).

If you allow these and the dozens of other "filters" to eliminate other-wise extremely qualified people, your management team will have ex-tremely limited vision and your company will suffer.

This Venn diagram illustrates the classical manufacturing operation. It is important that you sketch your own company's overlapping disciplines so that you can intelligently interview management candidates to deter-mine their empathies and understanding of adjacent disciplines. How many sales managers do you know who are sales oriented (instead of profits oriented), how many manufacturing types consider QA a natural

---

[1] If you want a real eye opener of the effects of ignoring Axiom eight, look at the bureau-cratic operations of our civil service. The government bureaus disapprove of this axiom and therefore attempt to ignore it. The effects of ignoring it are so apparent that I for one am ready to plead that we go back to the spoils system because graft was never so expensive and inefficient as our civil service.

As a rule of thumb, when we consultants estimate a bureau's expenses for a specific task, we first calculate what the job would cost if it were performed efficiently and with fiscal responsibility. We then multiply that figure by 100 and we have a pretty close estimate of what it will cost our government. In other words, for every dollar that we pay in taxes, we can expect one penny of results.

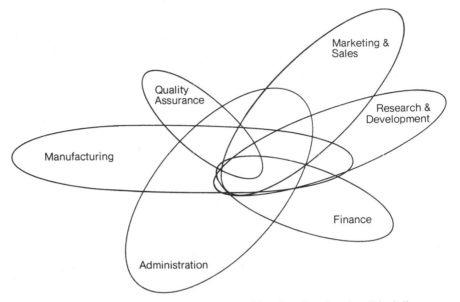

Figure 6-1: An Example of a Venn Diagram Showing Overlapping Disciplines.

enemy, how many R&D persons ignore manufacturing, how many administration types have absolutely no feel for operations, and how many finance people enforce systems and controls which stunt growth?
Note the central core must be common to all disciplines. This center should be your company's goals, objectives, and philosophies. As soon as a department is divorced from this core, your problems begin.

THE AVAILABILITY OF QUALIFIED CO-FOUNDERS   M, IS, RS, F

There is an excess of qualified candidates available to any viable start-up. At any one time, I'll bet that there are over 1,000 presidents, 10,000 vice presidents, and 200,000 engineers, scientists, managers, lawyers, accountants, consultants, marketing specialists, salesmen, and people from the other disciplines essential for your team. These candidates will jump at the opportunity to "moonlight" without pay for the opportunity of joining a winner on the ground floor.

To illustrate my point, Business Solutions is in no way in the executive recruiting business. Yet each month, we receive hundreds of resumes from highly qualified people to be considered in a start-up. Our clients rake these resumes to select co-founders.

Minor Point 6-1: A Warning   M, IS, RS, F

In the shake out that will occur as your management team matures and clears milestones, a natural leader will emerge. If you are on an ego trip and want the title of "President," you will not get it unless you are the best man and the natural leader. If the ego trip means more to you than developing the strongest and most dynamic team possible, skip the balance of this chapter.

AXIOM TEN: REGARDLESS OF HOW LARGE, HOW OLD, OR HOW ESTABLISHED YOUR COMPANY BECOMES, THERE IS ROOM FOR ONLY ONE MANAGEMENT TEAM.

This obvious axiom is not only ignored by many start-ups, it is frequently overlooked by many established companies . . . and do they pay a premium for ignoring it! There should never be factions. Your departmental goals should always mesh with your company goals or give yourself an "F" grade in Management-By-Objective (MBO), Management-By-Exceptions (MBE) and Management-By-Motivations (MBM) control systems. However, regardless of how good your control systems are, unless your co-founders mesh in their personal objectives, Axiom Ten will always be strained.

THEOREM TWO: IT IS ESSENTIAL THAT ALL OF YOUR MANAGERS HAVE MUTUAL RESPECT FOR EACH OTHER . . . AND IT HELPS A LOT IF THEY ALSO LIKE EACH OTHER.

Some idiot at sometime must have said that you cannot receive both friendship and respect at the same time from the same person,[2] and we all bought this hackneyed notion as an axiom. Believe me, respect and friendship aren't disharmonious.[3] When you select co-founders, select

[2] Probably one of the biggest causes of the decline of the British Empire was its training of its diplomatic corps to believe that "Familiarity breeds contempt." This false bromide soon degraded into, "You may either be respected or you may be liked, but never both." Since British diplomats always opted for respect at the price of friendship, their wards disliked them. Respect had to be insured through "gunboat diplomacy" until this technique became unviable and then the Empire began its decline.

Unfortunately, we American businessmen bought these false notions and attempted to use them on our wards (our workers). Our respect was enforced through blacklists and pink slips. Though unions and legislation made these tactics obsolete, there is still a "them" and "us" attitude between management and employees and both sides know it. Everyone pays a high price for maintaining these factions.

[3] If you are a weak or incomplete person, then seriously consider applying this bromide as a tool to hide your imperfections. Shut yourself off from your team members, communicate through memos instead of the give and take of other forms of communications, and it will take your superiors, peers, and subordinates a long time to discover your insecurities.

only those who will mutually like and respect each other. This is important because to get the effort that your company requires, everyone must make a dedicated commitment to see the jobs through. The work atmosphere must be free of conflicts. It will never come off without the mutual respect and warmth of all team members.

Minor Point 6-2: Keep Roles Clear   M, IS, RS, F

Before you are ready to interview prospective candidates, distinguish the differences between your management team, your key employee teams, and your board of directors. If you blur the differences between these functions, your selection of candidates can be very damaging.

As examples: if you "promote" an outstanding scientist to R&D Manager, too frequently you'll lose an outstanding scientist and gain a poor administrator. The most frequent blunder occurs in "advancing" your top salesmen to sales managers or marketing directors. The talents and disciplines that are real assets in sales are frequently liabilities when imposed on your management team.

Actually, most of our clients distinguish their groups by the following classifications: (1) directors, (2) managers, (3) key employees, (4) key non-key employees, and (5) non-key employees.[4] We will discuss in detail these classifications later; however for now, realize that there are differences.

> THEOREM THREE: IF HIS VALUE TO YOUR COMPANY IS GREATER A KEY EMPLOYEE SHOULD MAKE MORE MONEY AND RECEIVE GREATER INCENTIVE REWARDS THAN HIS BOSS (A MANAGER).

This theorem only applies to the upper two-thirds of the organization pyramid. If you'll incorporate this theorem into your start-up you'll discover that square pegs stay in square holes and round pegs in round holes. In most companies, managers always realize the greatest benefits and therefore talented specialists attempt to desert their specialities to become managers, regardless of whether they are qualified or not. Reward on value and you'll eliminate many of the causes of the "Peter Principle."[5]

---

[4] Every time I broach the subject of key employees, company personnel managers are quick to state that in their companies everyone is a key employee. This sounds very democratic and nice but if you delve slightly deeper, you'll discover that since everyone is key, no one is key and the incentives and rewards which inspire excellence do not exist.

[5] For those of you who may not have read Dr. Peter's book, *The Peter Principle,* allow me to tersely paraphrase it:

People are promoted until they reach the level just beyond their capabilities and effectiveness. Once they become ineffective, their promotions stop and they become fearful of their job security. This fear generates a multitude of problems.

Minor Point 6-3: A Few Legal Considerations

Unfortunately, there is a lot of poor legal advice around, so allow me to pass on a few recommendations that the better lawyers have passed on to our clients.

The first is that instead of having one long founders' contract, seriously consider having many short single-point contracts. From an operational standpoint, this allows you to obsolete or change a single point without jeopardizing the intent of the other contracts. From a legal standpoint, it gives your company's lawyer more options in enforcing the agreements. He has the option of just utilizing the single-point contract or he can combine several single-point contracts in his courtroom tactics.

The second recommendation is never combine all of the co founders in the same contract. Arrange a separate contract between the company and each founder. Therefore, if your lawyer has to enforce an agreement against one co-founder, he can do so without involving all the other co-founders.

The following examples of essential co-founders' agreements illustrate these two points.

Example 6-1: The Founders' Partnership Agreement
M, IS, RS, F

I, _____, as a co-founder and co-owner of _____, realize that we must operate as a partnership in the public's eyes until we are ready to incorporate. I realize that my co-founders and co-owners are placed in jeopardy by my actions and by my commitments. Therefore, I agree not to spend over $_____ in cash purchases or to commit my company to over $_____ in any agreement without the prior approval of the board of directors.

Signature	Date

Witness	Date

Witness	Date

Most of our clients allow up to $250 in cash purchases and up to $1,000 in commitments so that each co-founder has a certain degree of freedom in making decisions. If you feel that these figures are too limiting, allow the figures to increase, but I would draw the line at $10,000 for any unapproved commitment.

Many start-ups give their best negotiator the initial purchasing responsibilities. They then lower other co-founders' levels and add a clause that only purchasing can approve all buys.

Example 6-2: Preliminary Non-Disclosure Agreements   M, IS, RS, F

This agreement applies only to those who are to be interviewed for a co-founder's opening. It remains in effect forever if the candidate is not selected and will be replaced by example 6-3 if the candidate joins the founders' team.

I, _____, realize that I have been invited to present my qualifications as a candidate for the founders' team of _____. I realize that I am to be given proprietary and confidential information to allow me to determine whether or not I wish to join this founders' team. I hereby agree to treat this information as confidential and will not disclose it to anyone outside of the start-up.

_____   _____

Signature   .   Date

_____   _____

Witness   Date

Example 6-3: Co-Founders' Non-Disclosure Agreement

I, _____, as a co-founder and co-owner of _____, will have access to proprietary and confidential information. I hereby agree that I will not disclose this information to anyone outside of the company without prior approval of the board of directors.

This contract will remain valid for a period of three years after I leave this company.

_____   _____

Signature   Date

_____   _____

Witness   Date

_____   _____

Witness   Date

Have all co-founders witness each co-founder's agreement.

Example 6-4: Co-Founders' Non-Competition Agreement

If your start-up is addressing a viable market gap, realize that there is a very real temptation for co-founders to quit and go into the market in competition with you. You might consider the following agreement:

I, _____, have been accepted to the founders' team of _____ and have been made privy to extremely confidential and valuable information. I realize that this information has been gathered at considerable expense to others and given to me so that I may perform.

I hereby agree that I will not enter into competition with this company in the following specific areas: (Here list the specific products and service areas that the start-up will address.)

I have received adequate financial compensation and adequate stock for signing this agreement.

Signature	Date
Witness	Date
Witness	Date

CAMEO 6-1: THE PUSHER

The chief engineer for a construction equipment manufacturer became unhappy and decided to start up his own company. At that time, the major growth area in highway construction equipment was the pusher. These enormous tractor type machines pushed scrapers, earth movers, and tractors. The firm that offered the most powerful pusher would realize the bulk of the sales.

The engineer developed a unique brute that was by far the most powerful in the industry and started seeking the capital to produce it. The venture capitalists of course checked with his old employer to see if the contracts that he had signed would curtail his start-up and learned that he had signed the conventional engineer's agreement. When his former employer learned of his intentions, they brought suit against him to stop his start-up. The courts ruled in favor of his old employer.

In frustration, the engineer went to a competitor with his unique design and again the old employer went to court to block his giving his design to their competitor. This time the courts ruled that the old employer was attempting to block the engineer's ability to earn a living and declared the original contract invalid.

Since the second court decision overturned the first court's ruling, the engineer was now free to start up his own company. He attracted his venture capital, started developing production and marketing capabilities, and was well on his way to beginning a successful operation when his old employer offered to buy him out. Within 11 months after the second court decision, he sold his company and became general manager of the new division.

LEADERS VS. FOLLOWERS   M, IS, RS, F

Many authors and business managers feel that there is room for only one entrepreneur on a management team. He leads and everyone else follows. If he is a truly talented individual, the company's success will mirror his efforts. If he is less talented, the company will be less successful. Though there have been hundreds of success stories with this kind of top management organization (Ford Motor Company, ITT, Standard Oil, J. P. Morgan and Associates, Chase Manhatten, etc.), please realize that these companies were one-man shows until the companies grew too large for the men. Also, realize that for every success story, there are several failure stories.

Most of our clients are made up of extremely strong men who band together for common causes. A team of strong men replace the single entrepreneur and this team is unbeatable.

Realize that if you opt for the team approach and select only strong candidates for the top levels, there will be the frequent clashes that always occur when strong willed people disagree. There may frequently be blood spilled on your carpets; however, if your people are mature, knowledgeable, energetic, honest, motivated, and dedicated, these clashes will not splinter your team. Add these attributes to company goals which all team members want and you can't fail.

SECTION TWO: THE MECHANICS OF INTERVIEWING AND TESTING CANDIDATES

DEVELOP A QUALIFICATIONS OUTLINE FOR EACH OPENING   M, IS, RS, F

Before you can intelligently search for qualified candidates, you must define for yourself what you are looking for. Shoot high in your qualifications' demands. Remember Ross Perot became a multi-millionaire from following his slogan, "Doves, sparrows, and other low flying birds flock together and can be caught in bunches. However, eagles soar alone and must be gathered one at a time." Your specifications will determine where you should look for your eagles.

Example 6-5: A Typical Qualifications Outline   M, IS, RS, F

A typical qualifications outline for a marketing manager is:

I.   The candidate must be: (1) profit oriented as well as sales oriented, (2) marketing oriented, (3) ethical, (4) honest, (5) healthy, (6) energetic, (7) vigorous, (8) dynamic, (9) innovative, (10) flexible, (11) organized, (12) a decision maker, (13) a good communicator, and (14) domineering.

II.   Since our company will be a customer oriented firm, he must lead our other managers to want to serve our industry properly. This man must be the second strongest man on our management team. He will also sit on our board of directors.

III.   This man must have a working knowledge and empathy for: R&D, Manufacturing, Quality Assurance, Field Service, Finance, and Administration. He must command the respect of all of the managers of these departments and their staffs.

IV.   The successful candidate must have in-depth knowledge and understanding in the following areas: (1) our industry, (2) manufacturers' representatives, (3) sales agents, (4) distributors, (5) retailers, (6) direct salesmen, (7) industrial sales, (8) foreign sales, (9) commercial sales, and (10) high-reliability sales. *Be specific:* it forces you to define the job function tightly.

V.   The successful candidate will be responsible for: (1) setting up, training, motivating, and sustaining our sales networks, (2) short-term and long-term forecasting, (3) short-term and long-term quotas, (4) advertising, (5) public relations, (6) promotions, (7) market analysis, (8) gap analysis, (9) market testing, (10) applications engineering, (11) tracking growth industries, (12) implementing profitable targets-of-opportunity, (13) pioneering new product sales, (14) establishing and meeting sales budgets, (15) setting up and sustaining an effective competitive evaluation program, (16) communicating marketing and sales information throughout our company, and (17) supervising his staff.

VI.   This man should be a no-nonsense "work smart . . . not hard" type of individual who will "sell . . . not tell" our company's policies, philosophies, and procedures to our sales networks and customers.

VII.   This man will assume 50% responsibility for developing our business plan and 75% responsibility for presenting it properly to the financial community.

VIII.   This man will assume 50% responsibility for turning cash within 60 days after we form. We wish to have the image of an on-going company prior to seeking venture capital.

IX.   The successful candidate will receive no salary until we are funded, however he will receive 10% of the profits that we realize from our initial cash-turning profit centers. This man must hold his present job until we can afford to pay him amounts large enough to sustain his life style needs. In addition to his regular job, he must invest a minimum of 16 hours per week on our venture.

These rather broad-brush specifications will greatly help you in your preliminary pre-screening interviews. Note also that they dictate where to look for such a man.

Obviously, you won't locate a man with all of the qualifications. Any man young enough to meet your energy and health requirements will not have all the in-depth experience you defined in IV. You'll therefore have to compromise. However, I wouldn't even consider a man who did not meet all of the requirements of I, II, VI, VII, VIII, and IX.

WHERE TO LOCATE CO-FOUNDERS   M, IS, RS, F

I like to see start-ups gather from three to five extremely qualified candidates for every management opening and at least two candidates for each key employee slot. First of all, the competition for each opening makes the candidate realize that if he had to hustle to get the opportunity, he'll really have to perform to keep it. Then, if you utilize the interactive testing described later in this chapter, your other founders will have a greater selection to choose from. Finally, many who might be unsuccessful candidates for the top slots will want to work with you in lower positions. In almost every case where there are a great number of candidates, the start-up realizes from 6 to 20 very talented men for lower slots and really develops fast.

Most start-ups search for their founders and key personnel in the following areas: (a) parallel companies which manufacture similar products, (b) competitive companies (be careful on this one—you run the risk of performing your competitor's R&D and market research if the candidate isn't loyal to you), (c) college and night school campuses, (d) consultants (not only do consultants have extensive knowledge of promising people within their clients' companies, you'll discover that many consultants will work as a cofounder for equity only to satsify their desire to acquire line responsibilities—the ''staff'' personality of consulting can grow tiresome), (e) associations and societies, (f) referrals from bankers, lawyers, accountants, venture capitalists, management associations, friends, and contacts, (g) recruitment agencies (don't forget Forty Plus for your lower and middle management slots), and (h) advertisements (*Wall Street Journal, Electronic News, New York Times,* etc.).

TECHNIQUES FOR INTERVIEWING CANDIDATES
M, IS, RS, F

It is surprising that very few people know the techniques for getting to the very inner being of a candidate. And if you are going to select individuals whose decisions and performances will make or break your company, then you must literally get into each serious candidate's shoes before you can intelligently select or reject him. I utilize the following techniques.

I meet the candidate for breakfast or lunch so that I can observe his social graces while we both effectively utilize this personal down time. Remember, your founders will have to eat with venture capitalists, customers, and with each other so if you acquire a clod with no social graces, it's a minor handicap.

I accept the man's resume but never even glance at it during the interview. Time is too precious to waste reading a resume and I don't want to be distracted from my objectives of the interview.

I put the candidate totally at ease by thanking him for his time and then I give him a briefing on the start-up, its objectives, and its goals. I let the man know that we are searching for only the very best to join us.

I then tell the candidate that this isn't going to be the usual warm-body type of interview because I have only about an hour to really get an accurate feel as to what kind of man that he is. Then I start out the questioning with a simple question that any mature man can readily answer. "Joe, what do you want from this thing that we call life?" Though the answer to this question is of real interest to me, because the start-up must meet the needs that he defines, I also pay a great deal of attention to his ability to communicate, to be forceful, and his mental organization.

Now that he is loose, I hit him with tougher questions (see Example 6-6) and really get a feel for what makes him tick, what kind of man he is, how innovative he is, how flexible he is, whether he has the necessary knowledge, experience, and common sense, and what his priorities are.

By the time we have gotten through the bulk of the questions shown in Example 6-6, the lunch hour is pretty near over and I've drawn an opinion as to whether or not the start-up can use him.

If I am interested, I tell him so and briefly explain the interactive testing that we'll perform. I ask him to think about the start-up and if he is interested in joining it, please telephone me and let me know his decision.

If I am not interested in the man, I usually tell him so and why. Though I've made a few enemies by being blunt, I don't believe in stringing anyone along.

I study the man's resume in-depth, call his references, and do my homework on him. If there are any questions, I'll ask them when he telephones me his acceptance.

Example 6-6: Penetrating Interview Questions   M, IS, RS, F

Try these questions on for size. By answering them, your candidate will give you insights into himself that are far deeper than the company for whom he has worked for decades sees. Observe that there are no right nor wrong answers—just answers that are in harmony or discord with your plans.

(1)   You are my boss. I am your office manager and have seven secretaries reporting to me. I have always allowed each secretary to file "her way" and therefore we have seven different filing systems. This is causing major problems. How would you like to see me solve my problem?

(2)   You are our controller and the only member of the management team in town. The rest of us are in Europe setting up distribution. The lead foreman rushes into your office and states, "Production station three is down and it looks like it will remain down for four weeks. What should I do?" You know that all of the production and QA people can do nothing until station three comes back up and we'll experience expensive cancellations with the four-week delay. What would you do?

(3)   When should a man be fired?

(4)   How do you control purchasing?

(5)   I am your boss. You discover that I have a conflict of interests which I haven't disclosed to our company and which is costing us 10% more in purchases. What would you do?

(6)   I am three tiers in management below you. I have worked extra hours and innovatively solved a problem that has cost our company major dollars and problems. What would you do?

(7)   Should field service report to administration, QA, manufacturing, sales, or who?

(8)   What inventory control systems would you recommend to assure us of 12 times yearly turnover without jeopardizing our production flows?

(9)   What do you want from this thing we call life?

(10)   What must our company supply you now . . . in 3 years . . . in 10 years . . . in 20 years from now?

(11)   How should we set up and sustain new product development? Who should be responsible for its administration?

(12)   How should we set up an effective quality assurance program? Who should QA report to?

(13)   How should we motivate and sustain our non-key workers?

There are no single correct answers to these questions. However, when a candidate answers them, you'll have a pretty good feel of what kind of guy he is, how well he expresses himself, how confident he is in his abilities, how knowledgeable and experienced he is, how profit motivated he is, and what makes him tick. In one hour, you probably know him better than you would if you worked next to him for six months.

Did you try to answer these questions for yourself? See how this kind of track will allow you to get into the guts of a candidate to determine what kind of man he is.

Once a person clears this preliminary screening, you'll really test the temper of his steel in the fifth session of the interactive testing (Example 6-7). When he completes that, you may know more about him than even his wife knows.

CAMEO 6-2: THE THOMAS EDISON TECHNIQUE

Thomas Edison liked to hire young engineers and scientists to work in his laboratories because he felt that the young mind was the uncontaminated mind. Also, young people made him stay young.

However, he had a great deal of trouble determining how much common sense his job applicants had until he fell upon the following very simple test.

When a young man fresh from college applied, Mr. Edison would hand him a light bulb and ask the man to determine the volume of air inside the bulb. If the applicant took a pair of calipers, measured the bulb's many dimensions, and tried to calculate the volume mathematically he usually wouldn't be hired. However, if the applicant thought for a minute and then filled the bulb with water and then measured that water's volume, he had a job.

Minor Point 6-4: Simultaneous Team Development   M, IS

Before we get into interactive testing, you may want to seriously consider the advisability of setting up your management team, your key employee teams, and the nucleus of your board of directors simultaneously. I've noticed that those teams which do this usually move much faster, have fewer problems in raising capital, and make fewer mistakes.

The only drawbacks are that you initially have to give up much greater percentages of founders' stock (however, the speed in which you will move offsets this factor by producing much higher profits much faster), and that you will have to invest a greater percentage of your time administering all of the simultaneous efforts.

INTERACTIVE TESTING   M, IS, RS, F

We are now going to invest several pages to the various interactive testing techniques. We must spend this much time on these techniques because so few companies practice them and therefore so few people know about them.

If properly administered, interactive testing will place each candidate into a realistic work atmosphere and allow you to observe his:

(a)	maturity	(e)	knowledge	(i)	ability to communicate
(b)	confidence	(f)	experience	(j)	personal strength
(c)	flexibility	(g)	stability	(k)	teamsmanship
(d)	leadership	(h)	organization	(l)	objectives

THE SIX-STEP INTERACTIVE TEST   M, IS, RS, F

The six-step method is particularly effective for a start-up because it allows each candidate to select his bosses, peers, and subordinates. Basically, it works as follows.

Rent a motel conference room for a weekend (usual costs range from $50 to $200). Additional costs of approximately $15 per candidate will include: Saturday's breakfast and lunch; Sunday's brunch (combination breakfast and lunch); and a champagne toast during the sixth session. Drinks and dinners are usually on a no-host basis.

The stages of the sessions are:

Step One: Breaking the ice and establishing the importance of the decisions to be made.
Step Two: Candidate introductions and brief breakdown of each individual's qualifications.
Step Three: One-to-one interviews. When this is complete, everyone knows and has some rapport with everyone else.
Step Four: Departmental team building and testing.
Step Five: Development of total team (the company) and testing.
Step Six: Each candidate selects his bosses, his peers, and his subordinates.

Now that we see this overview, let's look at each step more deeply.

Session I: Saturday Breakfast

While everyone eats, give a brief rundown on your start-up, its products, its services, its goals, and its markets. Then state that the primary reason for this meeting is to allow everyone to interview everyone else, see all candidates perform in their areas of expertise, and then to select those with whom they would like to work. Emphasize that the decisions that they will make this weekend will probably be the most important decisions that they will ever make for their company.

End this meeting by giving several examples of other start-ups and how they prospered or failed.

Session II: Introduction of Candidates

Adjourn to the conference room which is set up with auditorium or classroom seating. On each seat is a packet which contains: (1) two unsigned non-disclosure agreements (see Example 6-2), (2) a candidate's worksheet which gives each candidate's name, a brief description of each candidate's accomplishments and qualifications, and adequate space for making notes, (3) each session's agenda (including starting and stopping times), (4) a brief summary of your start-up, and (5) the ballot that each candidate will turn in during the sixth session. It helps to add several sheets of blank paper in each packet.

Make certain that everyone signs your copy of the non-disclosure agreements and make certain that they are all properly witnessed before you proceed further.

The balance of the second session is devoted to each candidate coming up to the podium and giving a brief 10-minute biography about himself, his accomplishments, his goals and objectives, and any other pertinent information that you feel is necessary. After each candidate talks, add any other comments that you may have gleaned from his resume or your pre-screening interview.

When the second session is complete, you have just broken the ice and all participants feel that they know each other. While you are adjourned for lunch, have the motel set up the conference room for musical chairs in session three.

Lunch

Ask the motel to arrange the luncheon at a single table so that everyone feels a part of the group. Though the luncheon is informal (no presentations are to be given), observe how the candidates segregate themselves. You'll observe potential directors singling out other potential directors to sit next to, scientists selecting other scientists, salesmen near salesmen, etc.

Session III: One-to-One Interviews

For the next three to four hours have your candidates play musical chairs, interviewing each other on a one-to-one basis. Place a chart at one end of the conference room to make certain that no one skips anyone in these interviews. Control the time lengths of these interviews and make certain that every interview lasts at least 10 minutes.

While the interviews are taking place, observe them without interfering. Observe who is dominant, who is shallow in his questions, who has poor chemistry with whom, etc.

When this session is complete, you'll observe that everyone is exhausted and any further work will be counter productive. You'll also note that everyone feels that he knows everyone else in depth. If you did a good job in selecting highly qualified candidates, most will feel honored that they were invited and will have a real desire to be associated with other highly qualified people.

The first three sessions, a complete day, accomplished the foundation for the tough fourth and fifth sessions. So far, all you have is a group of highly qualified individuals. But you have completed the spade work for building your team.

Sunday Brunch

The primary reason for the Sunday brunch is to take up the slack in people's arrivals on Sunday morning. You want everyone present for the real interactive testing sessions.

Session IV: Form and Test Your Departmental Teams

Arrange to have a series of tables placed in your conference room. To each table, assign a department (example: Table A, Manufacturing; Table B, R&D; Table C, Marketing; Table D, Administration; Table E, Finance; Table F, QA and Reliability; Table G, Directors). Assign each candidate a seat at the department table which applies.

When everyone is seated, tell them that you are giving each discipline assignments which are designed so that all may observe each candidate in his areas of expertise. The solutions are really impossible without research and management directives, however the assignments should bring out the best and the worst in everyone.

Allow one hour for each department to:

(1) Define departmental goals and objectives for the next three years.

(2) Work up a milestone outline which shows the essential steps to meet these goals and objectives.

(3) Allocate departmental priorities.

(4) Establish rough estimates (in both dollars and man hours) to meet these priorities.

(5) Develop the image that each department would like to establish in: (a) the market's eyes, (b) the company's eyes, and (c) the department's eyes.

(6) After the hour's time, select a spokesman to come to the podium and present the decisions to the general audience.

This is a pretty inclusive assignment for just an hour's time. It forces all to rapidly chip in and get the job done. As this session progresses, walk around and observe the teams begin to form. By the time that they complete the fifth assignment, the members of each team have a pretty good feel to the other members' capabilities and strengths.

Session V: Form and Test Your Company Team

Now that you have developed individual rapport and your departmental chemistry, you are ready to test each candidate in both his department and in the total company.

In Example 6-7 there is a complete list of assignments which are designed to allow each candidate to display his competence. Note that the assignments force each department to delegate responsibilities to each candidate. Also note that there will be a considerable amount of negotiations between all of the departments. Allow approximately two hours for these assignments to be completed and an additional hour for each member to present his decisions to his department and get its approval. If the individual can't get the approval, then he must renegotiate with the other departments until he gains an acceptable conclusion.

When this is complete, have each candidate go to the podium and spend a maximum of five minutes explaining and defending his decisions.

At the end of this session, every candidate will have an in-depth feel about every other candidate's total capabilities and team chemistry. You are for the first time qualified to select the best for your founders' team.

Session VI: The Candidates' Sealed Selections

After a champagne toast to the infant company, its growth potentials, and the prosperity of the founders, ask each candidate to:

(1) State whether he is interested in joining the founders' team.
(2) Go down the ballot list and disqualify any candidates who he does not want to work with.
(3) Go down the list and put titles and job descriptions behind each candidate's name.
(4) Sign the ballots.
(5) Seal them and give them to you.

It is important that you have them sign their ballots for the following reasons: (1) you get a deeper insight into the individual (if he selects weak people, you could have problems with the man when he selects second generation employees), (2) it will allow you to weight "blackballs" more effectively (if the manager of R&D opposes a scientist, it will carry more weight than if a salesman "blackballs" the scientist), and (3) if you decide to override the "blackball" and choose the marked man, you'll be aware of the calculated risk that you are taking and take swift corrective actions if you lose the gamble. The obvious reason for signing ballots that you tell everyone is that you need to know their names if they stated that they weren't interested in joining your team.

BALLOT OUTCOME   M, IS, RS, F

Though you will probably not follow completely democratic procedures in your final selection of successful candidates, you will discover that the strongest and best qualified almost always win the top positions by a landslide.

Never count the ballots in the presence of the candidates. Wait until you are totally alone and work up your organization chart undistracted. Telephone the winners first and make certain that they are still interested in joining. Then discuss the losers with the winners and see if there are any lower spots that you might offer them. Then telephone the losers and either offer them the lower positions or reject them.

CAMEO 6-3: INTERACTIVE TESTING RESULTS   M, IS, RS, F

We are aware of approximately 250 companies which utilized the six-step interactive test technique and the following results were observed:

In almost every case, there was at least one candidate eliminated because he mis-represented his capabilities, his intentions, or his experience.

So far, there has yet to be one start-up that has experienced an explosive team splintering in which a fragment spun-off to enter competition with the parent start-up. Not one team which formed under this technique has yet entered the courts to sue other co-founders.

In every case where venture capitalists were invited to participate as board members, the capitalists have either invested in the start-up or introduced the co-founders to their investors.

In five cases where the fifth and sixth sessions were attempted without the foundation laying of the first four sessions, the teams never formed.

In several cases, session five erupted into a fist fight. In one case where free drinks were offered throughout the session, the participants ended in jail after the fight. That fifth session can really puncture an inflated ego.

In almost every case, the participants found the six-step session technique one of their most interesting and stimulating experiences. It is rarely dull.

CAMEO 6-4: TWO TYPICAL EXAMPLES   M, IS, RS, F

Advanced American Teleprocessing & Technology had 31 candidates to fill its 6 management posts. Most of the candidates had successful track records, made well over $18,000 a year, had at least two college degrees, and were in all other respects highly qualified individuals. The company ran the six-step method and had 19 of their candidates vote for the same 5 men and 24 candidates vote for the same 4 men.

Universal Sales Applications had 27 candidates for 8 positions. The chemistry between 24 of these men was so excellent that they scrapped the titles and started up with all 24 on their team. Within three weeks, this firm started turning cash and within three months, was realizing over $1,000 a week in profits.

When Universal Sales was first formed, they thought that they would have to go out for almost $1,000,000 in venture capital. By the time their business plan was completed (nine months later), they discovered that they had ample cash flows to meet their ongoing needs. So they accepted two $25,000 offers from two separate venture capital avenues (for 2% of their stock) and have yet to seek another dime.

Example 6-7: Interactive Test Assignments for the Fifth Session   M, IS, RS, F

The following assignments have been used by 13 manufacturing start-ups with excellent results:

I. Assignments to the Marketing Team:

   (a) *With R&D,* set up the procedures for new product development.
   (b) *With Finance,* set up the technqiues that will be utilized for sales forecasting and establishing sales quotas.
   (c) *With QA and Manufacturing,* set up the procedures, philosophies, and guidelines for field service.
   (d) *With Administration,* establish the policies for supporting field sales.

II. Assignments to the Manufacturing Team:

   (a) *With QA,* establish the policies of the material review board, production yield monitoring systems, and scrap policies.
   (b) *With Finance,* develop the "make or buy" profit center concepts.
   (c) *With Administration,* develop the inventory control systems and purchasing policies which will assure 12 times yearly inventory turnover without jeopardizing production flows.
   (d) *With both Administration and Finance,* develop employee policies, non-key employee incentives, and internal public relations which will aid labor harmony.

III. Assignments to Research & Development (R&D):

    (a) *With Manufacturing,* establish operating procedures and systems for turning over responsibilities for new products from R&D to manufacturing.

    (b) *With Administration,* develop a security system for our engineering drawings (microfilm protection against fire or flood, vault system against theft, etc.).

    (c) *With Marketing,* set up an effective competition evaluation system.

    (d) *With Finance and Administration,* establish a milestones budget system for new product developments.

IV. Assignment to Quality Assurance (QA) Team:

    (a) *With Marketing,* set up the essential procedures which will allow us to sell to the military, AEC, and NASA.

    (b) *With Administration, Finance, and Manufacturing,* establish the role of QA and Reliability within our company.

    (c) *With Administration,* establish vendor control procedures.

    (d) *With R&D,* establish the procedures which will assure that both quality and reliability are designed into our products . . . not just inspected into them.

V. Assignment to Administrative Team:

    (a) *With Finance,* establish monitoring systems for purchasing, inventory, security, employee conflicts of interests, departmental petty cash reserves, and employee honesty.

    (b) *With All Departments,* establish organizational charts (company and departmental).

    (c) *With the Board of Directors,* establish guidelines for: (1) management incentives, (2) key-employee incentives, (3) non-key-employee incentives, (4) founders' incentives, (5) incorporation by-laws, and (6) our company's short-term and long-term objectives.

    (d) *With All Departments,* set up the management-by-objectives, management-by-exceptions, and management-by-motivations systems.

VI. Assignment for the Finance Team:

    (a) *With Administration,* develop profit center control systems.

    (b) *With the Board of Directors,* determine finance's role in attracting venture capital.

    (c) *With All Departments,* develop flexible budget philosophies and rigorous controls.

(d) *With Administration and the Board of Directors,* develop financial communication systems, determine security techniques, and establish the frequencies with which both actual and proforma reports are needed.

VII. Assignments to the Board of Directors:

(a) *With Administration,* determine the avenues that we should pursue for our initial financing, our secondary financing, etc.
(b) *With Finance,* determine the leveraging principles that we should follow.
(c) *With All Departments,* determine who should be responsible for what in our business plan.
(d) *With Marketing,* determine the options that we should pursue for additional profit centers and targets-of-opportunity.
(e) *With Administration,* develop the overall time base for our company's growth, its rate of growth, and the cash injections that it will need for these accomplishments.

Comments on the Above Assignments:

(1) These are pretty emotional assignments because there are so many correct ways of accomplishing them. The technique which an individual selects will give you a real insight into him.

(2) These are pretty comprehensive assignments for even the most knowledgeable to complete in just two hours. The bluff artist doesn't hold up long and will feign illness or an important appointment rather than disclose his lack of depth.

(3) These assignments are intended to show a candidate's flexibility, ability to communicate, agility, experience, knowledge, innovativeness, and teamsmanship. If he is "snowed" by terms, either freely define them or change the assignment to one that he can work with. As an example, if the term "profit center" stumps your financial group, then allow them to set you up on the old cost center basis in this exercise.

(4) As you can see, there are no single correct solutions. Expect to see fireworks from your stronger candidates because the decisions, though just an exercise, are far from trivial.

(5) As stated in the body of this chapter, we frequently invite venture capitalists to these sessions and put them to work. Not only do most of them enjoy it, it gives them a good insight into your candidates' capabilities and it likewise gives you a good insight if you want them on your directors' team.

(6) These questions are designed for departmental teams of five to six individuals. If you have more, either add more questions or decrease the

time length. If you have fewer candidates, decrease the questions or increase the time. One start-up tried these tests by mail and had successful results.

(7) Since the assignments force each department to interreact with all of the other departments, there is a great deal of noise, traffic, and confusion. Consider recommending that each departmental team leave a minimum of two candidates at the departmental conference table to "field" questions. Also, continually announce the time remaining so that all assignments will be completed on time.

Other Comments on the Six-Step Method　　　M, IS, RS, F

Whether you realize it or not, the assignments you give the candidates in the fifth session can make the sparks fly. If you attempt them without the essential spade work performed in the first four sessions, you run a great risk of seeing your team splinter before it forms.

Though the decisions to the assignments can't really come from a two-day session, a surprising number of start-ups found them quite close to their researched decisions. Realize that you are performing a lot of the essential spade work for your business plan.

We'll discuss whetting venture capitalists' appetites later, however usually we invite several venture capital groups to participate as "board members" in the interactive testing. In many cases, these capitalists have continued to act as consultants to the start-up during its formulative stages and then invested heavily in them.

The assignments of example 6-7 have been used by 13 start-ups with unusually successful results. Eight of the 13 taped these sessions and used their findings as the bulk of their business plan. All eight were funded from $800,000 to $6,500,000 essentially for the work they did in these basic sessions.

ALTERNATE INTERACTIVE TESTING
TECHNIQUES　　　M, IS, RS, F

There have been many successful start-ups which performed their interactive testing as follows:

(1) If in the pre-screening interview, the interviewer feels that a candidate is extremely qualified, he'll arrange an intermediate appointment for the candidate to meet the rest of the founders.

(2) At this intermediate session, considerable interactive testing is performed and both the candidate and the founders determine if there is a fit. If the fit looks good and the candidate is interested, they give him several assignments to perform for the start-up.

(3) If the candidate performs the assignments to the founders' liking, he is invited to become a full-fledged member.

Another technique is to hire the candidate at the initial interview and depend upon the incentives and the assignments to make him a permanent or just a temporary founder. If he jells, he is accepted. If he doesn't, you'll search for another to take his place.

Though these techniques are considerably faster than the six-step method, realize that you are giving up the absolute veto powers of who joins your team. You are reduced to a single vote.

CONTINUED MANAGEMENT TESTING   M, IS, RS, F

Let's face it, the techniques that you use to select your founders may be excellent but they are not infallible. You and the other team members will continually re-evaluate each member as your company matures. There is a high probability that you will have to replace one or more of the original founders, so devise the machinery so you can flag problem areas fast and take action before real damage is done. Some of the systems commonly used are described in Chapter Seven, however you may also want to consider the following additional techniques for continued evaluation.

I. Periodic Personnel Evaluation It's a good idea to hold periodic evaluations in which each founder is forced to evaluate his bosses, his peers, and his subordinates. These evaluations not only illuminate personality problems, they significantly dampen any ego trips which tend to crop up too frequently in start-ups. Since every founder knows that every other founder is continually evaluating him, he'll control his behavior much more closely. This is no bad thing for either a start-up or an established company.

II. Time Base Controls Though we will discuss time bases later, make every key employee and every manager know that he is being judged by how well he meets his milestone dates. Things tend to get done on time with this system.

Realize that just meeting schedules is far from the yardstick that you require for excellence. Any engineer can swiftly design something that works, but it takes a special engineer to design something that meets or exceeds all the objectives of the market, manufacturing, administration, QA, and finance.

III. Incentive Controls We'll discuss incentive much more closely in the next chapter, however be concerned with those who are underachieving in the rewards. Either the rewards are not rigged right or your founder isn't performing right.

IV. Harassment Tests You'll observe that there will be much self-appraising and much doubt by all founders until major cash flows begin. These unhealthy aspects, when coupled with holding down another full-time job and devoting major efforts on your start-up can make key men feel harassed. Judgments and performance can be adversely affected.

If you suspect that one or more of your co-founders are overloaded you might attempt a test as follows.

Example 6-8: Harassment Testing   M, IS, RS, F

Let's say that you are concerned about your marketing manager and suspect that he is overloaded. When someone reaches a harassment peak, you know he is prone to make rash and bad judgments. You might test him to see if he is reaching this peak as follows:

"George, I'm concerned about the expenses involved in our market testing. How about market testing in just Chicago instead of the eight geographical areas we initially planned upon?"

If he responds, "Great idea," instead of, "It won't work because Chicago's market testing won't tell us how New York, Los Angeles, San Francisco, Houston, Atlanta, Boston, or Philadelphia will buy," you have problems. In all probability, this man made a major decision error because he is harassed. His other decisions must now be considered "suspect" and the man's work more closely monitored. You, as boss, must address and solve the causes of the man's harassment.

CAMEO 6-5: THE COLORADO HIGHWAY PATROL TEST

When a recruit's aptitude test results indicate that he has a great deal of promise, the Colorado Highway Patrol will give him a series of special interactive tests to determine what kind of man he is. One of their more interesting tests is:

On the first day that the recruit reports to duty (before he knows anything about patrol work), they fake an emergency. They inform the recruit that they need all the trained men that they can raise and ask him to patrol a lonely stretch of highway to free a more qualified man. He is issued a uniform, a gun (that doesn't work), a patrol car (that has a radio that receives but doesn't transmit), and then he is sent on his way.

When the rookie arrives at his patrol assignment, he discovers a car parked along the side of the highway and two men fighting. One man is extremely drunk and the other is excessively vocal and argumentative. When the patrolman gets out of his patrol car, the argumentative man completely takes over and attracts the recruit's full attention. When the rookie's attention is on the first man, the drunk ambles over the patrol car, climbs in, locks the doors, and falls asleep. When the rookie discovers this and tries to talk the drunk out of his squad car, the argumentative man gets into the other car and drives away. If the recruit made a mistake and left his keys in the ignition (most do), then the drunk awakes, discovers the keys, starts the engine, and drives away. The rookie discovers himself alone on the side of the road.

This test is designed to agitate the man and then observe how he functions when he is angry. The fighters are patrolmen and the session is taped and photographed to determine how the recruit maintained his poise. If you think that this test might make a candidate emotional, it is tranquil next to the stress situation involved in testing extremely qualified men in the six-step interactive tests. Throw five extremely qualified and knowledgeable manufacturing engineers together and ask them to come to an agreement in priorities, in budgets, in techniques, in employment philosophies, in incentives, and in milestones and I'll guarantee that sparks will fly as they test each other's abilities.

SECTION THREE: GET YOUR TEAM OFF ON THE RIGHT FOOT

So far, all that you have accomplished is to pre-screen candidates to select only the very strong and to bring these individuals together to verify that they have the chemistry to work well together. It is now time to weld them together as a smooth, functioning team. Consider the following recommendations:

HAVE YOUR CO-FOUNDERS VERIFY YOUR INITIAL SPADE WORK   M, IS, RS

If you are wise, you'll insist that your new management team and key personnel verify your initial research for the following reasons:

(1)   If you made a mistake, they will rapidly uncover it before your company invests money and time on the error.

(2)   It forces your people to assume the responsibilities of meeting their research instead of just yours.

(3)   When the potential of your market is understood by your team, they'll work harder to make things work and will hang in there when the going gets tough.

(4)   It will force all founders to become start-up oriented, an essential ingredient for team harmony.

(5)   It will become the foundation upon which your team will build its milestones, time bases, priorities, management control systems, goals, and philosophies.

This verification stage should take only a fraction of the time that it originally took you.

MANAGEMENT CONTROL SYSTEMS   M, IS, RS, F

We'll delve into Management-By-Objectives (MBO), Management-By-Exceptions (MBE), and Management-By-Motivations (MBM) control systems in later chapters, but at the very beginning of your company formation, start these systems to work and monitor performances closely. Though you'll probably have to tailor these systems to fit your specific company's needs, it is wise to begin immediately with controls so that no one will fall into bad habits. All co-founders must perform or leave and the only way that you can professionally judge performances is to follow systems that everyone knows, approves, and understands.

Minor Point 6-5: Non-Performing Co-Founders   M, IS, RS, F

When a man is not an asset to your team and you judge that he cannot be turned around, be honest with your other founders, your company, yourself, and the individual and let him go. It is unfair to everyone to give any man a free ride because you hate the unpleasantness of firing a friend.

ESTABLISH YOUR FOUNDERS' STOCK DIVISIONS   M, IS, RS, F

You have attracted extremely qualified individuals "on the come" and these men will not very long give you their all without definite incentives and definite stock definitions. In the next chapter, we discuss several techniques for founders' stock divisions. Establish a task force team immediately to study these and other techniques and make recommendations. Keep everyone informed on this task force's progress.

Minor Point 6-6: Meetings vs. Sessions   M, IS, RS, F

In every start-up that I know, the early stages of development involved a great number of meetings to establish each company's goals, priorities, budgets, philosophies, images, and to get things rolling. If you are wise, you will immediately define for all founders the differences between a meeting and a session and run both professionally and efficiently. There is no factor that I know that is more irritating than a poorly run and time-consuming meeting.

Oddly enough, very few people know the differences between a meeting and a session. This ignorance can waste significant man hours. In short, meetings are close-ended occurrences which are confined to specific agendas and topics and are run with discipline. The primary intent of a meeting is to make final decisions and to hear status reports on pending tasks. On the other hand, sessions are open-ended in nature and are frequently creative in scope. Brainstorming sessions, value engineering sessions, strategy sessions, philosophy development sessions, and even work sessions are called to start the creative juices flowing and to cross-fertilize minds. The disciplines required to conduct good meetings are too frequently counter-productive in sessions because they restrict innovation and problem solving.

If you are wise, you'll lay down ground rules for all meetings. All meetings should start and stop on time. The agendas for all meetings should be given to all invited several days before the meeting is to occur. Each founder who is responsible for a specific item on the agenda will be asked for the amount of time necessary for his items, and these times will be typed on the agenda and enforced at the meeting. If discussions on a specific item are not completed when that item's time is up, then the discussion will be deferred until the balance of the items are covered. After each discussion is completed, decisions will be made and actions initiated. Finally, no meeting will be allowed to develop into a session.

Most of our clients also add a few other "kickers" which may interest you. Anyone who misses a meeting and is unexcused is fined $25. Anyone who is late for a meeting is fined $10. Anyone who is poorly prepared for his item is fined $50. And anyone who calls a meeting and doesn't conduct it professionally is fined $100. You would be surprised how these "kickers" improve meetings and save everyone's time.

Minor Point 6-7: Disharmony Factors   M, IS, RS, F

Nothing will destroy a start-up faster than pettiness, one-upmanship, internal politics, or dishonesties. Show little patience with gossip and ego trips and take instant corrective actions with all forms of dishonesties.

When you have a personnel problem (and you will probably have many), talk to the offender in private and keep the discussion between the two of you.

Minor Point 6-8: Premature Incorporation   M, IS, RS, F

Most sophisticated start-ups refrain from incorporating until they have properly researched the ideal corporate structure for their company and until the timing is right. Premature incorporation usually brings a large number of headaches.

For instance, since federal, state, city, and county inspectors use incorporation applications as a "flag" to notify them to research you, you'll observe a covey of auditors and inspectors descending upon you for business licenses, zoning compliance, and to make certain that you are conforming to all the ordinances and laws. Not only will you be forced to fill out dozens of forms and pay immediately for a host of licenses, since these people only work during your prime hours, you'll be forced to invest many of these hours satisfying them.

Unfortunately, many of these bureaucratic clerks have no empathy or common sense in business matters. Their primary interest is to get their forms filled out correctly. I've seen investigators break into a sensitive sales-close situation to ask a question that the founders do not want their customers to know. In one particular case, the investigator interrupted a sales close to ask the president how much money the firm had in the bank. When the president winked at the inspector and nodded at his customer, the hint went unobserved and the inspector repeated his question. This time the president told the clerk that he was with a customer and would answer the clerk's question after the customer left. The clerk, who didn't want to wait, said, "Well obviously you have something to hide or you wouldn't be afraid to answer."

Credit research firms frequently use the public domain incorporation information to establish a preliminary line of credit on your firm. This information will be given to all of their subscribers and you will lose some of your money-leveraging options (i.e., your vendors may place you on a COD basis).

The costs of properly incorporating and the hidden costs can really hurt a cash-poor start-up.

Too frequently, the founders did not consider some of the options open to them in raising capital (franchising options, holding company philosophies, etc.) and they must go through expensive reincorporation expenses after they mature.

The primary reason that the founders incorporated was for the limited liability protection of the corporation. They then learn that this protective shell can readily be penetrated and that the protection isn't really there until their company becomes sound.

Consider holding off incorporation until you know that you are ready.

Minor Point 6-9: Initial Office Facilities   M, IS, RS, F

Your kitchen table is far from the ideal place to start and run your company. You'll discover that your team's efficiencies increase by as much as 10 times when you move your company out of your home and into its own facility. Your team can then readily come from their offices to your office, all files are available to everyone, you acquire a mailing address for all to use, an answering service always helps, meetings and sessions are undisturbed by families, and your company begins to establish an image to the outside world. Customers and vendors take you more seriously.

Therefore, one of your first management decisions should be to locate and rent proper facilities.

Minor Point 6-10: Your Company's Name   M, IS, RS, F

If you are innovative in your name, you'll reap the rewards of greater customer penetrations and of greater investor demand when you decide to go public. Before you finalize on your name, remember the American habit of abbreviating or alphabetizing names and test your final decision for all conceivable conceptions.

If your people don't come up with a name swiftly, use an interim name so that your researchers will not be hampered with a no-name company. People will not seriously answer questions or buy from a firm with no name.

Before settling on a permanent name, be sure you are not infringing on a trademarked company name.

CAMEO 6-6: ITEK   M, IS

ITEK is a major conglomerate today, but initially it was a tiny start-up in the tiny microfilm industry. It was rumored that ITEK selected its name to stand for "I Took Eastman Kodak" after Mr. Eastman's rather blunt evaluation of ITEK's founders, of their capabilities, and of the future of commercial microfilming.

The story goes that Mr. Eastman said, "Not only is microfilm unproducible, unfeasible, unpatentable, unmarketable, unprofitable, and unreliable, I would like to know how several of our employees could invest our valuable research dollars and research time developing such a stupid concept?" One of the research scientists grabbed a piece of paper and swiftly wrote, "Since microfilming is unproducible, unfeasible, unpatentable, unmarketable, unprofitable, and unreliable, I, speaking for Eastman Kodak, hereby give up all rights to it." Mr. Eastman signed it and ITEK was born.

Though this story may not be true, it certainly helped ITEK salesmen get past the receptionists' desks to see prospective buyers.

CAMEO 6-7: QANTEL   M, IS

The founders of the Qantel Corporation intentionally left the "u" out of their name so that when their customers tried to correct the mis-spelling, they could state, "We put the "you" in our product instead of our name."

CAMEO 6-8: FJR   RS

This New York electronics distributor appeared, by most informed sources, to be entering the market at the wrong time. New York City appeared to be saturated with excellent electronics distributors and there seemed to be no room for a start-up.

The founders selected the name FJR, let it be known that it stood for "Four Jewish Rogues," and immediately captured 8% of their market (a spectacular initial penetration). The name tickled the New Yorker's sense of humor and the company was well rewarded.

CAMEO 6-9: BTU   M, IS, RS

The founders of this company were attempting to enter the old and well established industry of production furnaces. They decided to address the growth segment (electronic conveyor furnaces) but they knew it would be an uphill battle to get the opportunities to quote against the established names. So they selected the name "BTU" so that production facility people would confuse their name with the BTU symbol (which stands for British Thermal Unit) used in all heat transfer problems. The gambit worked because within five years after they opened their doors, BTU's name ranked first in name identification and second in electronic sales.

CAMEO 6-10: THE 500 GROUP   M, IS, RS, F

This is a dummy company founded six years ago by a group of marketing research people. They frequently needed a prestigious name and what sounds more prestigious than "The 500 Group"?

Oddly enough, this dummy company today receives the benefits of approximately 1,000 mailing lists. Every Christmas, their directors receive hams, cases of wines, free tickets to shows, and a host of other gifts. Last year, the directors also received a block of stock from a company (value of $12 a share), several dozen offers to join joint venture opportunities, many tickets to $100-a-plate banquets, expensive research books, and two invitations to testify before the State of California committees on venture capital controls. The corporation itself pays approximately $200 a year in taxes while each director receives approximately $1,400 in fringe benefits.

YOUR COMPANY IMAGE   M, IS, RS, F

Unfortunately, the word "image" has a bad connotation and therefore is frequently scoffed at by entrepreneurs. Realize that your company is going to project an image regardless of whether you plan for it or not. That image is either going to help or hurt your salesmen, is going to attract or repel venture capitalists, is going to make you COD or thirty-day pay with your vendors, and is going to bring in or repel future key employees.

So your founders might as well face image from the beginning and decide what image they want to project.

Minor Point 6-11: Different Images from Different Viewpoints

Be aware that your start-up will develop different images to those with whom you come into contact. If you are wise, you'll work for the following images for each viewpoint.

(1) *Management Team and Key Employees:* "We are a stimulating but demanding company. All overachievers are going to become millionaires."

(2) *Non-Key Employees:* "It is a no-nonsense, fun place to work. Its managers are sharp and seem to really appreciate good work, good ideas, and good teamwork, regardless of where they come from. A man can get ahead here."

(3) *Sales Distribution Networks:* "Those guys are real pros who understand their industry and really appreciate professionalism in their sales distributors. Every one of them, regardless of how high or how low his job, really goes out of his way to close a sale and keep our customers happy. Every one of our salesmen knows every director's and every manager's home telephone number and they know to use it when there is a problem."

(4) *Customers:* "They are a young company but appear very professional. We haven't had any real problems yet but when we do, I think they will get things fixed right and will be just in their decisions. I get the feeling that these people will be leaders, not followers, in our industry because they are always asking what problems I have that need solving."

(5) *Vendors:* "They are tough and demanding but are professional enough to know exactly what they want and how to pay bottom dollar for it. I'd like to own stock in that company because they are really going somewhere."

(6) *Venture Capitalists and Other Investors:* "They are a real bunch of pros and are going to be a major growth company and make us all fortunes. However, the thing I like best about them is that they solve their problems before they come up and level with us on these problems. The next time they need financing, I hope that they come to us."

(7) *The Community:* "They are a small, hungry, and lean company but good neighbors."

Oddly enough, you can acquire 50% of these images by just telling people that this is the way that you are. It's the other 50% of the image (the proving that this is the way that you are through performance), that is tough.

FOUNDERS' INVESTMENTS   M, IS, RS, F

In the very early stages of many start-ups, it is not uncommon for all co-founders to invest seed money in their venture. I dread bringing up this viable avenue for initial funds because too frequently weak co-founder candidates with fat checkbooks are chosen over talent with thin resources. You want brains, not bucks, in the early stages because bucks are easy to raise with brains.

However, if your team decides to ask each co-founder to invest in your start-up, remember that small amounts of money can "talk" too heavily in decisions. If one co-founder can invest $20,000 while all of the others can afford only $2,000 each, then you run the risk that the $20,000 investor will speak 10 times stronger than the $2,000 investor.

If you must raise money from your co-founders, then raise equal amounts from each.

Minor Point 6-12: The Wife Problem   M, IS, RS, F

Fools rush in where angels fear to tread, and in attempting to address the wife problems involved in a start-up, I am truly getting into trouble. Yet if you ask me what the single largest pitfall for a start-up's management team is, I would have to unqualifyingly answer, "The wife problem."

Recognize it as a very real pitfall now and address it for your own wife as an individual and also address it as a company problem for your other co-founders' wives.

Remember that the wife of each co-founder will play a major role in that man's performance during the crucial development stages. Many wives swiftly lose heart when their husbands spend three nights a week and every weekend on a project which isn't bringing in immediate returns. If the family's savings also become involved, patience becomes even shorter.

When I learn of a strained relationship, I always recommend that the husband give his wife reading materials on entrepreneurship and case studies of firms that have made it big and firms which have failed. Many of our clients have participated in marriage encounter weekend retreats and found that the techniques of communicating drives and feelings that these retreats teach make their marriages blossom. One wife told me that such a weekend was like "an orgasm of the mind." The important part of the experience is that it allowed the founders to communicate their dreams and drives in such a way that their wives could share in the fun.

Many start-up clients have addressed this very real problem.

Besides keeping the founders informed on their companies' progress, they also went one step deeper and sent the founders' wives weekly progress reports.

Where "togetherness" works (and the chemistry between wives and founders must be excellent for it to work reliably), wives are invited into brainstorming sessions, strategy sessions, work sessions, and milestone celebrations. Instead of being on the sidelines, they are now an integral part of the dream.

Many give the wives small percentages of their stock when milestones are met. Besides the advantage of allowing the wives to become partial owners of their husbands' dreams, this technique broadcasts the milestones that their spouses must meet in the future. This will motivate them to help rather than hinder their husbands' efforts.

The most fail-safe wife appeaser is to swiftly generate significant cash flows and give each wife a small percentage of the profits.

Example 6-9: Some Techniques Utilized to Keep Founders' Wives Tranquil   M, IS, RS, F

Almost every one of our start-up clients generate cash flows extremely rapidly (within six weeks after the founders' team is formed). The following are a few techniques that they used to pacify their wives.

Many teams give their founders 10% of all profits in lieu of salaries. Several pay their wives an additional 10% of the profits. In one case, this amounted to well over $1,500 a month for each of the four founders and each of their wives.

One client start-up placed a percentage of its profits in a reserve for a gala vacation for all founders' families. The first year produced a week in Palm Springs, the second year a two-week vacation in the Bahamas, and this year they are considering sponsoring individual family trips to Europe for three weeks.

Several clients with less profitable operations give periodic "thank you presents" to each founder's wife. This includes color television sets, watches, jewelry, and insurance policies on the high end and sweaters, gloves, and tickets to plays on the low end.

Almost all clients hold champagne celebrations when major milestones are met. Founders' wives are always invited to these celebrations so that they can rejoice in their husbands' accomplishments.

The primary reason for the wife problem is that the wife isn't invited to participate or she doesn't feel appreciated for her efforts. Your start-up should realize this and address it.

7 · Rig Your Company's Incentives

PROLOGUE   M, IS, RS, F

What kind of output can you expect from your people?

AXIOM ELEVEN: YOU WILL REALIZE AS MUCH FROM YOUR PEOPLE AS YOU ALLOW THEM TO PRODUCE.

In other words, if you rig your company to: ONE reward your people, and TWO utilize the systems which make your incentives work, your people will give your start-up as much of themselves as they can.

Engineers measure an engine's performance by dividing the actual work of the engine by the work that the engine could do if it wasn't hampered by losses to friction, heat, incomplete combustion, etc. They call this ratio the engine's "Effective Efficiency." If an engine doesn't have a high enough effective efficiency, the engineers will redesign it to lower the causes of inefficiencies.

Unfortunately, engineers are far better with engines than we are with our people. The American Institute of Business Consultants attempted to measure peoples' "Effective Efficiency" and developed the following sad table:[1]

Category	Employee Effective Efficiencies
Bureaucracies	0.25%–1.0%
Large Utilities	0.25%–1.0%
Large Corporations (10,000 or more employees)	0.5% –2.5%
Medium Utilities	0.25%–1.5%
Medium Corporations (2,000 or more employees)	1.0% –3.5%
Small Companies (100 employees or more)	1.0% –5.0%
Tiny Companies (5 employees or more)	1.5% –8.0%

[1] *A Study of the Utilization of Talent in U.S. Government and Industry*. J. R. Blake Ph.D., M. T. Harper, Ph.D., and F. M. Jensen, Ph.D. Government Contract I.A.C. 69-140 H U D2094C- GS, final report 1973.

In other words, if you are a medium sized company and realize 3.5% of what your people have to offer, you are at the upper end of the spectrum. Very few companies are properly rigged to take advantage of their most important asset, their people. Though most progressive managements give "lip service" to their people's capabilities, the truth is that they can't handle innovation, creativity, dedication, pro-activeness (instead of reactiveness), loyalty, and the dozens of other attributes that good people want to give to their company. Since they don't have the systems and the rewards for these characteristics, they default on them and their companies pay the prices shown in the above table for this defaulting.

It is the intent of this chapter to show some of the incentives and the systems which make these incentives work. We'll do this by first laying the groundwork, then examine some of the systems which rig your company for management-by-objectives, management-by-exceptions, and management-by-motivations, and hope that these examples lead you into a tailored family of control systems which work for your personality and your industry's needs.

SECTION ONE: GROUNDWORK FOR MANAGEMENT CONTROL SYSTEMS

YOUR PEOPLES' NEEDS   M, IS, RS, F

People are not limited machines. They are complete, rational, and complex beings who have very real needs and demands far beyond monthly paychecks. Meet these needs and demands and you'll realize rewards that you never felt possible. Your start-up may reach 10%–15% employee effective efficiencies which means that you'll accomplish your goals with a fraction of the work force your competition requires. The savings realized usually more than pay for the costs of such a program.

What do people need? Most good people need:

(1)   Enough money to live their required life styles.

(2)   Opportunities to earn enough additional money to live their desired life styles.

(3)   The freedom to perform with excellence (along with the rewards for excellent performances and the punishments for poor performances).

(4)   The opportunity to meet their capabilities, to satisfy their talents, and to enforce their disciplines.

(5)   Meaningful challenges and worthwhile goals.

(6)   The chance to be pro-active (instead of reactive) and to work smart instead of just hard.

(7)   To satisfy their innovativeness to end-run old problems and to create new profit centers.

(8)   Meaningful recognition (earned respect) from their subordinates, their peers, and their bosses. Meaningful recognition always includes verbal thanks, and frequently it should be backed up with more tangible rewards.

(9)   A stimulating yet harmonious work atmosphere. This includes both physical surroundings and people.

(10)   To see and to understand "The Big Picture" and how their work functions fit into that overall effort.

(11)   To build an estate that is secure from government whims, economic trends, unions' manipulations, and all other outside forces over which your people have no controls.

(12)   Above all, they need the reliable management control systems which monitor and assure the above basic needs.

Very few companies (your competitors for top talents) even admit to these needs, much less try to fulfill them. If your start-up even attempts to satisfy them, you'll realize rewards beyond your wildest dreams in not only attracting and holding excellent people, but in getting results that will assure success. You'll realize the work-smart-instead-of-just-hard atmosphere in which success flourishes.

EARNED REWARDS   M, IS, RS, F

Make no mistake about it, the type of people you want are ones who want to earn their rewards, not receive them on a platter. All that we are discussing is opening up the avenues of opportunities so that those individuals who perform may realize the rewards of their extra performances. Those "warm bodies" who want to give their minimums from nine to five will receive rewards that are in proportion with their robot contributions.

Minor Point 7–1: The Life Style Incentive   M, IS, RS, F

Actually, a person's drive to live the life style that he wants is probably a bigger drive than salaries. What good is it to earn $200,000 a year if you can't get the time to enjoy it?

At present, there are several interesting experiments in satisfying this life style drive, however until these experiments prove reliable, we won't discuss them. Keep your eyes open to possibilities in your area. If they work, you'll pirate the cream of the employee crop without having to pay a premium.

CAMEO 7-1: FILLING A LIFE STYLE NEED   M, IS, RS, F

Two brothers, who were excellent auto mechanics, found an outstanding location for their shop and went into business for themselves. Since they were good and since their location was excellent, within three months they had more business than they could handle. So they borrowed enough money to double their facilities and started trying to get the other top drawer mechanics to quit their jobs and come to work for them. They offered top wages, excellent fringe benefits, profit sharing, and a professional atmosphere, and yet they couldn't talk one of their prospects into joining them.

Rather than lower their standards and accept second rate mechanics, the brothers drew back and asked themselves, "What can we offer the best to make them join us?" The answer was obvious.

Briefly, the best auto mechanics need an occasional escape from being auto mechanics. The grime, the frustrations, and the drudgeries involved in repairing cars either force a man into alcohol or into active sports (hunting, fishing, hiking, golf, camping, etc.).

So, the brothers offered four three-day shifts. On Mondays–Wednesdays the first shift worked from 11:45p.m. to 12:15p.m. while the second from 11:45a.m. to 12:15a.m. Then the third and fourth shifts repeated the same hours on Thursdays through Saturdays. There was a half an hour overlap in shifts so that work-in-process could be passed on. What avid sportsman won't take three days on and four days off. They had no problems in attracting two master mechanics for each shift and four apprentices to support them.

There are some other aspects which may interest you:

(1)   Since they had one of the few round-the-clock operations, they attracted a following that has kept them back ordered for the last two years. If they can't repair your car in 24 hours, they'll loan you a car until your car is running.

(2)   There is a freshness and an integrity about avid sportsmen which carries over into their work. The atmosphere of the shop is pleasant (there is a lot of kidding and warmth), and so far not one complaint has been registered against them with the Better Business Bureau (an outstanding accomplishment in the auto repair business).

(3)   Most of their customer base are repeat customers. They have confidence in the company and know that if only something minor needs to be repaired, only that will be repaired and the charge will be appropriately small.

(4)   The 24-hour service has induced several parts houses to place their parts in this company on a consignment basis. These parts houses realize significant additional sales from do-it-yourselfers who walk in after hours. Since the shop gets its parts on consignment, they don't have to tie up their cash in inventory. They also realize a commission on those parts sales.

(5)   Initially, the union was against the three-day weeks. They were concerned that these men might go out and hold down another job. When the union appeared to be about to outlaw the long shifts, every employee (mechanic and apprentice) threatened to quit the union and to make their shop an open shop. The union tabled their ruling for further study. It has been two years since their decision was tabled and since very few workers are holding second jobs, it's unlikely that the union will rule against them.

(6)   The bonuses that the master mechanics earn are approximately half of

their salaries. The brothers insist all apprentices have a professional, complete set of tools by the end of their first year with the shop, so all apprentice bonuses are given in expensive tools until they are fully equipped.

(7)   Promotions of apprentices are unfortunately closed since there is no turnover in master mechanics. Therefore, the brothers are unintentionally running a school for their apprentices. When an apprentice completes 18 months with the brothers, there isn't a garage in the area that won't hire the apprentice as a master mechanic. So far, the brothers haven't come up with an answer to this talent loss.

Minor Point 7-2: The Opportunity Requirement   M, IS, RS, F

Another major incentive frequently overlooked is the requirement that all employees need to feel that opportunity avenues are open to them. Too frequently, departments are frozen out of mainstream promotions. As an example, usually quality assurance, purchasing, personnel, marketing, computer groups, and research groups are never permitted promotions outside their little groups. Therefore, when a key man or a good man feels that his advancements have plateaued because the system won't allow him to advance further, he knows that he must quit or become stagnant. Consider breaking this freeze by allowing cross-training opportunities.

CAMEO 7-2: GETTING THE BEST BY OFFERING THE OPPORTUNITIES

U.S. Sales Applications, a 12-year-old marketing consulting firm, continually observed clients who improperly used their sales forces. One of the most frequent causes of lost sales was that these firms broke their salesmens' sales rhythms by forcing them to perform a myriad of essential non-sales tasks, yet did not equip their salesmen properly to perform these tasks. As an example, many sales organizations force their salesmen to invest up to 10% of their sales time in writing expense reports, sales call reports, short-range, mid-range, and long-range forecasting reports, quality reports, service reports, installation reports, and credit reports, and in expediting quotes and shipments. Though all of these non-sales tasks are essential, it is an expensive practice to tie up your salesmen in performing them.

So the consultants developed a computer concept that would not only perform these routine tasks, but would also allow each salesman to act as his territory's manager and conduct several parallel sales calls at the same time. Those sales forces which used this concept usually saw immediate increases in effective sales calls and increased sales of 10%–15%.

Though these consultants understood computers, they were certainly not equipped to design a reliable program which would be compatible with any computer system. They therefore needed the cream of system analysists and programmers. How could they attract the best for a short-term, two-year task?

Now working in a company's computer group is a dead-end job for many reasons. Most managers are so young that those under them must wait for 20 years for them to retire. The leading hardware manufacturers practice planned obsolescence of both equipment and computer languages so that by the time you become an expert, you are obsolete. The path out of the computer group into other disciplines is usually non-existent because most personnel departments and managers distrust computer specialists.

Therefore, U.S. Sales had their choice of the best by offering to teach these men marketing as no one else could teach it. As consultants' aids, these men got to see every aspect of both marketing and sales inside each client firm and to get a foundation second to none. Of the five men selected, two are now marketing managers of their own companies, two were invited to remain with U.S. Sales as associate partners, and one started his own advertising agency. These individuals would never have had these opportunities to advance if they had remained buried within their computer groups.

SECTION TWO: THE FOUNDERS' STOCK SYSTEMS

THE BASIC REQUIREMENTS FOR A GOOD FOUNDERS' STOCK AGREEMENT   M, IS, RS, F

Beware of any start-up founders' agreement which doesn't have all of the following essential requirements:

(1)   The agreement must allow your company an escape path for poor co-founders. If you made an error by selecting the wrong individual for your team, then the system must allow you to replace this weak individual without hurting your company. (Approximately 90% of co-founders' agreements overlook this requirement).

(2)   There must be performance incentives. Those co-founders who do not perform to your company's needs not only should not receive their rewards, they should receive punishments (negative rewards).

(3)   Your stock system should be tailored so that your team members are rewarded for individual performance and also for team (company) performances.

(4)   Your system should be rigged so that those who took the greatest risks and who gave the most during the start-up stages receive greater rewards than those who joined later and took smaller risks.

(5)   Your system should impose controls upon yourselves (and the monitoring techniques to judge your performances) in such a way that they are acceptable to your venture capitalists. If you do not impose these control systems upon yourself, the venture capitalists will impose their own controls upon you.

Section Two will discuss in depth three basic systems that are practiced by many start-ups. These systems will allow you to develop your own stock agreement tailored for your own company's needs.

THE IBM SPIN-OFF INCENTIVE SYSTEM   M, IS

This is a simple system which has worked extremely well for dozens of start-ups. Briefly, each founder was assigned a stock ceiling which he would achieve in quarterly payments over a five-year period (See example 7-1). If the venture capitalists invested heavily enough initially to own more released stock than the founders, then matching voting shares were released to the founders so that they owned 50.1% of the voting power.

This was a brilliant first step because it allowed the founders to replace a non-performing founder with a better man and use the original founder's stock as the replacement's incentives. However, the main incentive was only calendar time. You were rewarded in founders' stock only by the length of time you stayed with the start-up.

Example 7-1:   The IBM Spin-Off Founders' System   M, IS

In the IBM spin-off system, the founders received ownership of their stock on a linear (straight line) basis according to the time they remained with their company. Usually, this ownership was passed on quarterly until they reached their stock ceiling. In many cases, the founders split the founders' quadrant evenly (i.e., five founders divided 25% of the stock evenly so that each had a ceiling of 5% of the stock).

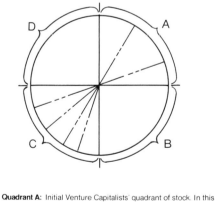

Quadrant A: Initial Venture Capitalists' quadrant of stock. In this example, three venture capital avenues are being addressed.
Quadrant B: Reserve of stock for future rounds of financing.
Quadrant C: Founders' quadrant. In this example, there are five founders.
Quadrant D: Reserve of stock for future key employees, for management incentives, for addressing new profit centers, for holding company options, etc.

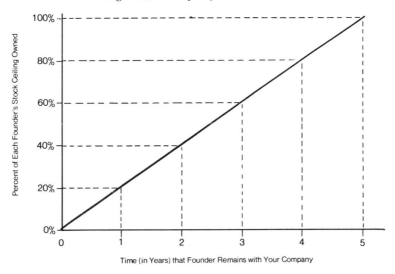

Figure 7-2: Distribution of Stock to Each Founder

THE LING-HINDERMANN INCENTIVE SYSTEM   M, IS

Doctors Ling and Hindermann made significant refinements of the IBM system. Instead of making stock payments by calendar time, they made payments by the man hours each founder invested in the start-up. The usual payments were 10 shares an hour for individual performance.

In addition, these men split each founder's stock slice into halves. Half of the stock was earned from individual performance (10 shares an hour) and half was earned from calendar time (shares were paid monthly instead of quarterly). The doctors were the first to reward both individual and team performances.

In theory, the Ling-Hindermann system was a brilliant piece of work, however it never succeeded in actual practice the way they hoped it would. Business Solutions took the ground that these men plowed, made several minor adjustments, and asked these men whether we could use their names on our third-generation system. They declined, so we named the system, The Business Solutions Milestone Incentive System. However, I would like you to know that Doctors Ling and Hindermann did the major work and all the consultants at Business Solutions did was make their idea suceed.

Example 7-2: The Ling-Hindermann System   M, IS

This second-generation founders' stock division system is basically identical to its parent, the IBM system, except for the founders' quadrant.

Each founder's slice was divided into two equal segments with the resulting distribution:

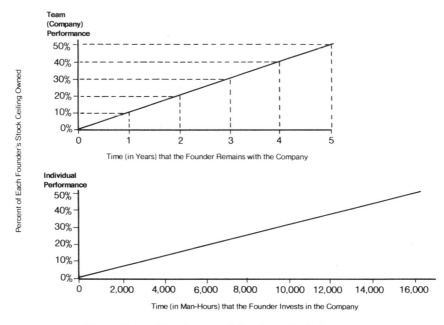

Figure 7-3:   Distribution of Stock to Each Founder

THE BUSINESS SOLUTIONS MILESTONE INCENTIVE SYSTEM

The system works as follows:

1. *Utilize Corporation Structure:* Though you will not incorporate until you are ready for it, from day one work on ownership slices as though your company is a corporation. What the founders are doing is earning stock in a partnership which will be converted to corporation stock eventually.

2. *Allow Ample Stock Reserves for Future Needs:* Consider dividing the stock slices along the following rough guidelines:

    (a) Approximately 50% is immediately placed in a reserve for utilization when your company needs second through fifth round financing.

    (b) Place approximately 15% in an additional reserve for future profit centers, future targets-of-opportunity, for incentive systems to those who contribute significant profits, and as an additional reserve for those founders who exceed their founders' stock ceilings.

    (c) Place approximately 10% in a third reserve for: attracting future key employees, for non-key employee incentives, for non-company people who contribute heavily to your firm's success, and to take up the difference between your asking and taking price for initial investors.

(d) Set aside approximately 12.5% to offer venture capitalists for first-round financing.

(e) The remainder (approximately 12.5%) is assigned to the founders. Though you may allow the founders full voting rights on their assigned stock, the actual ownership will not be passed to them until they earn it. If a founder should leave you for any reason, you can use the unearned balance to attract a replacement.

3. *Assign an Internal Value to Your No Par Stock:* Most start-ups assign a $1 value to their stock and immediately treat it as if it were worth that value. The reason that you want to force your stock to be worth that value is that you'll insist that the venture capitalists pay that amount for your first round financing. They will not pay it unless you and your founders likewise paid the value in accomplishments.

4. *Determine the Amount of Money You Will Initially Need and Set Your Quantities of Stock Accordingly:* If your start-up needs approximately $2,500,000 in seed money and initial financing, if you assign a $1 value to each share, and if you assigned 12.5% of your equity for this first round of financing, then you wish to get $2,500,000 for 2,500,000 shares. Therefore, your initial incorporation will be for 20,000,000 shares.

5. *Quantities vs. Percentages:* Start working with numbers of shares instead of percentages as soon as you can. You'll discover that people will make major efforts for 10,000 shares ($10,000 in value), whereas they will become discouraged for 0.05% of the stock (the same $10,000 value).

6. *Determine the Venture Capital Avenues That You'll Address and the Stock Divisions of Each Avenue:* We'll get into this in greater depth later on but right now you should realize that you'll want to divide that 12.5% from three to five different ways depending upon the number of avenues that you attract to invest in you. The only way that the capitalists can wrench management control away from you is by combining to vote against your management team. They won't be able to do this unless your management team isn't performing.

7. *The Founders' Incentives:*

(a) Divide the 12.5% among the founders. Please note that I didn't say equally. In all probability, some of your founders have greater value to your start-up and therefore should realize higher earning ceilings. If this should cause initial frictions, don't hesitate to show the unhappy founders the reserves that they can address after they reach their assigned ceilings.

(b) Divide each founder's slice into two parts (again not necessarily even). Define one part as individual performance and the other as team (company) performance.

(c) Individual Performance:

(1) Each founder will have specific tasks to perform. Each task has a specific value to the company. Assign that value to each task and pay the founder in stock when the task is reliably completed.

- One of the key words above is the word "value." The value of a task is directly proportional to the profits the company will realize when the task is completed. If a task will produce $100 a month in profits, then the value might be 36 × $100 or $3,600. As soon as the founder reliably completes the task, he has earned 3,600 shares for the profits your company will realize over the next three years.

- The second key word above is the word "reliably." A task isn't complete until its solution satisfies all groups and the customer. The usual method used to assure that the task is completed properly is to give 10% of the stock when the founder says the task is complete. Give 20% of the stock if the solution is working reliably after 30 days, 30% if the solution appears reliable after 60 days, and 40% after 90 days. If the project runs into snags before these time periods are up, then payments are stopped until the problem solver reliably resolves the problem. (These delays force design engineers to live with their designs through the production and marketing stages. If the design engineer can't make his design meet all specifications, then you may use the unreleased values to attract another engineer to solve the problem.)

(2) Drudgery tasks are common to all start-ups. Parts need assembling, offices need painting, toilets need fixing, deliveries need to be made, typing must be done, and a host of other drudgery tasks must be completed. Since you have limited money, the founders must perform these tasks. Consider assigning an hourly rate (X shares per hour) and expect all founders to chip in on these tasks. If you have a deadbeat in these dull tasks, also consider a negative value per hour for the "no shows." (One excellent tactic frequently used for meetings: All of those who are prepared for a meeting and attend it on time get X shares. Those who are absent, late, or poorly prepared, have minus X shares permanently removed from their founders' slice. This device produces excellent results.)

(3) Frequently, you'll discover that a few of your founders cannot meet their individual tasks (mini-milestones) for a multitude of reasons. Though frequently these excuses are justified, realize that your company's major milestones can't be met until the mini-milestones are completed. Therefore, the complete team must slip completion dates because a team member isn't doing his part. This system allows you the option of re-assigning the incompleted task to another founder and paying that founder from the delinquent founder's slice. Note how every founder's percentage of ownership can increase or decrease with performance?

(d) Team (or Company) Performance Incentives:

(1) Rough out your first five-year major milestones. Then determine the medium and mini-milestones essential to meet these major milestones. Assign a value of stock to each of the small, medium, and large milestones (see Example 7-4).

(2) Distribute the ownership of these shares when the milestones are met.

(3) Call these distributions team rewards and make certain that every founder realizes that he must be with the company and significantly contribute to its performance to realize these team rewards.

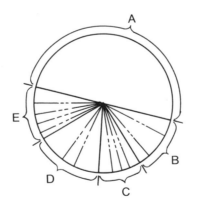

Stock **Segment A:** Reserves for second through fifth rounds of financing.

Stock **Segment B:** Reserves for first round financing.

Stock **Segment C:** Reserves for future key employees, non-company personnel incentives, non-key employee incentives, and the difference between asking and taking price for first round financing.

Stock **Segment D:** Reserves for future profit centers, management and key employee incentives.

Stock **Segment E:** Reserves for founders' stock. This slice usually equals the Stock Segment B slice.

Figure 7-4: Initial Stock Assignments

Example 7-3: The Business Solutions Milestone Incentive
   System   M, IS, RS, F

Note the future options and flexibilities open to your company. You have the option of going out for second through fifth rounds of financing when the money market is prime, you have the option of using holding-company pyramiding both upwards and downwards,[2] and you miss that old start-up pitfall of having to force your original investors to allow their stock percentages to be diluted when you must seek second through fifth rounds of financing.[3]

Note that in this particular example, the founder had a higher ceiling on his team performance than his individual performance. Disciplines like manufacturing, quality assurance administration, and marketing are more team oriented than individual oriented and you might consider rewarding each to its discipline's criteria. On the other hand, research, design, and finance are more individually oriented and teamsmanship is less important.

Minor Point 7-3: Other Benefits of the Business Solutions Milestone
   Stock System   M, IS, RS, F

Observe that this system gives you the essential fail-safe features if you should select the wrong founder. Usually you'll discover if a man is weak or lazy within the first three months. He'll leave with very little of your company's stock.

---

[2] If you keep the option of pyramiding holding and held corporations, you buy many options for later operations. Besides the obvious advantage of being able to almost "print money" in the form of subordinate corporation stock, you also have the option of: (1) setting up a franchise corporation and realizing some of your secondary financing through selling franchise stock to your franchisees, (2) setting up an operations corporation and giving its stock (in lieu of fees) to your vendors, jobbers, etc., (3) setting up a sales arm corporation and giving its stock in lieu of commissions, (4) when a profit center's operations grow to the extent that this center begins to conflict with the other centers, you can spin-off a corporation and have its management answer to your board, (5) the option to pyramid upwards is a definite club which you can hold over your venture capitalists' heads. If your capitalists are being unreasonable (it sometimes happens), then you have the ability to set up a higher holding company with your 50% reserves and outvote your investors, and (6) you have many complex but legal tax options open to you. Though this reasoning is premature at the start-up stage, you want to leave yourself as many options as possible for your future needs.

[3] One of the saddest things to see is a young, healthy, and dynamic company's growth stunted because its original venture capital groups either could not or would not give it the funds it needs. Frequently, these same investment groups will not allow their stock percentages to be diluted by the managers seeking funds from other sources. Then the management is forced to attempt extremely sloppy methods of raising capital (e.g., preferred stocks, warrants, limited common stocks, bonds, etc.) and these can be difficult and limited options in a tight money market. By selling small percentages (but large released stock percentages) initially, you miss this common pitfall.

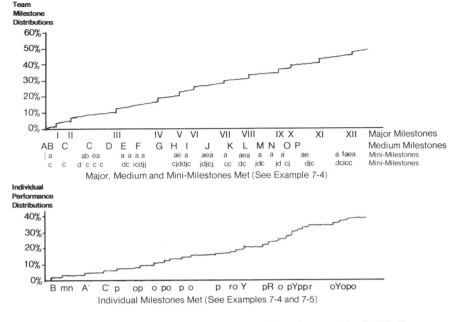

Figure 7-5:   The Distribution of Founders' Stock.   M, IS, RS, F

The milestone incentives get to the heart of what your start-up is trying to achieve. If these milestones are your company's objectives and goals, the rewards for meeting them outweigh individuals' personal goals (i.e., building an empire, taking an ego trip, always wanting the newest equipment when older, less expensive equipment will work, etc.).

Observe that this system forces your management team to establish your start-up's goals and objectives and then to determine the milestones essential to meet them. Though this planning initially takes a lot of time, it will reduce your start-up's time in writing your business plan, attracting your capital, and getting rolling. This planning also forces all founders to get their feet firmly on the ground and to become entrepreneur-oriented.

This founders' incentive system should not be the only incentive system open to the founders. They should all participate in the other incentive systems.

Note that your founders now have a concrete way of judging their performances prior to your having to take action. A lot of distasteful and damaging meetings are eliminated because the man who isn't meeting his commitments knows it and knows that everyone else knows it. The peer pressures can become extreme. Buck passing becomes difficult.

The reward-punishment aspect gives your milestones a double punch. Not only will a man not realize his rewards if a milestone isn't met, he'll be punished and lose his stock to the others who must complete his tasks.

The value aspect really brings your founders' feet down to earth. It forces them to priority those tasks which will bring the greatest benefits to your company for the energy invested. Too frequently, people want to do what they like best first instead of what is needed to be done. The calendar time of the IBM system or the man hours invested of the Ling-Hindermann system are poor rewards when compared to accomplishments.

Observe that the priorities are highlighted for all to see and to meet. This is the backbone of your management-by-objectives atmosphere. Confusion, frustration, and excessive meetings are eliminated. If you incorporate the right systems to complement this system, everyone knows where everyone else is going and when they should be there.

Please be aware that many of the mini, medium, and major milestones described in Example 7-4 are also warning flags for your management-by-exceptions systems. If you incorporate the milestones, you are forced to set up the systems which will monitor them. Once these systems are running smoothly, 50% of your management time and problems are eliminated.

When these warning flags described above "fly," the founder who is responsible for them has his dirty wash out for all founders and managers to see. This in itself is a significant incentive.

Be aware that the individual incentive systems described in 7c can be a discordant process unless they are tempered by the teamsmanship incentives of 7d. It isn't advisable to eliminate the healing ointments of team (company) incentives.

We have had several clients eliminate the individual incentives because they feared that the competition over founders' stock would splinter their team. These clients seemed to move a great deal slower than those clients who kept them both.

The people who administer these incentives must be both strong and just. Occasionally a task which seems to have minor value but which requires a great deal of time and effort must be completed before an important milestone can be addressed. In these cases, the founder who must complete the low value task should be rewarded for the time and effort he had to invest instead of the task's low value.

Be aware that this system can be extremely flexible. Frequently, a start-up wants to change its priorities to take advantage of an opportunity or another lucrative profit center. All the management has to do is insert the new milestones with the dates that they are to be completed and to slip the old milestone's dates. If swift reaction time is essential (it often is in bid situations), management can offer stock premiums if the rush dates are met.

Most of our clients who use this system open up similar systems for their managers, their key employees, and the non-key people. The rewards and punishments are scaled down according to the importance of each of these three groups. The effects of these additional programs are usually very rewarding. However, don't introduce them until you have the system debugged and calibrated to your company's needs. The program should be very stable and reliable before you invite your non-key workers to participate.

Make certain that the board of directors has the option of increasing the value of your stock in these programs. If you initially set up your company with 20,000,000 shares at an internal value of $1 a share, the stock's value will probably have doubled by the time your founders have earned 2,000,000 shares. It will probably have doubled again by the time they earn 3,000,000 shares. Do not freeze the value of your stock, because you'll want to command the increased worth when you go out for your second through fifth rounds of financing.

This system is an excellent reference point in your initial venture capital negotiations. Though it is probable that you'll have to make minor alterations in the give-and-take of the final negotiations, at least you'll be controlled by your own controls instead of the more rigorous ones usually implemented by these venture capitalists.

Almost all start-ups go through periods of doldrums. Everyone works hard, everyone works smart, there is a lot of activity, but nothing seems to be going right. If these periods last long, frustration begins, tempers shorten, and morale drops. This system is an effective tool for breaking the doldrums by announcing the minimilestones as they are met. Even tiny successes, when announced to all hands, give the founders heart and create a success atmosphere, which transmits to customers and employees alike and frequently kicks things off of dead center.

Example 7-4: Typical Milestones   M, IS, RS, F

The following major, medium, and mini-milestones are typical of a manufacturing start-up. Note how many of them can apply to almost any type of start-up. Feel free to alter, add, or delete these milestones to fit your company.

Major Milestones (10,000–50,000 shares)	*Stock Value*
I. Venture capital funds are received	25,000 shares
Ia. In lieu of investors funds, start-up generates enough cash to eliminate need of outside funds	50,000 shares
II. Company achieves profits for six months in a row	10,000 shares
III. Company realizes net profits of $25,000 (before taxes) for three consecutive months	10,000 shares
IV. For each $25,000 net profit increment thereafter	10,000 shares
V. Nationwide distribution set up, trained, and equipped	25,000 shares
VI. Market penetration exceeds 2% for three months in a row	20,000 shares

Major Milestones (10,000–50,000 shares)   *Stock Value*

VII.	For each 2% penetration increment thereafter	15,000 shares
VIII.	The 50th franchise is set up, trained, and equipped	25,000 shares
IX.	For every 25th franchise increment thereafter	10,000 shares
X.	When managers' and key employees' incentives exceed 50% of their salaries	20,000 shares
XI.	Each 25% increment thereafter	10,000 shares
XII.	When non-key employees receive 10% of their salaries in incentives	20,000 shares
XIII.	For each 10% increment thereafter	10,000 shares
XIV.	For each complete product (service) family ready for sales	20,000 shares
XV.	When employee turnover is less than ½% for a complete year	10,000 shares
XVI.	When company's stock value exceeds three times the initial value placed upon it	25,000 shares
XVII.	Every time the stock doubles in value thereafter	25,000 shares
XVIII.	Company successfully sold prior to each founder achieving his stock ceiling	50,000 shares
XIX.	Board of directors' discretion (up to 50,000 shares)	

Medium Milestones (500–5,000 shares)   *Stock Value*

A.	First product (service) ready for sales	1,000 shares
B.	Business plan completed	2,500 shares
C.	First month we turn a profit	1,000 shares
D.	First three months running that we turn a profit	5,000 shares
E.	Every month thereafter that we turn a profit	500 shares
F.	Cumulative cash flow reaches zero (all dollars received in profits equal all dollars invested)	5,000 shares
G.	Management-by-objectives systems have worked well for three months running	2,500 shares
H.	Management by exceptions systems have worked well for three months running	2,500 shares
I.	For every 250th customer realized in each quarter	2,000 shares
J.	For every 500th satisfied customer each quarter	2,000 shares
K.	For every 10th dissatisfied customer each quarter	−1,000 shares (minus)
L.	For every 1,000th order shipped on time each quarter	2,000 shares
M.	For every 20th order shipped late	−1,000 shares (minus)
N.	For every 10th franchise set up, trained, and equipped	2,000 shares
O.	For every 20th franchise properly supported each quarter	2,000 shares
P.	For every 4th franchise improperly supported	−1,000 shares (minus)
Q.	When sales, back orders, and profits dictate developing "in-house" production capabilities	5,000 shares

Medium Milestones (500–5,000 shares)   *Stock Value*

R. For every gross sales increment of $10,000/month   1,000 shares
S. For every net profit increment of $5,000/month   5,000 shares
T. When yearly inventory-to-sales ratios are met
    with no adverse effects   2,500 shares
U. When scrap/re-work/customer returns meet levels   2,500 shares
V. For every 1% increment improvement in U above   2,500 shares
W. For every 1% increment loss in U above   −2,500 shares (minus)
X. For every $25,000 in net profits realized at year's
    end   2,500 shares
Y. For every $5,000 loss at year's end   −5,000 shares (minus)
Z. When company's line-of-credit exceeds $50,000   2,500 shares
A' For every $50,000 line-of-credit increment there-
    after   1,000 shares
B' When there are a minimum of three approved
    vendors for each critical item   1,000 shares
C' For every $10,000 savings increment realized
    each year   500 shares
D' For every new growth industry properly ad-
    dressed   5,000 shares
E' For every new profit center addressed properly   1,000 shares
F' When the value of the company's stock reaches
    the value you initially set for it on the open market   5,000 shares
G' President's discretion (up to 5,000 shares)

Mini-Milestones (10–250 shares)   *Stock Value*

a. For each new customer brought on-line   10 shares
b. For each week with no late sales quotations   50 shares
c. For each late sales quotation   −25 shares (minus)
d. For each week with no late shipments   50 shares
e. For each late shipment   −25 shares (minus)
f. For each week that sales exceeds sales quotas   50 shares
g. For each month that sales are within 10% of the
    sales forecasts   100 shares
h. For each management meeting properly prepared
    for and attended on time   20 shares
i. For each management meeting improperly pre-
    pared for or attended late   −25 shares (minus)
j. For every "good try" recommendation rejected   25 shares
k. For every $1,000 net profits realized each month   200 shares
l. For every $1,000 in budgets not spent each
    quarter   100 shares
m. For every minor cost savings realized (10 shares
    for every $100 saved)
n. Profit Center Manager's discretion (up to 250
    shares)

FLOATING FOUNDERS' INCENTIVES

There are some milestones which will not accurately fit into the mini, medium, or major milestone classifications, however they are important because they force everyone to work for the company's goals. Three typical examples and rewards are:

(1)   Monthly profits (before taxes) from the primary profit centers:
  * 90% of the profits go into the company treasury and the founders divide the stock amongst themselves. (In other words, if your company has five founders and your company made $5,000 last month, then $4,500 goes into the company's treasury and each founder receives 900 shares for these profits.)
  * 10% of the profits are distributed in cash to the founders. (In our example above, each founder would receive $100 in cash for the month's work.)

(2)   Monthly profits (before taxes) from secondary profit centers and targets-of-opportunity:
  * 75% of the profits go into the company treasury, and the founders, who were responsible for generating the "accidental" cash flows, divide the stock.
  * 25% of the profits are divided among the participating founders.

(3)   Viable suggestions and recommendations implemented by the company:
  * 10% of the profits realized are paid monthly to the founder who made them for a three-year period.

The importance of the floating milestones is realized when your people begin to attempt to bring in cash. In many cases, you'll discover that founders make enough in incentives to quit their other jobs and work full time for your company. When your company really grows and matures, these floating incentives can easily exceed $100,000 a year to every founder.

Please observe that this system allows no one to receive anything until things happen. Also, note that many of these milestones are "flags" for your management-by-exception atmosphere.

SECTION THREE: OTHER CONTROL SYSTEMS

TIME BASE CONTROLS   M, IS, RS, F

Every major task (project) should be reduced to a time-base chart which lists the essential ingredients (mini-milestones) that are needed to complete that task. The dates these small tasks are to be completed should be shown, the manpower loading should be shown, the expenses involved should be estimated, and the value (stock payments) should be shown. Every month, the task manager (project manager) should update the time base and explain slippages and coverages.

Not only is a time base an excellent worksheet to prepare for a task, it has real value in eliminating those expensive status meetings because the worksheet in itself communicates all, in allowing your financial people to allocate funds when and where they are needed, and in allowing management to reshift priorities and meet manpower needs.

Another excellent time-base control system is the PERT system developed by our aerospace companies. Since there are many excellent books on PERT, we won't discuss it further.

Example 7-5: Time Base Worksheets   M, IS, RS, F

This worksheet form is used by the gross by most of our start-up clients. Observe that the project manager not only should list the task to be accomplished but is forced to list each minor step in accomplishing his task. This practice allows all other managers to see each step's progress so that they can more readily intermesh their tasks to fit. This practice also forces each manager to thoroughly plan before he commits your dollars and man hours to the task.

Please refer to the attached worksheets of Advanced American for the balance of the example.

CAMEO 7-3: ADVANCED AMERICAN TELEPROCESSING AND TECHNOLOGIES' EXAMPLE TIMEBASE   M, IS, RS, F

AAT&T allowed me to use one of their monthly time bases to illustrate its value. This computer services company averaged only one management team meeting a month because it used systems which obsoleted the need for meetings. Every co-founder knew every other co-founder's progress through their time-base control system. (See page 128 for the balance of this cameo.)

THE PIPS SYSTEM   M, IS, RS, F

The PIPS system stands for Purchasing-Inventory-Production-Sales & Shipping single system. This effective management-by-exceptions system literally allows you to see at a glance every order's status, where you lead and where you lag. I like it for several reasons. It allows you the opportunity of taking corrective action as soon as a problem surfaces. It is an instant communicator to all people involved. It forces purchasing, inventory, production, and sales to have a common system which cuts expediting time to a fraction. It gives your sales group the opportunity to "pull

Business Solutions Inc.
1961 The Alameda, San Jose, Ca. 95126
Telephone: (408) 249-7030

AUTHOR: R.D.B.   DATE: March 28

GROUP: Finance   APPROVER: ——

ROUTE TO: All   PAGE: 1 of 1

DESCRIPTION OF TASK	DATES BEGUN	DATES COMPL'TN	DOLLARS BUDGET TO-DATE	MAN-HOURS EST'D	MAN-HOURS TO-DATE	STOCK VALUE	3/3	3/10	3/17	3/24	3/31	PERCENT COMPLETE	NOTES
1. Financial Projection of Business Plan	8/67	3/68	0	100	310	10,000						100%	①
2. Bylaws, SBEC Negotiations	7/68	?	100	50	80	25,000						50%	②
3. SBA Loan	1/68	?	100	100	10	10,000						0%	③
4. V.C. Prospect	1/68	?	100	1000	250	25,000						?	④
5. Incorporation	3/67	4/68	750	1000	750	4,000						99	⑤
6. Foster Mercantile Orders	3/68	3/68	0	25	20	1,000						100	⑥
7. On-Going Tasks													
Controller	—	—	100/mo	20/mo	5	6,000							⑦
M-B-O Systems	—	—	100/mo	20/mo	25	4,000							"
CO-B-E "	—	—	100/mo	20/mo	10	1,000							"
M-B-M "	—	—	100/mo	20/mo	1	4,000							"

TOTALS:

COMMENTS: ① John - By A has committed $50,000 but need that final business plan draft. His shipping is killing him. ② SBA loan developed — will get citizens by Aug. the gentlemen. ③ Have 2 commitments at $50,000 each. That Mercurek contract over Feb 1. ④ Increments in meeting slowly - increase. Maybe we'll get the final approval in April. ⑤ By A Loan $25,000 at 8½% interest. We contract a with $25,000 of we need it. ⑥ All control systems appear to me to be working right. Any complaints? R.D.B.

Thanks for your help, gentlemen.

Business Solutions Inc.
1961 The Alameda, San Jose, Ca. 95126
Telephone: (408) 249-4030

AUTHOR: *J.J.*　DATE: **3/31/68**

GROUP: *Marketing*　APPROVED: —

ROUTE TO: *All Co-Founders*

PAGE: **1 of 2**

DESCRIPTION OF TASK	DATES BEGUN	DATES COMPL'TN	DOLLARS BUDGET	DOLLARS TO-DATE	MAN-HOURS EST'D	MAN-HOURS TO-DATE	STOCK VALUE	3/3	3/10	3/17	3/24	3/31	PERCENT COMPLETE	NOTES
I. Market Research	5/67	3/68											100%	①
A. Time Sharing	5/67	3/67	1000	20	500	100								
B. Data Base Services	5/67	7/67	1000	10	500	10								
C. Programming "	5/67	4/67	1000	10	500	10								
D. Hardware "	5/67	9/67	1000	200	500	100								
E. Stock Market "	5/67	6/67	1000	0	500	10							②	
F. Small Bus. Accounting	5/67	3/68	1000	3800	500	1200	2000							
G. Small Manufacturing Ser.	5/67	7/67	1000	100	500	80								
H. Stadium Crowd Ser.	1/68	3/68	1000	450	500	250							③	
I. Oem Services	5/67	3/68	1000	2300	500	1400							④	
J. Gap A-3	3/68	5/68	1000	650	0	210								
K. Gap A-1	11/67	3/68	200	200	100	100							100%	
II. Business Plan	5/67	3/68	500	50	100	250	1000						100%	⑤
III. Business Plan	2/68	3/68	0	0	0	0	—						0%	⑥
Rehearsals														
TOTALS:														

WEEK OF

COMMENTS: ① Though the VC like timesharing, every flag is up showing it to peak in 1970 & begin decaying.

② Though Market Research isn't promising here, Small Business Accounting is now generating $6,000/month
   for Valid Sales ($12,500 in Profits). Let's either get into H/Right or get out. ⑧ Picked up one
   10th customer this month. Sales are up to $4,500/100.

④ We feel into this one & got Menadrex at -5,000/mo for 12 months. We'll have A1 outline on
   4-4. We fell into this one (N 2,500,000) and Addrex by 4-15 (8 6,500/mo). We need 2 salesmens' 4 support people.

   East. Details will be discussed at 4-2 meetings. This is going to hit big!
   ⑤ Stop by & pick up your copy of the last re-write. It's an excellent plan.

⑥ Gentlemen — We stink here. Rehearsals are going to continue until we can present
   ourselves professionally. Schedule Next Tuesday & Thursday evenings from 6 pm - P.

Business Solutions Inc.
1961 The Alameda, San Jose, Ca. 95126
Telephone: (408) 249-4030

AUTHOR: J.J. DATE: 3/31 PAGE: 2 OF 2

GROUP: MARKETING APPROVED: — ROUTE TO: ALL CO-FOUNDERS

DESCRIPTION OF TASK	DATES BEGIN	COMPL'TN	DOLLARS BUDGET	TO-DATE	MAN-HOURS EST'D	TO-DATE	STOCK VALUE	3/3	3/10	3/17	3/24	3/31	PERCENT COMPLETE	NOTES
II. ON-GOING SALES														
A PROGRAMMING	—	—	50/mo	3100/mo	80/mo	320/mo	1450							A
B SMALL BUS. ACCTING	—	—	400/mo.	410/mo.	80/mo.	410/mo.	2500							B
C STORE MANUFACTURING	—	—	350/mo.	410/mo.	40/mo.	20/mo.	900							C
D STADIUM PROJECT	—	—	200/mo.	0/mo.	40/mo.	0/mo.	1100							D
E OEM SERVICES	—	—	100/mo	600/mo.	80/mo.	80/mo.	1400							E
F GAP A-1	—	—	400/mo.	410/mo.	100/mo.	100/mo.	4200							F
G GAP A-3	—	—	—	1350	—	80	3500							G
I. TARGETS-OF-OPPORTUNITIES														
A GLEASON'S	—	—	1000	820	200	40	5700							H
B S.C. #1	—	—	500	700	200	500	550							I
C S.C. #2	—	—	1100	650	250	1125	(1400)							J
D CONSULTING	—	—	500	0	100	310	4200							K

TOTALS:

COMMENTS:
Ⓐ 1100 SALES (450 PROFITS), Ⓑ 4550 SALES (1450 PROFITS), Ⓑ 6000 SALES (2500 PROFITS), Ⓒ 2200 SALES (900 PROFITS),
Ⓓ 1100 SALES (1100 PROFITS), Ⓔ 5100 SALES (1400 PROFITS), Ⓔ 7500 SALES (4200 PROFITS),
Ⓕ 5000 SALES (3500 PROFITS), Ⓗ 41,000 SALES (5700 PROFITS), Ⓘ 6300 SALES (250 PROFITS),
Ⓙ 1100 SALES (1400 LOSES), Ⓚ 17,800 SALES (4200 PROFITS).
Ⓜ WE'RE GOING TO BE SUED UNLESS WE CAN STRAIGHTEN THIS ONE OUT. SCHEDULE ME 15 MINUTES
AT 4:14 MEETING. SAM, I NEED FRED & DAVID AT CUSTOMER'S FACILITY UNTIL WE MAKE THINGS
WORK. DEAL BUDGET 2,000 LOSS FOR APRIL.
Ⓖ EVERYONE COME TO 4/2/68 MEETING ON A-3. IT'S BIG IF WE NEED DECISIONS. SEE ATTACHED
AGENDA.

your chestnuts out of the fire'' with your customers when you have problems. It's an extremely inexpensive and simple system to install and run, and when your start-up finally grows so large that a computer becomes justified, the system falls onto a computer with minimal programming efforts.

Briefly, the PIPS system works as follows:

(1) When your sales department receives an order, they begin the control system by initiating the paperwork with the model ordered, the quantity ordered, the first six letters of the customer's name, the last six digits of the customer's purchase order number, the date the order was received, and the date it is to be shipped. The paperwork then goes to production while administration is notified to check the customer's credit.

(2) Production then completes the last part of the control number by adding the production stations to the part number and then placing the control number on a large magnetic board (the production control board). This board is mounted on the wall for all to see. The production station numbers should show the usual lead times of each station. (As an example, let's assume that your product must go through four production stations and then a final inspection station. The numbers that your production group adds might read: "5A3, 7A1, 9A2, 14A½, and 2F1. If you total the last numbers, you know that it takes $3 + 1 + 2 + ½$ or 6½ days for production time and 1 day for QA inspection. If your company is committed to a 3-week delivery date, then your purchasing department knows that it has only 8½ working days to get the necessary production components before due dates must be slipped.

The production department then adds the list of raw materials needed and the production and QA station instructions to the work packet and forwards it to inventory.

(3) Inventory checks the unassigned raw inventory bins to see if you have the materials to complete the orders and then passes the control sheet to purchasing. Inventory removes the station instructions and places them in an active file. When the materials are gathered into production lot kits, the station instructions will accompany the kits to the production floor.

(4) Purchasing now orders the raw materials to the dates that they are needed. If administration is unhappy with the customer's credit, they can stop the orders at this stage until agreeable terms are negotiated with the customer. So far, this whole process should have taken a matter of hours. If purchasing gets its paperwork a day or two after the order was received (remember, the order date is in the control number), then they should have instructions to notify administration of the delay and the guilty party should be fined incentive stock. If the guilty party isn't a founder, then the founder who supervises the guilty party should also be fined incentive stock. You would be amazed at how fast paper can flow after several finings.

(5) Meanwhile, back at the production control magnetic board, every production order is initially preceeded by the initials "P," "I," "P," and "S." When the raw materials have been received, the first "P" is removed and the board reader realizes that the order's bottleneck is now inventory instead of purchasing. When the letter "I" is removed from the board, everyone knows that inventory has delivered the raw materials and station instructions to production station "3A3" and production is the bottleneck. When station "3A3" has completed its work, it is removed from the magnetic board, and all board readers know that the production lot can be found at station "7A1." This process continues until all production and quality assurance stations are completed and then the second "P" is removed and everyone knows that sales and shipping are the bottlenecks. Sales types the bill of lading and the billing invoices and forwards them to shipping. When the parts go out the door, the final "S" can be removed and the order's control number taken from the magnetic board.

FURTHER COMMENTS ON THE PIPS SYSTEM

(1) If you are wise, you'll encourage every founder and every manager to visit the magnetic control board daily. When all of the bosses take an interest in your company's performance, you can bet that everyone else takes an interest also.

(2) You'll note that the customer's name and purchase order number are an integral part of your control number. When your customers or your salesmen call to determine the status of their orders, you can immediately refer to your control number without the delays involved in cross referencing their numbers to your control numbers. This impresses them and gives them the feeling that you are really looking out for their orders. They have the feeling that you are giving them special treatment and this translates into future orders.

(3) One glance at the control board tells you where everything should be. If an order begins to slip, you know immediately whom to contact.

(4) Note that a considerable amount of paperwork is eliminated. Since all departments use the same control numbers, there is little reason to have each department maintain duplicate files. Actually, several clients take a polaroid snapshot of their control board each evening and that photo is their record.

(5) The critical thing is that the control board must be updated almost hourly. If you allow it to become non-current, you lose control.

(6) The warning flags are always in plain view for all to see. If you use the reward-punishment incentive systems, the control board can also be slightly altered to monitor performances.

(7) The PIPS system initially places the greatest burden upon your

purchasing people. However, as soon as your start-up matures, these people get to know your vendors so well that they rarely run into trouble. Then the greatest pressure is placed on the production groups. However, they also rapidly mature and learn each production station's lead time and their people's capabilities and can stay on schedule. Then the greatest pressure falls and remains on your sales department. How can they keep production and purchasing from sandbagging lead times and thus losing orders? You will always have the eternal battle of sales to shorten lead times so that they can get you more orders. There is no clean answer to this problem. However, beware of excessive pressures by sales to over-inventory you (and therefore tie up your spendable dollars) to reduce lead times. Make the sales manager assume the responsibility of moving the inventory at acceptable rates before you surrender to his pleas.

(8) Note that if you decide to utilize the ongoing incentive system for your non-key employees, it is a minor change to add scrap/rework figures to your control board.

(9) Observe that the PIPS system will place a great deal of pressure upon your quality assurance group. Your QA people need a strong backbone to withstand production and shipping pressures to send out defective merchandise on time rather than send out reliable products late. You can't tolerate shipping less than top quality products so select strong individuals who can say ''no'' under pressure and reward and punish them accordingly.

(10) Perhaps the greatest benefit of the PIPS system is that it allows your sales department to see problems as soon as they occur. If the sales group learns that you are going to slip shipment, they have the option of contacting the customer to learn how critical a delivery date is long before it is slipped. Good sales groups can buy you the time that you need (without expensive overtime or premium purchasing prices) by convincing the customer to take partial shipments, by determining that the requested delivery date is really not necessary, or by talking another customer into accepting his shipments late so that you can pirate from his production order to ship the critical order. But this usually takes some time and unless you have a system to give sales that time, they can only react and insist upon expensive overtime.

Minor Point 7-4: The PIPS Magnetic Board   M, IS, RS, F

You can get full wall (24' × 8') magnetic board coverage by the following trick. Order six 8' × 4' sheets of sixteen-gauge steel and attach them to your production wall (epoxy cement works well). Then order rubber magnet strips (usually pennies per foot) and cut these strips into the desired lengths with household scissors. To the strips, attach your letters, spray paint the steel sheets, use colored tape (electrical tape) for your board's permanent horizontal and vertical lines, and you are in business. The usual magnetic board costs less than $100 and takes four man hours to install.

BLIND PERFORMANCE REVIEWS   M, IS, RS, F

Blind performance reviews usually work well because they tend to keep everyone extremely honest in his relationship with his boss, peers, and subordinates. Too frequently, the view of a man by subordinates is totally different than it is by bosses. (Example: Cliff Nelson is a fictitious sales manager. The Marketing VP might say, "Cliff is one heck of an administrator. He has his thumb on everything." A sales engineer under Cliff might say, "I certainly hope that Cliff is promoted into another department so that I can start doing my job right. Cliff doesn't understand sales so he is trying to make up for this void by over-administering us. He is more interested in blame for a lost sales report than he is in allowing us to make sales calls. His demands are tearing up our sales rhythms. If he would leave us alone, we could meet our sales quotas." A peer in another department might say, "Cliff Nelson is the most vindictive man in the company. No one had better cross this man or get in his way for promotions or he'll kill him." If Cliff Nelson knew that he was going to be continually reviewed from all angles, he probably would conduct himself totally differently. If he doesn't change, you have all the warning flags necessary to take corrective actions.)

If you are wise, you'll require everyone to review everyone else on a monthly or quarterly basis. If you make these reviews "blind" (the author doesn't have to sign his name), you'll receive a lot of information that you otherwise wouldn't receive if you force signatures. Also, if you're wise, you'll include your own name to be reviewed. Consider changing your questions each month so that your people can't get a tight handle on what exactly to expect. Leave plenty of writing space for the constant last question, "Observations and recommendations on how this man can improve?"

BLIND COMPANY-PERFORMANCE REVIEW   M, IS, RS, F

Consider a quarterly company review (again blind) in which all personnel are asked to make evaluations on the company's management, its systems, its atmosphere, its incentives, and its products. Request suggestions and recommendations on how your company could be improved. You'll be surprised at what will come out of the woodwork.

MEMORY TICKLER SYSTEMS   M, IS, RS, F

The biggest sin that a manager can commit is to lose his personal organization. To always be organized is not too hard a discipline when a key employee or manager works for an established company which utilizes the proper supports (secretaries, banks of filing cabinets, microfilm retrieval systems, on-line computers, etc.). However, as a start-up, you don't have the money to spend on these supports. Furthermore, you compound the problem by forcing your founders to wear many hats. Most founders carry several responsibilities in several different departments until their company matures and grows. The probability that your founders will therefore frequently become disorganized increases significantly. Yet you cannot afford disorganization in anyone.

Consider installing a memory tickler system which will allow your people to feed in information and forget about it until an event or date flags the information and tells them about it. For instance, "If the model 101 scrap rate exceeds ½%, notify me immediately." The man who asked this can now completely forget about the model 101's scrap rate because he knows that he will be notified when his flag is exceeded once he's established that his flag system *works*. "Remind me on the 17th of my luncheon appointment with Mr. X on the 18th." "General Electric's Request For Quotation Number AQX 388782-BQ19 must be typed and mailed by the 11th. Notify me if Engineering's estimates are not completed by the 7th." "Notify me every Thursday of the Materials Review Committee meeting." All of these are typical examples of the inputs your founders will make each week. If you are wise, you'll install a fool-proof system which will allow them confidence in remembering.

For the time tickler system, place 31 bins in a central location. All employees who want to be reminded of a date need only to place their reminder in the date bin applicable. Then, each morning, a clerk pulls all of the reminders from the day's bin and distributes them. This system isn't very sophisticated but it works. We have had clients with as many as 400 employees use three shelves with 31 shoe boxes on each shelf. The clerk whose job it is to distribute these date ticklers states that almost all 400 use it consistently.

The event tickler system is the when-something-occurs, notify-me-immediately system. It isn't quite as easy as the others, but it isn't difficult. Instead of establishing just one system for the whole company, you usually must maintain a system for each department or discipline. As an example, if the president wants to be notified when the model 101's scrap rate exceeds ½%, the production control card can carry this figure. Let's say that a thousand pieces of the 101 start down the line. The first production station that receives less than 995 assemblies must notify the president (you would be surprised how this flag affects production managers and workers. Almost every time, 995 assemblies will make it to final inspection).

Wherever there is a significant "flag" that you must have in a management-by-exceptions atmosphere, there should be a reliable system to police that flag.

CAMEO 7-4: THE "I'M NEEDED" INCENTIVE   IS

Three commercial artists had always wanted to produce paintings of value but since their families needed support, none could afford to quit his job and devote his life to painting. Their problem wasn't ability, it was marketing, and until they addressed and solved their sales problem, they would always remain "hack" commercial artists.

We worked out a marketing system which would allow them to pre-sell their work (at approximately $250 a painting). When the marketing machinery was 3 months old, they had enough orders to allow one of them to quit his job and work full time painting; when it was 5 months old, another was able to quit; and when 6 months passed, the third quit. All went well until the start-up was approximately 9 months old. Sales then began to take off and the artists could not keep up. By the time the firm was 12 months old, orders doubled the artists' ability to produce and their distribution machinery was getting into trouble because of their late shipments. They needed more paintings to sell.

Now most artists spend a lifetime trying to build up a large enough following to allow them to live decently. These three artists told me that the average artist is 55 years old before he can earn even $20,000 a year. Through their unique marketing, these three artists were accomplishing in months what it took others years to accomplish and the art community was proud of them. Now, the men were in trouble and they were not afraid to say, "I need your help" to their fellow artists. Within two weeks after they sent out their SOS, the other artists had brought in their surplus paintings and all back orders were filled.

This young company is now 16 months old and they employ five full-time artists (on commissions) and nine part-time artists. Of all our clients, I think that these people have the happiest work atmosphere of all. Everyone is turning out the best work he or she is capable of and their customers appreciate the quality of this work. Though the founders of this firm will probably never be millionaires, they are living a good life and doing what they like and are best at.

KEY NON-KEY INCENTIVES   M, IS, RS, F

Be aware that there are always going to be non-key people, who by their job needs, are key to your company's success. People who continuously come into contact with your customers (waitresses, salesmen, sales clerks, debt collectors, etc.) are frequently classified as non-key people, but in truth, they are extremely important. Also, there are natural leaders who, through their leadership abilities, bring their fellow workers' performances either up or down. These people can be key non-key people. You'll also observe that there are always a few gifted non-key people, who by their personalities and their cheery dispositions, create the work atmosphere that you want. If you promote these people to key-employee status, you'll dilute your key status. Yet if you don't recognize and reward (or punish) these people, you don't establish their incentives to create the atmosphere you need. Have you ever gone into a restaurant and had a waitress who truly enjoyed people, liked her job and felt serving you was important, and tried her best to make your meal an occasion instead of just another meal? Have you ever tried to buy a train or bus ticket from a clerk who didn't care whether you got serviced or not? These two examples of key non-key individuals either encouraged you to return or forced you away from their employers.

The trick to incentive systems for this type of individual is to give them frequent reviews accompanied with the frequent rewards and punishments involved in their accomplishments. Though your reviews might be subjective in nature, these people know that they are constantly being appreciated. As an example for Susie Waitress, it might be, "Susie, it has been two weeks since I last reviewed you and I want you to know that I have observed the following: First, I want to compliment you on the way that you remember our customers' names. Here's a coupon for $5 for this attribute. Susie, you have a truly cheery nature that makes those you serve come back. You're great in this area and here is a $10 coupon for our appreciation of this characteristic. Next, I've noticed that you are slightly lax on your appearance. Several times you have worn a soiled uniform and occasionally you forget to clean your fingernails as they should be cleaned. Here is a minus $2 coupon for this attribute. Tonight, when you come up to the cash register for your pay, please turn in these coupons and get $13 additional."

NON-KEY INCENTIVES

This is the hardest part of the book to write because the non-key segments of organizational charts are the least tapped for incentive contributions. The first company to effectively tap this enormous reserve of desire and talent will sink us all for being obsolete.

Let's be honest with ourselves. We hire non-key people to perform routine tasks which complete our essential ongoing work. We may throw up smoke screens such as titles, invitations to management club meetings, frequent and loud lip service, trying to install professionalism in their arts and trades, frequent pats on the backs (or swats slightly lower), and a dozen other shallow disguises, but when all the shouting is done, we want them to perform X amount of routine work so that we can realize Y amount of sales and Z amount of profits. You know this, they know this, and there is nothing that either of you can do because the routine work must be completed and there aren't enough hours left over for them to offer you their other abilities.

The following are some of the non-key incentive systems which have proved reliable:

Occurrence Rewards: Every time an employee or an employee team (e.g., a production line) meets your standards in output, give a reward of coupons. Every time the employee or employee team falls below the standards, punish with negative coupons. In the case of production, these coupons are passed out with each production lot. In the case of national industrial service, they are passed out with every customer transaction. In the case of retail sales and service, they are passed out at the end of each day or week.

Excellence Rewards: Establish excellence levels above your standards. Every time these levels of excellence are met, give larger coupons. You can also have the mirror image of these standards below the standards. When performance falls short of these lower-than-norm levels, larger negative coupons are passed out.

Extra Job Rewards: Encourage your non-key people to assume responsibilities for additional tasks and reward them accordingly. As an example, most of our clients put a value on housekeeping and offer to either hire a janitor or pay their regular employees the janitor's wages if they'll keep the facilities neat. You'll discover that many will grab a broom and sweep up after work. When your facility needs painting, offer the painting contractor's fees to your people if they will come in on weekends to paint. The average non-key employee should be able to realize several hundred dollars extra each month for these options.

Promotions from Within: The theory that no man can be promoted unless he has trained at least two men to take his place is an excellent policy because it forces everyone to continually train both upwards and downwards. One promotion high up causes a chain of promotions which helps morale at all levels.

However, in actual practice, you'll probably replace a manager with the best man that you can find and frequently that man will come in from outside your company. Show me a company which only promotes from within and I'll show you a company with limited management vision.

Additional Profit Center Opportunities: Invite your non-key people to participate in your additional profit centers and targets-of-opportunity when these centers are extremely young. They can participate in these new projects on a part-time basis (or even a moonlighting basis) and are rewarded from that center's profits. Not only do these new and challenging projects keep everyone young, dynamic, and vigorous, they frequently are an avenue for even your lowest non-key people to assume minor profit center management experience. Frequently, you'll discover diamonds among your lowest people, who grow with their profit centers into key-employees and top managers. The important thing is that you have offered them an avenue up and the best will jump at the chance.

ADDITIONAL COMMENTS ON NON-KEY PEOPLE   M, IS, RS, F

I am going to skip the usual comments on leadership theory because I assume that you know what works best for your own personality and your own start-up, however I would like to touch upon a few points frequently overlooked by entrepreneurs:

(1) A person has a name and likes to be thought of and referred to by that name. Never allow your accounting clerks to give your people an accounting number which appears on paychecks, insurance contracts, employment contracts, or security badges. If your accounting clerks need numbers, let them develop a look-up table and keep those numbers only in the accounting office. You can't expect any man to feel that he is part of the company family and an essential team member if he feels that top management knows him only by a number.

(2) People like to accomplish things that are meaningful to humanity. Even a welder who must make the same weld 1,000 times each day has to believe that his welds are essential to the product's performance and that the product has real value to the user. Never allow any manager or key employee to "knock" the value of the man's contribution or your product's real worth to the user. Keep your people informed on how your product is being used.

(3) All people like to be treated as equals when they have earned your respect. All people like challenges and if you'll allow your problems to be known at the lowest levels, people at these levels will do their darndest to help you find the causes and the solutions to the problems. When they do define the causes and the solutions, if you recognize and reward their efforts, you'll buy dedication, loyalty, and innovativeness that you never knew was available.

(4) Respect and rewards must be earned both upwards and downwards on a continuing basis. If you give it or receive it for nothing, that is its value . . . it's worth nothing.

(5) The avenues for advancement, additional challenges, self-improvement, recognition, reward, and punishment must always be kept open and must be kept reliable.

(6) Some idiot at some time must have said that advancement is a one-way street. People can only go upwards, never downwards. If you promote someone beyond their capabilities be honest with him and yourself and demote him to where he can be most effective. Then, when

he develops himself so that he can handle the next rung, give him another crack at it.

(7)   Have as short a memory for foul-ups as you have for accomplishments. After the punishment (or reward), a new leaf is turned and the incident is forgotten. I've never understood the practice of permanently filing notes in a man's employment records.

(8)   Believe it or not, the frequencies of rewards and punishments are more important than the size of the pats or swats. A monthly review is far more than 12 times as effective as the yearly review. If you earned $250 last month in coupons, from many accomplishments, that $250 means a lot more to you than that $3,000 that you'll earn once yearly.

(9)   People like to feel that they are part of an intimate family. While you are small, this family atmosphere is relatively easy to maintain. When you grow to several thousand employees, you might consider establishing as many family groups as are necessary to make things work right.

(10)   It's an old cliché but in most cases it's true. People are your most important resource. If you have the best, you'll always succeed. If you have less than the best, you'll always have problems.

(11)   One of the best slogans to remember is, when a man has to be fired, there should be two men fired. If it's a new man, then the man should be fired along with the man who hired him. If it's an old employee, then the man should be fired along with the man who supervised him. In all cases, the chain reaction leads all the way up to your managers, your founders, and yourself. When a man needs to be fired, then you are flagged that a series of people failed and you should take corrective actions.

In theory, this policy sounds good but in actual practice it doesn't work too well. However, I like to see it given lots of lip service because most people on the lower rungs feel so strongly that it is true.

CAMEO 7-5: THE NEED TO PRODUCE SOMETHING
OF VALUE   M

This experience showed me that people need a lot more than just pay checks. A potentiometer client had a major production problem on one of his bread and butter lines. His model RJ 24 line had gone through a redesign and the production yields were very bad. Every manufacturing, facility, and QA engineer was busy trying to get this production line going right and nothing seemed to work.

It's hard to be a production worker when you know that half of your work will end up in the scrap barrel. The morale on this line was extremely low when a brief note was passed down from worker to worker. It read:

"As you know, for the last four months, we have been shipping significant quantities of our RJ 24 to Hazeltine. This potentiometer is being installed in a secret instrument to be used by our boys in Vietnam. Last week, the first Hazeltine units were received in Vietnam and two days ago, the following episode occurred.

"A platoon of 43 Americans were just leaving their camp for a combat patrol. The 'point man' of this patrol was carrying the Hazeltine instrument. When this man was just 50 yards from his camp (a position well behind our lines), the Hazeltine detector began to warn him of a pending ambush. The detector pinpointed where the ambush forces were located. Though the point man and his commander were certain that the instrument was malfunctioning and giving false readings, they radioed their company commander and asked for instructions. They were ordered to hold their positions until the accuracy of the reading was determined. Another platoon was dispatched on a flanking movement to investigate the 'false' reading. They uncovered 83 Viet Cong soldiers who would have ambushed and wiped out the first patrol.

"The secret Hazeltine detector uses six of our model RJ 24's. If it hadn't been for this reliable potentiometer, 43 American men would be dead today."

The 30 production people on the RJ 24 line read the note and glowed. For awhile, there was all kind of conjecture on the significance of their contributions. Forty-three wives with probably 86 children wouldn't have to spend 1,290 Christmas Eves without a husband and a father; 21 children might realize college educations because their dads were still around to pay the bills; perhaps even 2 of those 21 might become doctors, school teachers, or scientists, and think of the good everyone will get from them; 43 mothers would be spared the tears of lost sons. Was this note worth the three minutes that it took to dictate?

Minor Point 7-5: Management-By-Motivation Systems In Established Companies   M, IS, RS, F

Since most of the systems discussed in this book are written for the start-up and young companies, we have primarily mentioned control systems which replace dollar rewards for stock rewards. Never make the mistake of thinking that the old established companies (whose stock cannot be used) cannot convert to these profitable systems. They can. These companies (your competitors) can very readily cure their tired-blood problems by offering milestone incentives to their people. In the past eight years, we have introduced management-by-motivations systems into 22 manufacturing firms with the following results:

(a) In all cases, their management stated that they observed significant employee improvements.

(b) In almost all cases, there was a relatively high turnover of employees for the first six months. Thereafter, employee turnover dropped to new lows. In the majority of cases, the employees who left were the underachievers and were replaced with superior people.

(c) In 2 cases, the rewards were not commensurate with the demands placed upon the workers. These two firms received marginal benefits from the system.

(d) In 18 cases, the employees' incentive payments reached 20% of their salaries, in 9 cases, the incentives reached 50%, and in 2 cases, the incentives exceeded salaries.

(e) In 15 cases, the expenses involved in the incentive systems were less than half of the added profits the system generated.

(f) In 20 cases, the clients incorporated both the rewards and punishment features. Late shipments, poor quality, poor scrap rates, tardiness, poor housekeeping, and other poor performances were punished. However, since the rewards for good performances outweighed the punishments, few employees complained. In all cases bad habits were broken.

(g) The peer pressures placed on marginal performances were extreme. Since the complete production line lost incentive rewards (and therefore was punished) for scrap/rework/customer returns, those who generated them heard from their fellow workers long before management had the opportunity to react.

(h) Though none of these clients had stock to offer as incentives, they developed meaningful incentives through (1) establishing non-profit employee companies and building meaningful pension systems through these companies, (2) offering coupons which can either be redeemed in cash or merchandise (two companies even used trading stamps), (3) using the incentive percent of the profits to purchase stock for distribution to the employees, or (4) paying their people cash.

(i) In several cases, the companies offered to match the employees' incentives for their children's college educations.

(j) Though seven of these clients were unionized, in only four cases did the unions object.

Minor Point 7-6: An Insight into Union Priorities   M, IS, RS, F

Joan Thall, a consultant to labor negotiations, gave me an insight into a union's priorities which may interest you. Before you ever work with a union, realize that union's priorities or you'll be crucified. These priorities are:

First: The union's survival.
Second: The union's growth.
Third: The union's profits.
Fourth: The union's power.
Fifth: The benefits that the union's members receive.
Sixth: The union's image.
Seventh: The health of your company.
Eighth: A combination of minor priorities such as the effects of your labor contract on your company's customers, its effects on our economy, etc.

This is usually quite an insight for most who are encountering union negotiations for the first time. Do you see how this book's systems are in harmony with the fifth, seventh, and eighth priorities, while in conflict with the balance? Since these systems make your people loyal to your company instead of to the union, a union's days are numbered if they allow you to implement them and they know it. Therefore, if yours is an established company with union contracts, expect problems. Some companies have gotten around these problems in the following legal and illegal methods:

(1)   Sponsor a non-union spin-off which, after the controls are installed, enters into competition with the parent. If the control systems are working properly, the union can never penetrate this spin-off because its workers won't accept it. The spin-off's profits are, of course, fed back to the holding company and eventually the child will replace the parent as the prim producer.

(2)   Make the incentive system known to the union and if they reject it, begin an intensive education program for the employees. Once the majority favor the incentive rewards, force an election and vote out the union.

(3)   Attract an outside union which will allow the incentives as a price for entry. Perform the employee education program and when the timing is ripe, force an election to replace the existing union. It is rumored that the Teamsters Union frequently accepts these types of offers.[4]

(4)   Threaten the incumbent union with the above options unless they conform.

(5)   Other legal options such as offering the incumbent union long-term contracts, percentages of the increased profits, flat rate commissions (such as our railroads do with piggybacking), etc.

(6)   Other illegal options such as bribes, kick-backs, slush funds, the Swiss bank account route, etc.[5]

Minor Point 7-7: Effort vs. Work   M, IS, RS, F

Never allow your people to confuse the words "effort" and "work." A man may give 100% of his energies, he may work 14 hours a day, 7 days a week, and he may go home so spent that all he can do is go to bed, however, unless he has accomplished things of real value, he has accomplished little work. Engineers define work as force times distance and

---

[4] This is in no way to be considered an endorsement of the Teamsters Union. Though the Teamsters isn't the worst union to try to work with, it is a long way from being the best.

[5] I used to never discuss unethical or illegal practices in our government or our unions until the venerable management consultant, Doctor Hangrove Smith-Elliott said, "Don't concern yourself with politicians and union officials' improprieties because they have definite economic values. If you dried-up bribing these people, you would close-up 10% of the Swiss bank accounts."

I think that this definition carries over pretty well into the management field. Let's change the word "force" to "efforts" (which includes manpower loading, expenses, facilities, equipment, and support) and let's change "distance" to "value" (increased profits, increased efficiencies, increased market penetrations, improved products) and we have a pretty fair definition of work. If you are receiving low values for major efforts, then you, your management team, and all people involved should be taken to task because you are receiving very little work. It's time to draw back and admit that you are working hard instead of smart and make the changes necessary.

Minor Point 7-8. A Trick to Shorten Meetings   M, IS, RS, F

Remove all the chairs from the conference room, lower the temperature to approximately 62°, and don't allow the air to get stale. You'll discover that stand-up meetings take about half the time as sit-down meetings.

CAMEO 7-6: USING STOCK INCENTIVES IN A LIMITED PARTNERSHIP   M, IS, RS, F

Approximately four years ago, four engineers formed their start-up to manufacture sophisticated plant security systems. They estimated that they would need $3,000,000 to "do it right" and they started immediately to write their business plan and complete their sophisticated designs.

Approximately one month after they formed, they realized that one of their sensors would make an excellent bicycle chain alarm. They therefore took a flyer in the mail order business and this alarm sold well. Approximately five weeks later, they realized that another sensor would detect smoke better than anything on the market so they took another flyer on it and it sold well. Likewise, they developed a very cheap but reliable apartment burglar alarm (a window alarm), a library chip that, unless degaused, would trip a theft alam, a clothing store shoplifting chip, and appliance alarms. All of these were accidental product fall-outs, but they all brought in cash. When the start-up was six months old, the engineers agreed that they knew little about sales so they attracted a top grade marketing man. In three months, their products were included in two of the nation's largest mail order catalogs, their products were being sold by three nationwide distribution chains, and several OEM manufacturers were installing them in their equipment.

By the time the company was a year old, the sophisticated plant security system was still on the boards, the business plan (though completed) couldn't be used because the primary product wasn't being produced, and the firm was clearing $85,000 a month. Since the engineers still weren't certain which direction their company was going (and therefore they weren't seeking venture capital), there was no reason to incorporate. They placed a considerable sum of their profits into a lawsuit reserve in case the unlimited partner was sued but no further action was taken.

Now, four years later, the firm has completed its sophisticated security system but can't sell it. No one wants it. However, they now have 22 cheap products which sell well. To this day, these men still job out all of their production, have their jobbers carry all of the inventory costs, never manufacture a single device unless there are committed purchase orders to assure that the devices will not sit on a shelf, and have yet to seek one dime of capital. They have cash reserves of approximately $350,000 and they are still a limited partnership. Since all of the founders are well under 40, it is improbable that they will not want to sell their company for another 20 years. They will therefore probably bide their time until the money market is prime, they'll then incorporate and immediately go public, and all will become millionaires. Until that time, they'll continue to follow their milestone incentives and each earn more and more "internal shares" of their limited partnership.

Minor Point 7-9: The Options' Decision Systems   M, IS, RS, F

Though this is a personal (instead of company) decision system, it is the one primarily used by management consultants and better managers and should be briefly mentioned.

First, realize that there are very few non-routine management decisions that must be made immediately. Usually, you have from an hour to several days before your decision is essential. Therefore, when you are confronted with a problem, immediately determine when your decision is needed.

Next, with the time that you have, lay out all the options open to you without making judgments on any. When you have completed listing all the options open to you, then determine the effects and costs of each. The best option usually becomes very obvious.

When you have practiced this personal options system for awhile, you'll observe that 10% of the time, you'll completely end run the problem with a brilliant solution, that the first solution is the best solution only 25% of the time, and that you'll keep your competitors off balance because you aren't predictable.

OTHER MANAGEMENT-BY-OBJECTIVES AND MANAGEMENT-BY-EXCEPTIONS SYSTEMS   M, IS, RS, F

Profit center systems will be discussed in the next chapter. We feel that they are so important to a start-up that they deserve their own chapter.

There are dozens of other excellent systems which are hard not to discuss in this book. Actually, in an earlier draft of this book, I attempted to discuss in depth approximately 65 systems which ranged from inventory "FIFO" (First In–First Out) to the IBM competitive evaluation system. These systems make good reading and are fun to present but a discussion of them would make this text too long and too expensive. The systems presented above have proven extremely reliable for hundreds of start-ups and will probably carry you until you realize several millions in yearly sales. When they begin to become strained and you need to attach additional systems to control your incentives, you'll find many excellent texts in the business section of your main library. You'll discover that the authors of most of these texts have ignored the incentives but with minor modifications, you can build motivators into their systems.

8 · Profit Center Controls

PRELIMINARY NOTE

This chapter has been rewritten 17 times for readability and understanding. Accounting is a difficult subject into which to breath life, so after each draft, several non-accounting people (secretaries, salesmen, production personnel, etc.) were asked to read it. After the 17th attempt, we finally were satisfied that it was both interesting and understandable.

I went to this trouble because I hope you do not see the word "accounting" and skip to the next chapter. Most entrepreneurs and managers dislike accounting and therefore assign all responsibilities to "a qualified accountant." This logic would be acceptable except three-quarters of the "qualified accountants" that I know are truly poor businessmen and practice the same philosophies used by their grandfathers 50 years ago. Therefore, you can easily inherit an antiquated control system which will stunt your company's growth potentials. Your management team will be forced to be reactive (instead of pro-active) because most accounting systems lag, instead of lead, decisions.

This chapter is not written to teach anyone bookkeeping. Its only intent is to show you what is available to you in management tools so that when you interview a prospective controller, you can ask him intelligent questions and select the candidate who will work best for your team.

PROLOGUE   M, IS, RS, F

Profit center philosophies run far deeper than the shallow "make or buy" systems which many accountants define as "profit center controls."

147

Your profit center control system should allow you to look into the very bowels of your operations, forecast problems before they translate into expenses, and should be the backbone of your management-by-objectives, management-by-exceptions, and management-by-motivations systems.

It is unfortunate that many accountants have just taken the term "profit centers" and applied this term to their old cost center system without implementing the essential ingredients which make profit center controls work. Profit center controls go far deeper than just the shallow "make or buy" feature that most accountants attribute to them. It is the intent of this chapter to show you true profit center controls and what they will give you . . . not the shallow compromises that will force your company to fall short of its mark.

Let's first examine the theory and then look at some of the practical applications of profit center controls.

SECTION ONE: THE THEORIES BEHIND PROFIT CENTER CONTROLS

THE MINIMUM REQUIREMENTS OF A GOOD ACCOUNTING CONTROL SYSTEM   M, IS, RS, F

A good accounting system is far more than just an accounting system. It is a true management control system. You should expect the following minimums:

(1) You should get both present and future probable performances instead of just past performances. This includes the present month, next month, the next quarter, the next half year, and the next year. These projected (proforma) predictions are actually more important to you than your past performances because they allow you to intelligently establish your priorities, correct problems that will occur, and allow you to "close the barn door before the horse escapes."

(2) You should get a readable warning-flag report (exceptions forecast) which will predict the impact of problems unless corrective actions are taken.

(3) You should get a built-in security system which will allow information to flow to even the lowest of employee levels on an as-needed basis without concerning yourself with confidential information getting to your competitors. Once this security system is reliable, your profit center control system is an effective tool to disseminate meaningful information to all levels of management. The savings in meetings and conferences is significant.

(4) You should establish a relatively tamper-proof system. The checks and balances are there to discourage dishonesties, paddings, disguisings, and buck passing.

(5)   Your accounting system should be the foundation of your incentives (both rewards and punishments) systems. It keeps the scores and disburses the earned incentives.

(6)   Your control system should "float" with conditions as they exist and will exist. If sales are going to increase, the budgets for each group will likewise increase when the timing (a management decision) is correct. The floating budgets and reserves can be made so that they neither lead nor lag conditions.

(7)   Your system should give you frequent (about twice weekly) scan reports on who and what is generating your profits and your losses.

(8)   You should receive reports on your past performances that are accurate and on time.

These minimums are so obvious and so simple that I hate to waste your time reading them, however since so few accountants even strive for all of them, they must be mentioned. Do you see how essential they are to keep your management team informed and on course? Those firms which accept less than these minimums force their management to shoot in the dark.

Observe that these minimums put your management information into one clean envelope. Your "accounting machinery" not only combines all departments' and groups' performances in dollars and cents terms, it also gives them back information in a usable format (Example 8-1).

Be aware that these are minimums. As your company grows, instead of hiring additional people to manage the additional operational workloads, you can force your profit center controls to assume more of the workloads. It is a minor step to have a word processing unit added to this system, which automatically types and checks quotations, purchase orders, station instructions, bills of lading, letters, and sales presentations. A good word processing unit can replace 15 typists. When your company matures, this system will fall onto a computer system (either your own or a timesharing system) with a minimum of programming. The computer's memory and speed should replace all active files and an additional 20 to 50 clerks.

A Warning

For a start-up or a spin-off, profit center controls are just as easy and as inexpensive to establish as any other accounting-management system. However, once your company is set up with another accounting system (such as cost center controls), the transition to profit center controls can be extremely painful.

Profit center controls so expose inefficiencies, poor management judgments, blunders, and dishonesty that when an established company converts to it, usually the controller, his staff, the marketing manager, his staff, and several other managers and their key personnel are fired for past performances. So, rather than have poor management practices illuminated, most companies just use the name profit centers, add a few frills (such as minor make-or-buy decisions), and let things go at that.

If you are considering converting your already existing business to profit center controls, you must address the job security problem. Realize that most of the old accounting systems (e.g., cost center controls) do not give your managers enough information for them to make valid decisions. Therefore, their decisions may appear to be poor when illuminated in the glare of profit center controls. Therefore, you should expect your present managers to sabotage the conversion in an attempt to avoid the humiliations of having past poor decisions revealed.

Consider admitting that your past control system was inadequate and therefore all past decisions will not be challenged. Everyone starts with a clean slate.

SECTION TWO: SETTING UP PROFIT CENTER CONTROLS

THE MECHANICS OF SETTING UP PROFIT CENTER CONTROLS   M, IS, RS, F

A profit center is defined as any service, any product, or any family of products and services which generates profits. The steps involved in setting up your profit center controls are:

Step One: Assign one person as each profit center manager. This individual has both the responsibility and the authority to maximize the profits of his center. This manager should be a "buck stops here" type of guy.

AXIOM TWELVE: IF EVERYONE IS RESPONSIBLE FOR A TASK, THEN IN TRUTH NO ONE IS RESPONSIBLE, AND THE TASK WILL NOT BE COMPLETED PROPERLY.

Step Two: Segment your company into its cash producing components (profit centers) and treat each center as a separate division or company. Each center must have its own set of books to which its manager must answer.

Step Three: Utilize simple accounting for each center by divorcing all ledgers over which the profit center manager has no controls. In this step you are breaking out all overhead, G&A, facilities, support staffs, service staffs, taxes, and that capital equipment shared by more than one single profit center. This action forces all overhead people to be evaluated alone.[1]

Step Four: Divide each profit center's materials and production stages into their smallest increments. Give each increment full ledger status. In other words, if your profit center has four production stations, one QA station, and is made up of six parts, then this profit center has 11 ledgers for these 11 items.[2]

Step Five: Introduce a ledger linkage system which will allow your accountants to combine ledgers of identical items used by the various profit centers. This linkage will allow your purchasing department to combine identical items for quantity discounts, it will allow your administration to optimize manpower loading, it will allow your production people to more efficiently schedule work stations and inventory, and it will allow your sales people to priority key customers' deliveries.

Step Six: Establish a security system which will allow information to disseminate to all levels on a need-to-know basis. The usual security system is to classify each ledger on a 1-to-10 basis. See Example 8-2 for this system.

---

[1] This third step is usually disliked by most non-operations people because it forces them to become competitive with outside services. Since each profit center manager and each profit center team is rewarded (or punished) by his center's profits, these people become pretty hardnosed in their make-or-buy decisions. As soon as your staff or service groups acquire excess fat, then their costs go up and they must charge profit centers a higher fee. As soon as these fees exceed outside services, your center managers will go outside until the support groups lose their fat and lower their fees. It is impossible to build an empire under this system. Another reason that many staff people don't like this step is that it forces them to develop a service attitude to the operations groups. Since the operations people are their customers, they must either satisfy them or lose them. This is no bad thing for a lean and hungry company.

After approximately six months, the time usually necessary for the non-line groups to become efficient, you'll observe that your service groups suddenly like the new controls. Once they have lost their fat, these groups can usually perform their services at significant profits. Since these people also have the reward incentives that line people have, their take-home pay increases so significantly that they will never want to return to the old bureaucratic cost control system.

[2] Many accountants do not like this mini-ledger practice because they feel that it imposes too much extra work upon their department. They'll try to talk you out of it because it's "too expensive." However, since you are using your accounting system as a complete management control system, you can't afford to give in to accounting's request. You need these mini-ledgers so that you can assign "flags" for your management-by-exceptions program and you want these mini-ledgers to replace the records usually kept by purchasing, inventory, and production. Actually, from a company cost standpoint, this practice lowers expenses since you are replacing duplicate ledgers which had been forced on your other groups because accounting didn't want to keep these groups' records.

Step four has another side benefit which is valuable. It forces your accounting people to learn operations and it forces your operational people to understand accounting.

Step Seven: Develop a reliable system in which all "input" infor-
                    mation flows from the groups to accounting and all
                    "output" information flows from accounting back to
                    the groups. There are probably a dozen different ways
                    that you can accomplish this, however you'll be wise
                    to make it accounting's responsibility to make what-
                    ever way you select work.

Step Eight: Decide what kind of information you want from ac-
                    counting. Feel free to dictate the formats and leave am-
                    ple space for reader notes. You'll observe that your ac-
                    counting reports will gather all kinds of scribbled notes
                    and be sent back and forth in place of typed memos.

Step Nine: Determine the frequencies for each report. Some mar-
                    keting, inventory, production, purchasing, and ad-
                    ministration reports may be generated on almost a
                    daily basis, whereas some financial reports may be
                    needed only on a monthly or quarterly basis.

Step Ten: Establish your management-by-exceptions flags and
                    make certain that they are reliably tripped. Your ex-
                    ceptions reports will then become the backbone of
                    your operation's management.

Step Eleven: Implement your reward/punishment incentives into
                    this accounting system so that it will reliably dis-
                    burse both rewards and punishments.

Step Twelve: Since all past information is developed from actual
                    expenses and payments, your ledgers already handle
                    this aspect. However, since your proforma (projected)
                    management information comes from both back orders
                    and sales forecasts and the floating budgets to satisfy
                    these predicted sales, both your marketing and ac-
                    counting groups must work well together. Your short-
                    range sales forecasts should be within ±10%, your
                    mid-range forecasts should be within ±20%, and your
                    long-range forecasts should be within ±30%. Imple-
                    ment the forecasting systems which will give you these
                    reliabilities.

Step Thirteen: Establish a floating budget for each group. The bud-
                    get varies both upwards and downwards with sales.
                    Establish your lead/lag time periods with this floating
                    concept.

Step Fourteen: Determine what percentage of profits of each profit
                    center will flow into the company treasury. Deduct
                    this percentage plus the cost of sales percentages from
                    the selling price and that is the value at which each
                    profit center must sell the product or service to your

	company. This value minus the costs of producing the product is the profit the center realizes. This can be divided amongst the company and the center's team.
Step Fifteen:	Establish a series of mini-reserves and allow the proper level manager authority to release funds from these reserves. If "front money" is necessary to test a production cost savings idea, then the profit center managers and the production manager can withdraw funds from their respective reserves to determine the viability of the idea.[3]
Step Sixteen:	Agree to perform both periodic and random audits of this system. Though profit center controls have dozens of built-in checks and balances that make the system hard to beat, it should be policed by audits. Your accounting group can perform the periodic audits, however consider bringing in an outside CPA firm for the random audits so that everyone is kept honest.
Step Seventeen:	You have now developed a flexible system that restricts no one from performing company business. Therefore, there is no reason for anyone to try to disguise, pad, end run, shoot, or buck pass the system. Make it a well published company policy of how you'll deal with those who do attempt to violate your system.

GENERAL OBSERVATIONS ABOUT PROFIT CENTER CONTROLS   M, IS, RS, F

Did you observe that profit center accounting vertically segments your operations? As you are aware, cost center accounting divides your company into horizontal slices and makes it impossible for the manager to look down into any single income producer. The accounting system in horizontal segmentation (cost centers) invites disguising expenses. Frequently,

---

[3] A large number of mini-reserves are better than a few large reserves because it forces everyone to use a few dollars to prove viability before major dollars are invested.

Most accounting groups have one large contingency reserve in which a myriad of sins are buried, at the controller's discretion. Realize that your managers and key personnel are going to make mistakes and you must spend reserves to pay for these errors. Give every key man a personal reserve for errors and blunders. He can use this reserve to cover the small percentage of blunders that occur or he can use these funds in other ways. If you'll allow your people to horde their blunder reserves (in other words, don't take it away from them at the end of each fiscal period), you'll discover that people will take more and more calculated risks to improve things. I've seen marketing managers who have built "excessive" personal reserves use this money to test a lucrative target-of-opportunity. The "front money" used frequently brought in such additional profits that the company, the marketing manager, and those who were involved in the lucrative target really made money. Had the marketing managers not had considerable blunder reserves and the courage to use them, the targets may never had been addressed.

companies can run some profits centers in the red for years and never realize it. However, when you look down (instead of sideways) into your operations, you can always see what, who, and how much each increment adds to your company's profits and growth.

Note that you have instilled a series of checks and balances into your management-by-profit-objectives atmosphere. Let's look at a few of these checks and balances. If I try to hide a blunder by padding another ledger, I'll have real problems bypassing the system. Each ledger is extremely specific and if I tamper with it, I'll raise all kinds of warning flags on the exceptions reports. Since each profit center manager and every member of his team is rewarded (or punished) by that center's profits performances, if I attempt to violate their ledgers, their rewards suffer. It won't take them long to uncover my attempt at disguise and expose me. If I attempt to hide my error in a staff or service group's ledgers, then I am driving up their costs and robbing their incentive rewards. It won't take them long to uncover my attempt and disclose me. Since I have a blunder reserve, there is no reason for me to not use it. Finally, the periodic and random audits will probably expose me. In addition to these checks and balances, you have the common accounting double-entry checks and balances.

Observe that you really put the monkey on marketing's back to forecast correctly. Since the cornerstone of projected performances is your sales forecasts, it won't take them long to forecast accurately.

Observe that the major portion of your management efforts will be placed on present and future problems. There is little that you can do about last month's blunders but there is a lot that you can do about this month's errors.

Perhaps the strongest feature of profit center accounting is that it puts all groups and departments on the same footing, namely profit performances. Instead of just lip service, profits are now the foundation for all company priorities and the system insures profit maximizations. Since all groups have the same incentive goals, your management-by-objectives atmosphere is a profits atmosphere.

SPECIFIC EFFECTS OF PROFIT CENTER CONTROLS
M, IS, RS, F

(1)   They place a priority sequence on all problems to be solved. Usually people like to address problems that are fun to solve. Since this accounting control system now puts dollar values on problems, you'll find that now people will go after the most expensive problem first.

(2)   They highlight solving the effects instead of the cause of the problem: Problems usually don't go away until their causes are corrected. If you go off on a tangent and try to solve the effect instead of the cause, the problem will keep being flagged until you finally decide to define the cause

and correct it. It's hard to fall into "The Sick Company Syndrome" unless you ignore your flagging reports.

(3) Since you are allowing your accounting information to flow down to the lowest levels, you'll be surprised at how these levels will attempt to problem solve. Viable solutions seem to come out of the woodwork and everyone feels that he is a vital part of the company team.

(4) In over 50% of the cases, problems are solved by key and non-key personnel before management has an opportunity to act. Therefore your management's time can be invested in pro-active (instead of reactive) tasks.

(5) Since all personnel are rewarded from their center's performances and since that center's performances are contingent upon its sales, you'll observe that everyone is vitally interested in increasing his center's sales. All teams usually become extremely sales oriented and will run that extra mile to give the customer what he wants and needs. Repeat sales usually are significantly increased because of this customer satisfaction.

(6) Your profit center managers have a great deal of control over their sales. An innovative manager will use the tools at his disposal to insure proper sales efforts. He can threaten to terminate the sales department's support (remember that your sales group is nothing more than a service group to each center and they must either service that center properly or lose the acccount). The innovative manager can also sweeten the kitty to buy added sales efforts. We'll get into further discussions in the marketing chapter.

(7) Since every member of a profit center team is rewarded or punished by that center's performances, you'll observe that everyone becomes a QA and production inspector. The peer pressures on marginal performers is extreme. The individual at fault usually shapes up fast or is made so unhappy by his team members that he quits. Soon you'll have only top performers in each team.

(8) These same pressures can really hurt the egos of marginal managers and staff support people. The good old Anglo Saxon four-letter words will be used on everyone, regardless of his rank, who hurts a center's rewards. Expect to have your ego damaged when your blunder hurts a team. This is no bad thing for a lean and hungry company.

(9) As this system improves and matures your people's judgments, you'll observe that errors that were once considered minor begin to be considered real blunders. The firms that used to average 10% late shipments really get bent out of shape with even one late shipment a month. Marketing managers who used to be satisfied with 25% forecasting errors have been rung over the coals for 10% errors. Your team will sharpen to an extent that you once believed impossible.

(10) In almost every company which has several profit centers, we have observed rivalry between centers on their profits. The last week of each month is like world series time to see which center performs best.

Frequently, you'll discover that better production workers are approached by competing centers as a basketball league will try to pirate players from another league. Trades are not uncommon. It is a very meaningful thing for a production worker to have his skills recognized and appreciated by his peers.

Minor Point 8-1: Have Your Accounting Group Control
All Ledgers   M, IS, RS, F

An accounting group is set up and trained to handle ledgers far better than any other group in your company. Therefore, consider requiring them to handle all inventory, purchasing, production, quality assurance, marketing, and administrative ledgers and to have them give your groups the information that they need in the language that the group understands.

Example 8-1: Accounting Control of Inventory
Levels   M, RS, F

Why force your inventory people to control their inventory levels through maintaining their own ledgers? It is a minor additional requirement for your accounting group to report on inventory quantities in addition to dollar levels. They can then feed the essential information to your inventory, purchasing, and production groups in a manner such as follows:

Item	Description	On Hand	On Order	Committed	Comments
1.	RT22C2P102	1043	10000	14250	Warning Flag Pu 82
	Trimmer 1K	$2275	$22500		Warning Flag Pr 1 (3 wks)
2.	RT22C2P502	583	0	0	Warning Flag Ad 27
	Trimmer 5K	$1122	0	0	
3.	RT22C2P103	600	10000	9332	Warning
	Trimmer 10K	$1254	$22500		Flag Pr. 9 (lag 2 wks)

Do you see how valuable this type of scan report can be to initiate instant actions? In the above three items, the following action should occur.

Item 1: Purchasing (Pu) will observe that they must order more RT22C2P102's. They know that Production (Pr) has been alerted that this shortage will shut down the production lines in three weeks unless Purchasing can make up the deficiency in time.

Item 2: Administration (Ad) is being warned that you have $1,122 tied up in a 5K trimmer that isn't being used. Administration will probably approach R&D and ask permission to put these trimming resistors in series until the inventory is used. If this solution isn't viable, they may ask purchasing to try to return them to the trimmer manufacturer for credit on other trimmer orders. As a last resort, they may try to sell the excess inventory as best they can.

Item 3: Purchasing is notified that the RT22C2P103 manufacturer is lagging in his delivery promise by two weeks and unless the shipment is received in one week, production will cease.

This is a true management-by-exceptions report. Unless a warning flag is tripped, you need not invest time concerning yourself about it. It is an instant interdepartment communicator. Purchasing knows that Production will follow up unless the cause of the problem is swiftly defined and corrected.

CAMEO 8-1: PROFIT CENTER MANAGERS KEPT THEIR OWN BOOKS

In 1968, when this start-up began, they only had one man to handle finances. The founders wanted this man to devote full time to exploring their venture capital avenues, getting them a line of credit, and writing their business plan, so they decided to have each profit center manager keep his own books.

After the controller established their accounting system and trained all hands in using the system, he devoted his complete efforts to raising their initial capital. The last Thursday of every month, the other founders met to keep their books.

This evening session was quite an event. Since each founder had to account for his profit center's expenses, blood was almost spilt during the arguments of who spent what. Each session developed into a brainstorming session of how they could improve their performances.

Today this company has approximately 700 employees and could easily afford all of the accounting support that it needs. But the last Thursday of each month, all managers meet and account for their operations. Because of this practice, this company's team has always had its feet on the ground and driven for the same goals. One founder summed it up by saying, "God those meetings were hell. It's really hard on the ego to think that you were running things right and then discover that you wasted several hundred dollars. Everyone took pot shots at your blunders. However, after several months, the mistakes became fewer and fewer and the think sessions really began to pay off. Today, we have only three tiers of management and only 4% of our expenses go in overhead. We make healthy profits where our competitors break even. I still hate those sessions but I want to keep them because it forces us all to strive for the same things."

CAMEO 8-2: MAKE OR BUY　　M, IS, RS, F

This 15-year-old company was very proud of its verticle production capabilities. Though small (320 employees), it felt that it was extremely progressive and had the staff to attack any problem. Its track record appeared successful (its lowest growth year was 15%) and though it had the lowest profits-to-sales ratios in the industry, its stockholders were happy and tranquil.

However, the founders were not happy and decided to take the plunge from cost center accounting to profit center controls. The staff and service groups were divorced from the profit center accounting and the profit center managers received full make-or-buy authority.

Almost immediately, every manager decided to buy his services and support from outside the company. This alarmed the management because very talented staff people had little work to do. They looked closer at why the P.C. managers were going outside and discovered that in almost every case, internal support was three to five times more expensive than outside support. Specific examples:

(1)　The personnel department of 5 people had hired a total of 1 engineer and 11 production workers over the last year. They therefore had to quote a price of approximately $5,000 for every person hired. Since no profit center manager would allow this type of expense to be tacked to his center, all went to employment agencies for their hirings. Within two months, the personnel department had shrunk to one man.

(2)　The purchasing department had always had the practice of buying all production needs on a quarterly or semi-annual basis. No profit center manager would stand still for the interest expenses on inventories extended out six months in the future. They therefore forced purchasing to sign long-term purchasing contracts with deliveries scheduled weekly or twice monthly. The company realized $27,000 a year in interest savings (more than the budget for the salaries of the one-man purchasing department).

(3)　Many production operations were excessively expensive to run in-house. The heat treating, anodizing, plating, and casting operations were 10 times more expensive. Within two months, the company sold their expensive capital equipment and permanently jobbed these operations out.

(4)　The three-man advertising department, along with publishing equipment to print literature, was an extreme expense. Outside advertising agencies and print shops could perform the same work for 50% of the costs.

(5)　There were approximately 300 other major changes within the first six months.

In six months, this company's profits increased from 8% to 37%. In one year, it was over 40%. These additional profits more than paid for the incentive rewards paid to the employees. For six months, the morale was low but as the rewards began to become apparent, employees changed their attitude and defended the new deal. When the two unions which represented their employees decided to outlaw the changes, the unions were voted out.

One founder said, "We always felt that we were profit maximizers but darned if we weren't guilty of just giving it lip service. When we jumped into profit center controls, we opened the doors for our middle and lower management to take responsibility and darned if they didn't and showed us up. Thank God our major stockholders didn't run us all off when we discovered how poorly we were managing things.''

Example 8-2: The 1-to-10 Ledger Security System   M, IS, RS, F

If you are going to allow your accounting control system to filter down to all people who have a need to know, then you are going to have to develop a reliable security system to keep confidential information confidential. One of the simplest and most effective systems was developed by Doctor J. V. Robertson and it works as follows:

To each ledger, assign a 1-to-10 security classification. The classifications are:

Level 1:   President's eyes only.
Level 2:   President's and board of directors' eyes only.
Level 3:   Top management's eyes only.
Level 4:   Group managers may be given this information on a need-to-know basis only. This information may not be passed down to their staffs without the president's approval.
Level 5:   Profit center managers, according to their discretion, can let the information be known to staff members.
Level 6:   Staff managers and service managers can let the information be known to members of their staffs at the managers' discretions.
Level 7:   Ledger information is to be given to all profit center personnel without the manager's approval.
Level 8:   Ledger information is to be given to all staffs without the staff managers' approvals.
Level 9:   Ledger information is to be given to all employees, whether they have a need to know or not.
Level 10:   Ledger information may be used by marketing, administration, and personnel to be passed on to non-company persons (in PR, in attracting employees, in seminars, in sales literature, etc.).

Minor Point 8-2: Confidential Information   M, IS, RS, F

Since most entrepreneurs are extremely security conscious because of the pitfalls their start-up might fall into in the early stages, they retain this secretiveness in their accounting system. However, as their company matures and these men realize the dollars they lose and the hours their people must invest because ledger information is kept too classified, they tend to allow more and more information to pass down to all levels. After awhile, almost everything is classified level 10.

The ledgers that should remain classified are usually (1) specific salaries, (2) specific bonuses, (3) specific bonus losses (punishments), (4) specific profits and losses of each center, of each service group, and of each staff group, (5) accounts receivable (competition would love to get its hands on these ledgers), (6) a few of your accounts payable ledgers, (7) specific R&D project ledgers, and (8) all long-range and mid-range projected sales (anything further than six months out).

If you are in a ticklish union situation, you may wish to classify other ledgers.

Very little should be classified level 1 (instead of 2). The primary reason that the president might not want the board to see some information is that he questions the ledger's accuracy and wants it thoroughly investigated before allowing investors to learn about it. There are many R&D projects in which feasibilities must be checked out before getting the board's hopes up. On rare occasions, you may have a hostile board member from whom you wish to keep ammunition; however this should be rare.

You want to keep your staffs' profits from the profit center managers' eyes because since he has authority to bypass the staff and go outside, you don't want him to use the staff's profits as a wedge to lower their prices. A good staff group can usually undercut outside service bids and make significant profits (rewards) for their group. Since they are rewarded in real money for these profits, you do not want to destroy this efficiency incentive.

CAMEO 8-3: THE COTTAGE SYSTEM

We all have a tendency to make controls more complex and more expensive than is necessary. Too frequently the system, instead of the end results, becomes the important thing. Whenever we have a client who is going off the deep end with controls, I always tell the following cameo of a success with no controls.

A woman dropped out of high school to get married. Several years later her husband left her and their retarded child. Since the child needed almost constant supervision, the woman couldn't search for income in the normal way. She needed to bring in money by methods which would allow her to be at home.

She had one important asset. She had excellent finger dexterity and a flair for manual handicrafts (sewing, weaving, macrame, etc.). So she decided to capitalize on these abilities while tending her child. At first, she tried the usual technique with marginal success. She attempted to sell her production through mail order, through craft shops, through gift stores, and didn't make a go of it. Then she lit upon the idea of making artistic g-strings and pasties for the exotic dancers on the West Coast. Word-of-mouth advertising between the exotic dancers allowed her to realize approximately $150 a week in profits. This income kept the wolf from her door but was hardly what she wanted. She therefore also began teaching other Spanish-American girls her crafts in her home. She charged $40 for six sessions and then hired the most talented graduates as subcontractors to handle back orders.

This innovative young lady then fell upon the concept of decorating men's jock straps with her creations. Initially her sales were brisk as a woman's gift "to the man who had everything." She averaged $500 a week in profits, and employed four full-time graduates as subcontractors, and pulled from a pool of 32 other graduates for all other production back orders.

In 1973, sales quadrupled as men started buying her creations for themselves. It seems that if a male wore her athletic supporter under a tight fitting bathing suit, he appeared much better endowed than he really was. Today, this lady's profits are several thousand a week and she utilizes 31 subcontractors.

Though the cottage system that this woman utilizes went out of vogue in the eighteenth century, the most sophisticated production manager would envy her overhead costs, her production efficiencies, and her simple control systems. Let's examine her system:

(1) Every morning at 7:30, she stops by her post office box to pick up the day's orders, all bills, and all payments.

(2) At 8:30, all of her subcontractors stop by her home to deliver their previous day's production, drink coffee, chat, and help her ready their production for mailing. Since they all have children, she supplies the baby sitter, milk, and cookies.

(3) When this session is over, each subcontractor picks up what she thinks she can produce for the next day. Our female entrepreneur supplies them with kits of 10 jock straps, yarn, thread, etc.

(4) Between 10:00 and 1:30 is free time for her to tend her child and do whatever housework is necessary.

(5) At 1:30, her child takes his nap and she goes to the bank, makes whatever purchases are necessary, visits with her advertising agency, and does other business chores.

(6) From 3:00 to 7:30 she plays the role of mother again.

(7) At 7:30, she and her son watch television and build the next day's production kits.

(8) At approximately 8:30, her workday ends.

Her little company is run on a day-to-day basis. All orders received today will be built today and mailed tomorrow.

Her accounting is likewise simple. She gets between $12.50 and $20 for each creation. Though she will bill stores and distribution networks, all other customers must send their checks with their orders. Each supporter costs her approximately $2.25 in raw materials, $5 in subcontractor's labor, approximately 15¢ in shipping, and the balance goes into a reserve. She pays her subcontractors daily, her creditors weekly, and herself monthly. She does all business by checks so that the bank statements are her records.

Her marketing techniques are also unusual. Besides using a professional ad agency for her mail order business, she also has built up over 1,500 stores which sell her creations. She did this through writing the store owner, telling him that she was sending him a display for nothing and asking him to test her creations' salability. If the display rack sold out in one week, then he might be interested in ordering more creations. If it didn't sell out in a week, then the storeowner could keep the merchandise at no charge and not re-order. Only 137 stores which received these display cases didn't become regular customers.

Minor Point 8-3: Bonding Select Founders   M, IS, RS, F

Bonding a man will not make him honest but it will go a long way toward keeping him honest. Approximately 95% of our clients at least bond their presidents and their controllers for the following reasons: (1) it makes these responsible people realize that they will be prosecuted by an impersonal third party (the insurance company) if they mishandle your company's funds; (2) it forces these key men to fill out in-depth questionnaires and submit to thorough investigations at the insurance company's expense; (3) it allows the firm to tell its customers that its people are bonded; (4) it insures the start-up against losses due to dishonesty; and (5) it is relatively inexpensive.

Minor Point 8-4: Accountants vs. Operations People   M, IS, RS, F

Frequently, accountants and operations people mix like oil and water. Line people think accountants are primarily interested in the past whereas they (line people) are primarily interested in the present and future. "Our accounting system tells us where we blundered last month . . . not where we are apt to blunder this month," is a common complaint. Too frequently, this criticism is correct because the accounting reports read like yesterday's newspaper.

A second source of irritation is that most accountants do not truly understand their company's operations and therefore their reports do not sort the information so that it is meaningful. You hear the statement, "Our accountants make no attempt to work with us. They are like a baseball scorekeeper who doesn't understand baseball." If this analogy is true, then accountants could just as easily rebutt with, "You operations people are like baseball players who don't know how to keep score."

A third complaint by both sides is that budgets and the accounting system are too rigid and unflexible. Frequently, the small amounts of "front money" essential to address targets-of-opportunity, perform cost savings' experiments, test the viability of a new potential profit center, or do feasibility studies, can't be raised without a major effort. Rather than fight the internal battles necessary to shake loose the small amounts of front money, employees either end run the accounting system or shelve the idea permanently. The company therefore suffers.

Actually, this third cause isn't attributable to anyone other than top management. If the general manager wants a flexible system, any good accounting group can give him one. Many top managers don't want flexibility because it rocks the boat.

The fourth major irritant is that too frequently, accounting reports are considered extremely confidential and therefore only a few top managers and a few accounting clerks get to see them. A control system that is confined to so few makes a lousy management-by-objectives and management-by-exceptions tool.

CAMEO 8-4: THE HUNDRED-DOLLAR WATER COMPUTER

When I was a bright and brittle engineer entering business school, one of the first courses that I took was economic models. Since first semester MBA students seem to have the lowest priorities on the university's computer, I swiftly realized that 90% of this course's effort would be wasted in trial and error programs in the computer center. I therefore "borrowed" some equipment from the school's chemistry labs (glass tubing, beakers, valves, fittings, etc.) and proceeded to develop my own crude cash flow computer. It not only worked extremely well for the course, I've used it hundreds of times in consulting with excellent results. Therefore, I offer it to you for consideration.

Realize that cash flows are very similar to the first law of thermodynamics. Cash in must equal cash out. By equating one cubic centimeter of colored water to every thousand dollars, all that you have to do is pour water into the front end of your own water computer and watch its flow into the various beakers (expenses, reserves, profits, etc.). By varying the water flows (your company's priorities) you can optimize both profits and growths.

We always hook up this jury-rigged flow system for every client and let them adjust valves (change their budgets) until they are satisfied. Then, we check their final decision on our mathematical models and usually discover that they have optimized their operations. If you walk into our clients' presidents' offices, you'll discover that over half have hooked up their own Rube Goldberg water computer (usual costs are less than $100) and they never make a decision without seeing that decision's effects on profits. This system has one other benefit that I like. The tubing simulates your company's operations. The more complex and inefficient your organization is, the more of a nightmare this water computer's piping is. By straightening out the computer's piping, you are forced to straighten out your actual operations.

Many accountants don't like this system. It takes all of the mystique out of accounting.

9 • Your Business Plan

PROLOGUE   M, IS, RS, F

You should keep your eye on two goals while you write your business plan. These goals are: (1) your plan should be a working document (a blueprint for all founders, managers, and key employees to follow) on how you are going to build your company, and (2) your plan should be a sales document (an instrument to attract funds from sophisticated venture capitalists).

Approximately two-thirds of the business plans written ignore the first goal and therefore become only shallow sales material. The venture capitalists can spot these Walter Mitty pipe dreams in a matter of minutes and ignore them.

Approximately 10% of the business plans written lose sight of the first goal. These plans are usually complex, unreadable, and therefore not read.

It is the intent of this chapter to help you gather the material that you have developed in the earlier chapters (all of your homework has been completed if you followed the recommendations made in the preceeding chapters) and write a business plan which meets both goals. Let's first examine some of the basic ground rules, then discuss your business plan's ingredients, and finally examine some actual cases that worked.

SECTION ONE: THE BASIC SPADEWORK

VECTOR YOUR PLAN TOWARDS THE VENTURE CAPITAL AVENUES YOU WISH TO ADDRESS   M, IS, RS, F

There are many avenues open to you in attracting your capital. Each avenue will be discussed in Chapter Eleven, however realize that a slightly different approach should be made to each avenue. As an example, banks and bank-owned SBIC's like to see pages and pages of financial projections (proforma reports) so that they can run their ratio analysis studies. The government agencies (like SBA or EDA) like to see impact studies. What is the impact of your company on your community's environment, employment, economy, and so forth.

Since the most demanding and most professional of these many avenues open to you are the privately owned venture capital groups, this chapter will concentrate on how to write a plan to satisfy these groups. Once you have completed your plan to satisfy this demanding avenue, it is a minor task to make addendums and minor modifications to vector your plan towards the other avenues.

Minor Point 9-1: Using Someone Else's Business Plan as a Guide   M, IS, RS, F

I don't think I have ever had a client who hasn't requested someone else's business plan as a guide in helping him write his. At first, we used to keep a library of several hundred plans to meet this request, however we soon learned that this was a major mistake. Clients tended to plagiarize wording, formats, and graphs.

Realize that an excellent business plan is usually a closely guarded secret document. Your competitors will pay a handsome price for your plan because it saves them research and it tells them how you will behave. The only business plans that are available for everyones' eyes are the bad business plans and there are thousands of them.

Also realize that every major city has several proposal mills which grind out from 3 to 10 business plans a week for clients who are either too lazy or too stupid to write their own plans. For fees of from $1,500 to $25,000, these plans then make their ways through the same avenues and channels that your plan will follow. There is a sameness about these plans. The wording seems the same, the ratios are always ideal, the graphs appear the same, the milestones look the same, and even the covers come from the same source. The researchers, who must read these plans, can spot a proposal mill's verbiage from a mile off and since they know that it is a shallow sham to relieve them of their money, they don't give these plans much attention. If you should inadvertently use one of these documents as a guide, then your plan will also appear to be written by a proposal mill and will be ignored.

Write your plan yourself, use your own innovation to make it unique, make your company and its products and services "live," and keep your presentation simple and easy to follow. When the capitalist finally becomes convinced that you are beginning something that will be truly worthwhile, that you are going to follow the blueprint (your business plan) that you have laid out, and that you are determined to succeed, he'll raise the necessary funds to join you.

THE HURDLES THAT YOUR PLAN MUST CLEAR
M, IS, RS, F

Before we get into the "nuts and bolts" of a business plan, let's look at the hurdles that your plan must clear.

Hurdle One: The Initial Evaluation: The thoroughness of the thinking behind your plan is normally evaluated in the first reading. An extremely high percentage of plans never make it over this hurdle for the following reasons: (1) the plan is complex, unreadable, and therefore not read, (2) the plan has such obvious weaknesses that the capitalists' dismiss it out-of-hand because they assume that you and your founders' team must be poor managers to address something with such major weaknesses, (3) your products, services, or the industry which you are addressing doesn't interest the capital group, (4) the capital group feels that your product or service has no intuitive real value, (5) your start-up comes across as a "me-too" company which does little more than copy existing firms, or (6) the capital group does not have the funds to invest or they are so busy with other ventures that they don't have the time to invest in you.

Hurdle Two: Face-to-Face Presentations: When your plan clears the first hurdle, you and your fellow founders are usually invited to make oral presentations on your plan to answer questions. This "give-and-take" session gives the capitalist and his researchers a "gut feel" for what kind of people you are, how much you and your founders believe in what you are addressing, and the validity of your presentation and proposals. Expect to field "loaded questions" (we'll discuss this later) which will give them an insight into your dedication and determination.

Hurdle Three: Marketing Research: The capitalist's researchers will now begin to perform independent market tests to verify that there is a major demand for your products and services and that your industry will remain a growth industry for several years to come. Your products' features will be evaluated on their saleability and your proposed distribution machinery will be evaluated in-depth. The quality and ability of your probable competition to react will be investigated.

Fourth Hurdle: Your Management Team Capabilities: As stressed in the earlier chapters, this is your largest hurdle. Since most venture capitalists place a 50%–60% weighting on your management team, expect to undergo unending research until the capitalists know you. Your credit record, your criminal record, and your references will be checked. You'll have your home visited, your wife and children seen, your neighbors interviewed, and business acquaintances interrogated. The capitalists, before they will invest several million on your word, have to know that you are honest, have integrity, are flexible, are energetic, and are a problem solver.

Fifth Hurdle: Technical Research: Since most venture capital groups do not have the capabilities to perform their own technical research, they usually hire an engineering consultant to determine your product's design strength, producibility, reliability, and probable costs and problems. When you reach this hurdle, the venture capitalist must spend several thousand dollars for this consulting and you therefore know that he is interested.

Sixth Hurdle: Financial Evaluations: Though your plan probably underwent a pretty thorough financial analysis in the first hurdle, realize that venture capitalists know that most entrepreneurs have very little background in money leveraging, money controls, money timing, and forecasting essential for optimum profits and growths. These are the areas in which the capitalists excel. Therefore, you'll probably observe that your business plan is altered considerably so that proper reserves exist when and where they are needed. The timing of cash injections is usually determined from this hurdle.

Seventh Hurdle: Final Negotiations: Once you have cleared the six hurdles, it is time for the final negotiations on such things as stocks, changes in your incorporation by-laws and charter, changes in your company's board of directors, cash injection schedules, and so forth.

Now that we have seen the hurdles, it is pretty obvious how to write a plan to clear them.

SECTION TWO: HOW TO CONSTRUCT
YOUR BUSINESS PLAN

THE BASIC STRUCTURE OF A SALEABLE
BUSINESS PLAN   M, IS, RS, F

One of the most effective ways of writing a business plan is to make the body of the plan a very readable document for the capitalist and to make the appendixes for his researchers. There is no reason to burden the capitalist with the thousands of specifics which his researchers must use to determine your company's merits.

Consider making your plan's body a detailed summary and your appendixes present the detailed specifics. Most of our clients house each of their appendixes in its own booklet cover so that they can hold back highly proprietary details until the capitalist needs them and so that the capitalist's researchers use only specific addendums for specific research. When the researcher is examining the market aspects of your plan, then all he needs is the body and the marketing appendix. When they are ready to investigate the highly proprietary design of your product, then your R&D manager can hand carry the design appendix to the consulting engineer and make certain that this addendum doesn't visit a copying machine by sitting across from the researcher the complete time he studies your product's design. As Cameo 9-3 shows, this gives your R&D manager the opportunity to defend your design.

Minor Point 9-2: You Are an Equal   M, IS, RS, F

You are not superior to the venture capitalists, nor are you inferior to them. You are equals. You are an extremely sharp, innovative, honest, and competent entrepreneur and you are looking for equally professional people to invest in you and join your winning team.

The venture capitalists need you as much as you need them and the marriage will be an excellent mesh. Don't write your plan as if you are begging, and likewise don't write it as though you are tolerating an outsider leeching from your profits.

THE INGREDIENTS OF YOUR BUSINESS PLAN
M, IS, RS, F

A formal business plan usually contains the following *minimums:*

I.   *The Executive Summary:* In one to three pages, briefly describe the fundamental elements of your proposed venture. Describe the industry that you are selling to, your present and planned products and services, the unique features of these products and services, what investments are required, and the projected return on the investors' equity.

Make this summary extremely readable, concise, believable, and interesting. The primary function of this section is to whet the reader's appetite to read further.

II.   *The Table of Contents, Illustrations, Tables, and Graphs:* Do not skimp in this section. Most venture capitalists, after they read the summary, want to turn to six or eight specific details before they spend more time reading your prose. Give them the machinery to find these details fast and they will appreciate your foresight.

III.   *Brief Background and History of Your Start-up:* This also is an appetite-whetting section. Briefly describe how and why you formed your company, how it has developed so far, the new markets that it will open, the new technologies it is addressing, and where the company will go in the next 10 years. Make the reader want to join a worthwhile and winning team. You might even consider including a scenario format (Cameo 9-2).

IV.   *Products' and Services' Descriptions:* In layman's terms, describe your present and future product and service families' features that will make the customer want to buy from your company.

V. *Market Description:* Describe the classes of customers (and their buying profiles) for your products and services. Illustrate the total market; your segment of that market; your initial penetration projections, your degree of penetration in 1 year, 3 years, 5 years, and 10 years. Don't forget to illustrate the growth of your industry, what you project in additional customer demands with respect to time, and the personality of your industry.

VI. *Competititon:* Describe each competitor's personality, his strengths and weaknesses, and his ability to react. Consider a summary table showing your product's performance specifications against each competitor's models.

VII. *Marketing Strategies:* Describe your channels of distribution, your methods of setting up, training, motivating, and sustaining these networks, your marketing milestones, your projections of when you'll meet these milestones, the effective sales calls you project with respect to time, your sales forecasts for the first five years, and a summary of the budgets essential to meet these projections. You might also consider a brief presentation on the sales closes open to your product and how these closes will work on the various classes of customers. (Cameo 9-1).

VIII. *Manufacturing Plans:* Describe how each product will be initially produced and how it will be produced as soon as you develop in-house capabilities. Present your manufacturing milestones and make certain that they are in harmony with your sales forecasts.

IX. *Quality Assurance and Reliability Plans:* Describe your QA and reliability objectives and how you are going to meet them.

X. *Financial Plans:* This section should include summary tables on your projected (proforma) balance sheets and income statements (P&L statements) for the first five years. Refer the reader to the financial appendix for these projected statements done monthly for the first three years and quarterly for the fourth and fifth years. Make certain that the reader realizes that you developed the proforma reports from the sales forecasts, the budgets essential to meet those sales commitments, and the assumptions made in the assumption appendix.

This section should also show the summary cash flow projections. You might also include a brief description of the accounting system that your firm will utilize and the controls you have built into this system.

XI. *Money-Leveraging Strategies:* Describe how you will leverage the investors' money to get maximum benefits. This section is designed to show your fiscal responsibilities.

XII. *Proposed Distribution of Ownership:* Describe your company's structure (partnership, sole proprietorship, limited partnership, incorporation). Describe how you see this structure changing in the next 20 years.

Remember that no venture capitalist will invest in anything, regardless of how sound it might be, unless he can eventually sell his investment for significant profits. You might describe how you will go public when the investment market is at its best and solicit the venture capitalist's counsel in this matter.

XIII.   *The Organization and Its Founders:* Show an organization chart and define the responsibilities and authorities of each founder. Give a brief three-paragraph summary of each founder and each key employee. Don't get cute here, list the founders in their order of importance instead of alphabetical order. Refer the reader to the "Personnel Appendix" for complete resumes and letters of reference for each founder.

XIV.   *Founders' Stock Incentives:* If you bought my logic in the last two chapters, indicate the incentive systems, the milestones which generate those incentive rewards, the punishments, etc., for your founders, key employees, managers, and non-key employees. You are showing the reader the controls that you are implementing upon yourselves so that he won't have to impose additional limitations. Refer the reader to the incentive appendix for the actual details and the signed agreements of all the founders and employees.

XV.   *The Appendixes:*

A.   *The Products and Services:* This appendix should be written and signed by the manager of engineering in a manufacturing start-up or the operations manager in a service start-up. This highly proprietary addendum should explain in detail the product' design, its components, its safety factors, areas of concern, and assumptions. Of course this section will remain in the vault and be hand carried in and out of the venture capitalist's office.

B.   *R&D:* This section should be written and signed by the R&D manager. It should cover the future products and services your company plans introducing, the levels of R&D efforts necessary to achieve them (this includes both manpower loading and dollars), the philosophy of the R&D department and how it must dovetail with the other groups, and the projected budgets for the next 10 years.

C.   *Manufacturing:* This section is written and signed by the production manager. It should describe how the product will be initially produced, the equipment necessary, the personnel necessary, and the controls to be implemented. Production milestones should be described contingent upon both R&D's milestones and the sales forecasts. Comments should be made about what will occur if the milestones are slipped or if the forecasts are exceeded or not met.

If manufacturing is responsible for service groups (Inventory Control, Shipping, Purchasing, etc.) and you have key people who are to run these groups, then these key people should contribute (in their own writing styles) their portions of this appendix.

Do not forget to include Production's philosophies, budgets for 10 years, how it will interphase with the other groups, and how it will be sales and customer oriented.

D. *Marketing:* This section should be written and signed by the marketing manager. It should give details on the marketing research performed, the market testing, the sales forecasts (and how these forecasts were derived), competition, competition's strengths and weaknesses, competition's profits realized in the market segment addressed, the distribution machinery that you will utilize, how you will motivate and sustain that distribution machinery, marketing milestones, sales milestones, both marketing and sales philosophies, how these groups will dovetail with each other and how they will interphase with the rest of the company, and their 10-year budgets.

E. *Finance:* This section should be written and signed by the controller. It should include finance's budget for the next 10 years, all departments' budgets for the next 5 years (the first 3 years on a monthly basis and the last 2 on a quarterly basis), and the proforma financial reports (income statements, balance sheets, and cash flows) for the first 3 years on a monthly basis and on a quarterly bais for the final 2 years.

In addition, leverage principles should be discussed in detail. The company's philosophies on money and profits should be given prime space.

Financial control systems should also be discussed in depth.

F. *Administration:* This section should be written and signed by the president. Besides showing how the administrative group will support, motivate, and sustain all of the other groups, this section should tie all of the other groups into a single company team. The overall company milestones, the major milestones, should be outlined and projected from the milestones of each department.

G. *Organization and Personnel:* Give a detailed organization chart and describe the responsibilities of each individual shown on this chart both by functions and by objectives.

In the personnel section of this addendum, include a very complete resume on each founder (usually 5–7 pages for managers and 3–5 pages for key employees). Leave out nothing that will help make each man a complete being. Include religion, personal goals, job experiences, problem solving capabilities, criminal past (include traffic tickets, arrests with no convictions, everything), dozens of professional and personal references, education, motivations, self-image, and family responsibilities. Since venture capitalists like to see ex-paperboys, I like to recommend that each founder list every job he ever had back to the time he earned his first dime. When the venture capitalist completes reading each founder's resume, that founder should be a very human person, a person to be both liked and respected.

Also, consider including several letters of reference for each founder from people the venture capitalist would respect and be impressed by. It's a common practice to write these letters for your references and ask them to change them as they see fit.

H. *Management-by-Objectives and Management-by-Exceptions Systems Utilized:* Spell out in detail all of the systems that you have incorporated in your company, how they are working, and how they will change as your company grows.

I. *List of Assumptions:* List the assumptions that you have made in your business plan and why you feel that these assumptions are valid. There are some assumptions over which you have no controls, and therefore don't try to prove validity in things such as inflationary spirals, possible changes in the law which might damage your sales, or changes in tax laws. This addendum is usually written and signed by both the controller and the president.

J. *Summary of Problem Areas:* List those problem areas that you have met or anticipate meeting and some of the alternatives that are open to you in solving them. Be very frank here because capitalists have financed hundreds of start-ups and expect problems. If you are pro-active enough to see them before they occur, you show entrepreneuring maturity.

K. *Parallel Case Histories:* Describe several other start-ups that are similar to your venture. Those that failed should be analyzed as to why they failed and you should suggest the corrective action that you will take to not duplicate their poor performances. Those that succeeded should also be evaluated and the return on the original investor's investments discussed. Most of our clients described five parallel start-ups—one failure, two moderate successes, and two extremely big successes.

L. *Distribution Letters of Reference:* This appendix seems to carry a lot of weight because an endorsement from people who wish to sell your product to their customers represents hard cold cash in the capitalists' eyes. If you can get 10 to 20 distributors to write you reference letters saying that what the world needs is a product with the unique features you can produce, it helps. If these distributors state that they will sell your product to the following customers (and list the larger customers in their territories), it adds more credibility. If they state that they will carry significant inventories, it adds further weight.

If you lay out your business plan in this manner, you are certain of clearing the first hurdle. Please observe that there is nothing in this plan which you haven't already accomplished if you followed the first eight chapters' advice.

WRITING STYLE   M, IS, RS, F

The body of your report should be written by the best author in your company. Write as if you are talking to the capitalist. Feel free to express yourself in the first person (example: "We are to be a customer oriented company. In my opinion, this attitude is essential in all employees if we are going to achieve the market penetrations described on page 7 and discussed in depth in the Marketing Appendix.")

Avoid superlatives such as "fantastic sales" or "tremendous profits." However, don't let this recommendation stand in the way of transmitting enthusiasm. It is easy to transmit enthusiasm without sounding like a high school cheer leader.

The writing styles of the appendixes should be in character with the personality and image of the departmental manager who is authoring the appendix. When the researcher completes studying an appendix, he'll feel that he knows the author of that addendum by his writing style.

PERSONALIZED APPROACH

It helps to personalize your business plan for the specific venture capitalist group. This is frequently done by putting a plan on a word processor (such as the IBM MCST or MTST). It is then a minor task to insert names, etc. into the body of your plan.

Another technique that you might consider is to individually personalize the foreword of the plan (Example 9-1).

Example 9-1: A Personalized Foreword   M, IS, RS, F

The following foreword is a fictitious example of how to personalize your plan to a specific venture capital group. This personalized approach has worked extremely well for our clients.

"Our business plan is a working document for our management team. Please consider it extremely secret and meant for Hambrecht & Quist personnel only.

"Though we have selected what we think are the very best operations people and management people in the microprocessor industry, we feel that we are weak in the area of finance. We have therefore done considerable research of personnel in this area and are approaching Hambrecht & Quist because besides being experienced venture capitalists, they have the contacts, experience, and knowledge that we need. We want Mr. George Quist, Mr. Ernest Ruehl, and Mr. William Timken to counsel us in raising our $4,000,000 and to sit on our board of directors and help guide our growth. We have seen how these men helped Tymshare Inc. and we want the same innovative aid."

This brief foreword shows George Quist and two of his nine researchers that you are not just interested in $4,000,000. You are interested in $4,000,000 and their abilities. They suspect that you have researched the other major venture capital firms and selected them for the way they will fit into your operations. They will swiftly check to see if you have sent out similar feelers to the other capitalists and they will check with Tymshare Inc.'s people to see how they were approached, but you have caught their interest. You'll be assured that they will at least read your executive summary, and if it's good, they will read your complete plan. If it's good but they can't personally participate, then they will probably help you locate another competent venture capital group.

If you are phony in the foreword they'll uncover your phonyness in short order and ignore you.

CAMEO 9-1: THE "SALES CLOSE APPENDIX"　　M, IS

As you know, there are approximately 20 basic sales closes and perhaps a thousand variations of each basic close. Though the sales closes that your salesmen use should be very carefully monitored, this topic usually isn't discussed in a business plan.

We had a client who was entering the very explosive market of hang-gliders. In the past three years, there have been hundreds of start-ups in this new sports field and they are all making money. However, most of these start-ups are extremely small and underfinanced garage operations. There was an opening for a dominant company. Our client wanted to be that leader.

These engineers had developed several unique design features that really turned on the enthusiasts. However, these features didn't seem to live in the business plan. To make these features come to life, we added a "Sales Close Appendix" and had 10 pages of typical sales situations and the close for each situation. It really highlighted each feature. In addition, we installed tape recorders in stores and taped actual sales situations which used these closes. The customers' enthusiasm really came across in these tapes. The tapes were then reproduced and sent, along with an inexpensive tape player, to the four venture capital groups who were considering this start-up. The effect of this was amazing. Even the most non-technical of these people were glibly talking about "the telescoping cantilever truss design which allowed a variable center of gravity." This start-up had little trouble getting its $210,000 on its founders' terms.

Minor Point 9-3: Your Milestone Graphs　　M, IS, RS

Your milestone graphs have a major impact on your future negotiations with venture capitalists. A pictorial illustration of what should happen when allows them to see when and how much cash injections are needed.

Let's say that your venture capitalist agrees to invest $500,000 in your start-up. Instead of agreeing to invest it on specific calendar dates, he'll agree to invest it when specific milestones are met. In other words, you may get $20,000 on good faith, $25,000 when you meet your first milestone, $150,000 when you meet your second milestone, $75,000 when you meet the third, and so forth until the complete $500,000 is invested.

If your milestones are conservative, this is a real advantage because it will force cash injections at a faster rate than setting calendar dates for them.

Minor Point 9-4: The Use of Photographs   M, IS

Most of our clients' business plans include from a dozen to several dozen 8″ × 10″ glossy photographs of the founders' team working together, their products (both being used and being displayed), the problems that their products solve, their facilities, their equipment, and anything else that furthers their cause. Photographs pay off because they change the proposal from an abstract concept to something very real and concrete.

Minor Point 9-5: The Quality of Your Business Plan's Book Covers   M, IS, RS, F

I have seen business plans housed in almost everything from a 5¢ schoolboy folder to a $50 gold bound leather book cover. We recommend housing your plan's body and each of your appendixes in a 50¢ imitation leather pocket folder (some people call them "peachies"). Make certain that your presentation's covers look rich (but not ostentatious) and have a rich feel.

Do not underestimate the importance of your plan's first impression. When you hand the plan to the capitalist, you are handing him something of real value and the cover conveys this value.

Minor Point 9-6: Letraset   M, IS, RS, F

There are sheets of letters that, when rubbed, will transfer to whatever you wish. These letters come in all styles and all sizes and will greatly improve your graphs, tables, and illustrations. Every art supply dealer usually carries an inventory of these transfer letters.

You'll also observe that these letters will allow you to do the artwork on your advertsing layouts and your stationcry. It's a pretty inexpensive matter to use these letters to design your advertising, then find a printer who will run you off a few hundred copies for less than $10, and to then test your literature. Once you have developed the literature that has the effect you wish, then you can pay a commercial artist (graphic artist) $20 an hour to do the mechanicals for color separations that you'll need for mass printing.

SECTION THREE: SOME PRACTICAL APPLICATIONS

CAMEO 9-2: THE SCENARIO APPROACH   M, IS

One particular start-up didn't have too much of a shot at the EDA loan that it wanted because of reverse racial discrimination. Since the founders were white and since most of the city and county officials were black, the venture had little opportunity to be placed first on the county's priorities list. However, the founders gave it a good shot by doing the following:

They saw and admitted that they were working at a disadvantage. The blacks who ran things would have to be converted if they hoped to get the EDA loan. Therefore, they rewrote their business plan, using scenarios to illustrate their candy company's effects on the black community. They described the jobs it would generate, they described the techniques that they would use to train their supervisors, they showed how their personnel department would work with the Black Muslim Society to locate employees, they promised commissions and bonuses to the local black churches and social groups, and they agreed to name their candy bars after black heros. It was a brilliant and sincere piece of work and had the community placed it first on their priorities list and had EDA funds been granted, I think that the founders would have carried through on their promises. Though this scenario gambit worked well in getting and holding official interest, though several church and social groups strongly endorsed the start-up, and though the plan was economically viable, it was a near miss. The start-up was placed fourth on the county's priorities list and was therefore not funded.

Example 9-2: Giving the Appearance of an Ongoing Company   M, IS, RS, F

Throughout this book, you have read recommendations and examples of how your firm should start turning cash immediately so that you will have the appearance of an ongoing company instead of just another unproven start-up. Usually by the time the founders have completed their homework and written their business plan, the start-up is generating enough money to make their money needs less. Time is then on the side of the start-up, instead of the venture capital groups, and the founders can be more selective in the terms that they accept.

If your company has taken this advice and is now generating major cash flows, show this information. Do not be afraid of including copies of large customer purchase orders, of projecting your growth without venture capital, and of bragging about your fiscal responsibilities. The following is a typical insert:

"Our firm has now been in business nine months and is averaging $1,100 a month in profits on $1,800 sales. We anticipate that sales will reach $3,500 a month in three months (see list of probable customers in

Table VIII of the Marketing Appendix) and we should be realizing sales of $10,000 a month in nine months. Since we are cash poor, it will take us approximately three years to reach a 2% market penetration of $1,000,000 a month in sales. However, as shown in graph III of the Marketing Appendix, we can reach this 2% penetration level in nine months if we can spend $90,000 developing a proper marketing network (refer to proposed Sales Budget I in the Marketing Appendix). You will note letters from our proposed distributors describing their performances and what these performances will be with proper support."

This type of insert will make venture capitalists extremely enthusiastic in giving you what you need.

Minor Point 9-7: The Failure-Through-Success Pitfall
M, IS, RS, F

There is an unexplainable pitfall that occurs in hundreds of start-ups each year and that has stung most venture capitalists. It's hard to explain but since it occurs so often, let's try. Frequently, all founders work well together until the start-up gets into the black and success seems probable. Then suddenly, the founders begin to spend their company's money foolishly. We have had clients struggle for months and months and then as soon as their operation got into the black, they bought company cars, they bought original oil paintings for their offices, they bought expensive but little used capital equipment, they hired support people who weren't properly used, and they invested in dozens of other silly frills. Frequently, they even became extremely selective in their customers and drove away those who caused inconveniences. The founders suddenly became "successes" and planned extended vacations. Then the bomb hit, their higher overheads coupled with their reduced sales put them in the red again and the companies were hard to save.

Though an incentive reward/punishment atmosphere punishes and therefore minimizes this pitfall, realize that venture capital groups are extremely touchy on this point and look very hard for signs that tip them of this failure made both before and after they invest.

Minor Point 9-8: The Executive Summary as an
Interest Mailer   M, IS, RS, F

It's a common practice for start-ups to mail their executive summaries to all venture capital groups and see who responds. Though this method works pretty well in determining who is interested and who isn't interested in your plan, I think that it does more harm than good. First of all, the venture capitalists know that you are running your concept "up the flag pole to see who salutes." This action shows them that you probably haven't done your homework in funding groups and are hoping that your summary will do the job for you. Then, venture capital groups usually keep the business plans submitted to them away from your potential competitors. However, the mail order business plan (mail them the summary and if they respond, mail them the business plan) isn't considered confidential and can make its way into the other companies that the venture capitalist owns (your competitors). Finally, I think that this technique forces a lot of "no's" that should be "maybe if's" from groups. In several cases where we had clients who used this system prior to coming with us, we have approached groups which stated that they had no interest and discovered that suddenly they were very interested.

SECURITY   M, IS, RS, F

Your business plan is a highly confidential document. If it gets into the wrong hands, it will cost you a fortune. Treat it according to its value and your venture capitalists will do likewise. Treat it like it is a piece of junk and your venture capitalists (if you can find any) will do likewise.

CAMEO 9-3: THE R&D MANAGER VS. THE TECHNICAL CONSULTANT   M, IS

Engineering consultants can be a strange breed. Too frequently, their egos and petty jealousies can stand in the way of telling a venture capital group that a good design is a good design. To overcome this pitfall, we always classify the product's design as top secret and insist that the inventor (or the R&D Manager) hand carry this secret appendix wherever it goes. This way you are assured that the secret design won't stop by a copying machine and a copy get into your competitors' hands. However, the best reason for this practice is that it allows the inventor to defend his design against the consultant.

We had a client who had developed an extremely innovative instrument in the medical electronics field. Three venture capital groups were forming a consortium to finance this start-up and had retained a Berkeley engineering firm to evaluate the design. The R&D manager had to hand carry his appendix into this consulting firm every morning and hand carry it home every evening for 10 days. Every day, he sat across from the engineer or scientist who was evaluating each aspect of his design. After the 10th day, the consulting firm wrote a report stating that the design was excellent, would do everything that the start-up stated that it would do, was producible at the production yields purported, was reliable, and could be built at the costs estimated. The start-up eventually received $2,600,000 from these financing groups.

However, the R&D manager was disgusted with the time that he wasted in babysitting his appendix. He commented that in those 10 days, he had answered only three comments and with the exception of those five minutes in answering those three questions, he had had to sit and watch others work. Here are the three questions and comments that he answered.

Question: "This is not a good design because you have used an unnecessary diode. Why?"

Answer: "Initially we didn't have that diode and we had failures. That diode protects these transistors against the back EMF generated by this cheap switch. A switch that is good enough not to generate the back EMF would cost us $6 more whereas this diode only costs 3¢."

Statement: "You have used excessive safety factors in your design. Your circuit only sees $1/16$th watt however you are using $1/4$th watt resistors and paying a premium for this selection."

Answer: "What you say would be true if we didn't lump our small production purchases onto Hewlett Packard's large production purchases. H.P. uses enormous quantities of $1/4$ watt resistors and therefore they buy them at a fraction of the costs that we would have to pay for $1/16$th watt resistors. By using the same components as H.P. and adding our orders to their orders, we realize major savings."

Question: "Your circuit's components cost only $3 and each instrument will cost you approximately $6 in labor. You are going to sell this instrument for $500. Don't you feel that this is an unethical and excessive profit?"

Answer: "You are retained by your client to make technical, not moral, judgments. If you wish to tell your client (our venture capitalists) that my design is weak because it will make unethical profits, this is your right. I have not made judgments on your taking 10 days to evaluate a simple design which should have only taken five days to evaluate. At $40 an hour, I could challenge your ethics, however I shouldn't and therefore won't. I don't think that you should challenge my design's ethics."

Though the R&D manager was inconvenienced for 10 days, do you think that his time was well invested?

Minor Point 9-9: The Regulatory Agency Phenomenon M, IS

Approximately one-fourth of the people who come through our doors are considering entering an industry that is very tightly controlled by regulatory agencies. These industries are usually extremely static, are dominated by old and tired companies, and are lush hunting grounds for market gap analysts. We turn most of these potential clients down because it is improbable that their competition will not utilize the regulatory agencies to freeze the start-up out.

Be aware of the truth of that favorite American management joke. If your company's management is weak and top heavy, if your operations are inefficient and expensive, if you want to save money by eliminating new product developments, if your top management is under stock holder pressures, and if you are too tired to define problems and take corrective actions, then solve your problem the American way, demand regulatory agencies to assure profits regardless of your incompetences. The machinery usually works as follows:

   I.   Form an industry "interest" group.
   II.   Use this group as a guise to attract government controls (regulatory agencies) over your industry.
  III. Staff these agencies with industry personnel.
  IV. Use the agency as your tool to
      (a)   control prices,
      (b)   attract government subsidies,
      (c)   induce legislation to prevent competition, new products, new innovations, and any outside forces which shake your industry's status quo,
      (d)   establish policing capabilities to insure this status quo.

This joke seemed a little too cute and pat to be true until we had two clients crushed by these agencies. If you do not believe me, take a good look at the building industry. Every year there are thousands of potential start-ups which fail because of the rigorous controls to maintain the industry's status quo. Building codes outlaw new innovations, unions (along with city, state, and federal support) kill cost-saving concepts, and contractors (who know that they will lose all government contracts if they step out of line) fear new ideas.

If you have the combination to making the controls work for you, these industries are lush with opportunities and profits. However, if you do not have the contacts and the influence to get beyond the agencies' hurdles, then seriously consider addressing an industry under less government control.

FINAL COMMENT   M, IS, RS, F

Make certain that all disciplines' plans intermesh perfectly and that if sales should either lead or lag your forecasts, the other disciplines' milestones track these sales requirements.

10 · Your Financial Projections

A good financial man can evaluate your financial projections and tell you more about yourself than you would think possible. He'll get a deep insight into what kind of guy you are, your fiscal responsibilities, your practicalness, your management experience, and your objectives. And make no mistake about it, venture capitalists are excellent financial men who employ every trick in the book to determine what kind of guy you are.

It is the intent of this chapter to show you the only valid way that you can develop your financial projections to pass these fiscal tests and then to give you an insight into the actual tests that will be performed on your proforma financial reports.

Though I strongly feel that these tests are an essential part of this text, in a way I hate to disclose them because it will be a very real temptation for you to by-pass all of your management decisions, all of your company objectives and goals, and "shoot" your projected reports so that they will pass the tests. This "dry-labbing" approach[1] is usually so obvious (it is practiced by almost every proposal mill that grinds out business plans by

---

[1] Do you remember, in college, the clown who used to cut his laboratory classes and then turn in perfect data from the experiments he never ran? While you smelled of hydrogen sulfide and missed the big football game trying to make your tests work, he dated your best girl and laughed at your stupidity. Then came the day of reckoning. The professors, who had seen through this character's "dry-labbing," gave you an "A" for imperfect test results and him an "F" for cheating. In college, he could get a second chance by repeating the course. In seeking capital, there is rarely that second chance because venture capitalists will never stake their dollars and become vulnerable to the cheater.

the dozens) that when the venture capitalist sees perfect tests, he usually suspects the plan as being only a sales document and therefore ignores it.

SECTION ONE: THE EVOLUTION OF YOUR FINANCIAL PROJECTIONS

HOW YOUR FINANCIAL PROJECTIONS SHOULD EVOLVE   M, IS, RS, F

Proforma (projected) financial reports are little more than your projected cash-in (sales forecasts) less cash-out (the departmental budgets to meet those sales forecasts). If you have any money left over, you have profits. If you don't, you have losses.

This is pretty simple but would you believe that greater than half of the clients who came through our doors hadn't attempted this evolution sequence. As an example, if they were engineers, they frequently developed optimum manufacturing conditions, made this the cornerstone of their business plan and made the invalid assumption that sales can sell everything they can produce (or even worse, customers would buy their optimum production quantities without sales efforts). These optimum production quantities became their sales forecasts. If these start-ups were run by administrators, their forecasts usually evolved from the profits that the founders wanted to realize. The desired profits therefore became the cornerstone and the founders worked back to the sales essential to produce those profits. The third most common error is forecasts developed by a sales type of individual. This type either states that he can sell a "jillion of em" or "In X months, we'll realize 1% penetration, in Y months 2% penetration, and in Z months 5% market penetration." The forecasts are valueless and since your business plan is built on sales forecasts, it too becomes valueless. We'll examine sales forecasting in-depth in Chapter Seventeen but for now, realize that the following evolution is essential for financial projections.

Stage One: Define your company's goals, objectives, milestones, incentives, leveraging strategies, etc. You have already done this if you've taken the advice of earlier chapters, however realize that if these essentials have any meaning, they'll transfer themselves into your financial projections. Otherwise, they are shallow lip services and will be swiftly identified as such.

Stage Two: Define the market segment (or segments) that you will address first, the distribution networks essential to meet each market segment's needs, and finally, the sales strategies (sales prices, the sales close techniques, the sales support, etc.) that each market segment dictates. This is covered in later chapters.

Stage Three: Perform your sales forecasts (Chapter Seventeen). This forecast will convert into your company's cash-in.

Stage Four: Develop each group's budget necessary to meet the sales demand of stage three. The summation of these budgets converts into your company's cash-out.

Stage Five: Overlay all of your company's milestones, incentives, goals, objectives, and philosophies.

Stage Six: From stages three through five above, you have developed the foundations for your projected financial reports which will ring true to any analyst's tests. For your business plan, show your sales forecasts, the budgets essential to meet those forecasts, your balance sheets, your income reports (frequently called P&L Statements), and your cash flow projections on a monthly basis for 3 years and a quarterly basis for the following 2 years (5 years total). We advise many of our clients to also show semi-annual reports for the next 20 years. Though these long-range reports have little accuracy, we recommend this practice because it shows the investors (venture capitalists) that your founders are thinking of building a long-term involvement instead of selling out in a get-rich-quick scheme.

Stage Seven: Make certain that the end results are in harmony with both your personal objectives and your company's stated objectives.

Stage Eight: After everything looks right and defendable, perform the financial ratio tests described in the balance of this chapter. If these tests uncover an obvious error, correct the errors. If these tests show that you are out of line with the ''ideal'' start-up, don't worry too much. The ''ideal'' start-up that these tests define is far from ideal and the sophisticated capitalists know it. However, you are triggering ''flags'' for further questions and you and your partners should prepare yourself for these questions.

SECTION TWO: THE RATIO ANALYSIS THAT WILL BE PERFORMED UPON YOUR PROJECTIONS

It's easy to get bogged down in this section with a lot of definitions so to save ourselves complications, let's use the following example financial statement to illustrate those ratios studied by venture capitalists and bankers.

Example 10-1: Income Statement

SAMPLE MANUFACTURING COMPANY (1985)

NET SALES		$11,000,000
Cost of Sales & Operating Expenses		
Cost of Goods Sold	$8,200,000	
Depreciation	$ 300,000	
Selling & Administration Expenses	$1,400,000	
		$ 9,900,000

OPERATING PROFIT	$ 1,100,000

OTHER INCOME

Dividends & Interest	$ 50,000
Total Income	$ 1,015,000
Less Interest on Bonds	$ 135,000
Income before Federal Income Taxes	$ 1,015,000
Less Provisions for Taxes	$ 480,000
NET PROFITS AFTER TAXES	$ 535,000

Accumulated Retained Earnings Statement
(Earned Surplus Projected for 1985)

Balance, January 1, 1984	$ 1,315,000
Net Profits (Projected) for 1985	$ 535,000
TOTAL	$ 1,850,000

Less Dividends Paid On:		
Preferred Stock	$ 30,000	
Common Stock	$120,000	$ 150,000
BALANCE (PROJECTED) DECEMBER 31, 1985		$ 1,700,000

Example 10-2: Sample Balance Sheet and Income Statement:

ASSETS:

Current Assets:

Cash		$ 450,000
Marketable Securities at Cost		
(Present market value $890,000)		$ 850,000
Accounts Receivable	$2,100,000	
Less Reserve for Bad Debts	$ 100,000	$2,000,000
Inventories		$2,700,000
TOTAL CURRENT ASSETS		$6,000,000

Fixed Assets:

Land	$ 450,000	
Buildings	$3,800,000	
Machinery	$ 950,000	
Office Equipment	$ 100,000	
	$5,300,000	
Less Accumulated Depreciations	$1,800,000	

NET FIXED ASSETS | $3,500,000

Payments and Deferred charges | $ 100,000
Intangibles (Goodwill, patents, trademarks, etc) | $ 100,000

TOTAL ASSETS | $9,700,000

LIABILITIES

Current Liabilities:

Accounts Payable	$1,000,000
Notes Payable	$ 850,000
Accrued Expenses Payable	$ 330,000
Federal Income Tax Payable	$ 320,000

TOTAL CURRENT LIABILITIES | $2,500,000

Long Term Liabilities
First Mortgage Bonds, 5% interest due in 1988 | $2,700,000

TOTAL LIABILITIES | $5,200,000

Stockholders' Equity:

Preferred Stock, 5% Cumulative, $100.00 par value each on 6,000 shares	$ 600,000
Common Stock, $5 par value each authorized on 300,000 shares	$1,500,000
Capital Surplus	$ 700,000
Accumulated Retained Earnings	$1,700,000

FINANCIAL RATIO ANALYSIS   M, IS, RS, F

To better understand the tests which will be put to your business plan, let's look at the sample balance sheet and income statement shown in Example 10-1.

When the venture capitalist first gets your plan, he'll probably follow these steps to determine your plan's feasibilities and rewards:

Probably first he will multiply your net profits ($535,000) by 10 (conservative value of your company), then by 20 (standard value of your company) and then by 50 or 100 if you are addressing a growth or glamour industry.

Let's say that you are seeking $100,000 in seed money and for this you are willing to give him 10% of your stock. Therefore, conservatively speaking, your company will be worth $535,000 × 10 = $5,350,000. If he owns 10%, then he can realize $535,000 if he sells his 10%. He'll therefore realize a 5.35 to 1 investment growth on his capital with conservative estimates.

If the conservative estimate is under 5 to 1 in 5 years for start-up (seed money) investments, in all probability he will ignore your plan completely and search for more lucrative investments. However, if your company started turning cash and appears to him to be a safer first or second round investment, then he'll settle for 3.5 to 1 or 2.5 to 1 investment growths respectively. We have two clients who were able to project third round images and they had five different groups dickering for only 1.5 to 1 investment growths.

Next the reader will ratio your working capital (current assets of $6,000,000) against your current liabilities ($2,500,000). This ratio will be compared to your competition to see if you are in-line.

He will then determine your quick assets (current assets [$6,000,000] less inventories [$2,700,000]) and divide this figure by your current liabilities [$2,500,000]. This ratio is compared to that of your competition.

He'll then determine your net quick assets by subtracting your current liabilities ($2,500,000) from your quick assets ($6,000,000 − $2,700,000 = $3,300,000 − $2,500,000 = $800,000). If he invests $100,000 for 10%, then 10% of the net quick assets is $80,000 (or 80% of his initial investment). His downside risk is only 20% if you sold your firm at fire sale prices.

The capitalist will then divide your net sales ($11,000,000) by your inventory ($2,700,000) and compare this figure with your competition and your industry. Most of our start-up clients assume a reserve of 0.5% for bad debts. In actual practice, their bad debts are far less than 0.1% and even the Department of Commerce figures show a norm of 0.25%, however the capitalists seem to like the conservative figures. Expect to defend your system for bad debt collections regardless of what percentage you assume.

Next he will compare your fixed assets ($5,300,000) to your net sales ($11,000,000) to determine how leverage conscious you and your founders are. How much more would your cost of sales ($8,200,000) be increased if you jobbed your production out?

Venture capitalists and bankers differ greatly on the value of having large fixed assets. Bankers tend to like bricks, machinery, inventories, and properties because they state that these fixed assets increase the barriers to entry into your market. They assume that your competitors will have to match your fixed assets to compete. Venture capitalists say "hogwash," maintaining that bankers want you to invest in items that are foreclosable if you don't pay back your loans properly. Most privately owned venture capital groups want you to leverage their money to the optimum safe levels.

Next, the venture capitalist will compare your operating profit margin (operating profits [$1,100,000] to net sales [$11,000,000]). Expect to have your sales prices, your cost of sales, and your operating expenses challenged if this ratio is either too high or too low. It is a usual tactic to "brainstorm" how to command higher prices and how to lower costs in the course of your negotiations so that they can determine how solid these figures are.

Your net profit margin (net profit [$535,000] divided by net sales [$11,000,000]) is then compared to your industry and your competition. Once your start-up is projected significantly into the black, you'll observe that your net profits are approximately one-half of your operating profits if you calculated taxes correctly.

Your projected net profits for the next five years are compared to your competitors' performances over the past five years. Though this practice is darned invalid for a host of reasons, it's easy to do and therefore most investment groups do it. Many expect your fourth year of operations to have net profits of almost half that of established companies and a few extrapolate your net profit curves out to the seventh year to make certain that you equal competition. It's illogical but since they do it, you might just as well do it so that you can field questions.

Most venture capital firms which specialize in helping start-ups dislike seeing dividends for the first 10 years because they know how cash hungry young companies can be. In most cases, dividends can be a deterent to growth.

The capitalists now dig into your departmental budgets. Though the rules-of-thumb can get pretty hazy here because budgets vary so greatly from industry to industry and money philosophies vary so greatly from one investment group to the next, let's walk on thin ice and try to establish some guidelines in the budget areas. The only reason that I am venturing out on this thin ice is to give you a feel of what the capitalists look at so that you'll be properly prepared for the give and take of negotiations:

In most high technology companies, the selling expenses (commissions plus support expenses [salaries, travel, advertising, literature, etc.]) are usually from 10% to 30% of the net sales after the fourth year. In most low technology companies, these percentages increase to 25%–40% of net sales. Service companies vary too greatly to give guidelines. In franchise operations, usually the percentages are down around 1%–3% (because the franchisor carries the bulk of the sales expenses). Retail operations generally run in the 10%–15% range.

In manufacturing companies, the production salaries should not exceed 15% of the net sales.

In manufacturing and major service start-ups, the combined salaries of the marketing and sales groups should not exceed 5% of net sales after the fourth year. No comments can be made on retailing and franchise operations.

Generally the materials purchased in a manufacturing start-up should not exceed 10% of the net sales, according to most venture capitalists.[2]

Administration salaries should not exceed 3% of net sales after the fifth year.

---

[2] I rebel against this guideline. We have many clients who take off-the-shelf products, combine them for specific applications, and then sell or lease their combinations at a much higher price. Since there is minimal production, their purchased materials exceeded the 10%. However, each group had to defend their ratio so expect to yourself.

Finance salaries shouldn't exceed 0.5% of net sales after the second year.

R&D has few rules of thumb; however many capitalists grow concerned if R&D's budget drops too far below 10% in a manufacturing start-up or 15% in a high technology start-up. Twenty-percent budgets are not uncommon in high technology companies.

Capitalists become extremely concerned if they spot frills in your budgets. Though your sales group may have to put up a front to attract customers, items like original oil paintings, carpeting, drapes, directors' meetings in the Bahamas, company cars, employee gymnasiums, and recreation rooms, will always be challenged.

It is a standard practice in government and in large corporations for every department to always spend its complete budget. The philosophy is that if you don't spend your complete budget, you therefore made a management error by requesting that budget, and next year your budget will be cut accordingly. This practice leads to some pretty silly spending as the fiscal year nears its end. Therefore, at the bottom of each group's budget, we have our clients end with the following certification: "The above budget represents my best forecast of the expenses involved in meeting the sales forecasted on page x. All figures have been thoroughly evaluated and I hereby certify that they are as accurate as I can make them. I also certify that I will continue to search for new techniques, new materials, and new procedures which will lower my group's expenses. I further certify that any budget excesses will be turned back to the company at year's end."

This certification, signed by all group managers, may sound stupid, however its effect on venture capitalists is excellent. The last thing that they want is panic buying at year's end to justify budgets.

Your controller will have to answer significant questions on his various control systems. "Assume that one of your founders is dishonest and will try to steal profits. What flagging systems do you have to warn you? Next, assume that your controller is dishonest. What flags will expose him?"[3]

Minor Point 10-1: The Two Ingredients That Venture Capitalists Demand   M, IS, RS, F

Keep in mind that venture capital groups are primarily interested in investing in start-ups which will allow them to realize significant investment growths and to sell their equity when the timing is right.

The second point can be a hang-up for venture capital groups unless you

---

[3] In actual life, the probability of one of the primary founders being dishonest is relatively remote. The lower you go in management echelons, the more frequently you'll observe dishonesties. If you have an effective incentive system, it will not stop the thief from being a thief, however it will make his peers, whose incentive rewards he is also robbing, become policemen and quickly expose the culprit.

will allow your company to become an open corporation. They look for founders who will follow their guidance in going public when the timing is right. It is an expensive proposition to go public. You will need either to build significant reserves or seek more money through various other avenues to finance "going public."

Minor Point 10-2: The Value of Financial Ratio Analysis
M, IS, RS, F

If you stop to evaluate the rules of thumb described in this chapter, you'll observe that many of them are relatively shallow and therefore not very valuable. Also, it is a gross assumption to attempt to lump very different and very unique start-ups into one set of values. Therefore, in my opinion, the rules of thumb presented in this chapter aren't really worth the paper they are printed on. However, since most venture capital firms use these ratios as an instrument to trip warning flags of areas that have to be examined more closely, it is essential that you know these ratios.

We rarely have a client who doesn't violate several of these guidelines with successful results. As an example, we try to get our clients to receive their inventories on a consignment basis. They stock other people's products and don't pay for them until they use them. Therefore, many of our clients have extremely low inventory-to-sales ratios. Most of our clients turn cash within a relatively short time. By the time they are ready to attract their venture capital, they give the appearance of an ongoing company with similar smaller risks than just another start-up, and this pays dividends in equity negotiations. Most of these start-ups pay their founders 20% of the net profits (before taxes) instead of salaries. No venture capital group has yet to dislike this practice. Though the incentive reward/punishment systems allow you to realize a lot more work from a lot fewer people, they don't change the ratios too much because you pay those fewer people a lot more money. We have some clients who leverage their dollars to the extent that all the overhead they have is office rental. Our prize client turns $40,000 a month from less than $300 in expenses. He doesn't have one ratio that is even close to the guidelines, however there are six firms who have asked to invest in this client if and when he does need capital.

Therefore, violate these ratio guidelines at will, but expect to answer questions when you do.

SECTION THREE: OTHER CONSIDERATIONS

Minor Point 10-3: Probable, Optimistic, and Pessimistic
Forecasts   M, IS, RS, F

Though most venture capitalist groups do not expect this, we recommend that you develop optimistic, pessimistic, and probable proforma reports. To develop your sales forecasts and your projected budgets to meet those sales demands, you must make a series of assumptions. Though your assumptions will be valid, they may not necessarily be accurate. There are too many variables which affect your future.

Therefore, when you develop your projections, evaluate them as if everything will go as you hope it will (optimistic), as if everything will go as you think it will (probable), and as if nothing will go well (pessimistic). In the latter case, you will of course be prepared to discuss alternate approaches.

Those clients who developed these additional forecasts in a separate appendix impressed their plans' readers and had considerable success.

The other advantage of this planning is that it forces you and your team members to be alert for trends and to move more rapidly into alternate courses of action when the situation warrants it.

CAMEO 10-1: DISHONESTIES AS SEEN BY A TURN-AROUND CONSULTANT

Frequently we are asked to aid those specialty consulting firms which do nothing but turn sick companies around. These specialty consultants are as hard as nails and have a nose for ferreting out dishonesties when they exist. I asked the best to give me a breakdown on dishonesties as his firm observed them and got the following candid letter.

Dear Rich,

In going through the past fifteen years of clients, I dug out the following percentages for your text. I took the liberty of rounding off to the nearest 5% because if someone sees 82.87%, they naturally assume a sample size much larger than one firm's clients over just a fifteen year span.

Rich, with the exception of just one client, we found dishonesties with every company. However, in only 40% of the cases did we discover levels significant enough to warrant prosecution. These major dishonesties occurred in the following classifications:

1.	Presidents and Board Chairmen	10%
2.	The Company's Lawyers	85%
3.	The Company's Auditing Accountants	5%
4.	The Controllers	25%
5.	Other Vice Presidents	35%
6.	Middle Management	55%
7.	Lower Management	20%
8.	The Chief Purchasing Agent	70%
9.	The Buyers	15%
10.	The Venture Capitalists	10%

In almost every case where we found gross dishonesties, the client firm invited them through either poor controls or no controls. Also, realize that these percentages are extremely high because the clients were suffering from significant sicknesses in other areas. Your reader should know that we are usually called in when the client company is one step away from bankruptcy. Since most of the employees (and owners for that matter) felt that they were on a sinking ship, they attempted to salvage whatever they could for themselves.

Rich, as you know, we always have a clause in our contracts that we may start criminal actions on any outside consultant and we go after the dishonest lawyers and auditors with a vengeance. In defense of the lawyers, though we constantly attempt to get them disbarred, in only one case were we ever successful in even slapping their wrists. We had one case where a legal firm collected $820,000 in advance for miscellaneous services not rendered. The lawyers involved were censored and the firm returned the money to our client. Therefore, the reader should realize that though we classify a lawyer as dishonest, his practices were legal however unethical. The reader should also realize that our total goal is to turn the company around and we receive our bonuses from our performances. Therefore, any action or practice that is against our client company's benefit is usually considered suspect of dishonesty.

I firmly feel that most dishonesty is an effect and not a cause of our clients' problems. It is easily cured by proper systems and a harmonious atmosphere. If your readers spot a man who cheats in little ways (i.e., comes late and leaves early, doesn't throw a nickle in the till when he pours himself a cup of coffee, pads his expense account, etc.) on their team, I suggest that they get rid of him fast. This kind of man won't carry his load in little ways so why should you expect him to be honest in the big things.

Very truly yours,

Minor Point 10-4: Debt Collections   M, IS, RS, F

It is a relatively common practice for many customers to attempt to work on your money as long as you allow them to get by with it. If you sell a company something and it takes you 90 days to collect, then you have in essence loaned your customer money for one-fourth of a year at zero interest. Late collections can kill your profits. Late payments by you can kill your credit rating but make your profits.

It is therefore important to have a collection system which shortens your debt collections. Consider the following.

The day you ship your products, you also mail your invoices. If you are wise, the sales department will automatically type the invoices when they enter the purchase order. It is a simple matter to stamp and mail the invoices as the products are shipped out the back door.

. All of our clients have a boiler plate on their invoices that all bills are to be paid within 10 days. If payment isn't received within 10 days, then an automatic interest rate of 1.5% will be applied each month. Though these companies never enforce this clause, they do circle it when their first past due notice is mailed (15 days after the first invoice), and after 30 days, they attach a little printed blurb to their follow-up warning the customer of this charge and stating that it will go into effect retroactively unless payment is received immediately.

Invent a name and put this name in charge of your "collection department." Make this fictitious name the heavy of your accounting department and the name all delinquent customers see. Never use the president's name or the marketing manager's name in debt collections.

Address all requests for payments to your customer's manager of the accounting department. Even if the customer is a little one-man shop, addressing an impersonal letter to his manager makes him feel that the request is impersonal. Therefore he shouldn't take offense and stop buying from your salesmen.

Forty days after the initial invoice goes out (10 days after the second warning) you should start to become concerned that a late payment might become a bad debt. Consider having your invented collections manager telephone your customer's finance department to determine what the problem is. A good opening is, "I think that we probably have a mail problem here because the check that you mailed us never arrived. Would you object to cancelling your first check and rushing us a second check as soon as possible?"

At this stage, your customer will either agree to rush you a "second" check or if there is a problem, he'll explain it to your invented collections' manager.

Approximately 0.5% of your accounts receivables will not be paid after step 5. If after 10 days (now 50 days after the first invoice) you haven't received payment, telegraph the man. No one ever ignores a telegram. They may not act upon it but they always read it.

If after an additional 5 days (now 55 days after the first invoice) you haven't received payment, telephone again. Now your invented collections manager can get rough because you don't need a customer who pays so late.

If after 75 days, payment still hasn't occurred, then go into the customer's finance department and come out with a check.

The important thing for a start-up to realize is that it doesn't want to get on his customers' slow-pay lists. The larger a company is, the more they attempt to bully their vendors into accepting slow payments. A young and hungry start-up is duck soup for a controller's slow-pay list unless the start-up exerts itself.

If your industry is notorious for slow payments, then you might consider utilizing Dunn & Bradstreet's collection services. No company, regardless of how large they are, wants to get on Dunn & Bradstreet's list as a poor credit risk. For a nominal fee, you can retain D&B's collection group to handle your slow pays.

11 · The Many Venture Capital Avenues Open to You

PROLOGUE   M, IS, RS, F

'It is the intent of this chapter to show you the many avenues open to a start-up for getting funds. You will discover that if your start-up is addressing a growth industry, if your management team is excellent, if your ideas are well thought through and viable, that these avenues are easy to follow. In fact, as you travel down them, you'll discover that money is searching just as hard for developed ideas as ideas are searching for money. You'll receive inquiries and proposals from sources that you didn't even know existed.

Next to every avenue, I am giving you some editorial opinions. These opinions have been developed over the years while we helped our clients search for capital. You'll find that none of these opinions are completely valid as you search and you'll also find that they aren't invalid. The only reason that I am encumbering you with them is so that you won't be as vulnerable and as unsophisticated as I was on my first trip down these avenues.

AXIOM THIRTEEN: THE MORE SUCCESSFUL A START-UP IS, THE GREATER WILL BE ITS NEEDS FOR LARGER AND MORE FREQUENT CASH INJECTIONS.

There isn't a man in business who isn't painfully aware of this axiom. Yet approximately one-fourth of the clients who walk through our doors make the mistake of thinking that all they will need is one single loan or one investor to invest only once and then everything will be clover.

193

As a businessman, you are going to have to live with the financial institutions all of your life. If you are wise, you won't limit your resources to just one financial avenue.

SECTION ONE: THE VENTURE CAPITAL AVENUES

THE PRIVATELY OWNED VENTURE CAPITAL FIRMS
M, IS, RS, F

There are several hundred privately owned venture capital firms which invest between $750,000,000 and $900,000,000 each year in start-up through third-round financing. These groups vary so greatly in size, operations, goals, interests, philosophies, and support that it is impossible to put them into a nice neat package and define them for you.

Most venture capital groups are run by salaried people. These people are frequently either MBA's (Masters of Business Administration graduates) or ex-entrepreneurs. They receive excellent bonuses for excellent investments. Many are searching for an opportunity to join a founders' team of a major growth company.

Until recently, it was accurate to state that most of the money these groups invested came from their own founders. However, now there is a major trend for cash-rich countries (Japan, the Arab nations, etc.), some cash-rich individuals (some South American, Far Eastern, African, and European dignitaries), and some cash-rich companies (oil companies, insurance companies, real estate developers, etc.), to use the expertise of venture capital firms in investments. Some of the rumored machinery to channel money from all over the world reads like a detective novel. The secretiveness is all very legal and ethical but it can be tricky for a start-up if the start-up doesn't know who its investors really are. It doesn't matter as long as the professionals of your venture capital firms keep their investors happy. However, as this trend increases, you should see these firms double their investment capabilities.

Most venture capital groups have very tight investment objectives. They are: (1) the upside profits must be far greater than the downside risks, (2) most groups want their investment portfolios to double in value every four years, (3) they have minimum/preferred loan sizes (the norm is $200,000/$600,000, (4) they prefer to invest in those industries that they track very closely, (5) they tend to be pro-active (instead of reactive) in these preferred industries, (6) many like to form joint ventures with other capital groups to spread the risks, (7) they are usually extremely ethical, moral, thorough, and run by human people, and (8) many offer very essential additional services to the start-up. In almost every case, the venture capital group likes to feel that it is very involved with building something of significance while realizing profits.

This is a very important aspect that all founders should consider in whetting the capital group's appetites.

Very few venture capital groups want a majority of your stock for management controls. However, they do insist on paragraphs and clauses which will allow them to replace you and your team if you don't perform. Most will accept the restraints discussed earlier in this book as a replacement for their usual restraints.

Though the majority of venture capital firms still state that they are interested in the start-up, recently there has been a trend away from start-up funding (frequently called "seed money") into first- through third-round financing. If your start-up is turning cash and you give the image of an ongoing company, you not only increase your strength in equity negotiating, you also increase by a factor of eight the number of venture capital firms which will consider you.

There still are a few firms which prefer the start-up to the more safe but less profitable ongoing firms. However, the recent recessions have hurt many of these firms.

The more sophisticated firms mix their investments. They invest 10% of their monies in start-ups, 40% in first-round, 40% in second-round, and 10% in third-round financing. It is becoming a trend for many of these firms to only consider those start-ups which stand a good chance of giving them a 10 times investment growth in five years.

Almost all of these firms are run by extremely confident and competent individuals. Almost all feel that their start-ups couldn't make it without the wise counsel of their people. Almost all feel that there is a great deal of "hand holding" necessary in supporting every start-up and first-round investment. Therefore, most are insulted if you approach their company with an attitude of just give me $X and leave me alone. Almost all feel that $X from their firm is really worth $2X from a non-supporting source.

Almost none have any patience with dishonesty, laziness, or weak people. Every venture capitalist that I know considers himself an excellent judge of people, and in a relatively short time will tag those with whom they come into contact pretty accurately. They develop a "hunch" on a man and on a team and frequently this hunch will override all of the research and all of the testing.

COMMERCIAL BANKS   M, IS, RS, F

Realize that there are federal, state, and local laws which restrict the banking arm of a bank to own stock in your venture. These same regulatory agencies also restrict a bank from granting you loans unless you have significant collateral to cover those loans. Because of these restrictions, many founders tend to ignore the banking avenue in their search for funds. This is an error.

We recommend that our clients visit the loan officers of both their branch and their main bank (see Minor Point 11-5) because:

(1)   The loan officers are in contact with many money sources. Though these officers rarely recommend that you visit these sources, if you impress them they will recommend that their sources contact you. Many of our clients have received inquiries from will executors, from wealthy families, and from the suddenly rich.

(2)   You are going to want to establish a line of credit. Unless you have assets when you make this first visit, you won't be able to do this, however if you impress the loan officer, the foundation is laid for later months. They seem to take pride in being able to say, "Those people saw me before they turned their first dime and now they have built their firm so that they have an open line of credit worth well over $50,000." Give the loan officer your present financial reports and give him your projected performances. As you meet these projections, bring this accomplishment to his attention and you'll see your line of credit increase. Remember, if you can borrow $X, then that is $X less that you'll have to raise and give away stock for.

(3)   Many banks have SBIC divisions (Small Business Investment Corporations). Your loan officer should be able to give you a letter of introduction to this division. You'll find him a gold mine of suggestions and recommendations as to how best to approach this division. We'll discuss SBIC's later.

(4)   Many banks have SBA (Small Business Administration) loan groups which work very well with our government in SBA guaranteed bank loans. We'll discuss this later.

(5)   In recent years, most blue chip banks have gone into factoring in a major way. Though once factoring was looked down upon as beneath a banker's dignity, most now realize that it is one of the highest security loans that they can make. We'll get into factoring later.

INVESTMENT BANKERS   M, IS

The scream of "I've been raped" used to be heard across the nation. Young companies, when they were finally ready to go public, saw their initial stock releases double and triple in value within days after the stock first hit the market. If you went public with 10,000,000 shares for $10,000,000 and saw that stock jump in value to $30,000,000 in a few days, then you have left $20,000,000 on the table. Thus, the founders had to give up three times as much equity as they should have for cash.

The profits and competition of helping young companies go public are extreme, and today many of the better investment bankers are searching for lucrative start-ups long before they are ready to go public. Firms like Paine, Webber, Jackson, & Curtis have established venture capital arms in hope of grooming promising start-ups so that they, the investor, will realize the rich rewards when the young company does go public.

BANK OWNED SBICs (SMALL BUSINESS INVESTMENT CORPORATIONS)   M, IS, RS, F

The government realized some years ago that investment machinery for start-ups was essential and started the SBIC program. The government will loan any SBIC $750,000 for every $250,000 it raises to invest in young companies.

Many banks were quick to establish SBIC divisions because they not only were now allowed to own equity in companies, they realized major money-leveraging capabilities in acquiring this equity. Also, the company which uses a bank's SBIC capabilities will probably do its normal banking with that bank and therefore additional profits are realized.

Unfortunately, many banks staffed their SBIC division with ex-loan officers. The extreme conservativeness of bank loans frequently spilled over into the higher risk venture capital investments. These job-security-oriented individuals develop ulcers when they recommend that their division take a flyer.

Many of these conservative individuals will attempt to force you to spend your money on collateral so that if you fail, the bank will not lose everything. This can hamper your money-leveraging plans and stunt your growth.

PRIVATELY OWNED SBICs   M, IS, RS, F

These firms operate under the same legislation and controls as a bank-owned SBIC, however most of them have the goals and philosophies of a private venture capital firm.

There is a trend for private venture capital firms to set up one or more divisions of privately owned SBICs.

BANK OWNED AND PRIVATELY OWNED MESBICs (MINORITY ENTERPRISE SBICs)   M, IS, RS, F

The SBIC rules and qualifications are relaxed significantly and the money-leveraging capabilities are increased significantly for these firms. They must invest only in minority owned and managed firms.

Unfortunately, if the criteria for investment is the color of your skin, then you should expect significant failures. Though there are still quite a few MESBIC firms on the books, most of the money in this avenue has dried up. Out of 12 MESBICs investigated for this book, only 1 had invested in a new firm in the last two years. The balance had all of their funds committed and their portfolios were not growing fast enough to allow them to sell out and reinvest.

A few of the major banks are still investing small amounts in small minority start-ups such as barber shops or shoe repair shops. The bank officer stated that they will continue to do this as a form of charity to the hard-pressed areas.

COMMERCIAL BANK SBA LOANS (SMALL BUSINESS ADMINISTRATION):   M, IS, RS, F

The SBA has a budget that is rarely exhausted which will guarantee banks up to 90% of the loans that they make to small business without the collateral essential for standard bank loans. The government sets the interest rates that the banks can collect. This avenue is excellent, however there are a few things that you should realize before addressing it.

First, the SBA is a better-than-average government bureaucracy but it is still a bureaucracy. The bank must fill out significant paperwork and experience the usual delays involved in an SBA loan. This can be a relatively expensive operation. Therefore, many banks do not tolerate SBA's requirements and therefore do not realize their benefits.

Second, since the government guarantees up to 90% of the loan, they therefore do not feel that a bank should charge the higher interest rates that they usually charge to marginal borrowers. Therefore, the bank makes less profits on SBA loans.

Third, realize that the bank does not see any of the government guarantee until a loan defaults. Therefore, the bank must channel its assets from possibly more lucrative areas to give you an SBA loan.

Finally, if a bank's management is long ranged in thinking, they realize that if they loan you money, you'll keep your company's normal banking operations in their bank. This means additional profits for the bank.

SBA DIRECT LOANS   M, IS, RS, F

This is a great avenue because periodically the SBA is budgeted to make direct loans at interest rates far below the going rate. These long-term loans have helped many start-ups throughout the years. However, you should be aware of the following:

(1)   Usually there are four times as many loan candidates as there are dollars to lend. Therefore, within hours after the SBA budget has been released, its funds have dried up.

(2)   When this machinery was initially set up, the banks were con-

cerned about the government going into competition with them. There-fore, the SBA insists upon at least two turn-down letters from local commercial banks.

(3)   Though the SBA denies it, the bulk of its loans over the past years have gone to minority enterprises. Since they are a bureau of our government, they are sensitive to government pressures, and for the last 10 years our government has pressured them to give higher priorities to minority groups. This trend still remains, however there is also a significant trend to fund women entrepreneurs.

(4)   Unfortunately, many of the minority enterprises in which the SBA invested were not properly run and the enterprises failed. The repayments of the loans have been lost and consequently each period SBA's direct loan budgets have also dropped.

(5)   Though theoretically SBA is qualified to make loans up to EDA levels (up to $1,000,000), since the SBA budget is smaller and those requesting loans are greater, it tries to spread its budget over as many firms as it can. Since it can satisfy 20 $50,000 requests for every $1,000,000 request, loan sizes have diminished.

(6)   SBA likes to have its loans generate other loans and frequently will give priority to firms which are putting together large packages from various capital avenues.

(7)   As a typical government bureau, it is sensitive to local pressures. If the mayor, several city councilmen, several state senators, and your federal representative (congressman) put in a good word for your application, it does no harm.

(8)   Because of the large number of minority enterprise failures, SBA now utilizes professional management consultants (they pay approximately $200 a day for these consultants) to help their clients. In those cases where the management was capable to taking advice, this consulting has been invaluable.

(9)   After you have read this, never mention these points to your local SBA office. These points anger them.

Actually, direct SBA loans are one of the best avenues open to the start-up. Even though you can only get small amounts of low-interest, long term debts, every little bit helps. If you pay back your loans on time, the avenue remains open to you until you can no longer be classified as a small business.

You will find the SBA people a delight (when compared to other bureaucracies). They seem to genuinely care and want to help you. Their management and personnel are several cuts above bureaus like the IRS, EDA, Department of Commerce, etc. It's unfortunate that our government tried to force this agency to perform functions out of its scope and therefore limited it so greatly. If you don't try for a direct SBA loan, you are missing a golden opportunity.

EDA (ECONOMIC DEVELOPMENT AGENCY) LOANS   M, IS

EDA loans are usually long-term (20 to 30 years) loans which start at $1,000,000 (where the SBA is supposed to end) and go upwards to $5,000,000. Since President Kennedy started this agency, it has loaned billions. Interest rates are usually well below the prime rate.

EDA's written and unwritten rules are:

(1)   It will not loan money to firms which can secure loans from banks. Like the SBA, it is sensitive to the possible banker's complaint that the government is in competition with it.

(2)   It is authorized to loan up to 85% of the required capital. Of the remaining 15%, 5% must be raised from either the state or local community in which the start-up will be located, and 10% from other sources.

(3)   In actual practice, EDA rarely loans the 85%. They want to spread their budget out over as many investments as possible and therefore they rarely go above 55% (45% is the norm). The lower the percentage, the more likely you'll get the loan.

(4)   Since SBA rarely lends over $100,000, there is growing sentiment in EDA to change its minimum to $100,000 (instead of the million minimum). There have been several near misses in these lower loans and I expect we'll soon see more EDA loans for lower dollars.

(5)   The firm that is requesting the loan must be addressing a "growth industry." EDA's definition of "growth" is far less demanding than venture capital groups' definitions. If the industry that you are addressing equals or exceeds the projected GNA growth rates, then it is a growth industry. By this definition, there are very few industries that do not qualify as a "growth" industry.

(6)   The firm must be located in a high impact area (unemployment exceeds 5.5%) and the county must have submitted to EDA a community plan of where they want to go and what they want to achieve.

(7)   The firm must be compatible with the community. It cannot take business away from already existing companies within the community, it must help the community solve its employment problems, its ecology problems, its economic problems, and any other problem that is in vogue at the time you go for your loan.

(8)   The firm must be labor intensive. For every million dollars loaned, X people must get jobs. The variable X changes from year to year, however, it is usually around 14 people.

(9)   The community's people must want your start-up. Get local officials, state officials, federal representatives, the chamber of commerce, several church groups, local educational institutes, and local clubs and societies (such as the Elks, the Moose, the Masons, the Knights of Columbus) to endorse your plans.

(10) You and your management team must fill out a stack (approximately three feet high) of government forms. There is even a form on garbage collection.

(11) EDA is extremely sensitive to criticism and therefore attempts to keep a very low profile. Also, as a government bureau, it is vulnerable to government pressures. Those firms which have a black founders' team get a set of multipliers, those that have Mexican American founders get another multiplier, those that have mixed white, brown, yellow, and blacks, get another multiplier, those who want to build in EDA favored counties get another multiplier, etc. Because social problems are added to community problems, many firms are funded which attempt to solve these problems in place of making their company go and grow. Therefore, EDA's success rate has been less than admirable. Too many of its loan dollars are therefore never repaid and EDA's budgets for new loans are dropping.

(12) Unlike SBA, EDA is a relatively young bureaucracy and therefore is still relatively immature. Most of the people that are in EDA understand rules, understand forms, and have little or no understanding of business. I've seen top administrators completely misinterpret proforma balance sheets. I'll never forget trying to explain a leveraging principle only to have the administrator ask after the explanation what the word "leveraging" meant and then ask if this was a brand new management theory. Actually, I get the impression that EDA people don't care if the firms that they finance are successful or not. As long as the forms are filled out so that they satisfy Washington and as long as the founders don't embarrass EDA by spending its funds in Las Vegas, EDA seems to be happy. Though business plans impress EDA, I have yet to see a case where the plans were ever read. Only the forms are studied, and make no mistake, every line of every form is studied in depth.

(13) As with SBA, read these points and then keep them to yourself when working with EDA. Its loans are extremely attractive, and though this avenue takes a lot of work, it is worth it if you can land a loan.

INSURANCE COMPANIES   M, IS

Insurance companies have entered the venture capital field in a major way over the last few years. These cash-rich companies usually split their investment dollars between themselves and various of the larger venture capital groups.

Basically, most insurance firms operate very similarly to the private venture capital groups except they don't offer the support services or "hand holding" discussed earlier.

Be aware of the inverse equity agreements that many of these firms impose. They will come in for a small percentage of the equity initially and as your start-up meets its milestones and becomes a more and more lucrative property, they want to have first option of buying more and more equity. When your firm has matured and leads its industry, it can very easily become a wholly owned subsidiary. The insurance firm of course pays well for each equity slice.

PARALLEL MANUFACTURERS   M, IS

This is a tricky avenue but if the circumstances are right, it can be excellent. Briefly, by investing in your company and adding your products to their sales family (possibly under their own name), a parallel firm (a potential competitor) can have the use of top scientists and excellent administrators, and realize the fruits of expensive and innovative R&D, at a fraction of the cost that it would take them to develop a product (or service) identical to yours. Both you and the established company gain real benefits. The established company gains a product or service family which complements its sales in a fraction of the time at a fraction of the expense that it would otherwise take, and the start-up gains a sophisticated investor in the market which it addresses, gains an already established sales network, gains much faster sales penetrations, and gains a sizable negotiating arm with other venture capitalists (if a firm that is already in the industry wants to invest in your company and sell its products, then your products must be good and must have demand).

The risks of this avenue are obvious. The largest risk is the pettiness of the established company's R&D group. Jealousies may force them to attempt to pirate as much of your innovative work as they can get their hands on and then recommend to their management that they pass up the opportunity because their group can produce a better product in a very short time. I would only approach another company if I knew that their R&D group was heavily committed to another project and could not get around to duplicating your product for a long time.

The second big risk is that you may illuminate a major gap months before your potential competitor realizes that it exists. If they turn you down, you've given them months of market research information and reduced their lag time significantly.

The third liability is that since they are investors in your firm, they dictate some of your company's policies as long as your relationships exist. Their goals may not be your goals and if they carry too large an equity stick, your company may never have the opportunity to grow properly.

VENDORS AS INVESTORS   M, IS, RS, F

It is a relatively common practice for major vendors to supply products for equity in your company. If you need $50,000 worth of equipment, you could not care less if you get it in the equipment or in money so that you can buy equipment. Cash-rich vendors like the policy because it allows them to diversify and assures them that your company will continue to buy from them in a non-competitive situation.

Actually, I like to have our clients get their major vendors to invest in them because this practice frequently allows them to pay their bills to that vendor later than would be allowed otherwise and they can use the vendor as a reference to increase their line-of-credit ceilings. In many cases, valuable competitive information can be learned from this investor.

INVESTMENT GROUPS   M, IS, RS, F

Many doctors, lawyers, executives, cash-rich individuals, and cash-rich companies band together and form investment groups. Some of these groups are made up of individuals who have a tax problem and are looking for ways to minimize their tax payments while building an estate. These people are looking for limited partnerships so that they can realize the subchapter S tax write-offs.[1] Last year, over $50,000,000 was invested in start-ups from these groups.

FOUNDATIONS   M, IS

Foundations, as you know, have such tax advantages that they can build up sizable cash surpluses. Most of these surpluses are invested in stocks which will support the foundation when times get tough. Though the bulk of this investment is in the blue chip companies, frequently the wealthier firms will devote a small percentage to high-risk/high-profits stocks. Though these percentages are small, some of these non-profit companies cash surpluses are so large that even a 5% risk investment runs into millions of dollars.

If your product has real value in the foundation's field (i.e., medical electronics, education systems, humanities, etc.), it is a frequent practice for foundations to give cash grants for development projects, to loan money at low interest for modifications, and to buy high-risk stocks to finance a breakthrough. Most foundations are very tranquil venture capitalists.

MUTUAL FUNDS   M

This is an on-again, off-again avenue of which you should be aware. Periodically, high-risk mutual funds will invest in those start-ups which

---

[1] Subchapter S is a tax incentive for investors. This incentive allows investors to write off a company's losses as the investors' direct losses.

address major growth industries. The loyalty and stability of mutuals leaves a lot to be desired.

UNIVERSITIES   M, IS

This is a relatively new avenue for start-up funding. The costs of education are rising so rapidly that many of the wealthier colleges and universities realize that their low-risk, low-dividend portfolios will not keep up with the projected expenses of education. Therefore, many of these schools are now risking a percentage of their investment portfolios to high-risk start-ups. Though the investment amounts are still minor (the norm investment is only $40,000), the trend is growing. Two years ago there were only 6 universities investing in start-ups. The number now is 114.

PRIVATE MONEY SOURCES   M, IS, RS, F

There are thousands of estates, wealthy families, and unique consortiums who search for promising start-ups. Those start-ups which pursue the banks, the foundations, and the universities usually get dozens of inquiries from these unique money sources. The majority of them seem to have a "don't contact us, we'll contact you" attitude.

CASH-RICH CORPORATIONS   M, IS

Firms like Exxon, Phillips, General Motors, and Beckman, utilize both private venture capital groups and their corporate staffs to invest in promising start-ups. The trick with these firms is to offer services or products which address the same markets as they address. In other words, you wouldn't go to Exxon with a leisure industry product but you might gain their direct interest if your product was service-station oriented.

YOUR AUNT GERTRUDE   M, IS, RS, F

Though this source of capital is frequently used in start-ups, please realize that you arc inheriting a very unsophisticated investor who will be of little help in attracting future money.

FACTORING   M, IS, F

Though this isn't a true venture capital avenue, greater than half of our clients used it effectively prior to seeking their real capital sources. In the very early stages of your development, consider borrowing money using purchase orders received (accounts receivable) as collateral for your loans. When you first start up, most factoring houses will loan you up to 50% of each purchase order's value. When you build a reputation of being able to produce and rapidly pay back your factoring loans, the interest rates will drop and frequently these houses will loan up to 90% of your accounts receivables. Factoring is an excellent tool to build up your credit levels and therefore your lines of credit. We have had several clients who used this tool exclusively to start their companies up from a shoe lace into something of real worth. They pay a lot more in interest than most, however they still own 100% of their companies.

LINES OF CREDIT   M, IS, RS, F

This also isn't a true venture capital avenue but realize that every dollar you can borrow is one dollar less that you'll have to give up equity on. To establish and build a significant line of credit is usually one of your controller's first responsibilities. Borrow to your maximum levels frequently and pay it back fast. If you do things right, within 5 years you should build a line of credit equivalent to 25% of your yearly gross sales. After 10 years, this figure should equal your yearly sales.

FRANCHISING   M, IS, RS, F

It is unfortunate that in the last decade, franchising was the in-vogue thing and therefore many abuses occurred. Today, when you mention franchising as a viable solution to several problems, people seem to think that you are recommending an unethical practice.

Franchising, if performed properly, is a valid and ethical tool. It has the following drawbacks and strengths:

Drawbacks

(1)   Because of the many recent abuses by crooks who rode the bandwagon, most states have enacted very restrictive laws on franchising operations. These laws are not uniform and in many cases are so poorly written that they hinder an ethical and viable plan to the point where it may never work.

(2)   Because of its bad name, it is difficult to find qualified individuals to invest in a franchising company. Franchise selling costs have risen extremely. We recently had one client who had to spend over $350,000 for

every million dollars he attracted. Ten years ago, the average expense was $45,000 for every million raised.

(3)   There is a trend to pick only those who have enough money to buy a franchise. The key to successful franchise operations is to accept only highly qualified and motivated people. As soon as you accept an unqualified person, your company's operations and reputation will be damaged.

Strengths

(1)   People are paying you for the privilege of following your business plan. If your plan is sound and if you write your contracts so that the penalties for violating your plan are extreme, then you have as much (if not more) control over their operations than if you hired people direct and set up a factory office.

(2)   Assuming that you are extremely selective in accepting only qualified candidates, you can attract extremely talented and experienced entrepreneurs. These people are probably a cut above what you could attract in direct employees.

(3)   If you use a holding-company concept and sell shares along with the franchises, you have the machinery to raise major dollars without losing too much equity in the holding company. The franchisee will not only realize significant profits from following your business plan in his territory, he will also realize major profits as the held company prospers. You buy added loyalties.

(4)   I like to have parallel sales and service networks for market saturation. Franchise machinery is an effective and inexpensive secondary network.

SECTION TWO: SOME OTHER CONSIDERATIONS

CAPITAL RAISING TASK FORCE TEAM   M, IS, RS, F

You have now seen the basic avenues commonly followed for start-up funds. It is obvious that the bulk of your controller's efforts will be invested in investigating and selling these avenues on your start-up.

If you are wise, you'll consider setting up a special task force team to support your controller. Many of our clients make their controller the project manager of raising their funds and have their marketing manager, their president, and all administrative personnel as members of this team. If you are going to mix your venture capital avenues (it is recommended for future cash-raising abilities), then in all probability, your controller will be involved in as many as 10 avenues of finance simultaneously. It takes a lot of effort and time.

Minor Point 11-1: Money Promoters   M, IS, RS, F

I recommend that you raise your start-up's capital yourself. There are many promotors who go under different guises such as money finders, financial consultants, proposal brokers, or business plan expediters, who will offer to raise your capital for you on a commission basis My firm (Business Solutions) gets inquiries almost every day from these promoters.

The average promoter tries to promote 10 business plans a month. If he is successful on 1 plan every 18 months, he breaks even. If he can raise capital for 2 firms a year, he makes major money. Therefore, for every 180 plans that he promotes, he has to close 1 deal. For every 120 plans he promotes, he does extremely well if he closes 2 deals.

Frequently, those plans which he promotes and which fail to raise capital can never make it again because the water has been muddied too much by the promotion. Once your business plan has made the complete circuit without success, it's old news and second attempts don't stand too much of a chance.

Remember that between 50% and 60% of your concept's weighting is in your founders' team. Therefore, you are going to have to sell your plan yourself even if the promoter plays a role.

Also realize that most venture capitalists know all of the promoters extremely well. When the promoter starts pushing your plan, the capitalist knows that several hundred thousand dollars of his money will immediately be given to the promoter.

Minor Point 11-2: Mix Your Capital Sources   M, IS, RS, F

You should seriously consider mixing several different venture capital avenues in your start-up and first-round financing. This mixing concept has several advantages.

No one capitalist group has in-depth contacts or tracks the behavior of all the money avenues. Therefore, when you need to raise future rounds of financing, you'll have in-depth knowledge, experience, and contacts for many avenues instead of just one avenue.

Nowhere will you find men who are more experienced in start-ups than you'll find in these venture capital groups. Since these men will sit on your board of directors, you are in essence getting excellent consulting capabilities for nothing.

I am a firm believer in working your board of directors. As an example, when a director or an employee of that director's firm is flying to Chicago or New York, have that man visit a client for you or check out a credit rating. Since most venture capital firms do quite a bit of traveling, you'll inherit a lot of capabilities.

By mixing your capital groups, you are dividing one large segment of your stock holders. This segment will not combine against your management team unless your management team isn't performing and therefore needs replacement. Occasionally, venture capital firms get into financial problems and seek to make their investments liquid by forcing all sorts of compromises on their firms. If you have mixed your venture capital groups, the weak group can't force the other groups to force these compromises upon you.

Oddly enough, mixing groups is a very real appetite-whetting feature. If you tell an investment group that E DA is going to loan you $1,000,000 and Bank of America's SBEC is going to invest $200,000, then that investment group will be motivated into joining your team.

Example 11-1: Mixing Your Sources   M, IS, RS, F

Let's assume that you are starting-up a medical instrumentation manufacturing firm and at the end of three and a half years, you'll have a maximum negative cumulative cash flow of $5,000,000. Let's also assume that there is a good chance that you'll need another $5,000,000 in seven years to address a new market. You want to lay the foundation for attracting the second $5,000,000 at this time.

Before you approach your first venture capital group, you and your co-founders meet and lay out an ideal investment mix. Your logic may be something like the following.

A. For $5,000,000 we'll give up 25% of our company's total stock. Let's incorporate for 20,000,000 shares of no-par stock and sell each share for $1 for the first round. (I am assuming that your start-up is already generating cash and therefore can give the image of an ongoing company. It's very hard to raise $5,000,000 on the start-up round).

B. If we meet our five-year milestones, our stock should be worth $5 a share and therefore we will only have to give up 5% of our company for the second $5,000,000.

C. Of the $5,000,000 initially raised, let's attempt to do it as follows.
1. Twenty Percent ($1,000,000) will be raised from three privately owned venture capital groups. One group should be on the east coast, one in the midwest, and one on the west coast. Two of the three groups should be the type which invests private money, and the third should be a non-bank SBIC.
2. Twenty Percent ($1,000,000) will be raised from bank-owned SBICs.
3. Ten Percent ($500,000) will be raised from our vendors. These vendors will receive stock in lieu of full payments over the next five years.

4. Ten Percent ($500,000) will be raised from our distribution. They will accept stock as a partial payment of commissions over the next five years.
5. One Percent ($50,000) will be raised from our founders. Each will invest $5,000 initially and each will receive the balance over five years in lieu of complete salaries.
6. Four Percent ($200,000) will be raised from bank loans over the first five years. The stock (200,000 shares) will go to the management team when these loans are secured, used, and then paid back.
7. Thirty-Five Percent ($1,750,000) will be raised from government EDA loans. Though EDA loans do not include stock, the 1,750,000 shares involved will revert to the management team after the loan is secured, spent, and paid back. A portion of these 1,750,000 shares may have to be used as sweeteners for the other avenues.

D. The balance of the shares will be handled as follows:
1. Fifty Percent (10,000,000 shares) will be placed in reserve. It will take a majority vote of the board of directors to release any of this reserve.
2. Ten Percent (2,000,000 shares) will be placed in reserve to be earned by the founders' team. These shares will be released to the founders immediately for voting purposes, however their actual ownership will pass to the founders as the company meets its milestones.
3. Fifteen Percent (3,000,000 shares) will be placed in various reserves as manager incentives, key employee incentives, non-key employee incentives, to attract future critical personnel, and to be used in any other way approved by two-thirds of the board of directors.

This of course is a very idealistic mix and may not be possible at the time you search for capital (the venture capital industry is always fluid and changing). You'll have to compromise, there will be many features that you will not be allowed to use, new avenues will open and old avenues will dry up, however it's better to have a plan than to go around saying "We need $5,000,000 in the next three and a half years."

Minor Point 11-3: Preliminary Feelers   M, IS, RS, F

The newer a start-up is, usually the more impatient the founders are to go after capital. Frequently, you'll want to approach venture capitalists before your product or service is reliable and before your business plan is out of the rough draft stages.

The less prepared that you are, the less likely you'll get your money. However, I always recommend that founders investigate their venture capital sources as soon as they can.

Please, do yourself one favor and don't burn your bridges behind you. You'll swiftly learn that these investment groups are very sophisticated and can spot incomplete plans immediately. When you go into them, state that you are interviewing them to see if you are interested in having them on your team and go ahead and ask them all of the questions that you wish. If you are a salesman and have an intuitive feel that now is the time to close your sale (ask for money), go ahead. As you'll see in the sales chapter, a salesman can make dozens of sales-close attempts without permanently losing the customer. However, as soon as you are forced to bluff or to lie, you're getting into ground which can ruin you. Before the capitalist will sign the dotted line and agree to invest X million on specific dates, you and your plan are going to be investigated. Once you are caught in a lie or a bluff, you stand a chance of not only ruining yourself with that particular capital group, you stand a good chance of the word getting out and ruining you with the other groups also.

Minor Point 11-4: The Clubishness of Venture Capitalists
M, IS, RS, F

It's hard to explain, but realize that venture capitalists are extremely open and at the same time extremely closed with each other. They continually run into each other at board meetings, at conventions, or while performing research, and they seem to pass information quite freely. If you do not conduct yourself ethically and professionally the word seems to get around fast. We had one client who was so snowed with work that he literally forgot about an appointment that he had with a venture capital group. That evening, when he stopped by his bank to cash a check, the loan officer came over to him and asked why he stood-up the group. The next day, two other groups called him and asked why he at least didn't cancel his appointment. The statement "I just forgot about the darned appointment" didn't carry any water because a top-notch man is always so organized that he never overlooks an appointment. This client got black marks on both his courtesy and on his management capabilities. The venture capitalist wasted little time in getting the word out so that others would be aware of these weaknesses.

On the other hand, venture capitalists can be extremely secretive. If you come in with a money producing concept, the capitalists will guard the concept well. They may sit on the board of directors of a competing firm and never open their mouths. They will ask your permission to disclose your concept to another capitalist so that he can also invest in your start-up but they won't do it without your permission.

Minor Point 11-5: Bank Loan Officers   M, IS, RS, F

Realize that banks have two sets of management growth channels. One set is for the corporate officer candidates and the other is for branch management. People in the first group make significant salaries, while those in the second group frequently have salaries lower than engineers, supervisors, and salesmen. The banks give out vice presidencies to almost all who come into contact with wealthy clients (because the title helps their employees do business with the wealthy), but do not make the mistake of thinking that these "officers" have much authority or make much money.

When you talk to a branch loan officer, realize that he is extremely limited in his authority. By all means, talk to him but also talk with the primary loan officer in the bank's main office.

Minor Point 11-6: Both Sides of SBA   M, IS, RS, F

Almost all of our clients go for both SBA direct loans and SBA loans through banks. You might consider working both sides of the street as follows:

Step One: Select two banks which you know don't utilize SBA guaranteed loans. Since the paperwork involved is so extensive and the time delay in getting these loans is so long, almost half of the major banks choose not to use SBA (the loan officers will tell you their bank's policies).

Step Two: Once you have the turn-down in writing from these two banks, take these letters to SBA and fill out all of their application forms.

Step Three: Since SBA is like any other government agency, it is sensitive to government pressures. Select the local officials, state officials, and federal officials who will aid your cause and sell them on how beneficial your start-up will be to their communities. Ask these officials to write letters for you, telephone for you, and put the pressure on SBA to loan you the money. It doesn't do any harm to take the SBA officials out to your plant site and help them envision how your start-up will affect the community.

Step Four: In all probability, only a few other loan applicants have gone to this trouble and you'll get your loan when the next budget is released. However, it does no harm to check almost daily to see if the budget has been released.

Step Five: If you missed the loan on one budget, keep the pressures on. Have your people check into the "whys" you didn't get your loan and continue to follow up almost daily on the next budget release. SBA officers will grow so tired of this practice that they will make certain that you are on the next loan list to get rid of you.

Step Six: While you are working the direct side of the street, also work the other side by hitting all of the banks which do loan on the SBA guarantee program. When you get a turn-down from one of these institutions, get it in writing and add it to your file in the SBA so that they know that you are actively searching for funds.

Step Seven: As you search for funds on both sides of the SBA street, continue to turn cash and show fiscal responsibilities. Each month, bring your latest financial reports down to the bank loan officers to prove to them that you are a good risk. After a few months, these officers will grow interested in you or get tired of seeing you every month and will arrange for an SBA bank loan.

Step Eight: After one side of the street has been worked, continue to keep up your efforts on the other side. It may take several months more but of all of our clients which followed these steps, not one has yet failed to get loans from both sides.

CAMEO 11-1: WORKING BOTH SIDES OF SBA

A group of three engineers who were laid-off from the aerospace industry wanted to set up a game and toy manufacturing company. They needed, they felt, $80,000 in loans to attract $300,000 in venture capital investments on their terms. They followed the eight-step method outlined above and within four months received $65,000 in an SBA direct loan. Unfortunately, in the time length that they waited for this loan, the venture capital industry had changed significantly and their sources seemed to dry up. They therefore continued to work the bank side of the SBA street while they made their start-up produce $3,000 a month in profits. Within another five months, they managed to borrow $150,000 from a bank on an SBA guaranteed loan. With this money, they had little trouble attracting venture capital on their terms.

It should be pointed out that the engineers got a competent controller who spent all of his spare time in putting together this package. The controller averaged one hour a week in telephoning the SBA, he averaged two hours a week in visiting the eight banks they hoped to get loans from, and he averaged two hours a week re-doing the company's financial records to show their latest progress to both the bank and the SBA.

When this firm really got rolling, this controller refused to lose his contacts. In the last four years, this firm has received two more direct SBA loans, it now has a line of credit of $60,000, and though the company has gone through some agonizing problems, its sources for capital have never been hurt.

CAMEO 11-2: EDAs COMMUNITY PLAN
REQUIREMENT   M, IS, RS, F

We had a client who needed big money (approximately $6,500,000) to build a special sewage facility. This start-up had the technology of converting raw sewage into hydrogen and bypassing the methane stages. The process could take any organic material and generate pure hydrogen from it. The methane also thrown out would be used to power the plant and the excess could be used to generate power for other government facilities. The remainder of the sewage took the form of an extremely valuable white ash which could be used in road construction.

The founders developed a miniature desk top working prototype which generated approximately $10 worth of hydrogen a day from 2¢ in expenses. It was very dramatic, raised all kinds of interest, raised all kinds of talk, but not one thin dime in capital.

The founders decided to try for EDA funds. They located a county with all of the essential requirements except the county had never submitted a community plan. Therefore, EDA never visited the county. The founders requested that the county submit such a plan, in fact they offered to help the county write the plan. There was a lot of talk but no action. The founders therefore stated that they would write the plan for the county provided that they were placed first on its priorities' list. The county officials agreed.

The founders then went to all of the other countries in the state that had written a plan and borrowed their plans. Within two weeks, they had developed (plagiarized) a 1,100-page document, together with tables, graphs, and illustrations, that they knew would impress EDA. It did and within four days EDA officials were visitng the county officials. Unfortunately, the county officials had never even bothered to glance at their copies of the plan and therefore were totally in the dark about what they proposed for their county's future. The hoax was rapidly uncovered and EDA has yet to invest a nickle in the county.

It was a good try.

Minor Point 11-7: How to Build and Sustain Your Lines of Credit   M, IS, RS, F

First, realize that your lines of credit are with whatever firms that you do business and from whatever firms you borrow money. Every firm which sells you something on 30-day payment is giving you a 30-day loan at zero interest. The steps followed usually are:

(1)   Get off a COD basis as soon as you can with your major vendors.

(2)   Give your major vendors a whisper of your stock for extra "services rendered."

(3)   Give your vendors' controllers a whisper of your articles.

(4)   Give your vendors' salesmen a whisper of your stock.

(5)   Try to use steps 2–4 as a leverage to allow you to pay back after 30 days. (In many cases, 90 to 120 days are common because your firm is part of your vendors' families).

(6)   Introduce yourself to every bank loan officer that you can. Most of our clients have built up lines of credit with six or more banks.

(7)   Try to start with these loan officers by factoring your purchase

orders received. Initially they may send you to a factoring house, however after you gain the reputation of paying back your debts fast, they'll loan you money.

(8) Borrow up to your maximum and pay it back within days. After you have done this several times, you'll gain the reputation of being reliable.

(9) Keep your bankers informed of your progress and where you are going. Monthly reports do no harm.

(10) Show your appreciation to the loan officers. Tell them that you could never get where you are going without their help.

Minor Point 11-8: The Priorities of Payments   M, IS, RS, F

1st. Pay your bankers.
2nd. Pay other money loaners.
3rd. Pay your workers.
4th. Pay your other creditors.
5th. Pay yourself.

Example 11-2: Typical Loaded Questions Asked by Venture Capitalists   M, IS, RS, F

Before a venture capitalist will invest heavily in you, in your ideas, and in your abilities to convert your ideas into a viable company, he is going to get inside you to understand what makes you tick. Over the years, we have recorded several hundred loaded questions that our clients have been asked by capitalists to help the capitalists better understand the founders. Almost all negotiations included the following questions or variations of these questions.

(1) "Mister Jones, I am really impressed with you and your founders' abilities. You men would have no problems finding excellent jobs, would you?" After you assure him that you and your co-founders are the cream of the industry and would be welcomed with open arms in the best of companies, he'll counter with, "I know that you fellows are good. Tell me, what will keep you from throwing up your arms in frustration when the going gets tough and accepting one of those cushy, secure jobs? We, your investors, will then be left high and dry."

(2) "Mister Jones, I am really impressed with your business plan. I have a client who is looking to start-up his own firm and I know that he would be willing to pay you men at least $250,000 for your development. Shall I contact him and get you fellows together?" Or a variation of the above, "Mister Jones, I can see that you are far from a beginner as a man

of vision and a manager. I have a company, they make an entirely different product from the one that you propose, and I need a man of your abilities to run it. Would you accept a salary of say $50,000 a year, generous stock options, generous performance bonuses, and the usual fringe benefits such as country club, racquet club, company Cadillac, a half million in insurance, directors' meetings in the Bahamas, and so forth?"

If you think so little of your concepts as to sell out for peanuts, then why should he risk millions on you? You can bet your bottom dollars you are just being tested.

(3) "Mister Jones, I see where you and your co-founders have budgeted yourself for salaries of $50,000 a year. I also see where you are presently selling shoes at $6,000 a year. Could it be that you are trying to use me to pay for a significant promotion and pay raise?"

(4) "Mister Jones, I like everything that I see except two of your co-founders. You are extremely weak in both marketing and in finance. I (and my partners) are very interested in funding you except we want to replace these weak men with men of excellent qualifications. Do you object?"

Now this gambit is an extremely difficult one because as frequently as not, the investors are on the up and up and are not happy with your co-founders. They of course will not invest until they are satisfied that you have the horses to do the job. Therefore, if you agree with their evaluation that these particular co-founders are weak, you might agree to interview their particular candidates. On the other hand, if you are positive that you have selected extremely qualified and sound co-founders for the marketing and finance slots, you can be pretty positive that you are experiencing a trick question. You are being tested to show the investors that you have complete confidence in your co-founders. If you don't show this confidence in your own people, how can you expect the investors to put their dollars on these men?

(5) This isn't a question but very frequently occurs in negotiations. It's called the "Old Money Is Less Valuable Than Toilet Paper" routine. It's a long monolog which usually starts with something like this, "What this world needs is a medical instrument like you fellows have developed far more than me keeping a lousy two million dollars tucked away in my bank account doing nothing. You men are true explorers conquering new horizons and do I envy you . . . all I have ever done is inherit money from a rich father who inherited money from his father who inherited money from his father who was a pirate." This monolog usually progresses into areas about you developing new and meaningful challenges for thousands of workers, into you developing a company from scratch that will have really meaningful value for generations to come, and all you need is for the unworthy leeching venture capitalists to continually fill your pipelines with old worthless money. If you are wise, you'll let the monolog progress without ever agreeing that money isn't a very important commodity. Fi-

nally, when you feel the monolog stretching a bit too thin, interrupt the speaker with a statement like, "Sir, I am very concerned that we have a serious philosophical difference concerning money. Money has always been a very important thing to me and it will always be important to me. Ours will be a profit making company and as long as I am around, we are going to be a profit maximizing company. Every man selected for our team had to show a great deal of fiscal responsibility and respect for profits. What you say has validity in all aspects except profits. We are plowing new ground, we are building something of real value, we are going to be an industry leader, but first and foremost, we are going to make profits. If you disapprove of this practice, please tell us now so that we can search for another venture capital firm which approves of our goals!"

(6) While we are on the subject of monologs, realize that venture capitalists are past masters at spotting the co-founder who is on an ego trip, the snow artist, the dreamer, and the actor. If these types are holding relatively unimportant positions, it isn't too bad as long as they know that you know how to handle them. When they suspect that a founder isn't all that he purports, expect to see the old "let's inflate him and then puncture him" gambit. If you have any co-founders who are vulnerable to flattery, take them to the side before the negotiations begin and tell them of their problem. If you spot them falling into the trap during the presentation and the capitalists start the flattery process, then you do the puncturing before the man can be blown too large and cause an explosion when he pops. As soon as the capitalists see that you are aware of the problem and can control it, it then becomes a minor problem to them.

(7) I have yet to know of one capitalist investing into anything without first testing for ethical standards. There are perhaps three hundred basic questions with perhaps a thousand variations of each, so the list is too long to present, however the following combination will give you an idea of what to expect.

"I'm darned interested in investing in you men. There are just two favors that I want to ask. The first is, since I have to talk both of my partners (Sid and Harold) into matching my investments, I don't want egg all over my face when you fellows make errors. Therefore, I don't want you to ever tell them anything until I see it first and have the chance of filtering what they need to know. My second request is personal and no one is to know about it except you and me. You see, I have a worthless brother-in-law (and here he will tell you how this boob made so many blunders in life) who is just opening an electronics supply house. I'd appreciate it if you would let this dud quote on all of your electrical quotations. You don't have to give him much . . . just say half of your electrical purchases. If he is high in his quotes, you might let him see what everyone else is quoting and then he'll lower his bid . . . you know, the old last-look routine that everyone uses. Would you fellows do these two small favors for me?"

You can bet your bottom dollar that there is no brother-in-law and if there are a Sid and Harold, you can bet that this man tells them everything. Realize that once the capitalists invest in you, they are extremely vulnerable to your ethics and values. They have to trust you completely before they will invest.

(8)   The old life-style gambit is always used. Though most start-up founders are energetic and hungry in the early stages of the start-up, many become lazy and self-satisfied when their companies really get into the black. As stated earlier, many failures occur because of this syndrome. How long will you and your co-founders stay hungry after your company breaks into the black? Expect to see many searching questions, many pointed monologs, and many tricks to determine when you and your fellow founders will become satisfied men and slow down. Questions like, "What do you want from this thing that we call life ?"; "When will you want to sell your company and retire?"; "What are you going to do when you retire?"; "What epitaph do you want printed on your gravestone?" etc. If you are wise, you will not give glib answers but will reply, "I don't know, all my interests have been in building this company into something of real value. I'll worry about my retirement 20 years from now."

(9)   Throughout this whole negotiating process, the capitalists continually evaluate how enthusiastic you and your fellow workers are about your start-up. Before every negotiation, if you feel your enthusiasms dwindling, psych yourself up and review your objectives (both personal and company).

Minor Point 11-9: The EDA Offices   M, IS, RS, F

Like any government agency, EDA funding varies greatly within its various areas in funds available, competition for those funds, and priorities and objectives. In all probability, you will be interested in relocating to the areas which will fund you with major dollars at attractive long-range and low-interest rates. The following addresses will help you in determining which EDA area is best for your start-up.

ATLANTIC: 320 Walnut Street, Philadelphia, Pennsylvania 19106. Serves: Connecticut, Washington D.C., Maine, Maryland, Massachusetts, New Hampshire, New Jersey, New York, Pennsylvania, Puerto Rico, Rhode Island, Vermont.
MIDEASTERN: 517 Ninth Street, Chafin Bldg., Huntington, West Virginia 25701. Serves: Kentucky, North Carolina, Ohio, Virginia, West Virginia. Note: The Mideastern Area has received more funding than all of the other areas combined because of Appalachia's war on poverty. Their average loan is 2.75 times larger than the other areas' average loans.
SOUTHEASTERN: 904 Bob Wallace Avenue, Acuff Building, Huntsville, Alabama 35801. Serves: Alabama, Florida, Georgia, Mississippi, South Carolina, Tennessee.

MIDWESTERN: 32 Randolph Street, Chicago, Illinois 60601. Serves: Illinois, Indiana, Iowa, Michigan, Minnesota, Missouri, Nebraska, North Dakota, South Dakota, and Wisconsin.

SOUTHWESTERN: 702 Colorado Street, Austin, Texas 78701. Serves: Arizona, Kansas, Louisiana, Nevada, New Mexico, Oklahoma, Texas, Utah, and Wyoming.

WESTERN: 415 First Avenue, North, Seattle, Washington 98109. Serves: Alaska, California, Hawaii, Idaho, Montana, Oregon, Washington, and Samoa.

Recently, we have had several clients explore getting loans through several area offices at the same time. By approaching several offices at the same time, they hoped to attract their needed capital from whichever area had the money available for loans. Though all loans are cleared through a central office in Washington D.C., these start-ups have been relatively successful in getting through the preliminary stages to determine if an area office will fund them. They will of course relocate willingly to the first area which grants them their needed cash.

EDA is also a past master at lowering the amounts of their loans. In almost every case where a start-up has requested $X in loans, EDA begins negotiations with X-Y dollars. When the loan is finally approved, it is for considerably less then even X-Y dollars. However, if it is for well over $1,000,000 with excellent interest rates and unbelievable pay-back schedules, it is worth the headaches.

Minor Point 11-10: Using Study Grants as Your Funding Source   M, IS, RS, F

We have had two clients who were addressing medical instrumentation use this avenue with foundations to attract their capital. However, both start-ups had significant breakthrough products and though the funds were for feasibility studies, the foundations and the start-ups were pretty darned certain that the concepts were feasible long before funds were granted.

We have several scientists who are attempting to raise grant money from our government. These scientists write proposal after proposal to the various departments of our government with varying levels of results. One client averages three proposals a week and to date has received $63,000 on two accepted proposals. Research work keeps the founders alive while they are trying to make their company profitable. Another start-up included a great deal of proprietary information in one of its proposals. Since the proposal was unsolicited and was for considerable dollars, the department decided to go out for competitive bids. The proprietary information was passed along to all bidders.

A third client has worked the city and county departments with a great deal of success. In 22 unsolicited proposals and 8 solicited proposals, these people have hit on 6 awards totalling over $310,000. The key to their success is their timing. They always tend to put in an avalanche of unsolicited proposals towards the end of the fiscal year. All proposals are "modularized" so that the department can accept all or any part of any proposal. The reader should also be aware that this group spends a considerable percentage of their sales reserves in proper entertainment and other legal gifts to purchasers.

12 · The Entrepreneur Profile

PROLOGUE   M, IS, RS, F

We are all encumbered with preconceived notions of what personal profiles should fit what profession. Frequently we try to force the individual to conform to our mental stereotypes instead of seeing the individual for what he is.

Venture capitalists are no different from the rest of us. They have preconceived opinions on entrepreneur stereotypes and they like to see founders fit this profile before they invest their dollars in the man, his ideas, and his capabilities.

It therefore helps to know what profiles most venture capitalists like to see before you begin negotiating. It is the intent of this chapter to give you three brief profiles and then give you an insight into several successful entrepreneurs' profiles.

THE ENTREPRENEUR PROFILE AS SEEN BY THREE VENTURE CAPITAL GROUPS

There are probably as many entrepreneur profiles as there are venture capital groups, however, if you look closely, you'll observe a sameness, a common ground in the points necessary for success. The following three profiles were gathered from three venture capital groups which specialize in start-up and first-round financing. All three groups have offices within two blocks of each other and all three have several success stories behind them.

VENTURE CAPITAL GROUP ONE   M, IS, RS, F

"Ninety percent of the start-ups that we invest in are ramrodded by individuals who have either a bachelor's degree in engineering or no degree at all. Mechanical engineers and electronic engineers seem to have the entrepreneur bug more than any other profession. I wish we saw more chemists, more scientists, and more bachelor of arts graduates. We notice the following characteristics in those we invest in:

1.   They are darned honest with themselves. If there is a problem, they tend to get it out in the open fast and then stick with it until it is solved.

2.   If you look at their high school and college transcripts (we always do), you would notice that they either get A's or D's in everything. They work hard in what they consider important and ignore the other courses. A typical freshman transcript might be: Math–A, Physics–A, Chemistry–A, History–D, Philosophy–D, and English–B.

3.   They usually get frustrated after they have worked for a very large company for a couple of years. They grow less tolerant with mediocrity, slowness, inefficiency, and dishonesty as they grow older and most either quit or have been fired with fireworks from at least two companies.

4.   They all seem to have high energy levels. Working hard is fun and a way of life.

5.   Most have deep interests in the aspects of their lives over which they have control and tend to shun all subjects over which they have no control.

6.   All have a high degree of self confidence and all religiously follow their own standards.

7.   All want to gain control of their own destinies. This is probably the greatest prime mover of their inner selves. However, if you gave them complete control over their own time and finances, they would work as hard as they do today.

8.   Almost all have been married and have large families. Approximately half have been divorced. The other half have wives that they either totally dominate or totally ignore.

9.   All are extremely organized, communicate well, and delegate authority well.

10.   All are extremely goal directed.

11.   All love challenge, problems, and addressing new fields. Though almost all dislike routine tasks, they perform them until cash flows allow them to hire assistants.

12.   Almost all place complete confidence in their fellow founders and support them well. Once a founder loses this confidence or violates this trust, fireworks begin.

13.   All have an extremely low tolerance level with failure. Success is the only acceptable criteria.

14.   None will tolerate dishonesties of any nature.

15.   Most consider money as only a tool with which to accomplish goals and never an end in itself. Because of this characteristic, tight financial controls and continuous monitoring is needed.

16.   Almost none feel that they need any support from us other than cash injections. Almost all need from 5 to 20 man hours a week from our staff for their first two years.''

VENTURE CAPITAL GROUP TWO   M, IS, RS, F

''Most of those founders we invest in are extremely mature individuals. Almost all have at least masters degrees and many either have doctorate degrees or were well on their way to a doctorate degree before they decided to start their own firm. I've noticed the following characteristics in those founders whom we support:

1.   The leader is a true researcher and a perpetual student. He probably invests two hours a day in broadening his foundations.

2.   He usually became an entrepreneur by accident. Since the company for whom he worked would not or could not use the results of his research, he felt that he had to start his own firm so that he could continue his work.

3.   The man is a professional problem solver. The man has a great deal of common sense and though he may not have in-depth experience in all his start-up's disciplines (marketing, administration, manufacturing), he can usually see through a smoke screen and address a problem fast.

4.   He is extremely honest and has a built-in radar which warns him when others are being less than honest.

5.   He is usually either a bachelor or happily married. Many have wives who are dynamic, active, and interesting people. They expect their wives to run their end properly and be an inspiration to their successes.

6.   Most average one movie every two years, watch television perhaps an hour a week, and read trade journals perhaps 10 hours a week.

7.   Many are true introverts and must make major efforts to fulfill their entrepreneuring obligations. Though they must lead, they are not true leaders and will step down from the presidency when a natural leader emerges.

8.   Most do not care if you like them, however they work very hard to gain your respect.

9.   Most do not appreciably change their at-home life styles. They continue to live in middle class suburbs, drive their old cars, have low-key entertainment needs, and even their food and bar budgets remain low after they are wealthy.

10.   Almost all have excellent references. They have always been well liked and respected by their old bosses, peers, and subordinates.

11.   All show a great deal of empathy and understanding for those who work with them and for them. Though they don't demand, they expect and usually get professionalism and efforts from everyone on the start-up team.

12.   Honesty is an important attribute for all team members.

13.   All have a great deal of fiscal responsibility and tend to be too frugal in their cash disbursements. They therefore need a great deal of supervision and monitoring to make certain that they do not stunt their company's growth for lack of spending.

14.   Almost all need a great deal of encouragement and support during the first two years of their start-up.''

VENTURE CAPITAL GROUP THREE   M, IS, RS, F

''During the past 10 years, our firm has always selected scientific-manufacturing firms as start-up investments. Though we are changing our objectives now and beginning to invest in leisure, in television programming, and in other low-technology growth areas, our experience has always been with the scientist entrepreneur. We usually see the following characteristics in those founders in whom we invest.

1.   They were entrepreneurs by nature and scientists and engineers by accident. Most had developed a track record from the time they were eight years old and carried it well until now. As an example, at eight they had a paper route. The route started with perhaps 80 papers and by the time they quit, the route was up to 200 papers. In college, they probably had two minor jobs and several personal profit centers to keep them in cash.

2.   Most of them hated the large companies for which they worked. They jumped jobs from company to company until they matured enough to ask themselves, 'What's this thing called life all about?' They wanted to build a company that was lean, hungry, and flexible. They did and are running the britches off of their old companies.

3.   Many had taken 'flyers' on other start-ups. They did things wrong and got an excellent education on how to do things right.

4.   All are extremely honest with themselves and will not tolerate untruthfulness or dishonesty from anyone on their team.

5.   All expect problems and cure the problems' causes fast.

6.   Half married weak and either tolerate their wives or have gotten divorces. The other half have fulfilling home lives.

7.   All enjoy their work days and tend to put too many hours in at the plant. Those with children have problem children because of this neglect.

8.   All are extremely organized and take pride in their ability to get 16 hours work done in just 10 hours.

9.   All are self-confident and fast learners.

10.   Most are natural leaders who get a real kick out of life. They are fun people to be around.

11.   Almost all had a personal hero from the time they were very young. They imitate this hero. The heroes usually are: their fathers, their father's boss, a teacher or a scout leader.

12.   A large percentage prefer one-to-one sports over team sports. They prefer to be active in these sports instead of spectators. Winning is important.

13.   All communicate well and a significant number would probably like to teach someday.

14.   Almost all have a real zest for life and enjoy all of life's aspects. They tend to overdo everything (drive too fast, eat too fast, play too hard).

15.   Most consider profits as their essential measurement of performance. During the early stages of their company's development, negative cash flows make them impatient. Most tend to search for other avenues of cash flow so that their performances will appear better. This is allright if they don't dilute their efforts in their main projects. We have to discourage petty profit centers during the early stages.

16.   Patience is not their long suit. Usually, it takes twice as long to get a start-up in the black as most entrepreneurs project and this drains an impatient man's energies. Usually, the venture capitalist's role is to hold a start-up back instead of driving it to meet milestones. Premature products, half-developed services, and impatient decisions can really hurt a company.

17.   Actually, we usually have problems with too much (instead of too little) fiscal responsibility with most of the start-ups that we sponsor. Contingency reserves are intended to be spent when contingencies arise. We have to exert pressures to force our clients to spend these reserves.

18.   All of our clients tend to keep us overinformed instead of hiding things from us. They all have pro-active control systems which flag problems before they occur and they continually tell us of pending problems and their options for solving them. If we so much as miss a week in visiting them, they become concerned and visit us.

19.   Oddly, our relationships do not cease when we sell our interests in our start-ups. Our clients still request that we sit on their boards and they continue to come to us for management aid. They seem to want us to remain close friends even after they sell their interests and look for new opportunities.

20.   Most of our clients are very stable and extremely likeable people. One of the biggest fringe benefits of being a venture capitalist is that we have an active role in helping very worthwhile people grow and meet their life's needs. It sounds 'corny' but it is a very real thing.''

CAMEO 12-1: THE "HAVE TO MAKE IT OR ELSE" ENTREPRENEUR'S PROFILE   M, IS, RS, F

While in Korea, his father died, and fourteen months later (as he was mustering-out of the Marines) his mother was killed in an auto accident. This 21-year-old man inherited two kid sisters (ages 15 and 17), the family home (a large framed building located in the decaying part of the city that was appraised at $11,000), a bank balance of $485, and little else. The man had to see his sisters through college, wanted desperately to use his GI Bill to get a college education himself, and had to keep the remainder of his family a true family until his sisters married. But how could he do it with the things at hand? Here is what he did.

With his mustering-out pay and personal savings, he bought excellent bone china and silverware, complete linen supplies, every exotic-foods cookbook he could find, and restaurant-grade kitchen equipment. It was his intent to have his family live in the upstairs rooms of the house, convert the downstairs into a restaurant, have everyone go to school every day, spend their afternoons preparing a twelve-course exotic dinner (and studying while the sauces steeped), attract the carriage trade (the only segment which could afford the prices that he had to charge to make ends meet) into the decaying neighborhood, and make darned certain that his family remained close while his sisters finished high school, got their college educations, and got all of the necessities of life.

The concept of failure never occurred to the man. This was the only way open to him and his family and therefore it had to work. And work it did. Halfway through his first semester, they were booked every weekend and three-quarters filled every week night. By the end of his freshman year, the complete downstairs was filled every night and his customers were beginning to make appointments several weeks in advance. That summer vacation, the man reconverted the downstairs so that they could accommodate two catered parties and handle 10 tables of walk-in traffic. There was money left over to assure that the older sister could enter college.

By the end of his sophomore year, his two catered dining rooms were booked five weeks in advance and his home restaurant was averaging $600 a week in profits. That summer vacation, he moved his family into a "proper" home, converted his upstairs into small intimate dining rooms, and started an outside catering service (he hired college buddies to conduct these catered parties with the exotic food his restaurant prepared). When the second sister entered college, there were ample funds for all three students to not only realize the necessities but to enjoy a few niceties such as cars, trips, and tutors.

Since things were going well and he wanted to keep constant supervision over his younger sister while she was in college, he decided to get a masters degree and graduate with his younger sister. He then hoped to sell everything and get a proper job like every other college graduate. When he neared the completion of his MBA degree, he started interviewing with every major company that came onto campus. He got no job offers. Who would hire a man at $850 a month when that candidate was accustomed to moonlighting and making over $8,000 a month? Though this man never was hired by anyone, today he owns five firms, is a venture capitalist who helped over 30 start-ups, is an uncle of 12 children, and lives the life style he enjoys. He hasn't cooked a meal in 15 years, hates exotic food with a passion, and almost never eats out. He selects only start-ups who have founders who can't afford to even think of failure. "Success must be a matter of life and death to them," he says.

CAMEO 12-2: BACK TO OUR OKIE MECHANIC, PART 2
M, IS, RS, F

In 1943, a major eastern manufacturer decided to open a sheet metal manufacturing division in Tulsa. It built a half-million-dollar facility which was to produce war time consoles. All went well until the end of the Second World War. At the height of production, over 300 factory workers were employed. However, when the war time contracts began to peter out in 1945, profits dropped drastically, and by 1946, this division had 60 employees and was hopelessly in the red. Finally, the decision was made to sell the facilities, lay-off its employees, and close the division.

The Chamber of Commerce approached our Okie mechanic and asked him to try to save the factory. He visited the plant and saw one of the most modern sheet metal facilities in the Southwest. It seemed a shame to close the plant, so he negotiated an agreement where he would pay 90% of the value of the equipment (10% down and 5% per year for 18 years at zero interest). He then called the 60 production workers who remained and asked them to stay on at $200 a month and split the profits. Forty-five agreed.

The strange part of this case was the mechanic really didn't have the foggiest idea of what they should produce. He only knew that sheet metal was used in a lot of ways and this plant had the best equipment available. He had a hunch that they could locate a lucrative market.

Initially, they decided to produce pick-up truck utility bodies (tool boxes that mount on the sides of a small truck). Since they had no experience in this market, he bought several units made by competition and copied and improved upon them. Within three months, the small plant was selling 200 truck boxes a month and was making a modest profit. Within a year, they were producing 2,500/month and every employee was making $200/month in salary and $400/month in profit sharing. However, at the end of the first year, the mechanic's production equipment was only being used to 20% of capacity, so he looked for another product.

He decided to open a second company which would utilize the production equipment from 8:00 p.m. to 5:00 a.m. It was to be a modularized cabinet shop for industry. They built chassis for electronics manufacturers, they built metal kitchen cabinets, they built control consoles, and finally they went into instrument housing in a big way. Though it took this new company seven months to get into the black, it turned out to be the fifth largest industrial cabinet manufacturer within just six short years.

However, the plant's facilities still weren't being used completely. Both companies still only used less than 60% of the equipment's capabilities, so a third company was born. This company utilized dirt-cheap war surplus electric motors for truck-mounted cranes. The average motor and gear train cost them less than $10, while the completed cranes sold for from $1,000 to $3,500. Within two years, all three companies utilized the equipment to approximately 85% of capacity six days a week, 24 hours a day. Though the three firms did not equal the drilling rig profits, they did contribute approximately $4,000,000 a year. Not bad for a $500,000 investment spread out over 18 years.

When the mechanic died in the early 1960s, his will gave his employees the option of buying all the stock from their profit sharing earnings. Over 500 employees paid the mechanic's family $500,000 a year for five years. It was a bargain for everyone involved.

Minor Point 12-1: Our Okie Mechanic as an Entrepreneur
M, IS, RS, F

For this book, I filled out a resume of our Okie mechanic and sent it to the three firms that gave us an entrepreneur's profile. The resume would appear to the uninformed as a terrible resume. The man couldn't read or write, he had a second grade education, he was highly opinionated, he lacked most of the social skills (he never could master which fork or spoon to use), and though he pioneered many of the management systems that we use today, on paper he looked like a darned poor risk. I was certain that all of the entrepreneur firms would dismiss his resume in seconds and that I could report this in this chapter.

The funny part about it is that all three firms said that from the information they were given, they felt our oil field mechanic would make real money for whoever invested in him. Though none of the three venture capital companies were interested in funding his fictionalized start-up (I had to invent a cover story so that they wouldn't realize that they were being tested), the only reason that they declined was because they weren't interested in the oil industry as investment property.

So, you're wise to conclude that venture capitalists are pretty good judges of horse flesh and are not easily distracted by the meaningless qualities that are so frequently considered important by employment departments.

CAMEO 12-3: THE CRUSTY GRANDMOTHER   M, IS, RS, F

She is a crusty old lady of 84 today, but she has led quite a life. Born to moderate wealth, this lady attended the proper finishing schools, married the owner of a small cabinet factory, had three children, and lived the life of a typical housewife until the great depression of the 1930s wiped her husband out. I think her own words tell her story beautifully.

"I was a middle aged woman who had no practical knowledge when my husband's firm went bankrupt. I didn't know anything about anything except that if we were going to survive, I had to start humping fast. At first, I tried the usual stupid things that the ladies of those days always tried. I took in washing, I ironed, I sewed, and I tried to do a dozen other things that everyone in those rough days did for themselves, and I therefore failed. Then I decided to start using my finishing school education by tutoring children in their school subjects, I taught dancing, I taught the social graces, and I taught music. At 25¢ a lesson, I earned over $10 a week and then knew that we were going to make it. Ten dollars went a long way in 1930. Then my husband, Charlie, found a job that paid $35 a week and we had a cash surplus! Then I started tutoring Latin and French (at 35¢ a lesson) and we were absolutely wealthy.

"I always loved music and spent a great deal of my earnings on sheet music. In those days, a popular song's sheet music sold for 5¢ and unpopular and old songs sold for a penny. Over the years I built quite a library of sheet music. I then formed a mandolin orchestra, an all girls' jazz band, a swing-time choral and instrument group. I started booking them in all the towns within a hundred mile radius and earned another $20 a week. Then a music store owner who hired all three of my groups for a promotion went under before he paid us and Charlie and I bought him out for $832. We mortgaged our home, we borrowed from the bank, and we did everything we could to buy the place and stock it properly. Instead of just selling musical instruments and sheet music, we started stocking appliances. Radios were hitting in a big way and when our county got electricity, refrigerators and electric hand tools sold well. During the days, I manned the store while Charlie continued to work. Then in the evenings, I continued with my finishing school classes while Charlie and the children customized radio cabinets for our customers. When we finished paying off all of our debts and had pretty close to a thousand dollars in the bank, I heard about juke boxes and had a hunch they would help our record sales. I therefore spent everything to get the exclusive dealership in our three local counties and started putting juke boxes in every restaurant, ice cream parlor, and dance hall in the 11 towns in my three counties. I didn't know any better so I put the juke boxes in for free. For every nickle put in the machines, we got four cents and the restaurant owner got a penny. Now juke boxes in those days cost us $125 each (a small fortune). However, taking 80% of the take the way we did, they seemed to pay for themselves in just six short months. In the first three years that we had the exclusive franchise, we had installed over 1500 of them on our terms, paid off all debts, and were averaging $30,000 a month in profits. Now that wasn't hay in the depression years! Well, with that kind of money, we started going into business in a big way. We put up the first seven motels in our three counties, we built the first 11 drive-in movies in our counties, we bought exclusive distributorships in soft drinks, in beer, and in candy, and we were spread pretty thin. I made certain that my children ran some of these companies so that they wouldn't be as stupid as I was when they had to make ends meet.

"Well, the children grew up, went off to proper schools, married, and moved away to live their own lives. Charlie then died and I found myself 63, tired, old, and running 19 companies. So I got a good lawyer, transferred a lot of the ownership to my children, then sold the whole works and decided to retire. In six months, I aged 10 years so I decided that if I were going to live, I had better get off of my backsides and start humping again. . . only this time on a smaller scale.

"Remember the library of sheet music I told you about? Well, when Mr. Xerox came out with his copying machine, I decided to sell copies of my library at 25¢ a song. I put ads in music magazines and every month, I get from 6,000 to 12,000 requests for old sheet music from all over the world. My employees are my grandchildren. Each month, each gets $50 spending money and $150 in a trust fund for their college educations.

"This little company is fine but it was too easy and it didn't keep me occupied. So I went into partnership with my grandchildren in the vending machine business. We have school names printed on ball point pens and pencils and sell these and other items in vending machines on the school campuses. It may sound silly, but this little company is now on 1300 campuses and though we split the profits with the schools, each of those vending machines makes us over $10 a month. My grandchildren, the oldest one is 16 and the youngest is 2, have a tax problem. Every one of them that is over 6 has been bitten by the ownership bug and will have a pretty good appreciation of their own value when they go out into the world.

"I'm now playing with a new idea that is going to be fun. It's a mail order education kit which parents can buy to set up their children in business. If a child can earn just $50 a month before he is 10, then he'll always understand profits and will have the confidence in himself to take a chance on his abilities once in awhile."

13 • Venture Capital Appetite-Whetting Techniques

PROLOGUE   M, IS, RS, F

It is important to whet your investors' appetites prior to seeking funds for the following reasons:

(1) If they want to invest in your start-up badly enough, they'll demand less equity and less management control.

(2) If the capitalists have several months to prepare for your money requests, they can put together a better package.

(3) Make no mistake, every venture capital firm is flooded with proposals. Of these proposals, only 5% are viable, only 2% are seriously considered, and only 0.5% are acted upon. You must be part of the 0.5%.

It is the intent of this chapter to give you some of the commonly used techniques of whetting capitalists' appetites. This will be a short chapter because once a technique becomes a standard, it loses its appetite-whetting effect and can hinder, instead of help, your cause. I sincerely hope that you use these techniques as a springboard to develop your own innovative and unique approaches.

COMMONLY USED APPETITE-WHETTING TECHNIQUES   M, IS, RS, F

TECHNIQUE ONE: MASS MAILING OF THE BUSINESS PLAN

This is a common technique used by the proposal mills. Every week, dozens of business plans are manufactured by these firms and mass mailing techniques are used. Most venture capital firms have nice form letters which they sign and mail to the founders. The letters are kind but the plans are rarely read. If the founders think so little of the confidentiality of their plan, then there must not be much of value in it so why invest the man hours essential to study it.

TECHNIQUE TWO: THE BROADCAST LETTER

This technique came into vogue in the mid-sixties and today almost 25% of the start-ups attempt to use it. Briefly, the broadcast letter is a personalized letter which utilizes the executive summary in its body.

As stated earlier, $X from one investment group is frequently worth $2X from another investor. This technique shows the capitalist that you are running your concept up the flag pole to see who salutes and that you aren't really interested in his firm for its unique capabilities. Therefore, you'll usually get the very kind form letter response and no further consideration.

TECHNIQUE THREE: BRING THE CAPITAL GROUPS IN FROM DAY ONE

So far, this technique has always worked. The venture capital groups are invited to your interactive testing and play a role in both this testing and selecting your founders. Since they were in from the conception, they'll be happy to offer you counseling throughout your development stages. When the time is prime for financing, they are usually ready.

TECHNIQUE FOUR: THE INTERVIEWING TECHNIQUE

Long before you are ready for financing, personally interview each capital firm as if that firm is going to be an integral part of your management team. Ask them penetrating questions to see how they will perform when problems arise. Then select the best and let them know that they have been chosen for their professionalism. Work them hard during your development stages and let them know months before you need their financing.

TECHNIQUE FIVE: BUSINESS PLAN COUNSELING

Get several venture capital groups to advise you in your marketing research and business plan development. Get their help in developing your projected financial reports. When your business plan is finally completed, you don't have to worry about them reading it. They'll know what your plan states long before the final draft is complete. As far as the integrity of your marketing research, they'll know how you ran it and what the customer demand is and therefore will accept your results with a minimum of auditing.

TECHNIQUE SIX: A COMBINATION OF TECHNIQUES THREE THROUGH FIVE

So far, every client who has combined the above three techniques has been successful in getting the money that he needs on the terms that he wants. In several cases where the initial venture capital firms couldn't participate, they introduced the founders to groups that were ethical and were interested.

TECHNIQUE SEVEN: OFFER THE RESEARCHERS KEY POSITIONS OR OTHER SWEETENERS

I hold my breath every time a client tries this because I believe this technique can boomerang, however it has worked well for four of our clients. As stated earlier, many researchers are interested in joining a start-up with major growth potentials. By offering these highly qualified people key management positions once your firm is capable of meeting their salary demands, you add an additional incentive for them to report in your favor.

Realize, however, that you are forcing a conflict of interest on the researcher and may thus justly have the whole thing explode in your face.

TECHNIQUE EIGHT: USE YOUR PEOPLE MIX TO ATTRACT

Get a Nobel prize winner, a respected author, a celebrity, a politician, or anyone else who would attract venture capitalists to join your board of directors. The capitalists enjoy hobnobbing with these people and will want to join your board.

I don't know exactly how valid this technique is, however we use it continually and find it helps.

TECHNIQUE NINE: USE YOUR INVESTMENT MIX TO ATTRACT

Use commitments from your investors to attract other investors. As an example: ''As you see from our plan, we need $850,000. The Bank of

America is loaning us $100,000 (on an SBA loan), Wells Fargo's SBIC division is investing $150,000, H&Q Investment Corp. is investing $150,000, IBM Corp. has agreed to sell our machines and apply their first $200,000 in commissions to our stock, and I think XYZ is going to exercise an option to buy $200,000 worth of shares. We are coming to you because these firms state that they work with you on other start-ups and that they would like to work with you on our company.''

Do you see the attractiveness of this approach? If IBM is going to sell your product, if Bank of America, Wells Fargo, H&Q, and XYZ have investigated your concepts and are committed, then it looks like a winner.

TECHNIQUE TEN: SELL THE VENTURE CAPITALIST ON YOUR PRODUCT

This is a limited technique but when you can apply it, it is very valuable. Make the capitalist see that you have made a significant breakthrough and that your product's value by itself will put your company on the ground floor of a major industry.

We had a client who "loaned" his word processing prototypes to several venture capital firms. Within three weeks, these firms had used the equipment so much that it became an essential part of their operations. They therefore knew that it would become a foundation piece of equipment for every company which generated a lot of paper. They invested on the founders' terms.

TECHNIQUE ELEVEN: TURN SIGNIFICANT CASH BEFORE SEEKING INVESTORS

Of the firms that invest in companies, only 10% will take a risk on a start-up whereas 60% will invest in a young company going out for first-round financing. By all means, go after the 10% but also start turning cash fast so that your company will give the image of an ongoing company. Once you can establish this image and prove that you have fiscal responsibility, then your venture will not have the high risks of just another start-up. You can raise twice as much money for one-half of the equity.

CAMEO 13-1: TURNING CASH IMMEDIATELY   M, IS, RS, F

A promising start-up had attracted 13 extremely powerful individuals to their original founders' team. They planned on manufacturing a small electronics module which could be installed on automobile radios and allowed the owners to broadcast over the emergency frequencies. The FCC had approved the concept because it would enable the motorist to swiftly summon help when necessary.

Now this team had three outstanding marketing men (average salary of $50,000/year) who were in the process of price testing, distribution testing, etc., while the others readied the module for production. While price testing, they ran into a poorly run "Ma and Pa" electronics store that was for sale. Since the store averaged less than $100 a day in sales and less than 20% profits, the sales price was low. They discovered some antique equipment buried in the store room which was worth five times the asking price. The other inventory was worth twice the asking price.

These men lined up a buyer for all of the merchandise, then bought the store, and sold the stock for a considerable profit. However, when they were finished, they owned an empty store. They then studied the nature of the store's neighborhood and decided to start up an extremely unique quick-service grocery store. Once the store got on its feet they intended to sell it and get back to their original plans. They stocked it (on credit), opened its doors, and started searching for a buyer. The store's sales swiftly jumped to $800/day and profits rose to 25%. The selling price of the store rose with the store's new value. These men then started practicing their industrial marketing principles on the store's neighborhood ("we really didn't expect much of an increase but we were having a lot of fun") and sales soared to $1,900/day and profits rose to 28%. The store's selling price rose accordingly and this young electronics company (still without a salable product) found itself permanently in the food retail business. There were no Ma and Pa buyers who could afford their sales price. Since running a store full time detracted from their other more lucrative efforts, they decided to turn over the operations to a college fraternity house on a split-the-profits basis. This unique store soon became the "in" place for the college, and sales and profits rose slightly and then maintained themselves. Every day the company's treasury was blessed with approximately $300 from his accidental profit center ($2000/day in sales at 30% profit, realizing $600 dividend with the students). The marketing men then realized that they had developed a viable business plan for other Ma & Pa operations and approached others with a let's-share-the-profits proposal. Several stores took them up on the offer and an additional $1,100 a day was realized by the start-up before their first electronics product was really ready for sales.

It took approximately 16 months for the founders to complete their module design, set up the production job-shops to produce it, set up a viable national sales network, and attract the $5,000,000 they needed. Just when everything appeared to be put together, the FCC reversed its original sanctions and outlawed the module. The FCC was rightly concerned about pranksters using the device to overload and jam the emergency networks.

The team would probably have splintered and the start-up folded had it not been for the $1,400/day in profits that continually came in. Today, the team is busy developing another product which should have much greater demand and be much more profitable than the original module. The team also now realizes in excess of $2000/day from the additional accidental profit centers that their marketing group developed.

There isn't one venture capital group that has "tracked" this team that isn't interested in investing in it. What image would you say this start-up projects to venture capitalists? An untested start-up that needs seed money, a risky first-round investment, a less risky second-round investment, or a relatively safe third-round investment? How advantaged will this team be in ownership negotiations?

CAMEO 13-2: CYCLE CITY   RS, F

Two men who were frustrated automobile mechanics were also cycle enthusiasts. They decided to quit their jobs and open a cycle accessory shop. Their procedure might interest you because they were so innovative in making their business go. They did the following:

(1) They located an abandoned gasoline service station and rented it at a very low lease/purchase price.

(2) In the station's glass office, they opened a mail order profit center. Their customers could browse through catalogs and magazines and fill out order blanks for anything they wanted. The partners would then order from the factory and realize approximately a 30% commission on almost no overhead.

(3) In two of their three bays, they opened a do-it-yourself bike garage. They rented space ($1/hour), hand tools (at nominal fees), a welder (at $10/hour), a paint shop ($10/hour), steam cleaning equipment ($5/hour), and some metal bending equipment. The mechanics supervised all repairs or did the work themselves at $20/hour. Though this profit center only brought in about $750 a month in direct rentals, it was responsible for approximately $1,200 a month in parts and accessory profits.

(4) In the third bay, they displayed the hottest accessories. Initially, they had to buy this inventory, however they soon figured a way to get it on consignment.

(5) These three profit centers kept the doors open, although by themselves they contributed to only a marginally profitable business. However, when the mechanics bought a moving van (at $1,200) and rebuilt it into a reliable vehicle (costs $400 in parts, labor was considered free), their business really took off.

They converted the interior of the van into a bike repair shop and started making the circuits of weekend bike meets. In Northern California there is at least one bike meet on 50 out of 52 weekends.

To the rear of the van, they attached a canvas tent which measures 50 feet by 18 feet. When they set up at a bike meet, they extend this tent and hold a miniature bike accessory convention. Each participating manufacturer displays his latest equipment.

This fifth profit center made the rest. Not only do manufacturers pay these men for their display booths (from $250 to $400 per month), they also pay the men commissions on everything they sell and encourage them to carry large inventories by giving them their parts on consignment. The mechanics' overhead is now approximately 8% of their gross sales, and last year their tiny business netted well over $150,000.

Please realize that these men could never have made it without thoroughly enjoying their work. They consider their vacations their weekend bike meets, they truly enjoy working with manufacturers in displaying new and unique equipment, and they enjoy their ability to instruct any bike enthusiast in repairing bikes. They average a 6-day week with 12- to 14-hour days. Though they now have 7 part-time employees, you'll never find their shop without at least one founder always present.

CAMEO 13-3: THE WEST COAST COLLATOR   IS, RS

In the early twenties, every slick magazine was printed in the east and their west coast distribution had to receive the printed sheets, collate them, staple them, and then distribute the magazines. Since each magazine had to set up its own collating capabilities, it was an expensive operation.

A man who was a collator for *Punch* decided to open his own company and service all of the slick magazines. He attracted two magazine publishers to his concept, hired 4 men (at 25¢ an hour) and opened his doors. Within 5 years, his tiny firm had 15 magazines and employed 11 men. Our entrepreneur then wrenched his back and had to trust his men to run things right while he was in traction. When he returned after three months of bed rest, he found everything proper so he took a month's vacation to regain his strength. Upon returning, he attempted to lift a heavy load and again ended up in traction for three months. This time his doctor told him he had to retire.

Since the collating firm would not sell for enough money to allow the man to retire with confidence, he approached his workers with the following proposal. "I'll turn over ownership to you if you will guarantee me and my wife $5,000 a year until we die." The bargain was made and this tiny company changed personality overnight. The 11 men were no longer employees. . . they were owners.

Though there was not a high school diploma in the bunch, the new owners developed the most highly automated collating and binding operation in the nation. Much of their equipment was engineered and built in their homes. They pioneered pneumatics in the magazine industry and developed a reliable paper counter which paid them significant royalties through the 1940s. By 1933, this company had well over 80 magazines which depended upon them for their west coast collations. At this time, when people were standing in bread lines, these nine men were each realizing $1,200 a year in salaries and $8,500 in year-end profit sharing. In 1940, the peak of their company's profits, each man and six of their sons were realizing the same $1,200 in salaries and $26,000 in profit sharing. In 1941, when the unions heard that this firm was paying their employees only $100 a month, they began to picket them to stop truck deliveries and to free the oppressed slaves. The firm held a vote to pay union wages, but voted a non-union shop by the vote of 16–0.

Until this company was sold in the mid-1950s, it was an extremely unique place. Every worker came to work at 6:30 in a Cadillac, carried his own brown-bagged lunch, worked without supervision until the day's job was done (regardless of how long it took) and then went home. In the 1940s, when the major magazines opted to collate and bind their magazines on the east coast and ship the completed magazines to their distribution, not one man panicked. The little firm just changed its customer base from magazines to mail order catalogs, soft-backed books, and government manuals. The firm always had a waiting list of relatives who wanted to work for them, it always had excellent credit, and it always had satisfied customers.

14 · Making Marketing Make Sense

PROLOGUE   M, IS, RS, F

Earlier in the book we heard the hackneyed expression, "Build a better mousetrap and the world will beat a path to your door." No notion in the world could be more false. Probably the biggest cause of start-up failures is that the founders understand neither marketing nor sales. Good marketing is a carefully orchestrated program, and before your company can realize its growth potentials, you had better learn to apply its principles.

Most logical people discover that they make excellent marketing managers because the discipline of marketing is a very logical process. Most of the marketing rules can be reduced to plain syllogistic reasoning (major assumption, minor premise, valid conclusion). It is the intent of this chapter to give you the bulk of these assumptions and premises and let the obvious conclusions jump off of the page at you. By presenting marketing in this manner, we can cover in a few short pages the same ground on which volumes have been written.

Realize that to cover the amount of ground that we need to cover, we are just going to present the rules and ignore the exceptions to the rules. However, to pirate a reliability engineer's verbiage, "If you utilize the following premises, you'll be 75% confident that they will work properly 80% of the time."

SECTION ONE: THE MAJOR AND MINOR PREMISES OF MARKETING

MAJOR ASSUMPTIONS   M, IS, RS, F

Assumption I:

The words "marketing" and "sales" are in no way interchangeable. "Sales" is a developed art form (a craft) whereas "marketing" is an acquired discipline (an inexact science). Marketing men must understand sales (though frequently they make lousy salesmen), whereas even good salesmen rarely understand marketing (though many of them think they do).

Assumption II:

Never address (attack) your market universally. Before you can intelligently lay out your marketing strategies, you must develop your markets' profiles. First, segment your market into its many basic components. Second, determine the personalities, the buying profiles, and the needs of each segment. Third, determine the potential profitability of each segment. Fourth, determine the distribution machinery available to your start-up and what is needed to set up, train, motivate, and sustain that distribution. When you have completed this assignment, you have laid the foundation for a successful marketing program.

Assumption III

The majority of American companies (your potential competition) have had their marketing managers come up through the sales ranks. Therefore, though these companies have excellent sales departments, they are usually extremely weak in marketing. This weakness makes their customer base vulnerable to your start-up.

Assumption IV

Most of the industrial giants have extremely slow reaction times. It will take their marketing vice president six months to a year to even learn that you exist, another six months to a year to track your performances, and another six months to two years to move their sluggish machinery into position to compete effectively against you. Therefore, your major competition will come from the lean and hungry smaller companies in the first three years of your operations.

Assumption V

Most companies try to make their market subservient to their company's needs instead of their company subservient to their markets' needs. This characteristic gives your start-up a red carpet pathway into their customer base.

Assumption VI

Your product's value (sales price) has nothing to do with your costs of producing it. Your sales price is totally a function of your product's value in the eyes of your customers. Too low a sales price is just as detremental to sales as too high a sales price.

Assumption VII

Your sales volume will be directly proportional to the number of effective sales calls made by your sales force. The firm that realizes 5,000 effective sales calls a week will realize 100 times more sales than the start-up that realizes only 50 effective calls a week.

Assumption VIII

It usually takes about four years and major dollars to set-up a nationwide direct factory sales network. The time and expenses involved in recruiting, training, motivating, and sustaining direct salesmen is extreme. It usually takes a salesman a year to even learn his territory.

Assumption IX

It usually takes minor dollars and approximately six months to establish a nationwide agent/representative/distributor network, properly train it, motivate it, and realize significant sales. Because of this attribute most start-ups usually go this route and then replace these networks when sales justify company salaried salesmen.

Assumption X

If ASSUMPTION IX is valid for your start-up, then your major competition (and therefore sales efforts) will be the other manufacturers (principals that these commissioned sales forces represent). The real battle line in your sales war will be to earn your fair share of their sales time. Your start up will go nowhere until you win this sales time battle.

Assumption XI

If you understand, accept, and utilize the above assumptions, you have a head start over 50% of the established companies and 80% of the other start-ups.

MINOR PREMISES   M, IS, RS, F

Before you can put the major assumptions to work, you must understand the salesman who will sell your product. Salesmen, as a species, are both valuable and vulnerable. Once you understand the salesman, realize what makes him tick, and understand the price that you and your founders must pay to motivate and sustain him, you have licked half of your marketing problems. Therefore, almost all of the minor premises are made on salesmen as a species.

Minor Premise I

Like Gaul, the catagory of sales must be divided into three parts. No one individual can operate effectively in more than one part because the techniques are so different. These parts are:

(1) *High Pressure or One-Shot Salesmen:* Used car salesmen, insurance salesmen, door-to-door salesmen, and tourist area salesmen fall into this classification. If your product or service is a single-shot type of sales call, this type of sales may be essential for success. Most companies that lean on this type of sales develop several dozen "canned approaches" which their salesmen must know before they are allowed to sell. They then swiftly categorize each potential customer and use the "canned approach" which they think will work best on that customer.

This type of salesman is usually a disaster in all industries which require return sales calls.

(2) *Order Takers:* Most reps, agents, industrial salesmen, distributor salesmen, and clerks fall into this category. This type of salesman cannot sell unless there is a definite demand. He usually wears extremely well with his customers and given enough time can build a large following. However, realize that this type of salesman is a real handicap to a start-up with an innovative or pioneering product because he doesn't usually sell until the customer is ready to buy.

(3) *True Sales Engineers:* This type of individual (usually 1% of the pack) truly engineers your sales. He thrives on evaluating his customers' needs, tailoring your products or services to answer those needs, focuses his customers' appetites to want these solutions, closes the sales, and then services these sales closures.

The sales life expectancy of this type of individual is usually very short because the man either is pirated by his principals or customers, decides to start his own agency or rep firm, or degenerates into either of the other sales classifications if his principals can't keep him challenged with new products or customer problems.

If you can find one of these individuals to become your sales manager and have at least one in every agent/rep/distributor that you sign up, you'll be assured of swiftly progressing beyond the pioneering phase of marketing.

Minor Premise II

Salesmen tend to sell what sells easily. As a start-up, you're going to have to overcome this characteristic with techniques that we'll discuss later.

Minor Premise III

Salesmen are interested in gross sales, not net profits. Recognize this characteristic if you promote a sales type to marketing manager.

Minor Premise IV

Salesmen develop an uncanny ability to read their customers' minds and tell them what they want to hear. This is not a characteristic that they can turn on and turn off at will. Therefore, it will carry over into their dealings with you. The firm that leans only on their salesmen for sales forecasting, market testing, and customer feedback is vulnerable.

Minor Premise V

Agencies, manufacturers' representatives, and distributors feel that it is just as important to keep their principals (your start-up) sold as it is to keep their customers sold. Too many firms that were doing excellent sales work for their principals lost their principals by overlooking this minor premise. Therefore, if you get the best and most professional firms to sell for you, expect a significant number of smoke screens to keep you sold. You'll receive considerable amounts of busy work, glowing reports, and flack to keep you happy.

Minor Premise VI

Most salesmen have their pet accounts which they guard with their lives. They will not jeopardize their status in these accounts by introducing a new product or principal (this is *you,* until you earn their complete confidence).

Minor Premise VII

There are approximately 20 basic sales closes with perhaps a thousand variations of each. With the exception of high pressure salesmen, most salesmen know only four closes and practice only two. It is a profitable practice to go through these sales closes and their variations to determine which are acceptable to your product (or service) and to your company's image. You will probably select five basic closes with several hundred variations of each. Then train your salesmen in their use.

Minor Premise VIII

Most outstanding salesmen (approximately 2% of the pack) are relatively unstable individuals. Since one of these men is worth five adequate salesmen or 10 average salesmen, it behooves you to recognize the unstable characteristics and compensate for them. Examples:

(1) Most have extremely high drive and energy levels. They can sustain a 15-hour workday for weeks on end. Then they tend to "short circuit" until their body catches up with the drive. Learn to spot this short circuit cycle before it occurs and force the man to take off a few days until the cycle is over.

(2) They must sell all of the time. If they aren't selling customers, they

are selling you, their wives, or the nearest waitress. They are always "on stage" to prove themselves.

(3)   Though they appear to have a great deal of self confidence, they require continued adoration, attention, and respect. When you stop giving it to them, they'll look for another principal to fill this ego need.

(4)   Most have very little business sense (though they talk a good game). Though most make a great deal of money, they handle it poorly. They tend to spend for luxury items such as large houses, swimming pools, cars, or the latest clothing styles, and ignore the basics such as savings for childrens' educations or proper insurance. They tend to invest in the high-risk areas.

(5)   They need to dominate. Most either have subservient wives or are divorced.

(6)   They feel a definite need to leave permanent milestones for followers to admire. If they sell you on an idea or concept, they will knock themselves out to make certain that their customers buy your products which fill that concept.

(7)   Most are continuously looking for an employer who satisfies their inner needs. They'll change companies frequently in search of an ideal employer. However, once they think they have located the right chemistry, they'll stay forever.

(8)   These talented and unstable individuals will meet your sales quotas if you and your co-founders are willing to pay their emotional prices.

Minor Premise IX

Almost all new salesmen and many old timers feel very alone when they work their territories. Remember, when a salesman walks through your customer's doors, he sees dozens of people who seem to oppose his effort to sell your products. All that he has on his side is his briefcase.

If you can give him the feeling that you and your company are walking in spirit with him, that you are as close as the nearest telephone, that if he sells your product it will work reliably and make his next call on the customer easier, then he'll fight your sales battle rather than another principal's battle.

Minor Premise X

A salesman needs to feel that he knows more about what he is selling than the person to whom he is selling. This is so basic but so often overlooked. If a salesman just sells to purchasing departments, then his level of technical knowledge can be rather shallow, but if you want him to penetrate deeper to sell the design engineers, the manufacturing personnel, the research scientists, or top management, then your depth-of-training needs are multiplied. Salesman training is a never ending, ongoing process.

Minor Premise XI

Once a salesman gains experience in his territory and really penetrates his accounts, the "All Alone Syndrome" described in MINOR PREMISE IX is usually replaced with the "customer is my family" syndrome. The customer, who is just a name, a purchase order, and a set of problems to you, is truly family to him. He knows his customers well, knows their personal problems, has empathy with their goals, wants to satisfy their needs, and wants them to succeed. This is exactly the attitude that you want your salesmen to have.

Since he is now helping his family instead of selling them, you hurt your cause with non-performance, poor quality, late shipments, or broken promises on your part, or a "let's single-source the bastard and shaft him" attitude toward the customer. Realize the major incentive here is to help friends and then fill that incentive.

Minor Premise XII

All salesmen consider themselves true professionals and expect to be treated with professionalism. They have long memories of broken promises, silly blunders, alibies, and a "let's shaft the customer" attitude. Most good salesmen hate to be put in the position where they have to tell a lie to cover for you. They'll cover for you once to save their reputation with their customer but then they'll sell another principal until you reprove yourself.

Minor Premise XIII

Adequate salesmen (approximately 75% of the pack) develop a sales rhythm during their prime selling hours (8:30–3:00 in industrial sales). This sales rhythm allows them to meet their effective sales calls objectives. If your sales program complements this essential rhythm, they will work hard for you. If your program is not in harmony with this rhythm, expect to be ignored.

Minor Premise XIV

Salesmen like to sell. They do not like to be delivery boys, bad debt collectors, equipment installers, repairmen, or a host of other things that many principals request. Not only do these extra assignments break their sales rhythm described above, but also realize that you are forcing your sales people to become legal agents representing your company in areas where they aren't trained. If they make a mistake, you are liable.

A good commissioned salesman makes between $18,000 and $50,000 a year in commissions. This means that they must average between $4,000 and $10,000 a day in sales. They can't do it if you rob their time for other duties.

Minor Premise XV

Almost all agencies and manufacturers' representive firms feel a need to penetrate your company as deeply as they do their accounts. If you make your QA, Manufacturing, R&D, Administrative, and Financial co-founder managers available to them, then they'll have confidence that they can contact the right man if they get into trouble and your marketing and sales managers don't satisfy them.

We try to get all of the founders involved in the sales programs. Not only does this attribute help our clients' sales, it also keeps the sales departments honest while grounding all of the other departments in the market which they are serving.

Minor Premise XVI

Sales agencies and reps know that they will be terminated if they perform either too poorly or too well. In the first case, they'll be replaced with another commissioned firm and in the latter case they'll be replaced with a factory office. Therefore most firms will attempt to sell only the amount for which commissions equal 75% of the costs involved in setting up a direct office. There are several ways around this problem. The usual technique is to ignore it until you see your sales reach the 65% mark and observe sales efforts begin to level off. Then offer "sweeteners" to both the commissioned firm and to that firm's salesmen. An excellent technique is to bypass the rep firm's management with direct "sweeteners" to the salesmen and the salesmen's wives. This is a bridge that you'll have to cross in a couple of years after you open your doors.

The primary reason for bringing this point up at this time is because other principals that the reps are carrying are probably reaching this 75%

level and are not taking the necessary corrective actions. The salesmen now have excessive sales time open which your start-up can fill.

Minor Premise XVII

Sales agencies and manufacturers' rep firms grow and decay at alarming rates. When an agency starts a downhill slide, too frequently all of that agency's principals' sales slide with it. Never sign an exclusive territorial contract with more than a 30-day termination clause. Most reps like a six-month clause. If it takes you six months to get rid of a loser, it will take you a year to rebuild that territory's sales.

Minor Premise XVIII

All commissioned agencies and rep firms like to be paid their commission when the sale is closed. If you are wise, you'll pay them commissions when you get paid. This practice not only helps your cash flow problems, it tends to lower your bad debts.

Minor Premise XIX

Most good salesmen demand full responsibility for their accounts. To do an effective job, they must always be in the loop between you and their customers. Never end-run your salesmen or they will lose confidence in your start-up.

One of the biggest blunders continually repeated by almost all start-ups (and many established companies for that matter) is to send their quotes to a customer and just send a copy to the salesman. You are paying that salesman to sell and then you take away his opportunity to close the sale. Send a significant quote to your salesman and have him deliver it and close the sale—that is what you are paying him for.

Minor Premise XX

Sales is an "action" profession and most good salesmen are "action" people. They are well-organized decision makers who are constantly on the move and like it that way. Conversely, they tend to hate paperwork and therefore are at best marginal report writers, forecasters, letter writers, and record keepers. Force them "to ride a desk" and they will stop selling your products.

Now marry the 10 major assumptions to the 20 minor presmises and you can derive several thousand valid conclusions which most texts take hundreds of pages to cover.

SECTION TWO: SOME OBVIOUS CONCLUSIONS FREQUENTLY OVERLOOKED BY FOUNDERS

AXIOM FOURTEEN: A KEY TO MARKETING SUCCESS IS TO DETERMINE YOUR PRODUCT'S MARKETABLE DIFFERENCES AND STRESS THESE DIFFERENCES TO YOUR CUSTOMERS.

This axiom is so obvious that I feel guilty in wasting your time presenting it. However, approximately half of your salesmen and a quarter of the "marketing specialists" continually ignore it and sales suffer because of the oversight. Before you ever OK an advertisement, approve a sales presentation, or pass on a training course, make certain that these tools illuminate your firm's marketable differences.

Minor Point 14-1: An Advertisement's Goal   M, IS, RS

Usually, an advertisement's main goal is to make a potential customer expose himself as a potential customer so that your salesmen can call on him, make an in-depth presentation, and close the sale. With the exception of a few mail-order-type items, advertisements rarely, in themselves, close sales.

With this in mind, vector your advertisements so that the reader who is a potential buyer responds to them. The following advertising tactics work better than others.

Vector the ad for the specific market segment that the journal addresses. If the journal primarily is directed at production men, then you want your advertisement to be pointed at production managers. Though it is true that a few accountants, a few design engineers, and a few wives of production men will thumb through the journal, if you try to vector your ad to satisfy them also, your ad will be a "mish-mash" and appeal to no one.

Realize that the first goal of your ad is to catch the reader's attention for three seconds. If you fail in this goal, you will not reach your more important goals.

After you catch the reader's attention, you must whet his appetite enough to make him invest an additional 20 seconds. If you hope to keep the reader who has the responsibility to make decisions and purchases beyond this 20-second period, you're kidding yourself.

In this 20-second period, you can make your point or points. A good ad usually doesn't attempt to make more than one or two points before it whets the reader's appetite to seek more information.

Give the reader instructions on how to get more specific details. Do not be afraid to ask the reader to respond by sending you a request on his company's stationery if you are offering free literature in the guise of a reference book.

Most advertising men and most journal publishers push for quantity replies instead of quality replies. If you are going to use your advertising as a "bird-dogging technique" for your rep and agent salesmen, you want quality instead of quantity. I'd much rather have 50 viable leads than 50,000 responses from warm bodies. So vector your advertisements for the goals you wish to attain and spank your ad agency if it tries to change your direction for art's sake.

CAMEO 14-1: THE TRADE SHOW ADVERTISEMENT   M, IS

This particular client had a service start-up which was concentrating primarily on company controllers. They offered computer services for profit center accounting.

When they decided to open a booth at the American Management Association's convention, they were concerned about how they could attract only those controllers who had a need for their services and keep everyone else out of their booth. This start-up's founders needed to give in-depth presentations and did not want the usual booth literature hunters disturbing them. They developed the following brief advertisement:

"There is now a failproof and complete system for profit center controls. If you are a controller, visit booth 1018C at the AMA Convention for complete details."

This ad was placed in the *Wall Street Journal,* in the *New York Times,* on approximately 100 small billboards throughout the convention center, and placed on paper briefcases (which were given away at the convention hall's entrance to everyone who claimed to be a controller).

The booth was tastefully decorated with drapes, conference tables, the start-up's name, and a sign which stated "Controllers Only, Please." Next to this booth was a company which handled fleet leasing. They had free balloons, girls in bathing suits, audio-visual displays, 14 salesmen to handle the crowds, and a carnival barker to pull everyone who happened past into their booth.

At the end of three days, the start-up had only 385 visitors, of which 320 were controllers. They signed 18 customers and got approximately 75 viable follow-ups. The sales manager of the leasing booth boasted that his display had pulled in 22,000 visitors. However, one of his salesmen confided that of the several thousand visitors that he had tried to sell, only a handful had leasing responsibilities, only two were valid follow-ups, and not one sale was made. Which company had viable goals, the one which wanted visitors or the one which wanted valuable leads and orders?

Minor Point 14-2: Remove the Barriers To Purchasing   M, IS

Some companies are almost impossible to do business with because they create so many hurdles to purchasing. Let's examine a few do's and don'ts.

Make buying from you a pleasant experience. When a customer or salesman calls in an order, don't force him to sit through an inquisitive barrage of questions. Take all of the information that he has to offer in his format, not yours, and then after he has given you everything he can think of, ask the balance of questions in a cheery voice. "How do you want us to send you this material . . . by freight, rail, or air? I don't know if our rep explained this to you or not but you have your choice of shipping containers. Do you want a dozen to a box, 144 to a box, or would you like each to be individually boxed? The first two selections cause no added expenses, however we must charge an additional 5¢ for the individual pack."

When your people have completed taking the order over the telephone, make certain that they read it back so that any mistakes are caught at that time. After the order has been verbally verified, make certain that they thank the man for the order and give a brief pep talk on your company, your products, and your pride in meeting commitments. Then, the same day, verify the order in writing with a copy to your rep.

Always accept the order first and straighten out any problems after you "own" the order. This is important because you can always return an order but you can't always pick one up. Therefore instruct your order clerk to accept the order with errors first, verify the errors second, attempt to correct the errors third, and never turn back the order without top management approvals. If there is a pricing, delivery, credit, or specification problem, most good field salesmen can work them out face-to-face with the customer without jeopardizing the already committed order.

Make everything subservient to sales. When a customer needs something, it is first on the priority list. Always make it a practice to get your quotes out the same day you receive them. If this is impossible because production and engineering must work on the costs of the quotes, then get out a letter to the customer the same day thanking him for the opportunity of bidding on his request for quotation (RFQ) and saying you will submit your quote no later than a specific date. And then make heads roll if that date is slipped.

"I'll be over to talk to you about it" or "We'll have XYZ Rep Corp. over to talk about it" are two phrases that have made their users thousands of sales. When a person calls you with an inquiry, you stand a 75% chance that he is ready to buy. Don't fool around with mailing him literature, trying to sell him over the telephone, or trying to sell him by mail. Either go see the person the same day yourself or make an appointment for your sales force to get in.

Pass the credit for closed sales to your sales force. For some reason, factory clerks like to say, "I closed that order because I mailed the man a catalog and he bought" or "I just signed a $250,000 order with Firestone in Atlanta, Georgia." The poor man in Atlanta who made 20 calls on Firestone and paved the way for the close gets irritated with these clerks.

Sales is a carefully orchestrated team effort with the field salesman in the front lines. Never mail a significant quote directly to the customer. Always mail it to your salesman for him to hand carry in to the customer. A salesman's main strength is his ability to close sales. How can you expect him to close them if you rob him of the opportunity? Many of our start-ups will type several separate quotes and mail them all to the salesman. He can then walk into the customer, talk with him, determine which of the separate quotes will close the order, pull it out and close the order.

Give the customer the feeling that if something goes wrong, the buck stops at your desk. Never alibi by saying, "Our QA group sure dropped the ball on this one." Or, "Those clowns in our production department blew it." Or, "Our finance group held the order up pending your credit check and therefore we are late in shipping." To the customer, your company is one being and the last thing he wants to hear is buck passing. Have your people always say, "This is my fault and I'll correct it right now. Let me telephone you back in 15 minutes with the solution."

Use the editorial "we" in all cases except trouble. If the customer has a problem, have your people use the singular "I" or "me." In all other cases, it's "we," "our," etc. The editorial "we" gives the customer a feeling that a team is working for him instead of just one man behind a desk.

Always praise everyone else on your team in front of the customer. All people in your company are dedicated, professional, ethical, innovative, and interested individuals or else they shouldn't be on your team. Your company is not a bureaucracy like your competitors.

Minor Point 14-3: Consider Free Publicity Releases by Being a Newsmaker   M, IS, F

This is such an open area and can have such real benefits that I think it warrants discussion.

Publicity releases have excellent effect if you keep them simple and make only one point, make them of major interest, and make them applicable. Consider what your customers want to hear, vector your releases towards this direction, and then you'll reap the rewards.

For television and radio capsules, select a hot topic and then go "counter propaganda." If the government's news releases say one thing, consider having your company say the opposite. As an example, the government is pushing quotas in employment (both minorities and women). Our clients have been invited to sit on panel shows, have had up to 30-second free slots in news casts, etc., telling the harm this philosophy causes. As employers, they look for professional excellence first, ethics and desire second, and skin color and sex last. Or, when everyone else was laying-off in 1974–75, they were hiring. They got almost national coverage because they stated that this was the ideal time to hire because the best people are available. Two clients received national television coverage because of the way that they treat their employees' life style needs. In every release, the broadcaster usually introduced their company as the young innovative leader of the X industry.

For trade papers and journal releases, we have had considerable success by announcing awards. Specific key people of specific key accounts receive awards for their contributions in their industries. Specific sales firms receive awards for professionalism in specific areas. Not only do these awards grace office walls, they also are sought by other candidates.

New products releases are usually printed because the journal appreciates your advertising or hopes to attract your advertising. Make certain to mention the problem that your product solves in these news releases. If the journal is primarily sent to production people, vector the release to just production people. If it goes to purchasing, talk about prices and delivery. If it goes to R&D people, show how it will eliminate the need for other products while increasing reliability.

This strategy could be called the platform base. Publicity releases can be disguised as something other than a blatant attempt to get free advertising or to increase sales. We usually induce people the public thinks are unbiased to mention a product in a speech they are giving, in a federal investigation that is being held, or in a seminar panel discussion. Certain congressmen and senators are not averse to mentioning a specific company or a specific product on the floor of Congress so that the mention is recorded in the Congressional Record. This makes an excellent inclusion in your referral literature. One client's sales tripled when a federal investigator off-handedly mentioned his product as a solution to copier controls. Another saw sales multiply when his sugarless candy was endorsed by a dental group.

Many of our clients sit on local TV panel shows as experts in a subject. These men gain a celebrity status from these shows.

Speak at the drop of a hat at management club meetings, community meetings, and as a guest at a seminar. Select one gem to mention, make it highly quotable, release the quotes, and you'll get real coverage. As an example, we had a computer services client open a speech with, "I have just received the proof that computer sciences is the oldest profession. To those ladies of the evening, I know that this will come as a surprise, however my proof is so strong that I know it can't be disputed. In the first sentence of the first book of the Bible it states that computer sciences is the oldest profession. I quote this, 'In the beginning there was chaos.' Gentlemen, this description can only be about the computer industry." This quotable quote was printed in dozens of national magazines in the U.S.

Start an industry debate. Select a topic which could be controversial, investigate it thoroughly to make certain that you are on the right side, then release your findings to the trade papers. One trimmer manufacturer recently torpedoed the potentiometer industry by saying that the specification of noise during trimming was a phoney spec for which all pot users were paying a premium. When the smoke finally cleared, the company's sales had doubled and ⅓ of the design engineers who use pots were converted to this firm's philosophies.

Never be transparent in your publicity releases. Publishers' waste baskets are filled with "fluff" releases. Never be too frequent with a specific newspaper, trade paper, or mass media release. Keep a check list and when a paper uses your release, don't submit another to that paper for a month and then make it about a different subject.

Have every founder submit at least one article a quarter for publication. Frequently, these publications pay a nominal fee for excellent articles, however the real reason for the articles is that it gives your people the aura of being experts.

Minor Point 14-4: Color-Styling-Performance Priorities   M

The old-time clinché, "Color catches their eye, styling makes them buy, and performance makes them cry or re-buy," still has some validity today. The old-school salesmen state that the priorities for sales are:

Industrial Sales: (1) Performance, (2) Styling, and (3) Color.

Consumer Sales: (1) Styling, (2) Color, and (3) Performance.

Though we all realize that these are gross oversimplifications, only a fool would ignore the importance of both color and styling to profits.

Minor Point 14-5: Styling   M

There is a trend in start-ups to let manufacturing dictate styling lines from what is easiest for them to produce. Since simple and honest lines are usually the most accepted by customers and since these lines are frequently those most desired by manufacturing, frequently start-ups are lucky and accidentally get both good lines and good manufacturing practices.

Consider hiring a graphic artist for a few days to develop marketable profiles which satisfy both manufacturing and the customers. Frequently minor profile changes so greatly enhance the product's appearance that higher sales prices can be commanded.

Minor Point 14-6: Color   M

The old-time salesmen will always spout the following at you:

(1) Gold, silver, bronze, and royal blue give the image of quality and reliability.

(2)   Blues and greens denote tranquility.
(3)   Oranges, reds, and yellows transmit warmth.
(4)   Pastels give the image of femininity.
(5)   Browns and blacks transmit sadness and death.

Temper these sayings with the other variables of gloss, surface, materials, lighting, and shadows before you make your final decisions. Always evaluate colors on the actual surfaces and materials of your product. You'll discover that a color's language transmits a totally different image on your product than it did on the paper of the artist's sketches. If you are considering using a deep red on a plastic component, you'll discover that if the component has a dull finish and you overprint with black lettering, your component will appear cheap and will therefore be assumed to be unreliable. But if you use the exact same color but give it a glossy finish and overprint with white epoxy inks, your component will appear rich and will therefore be assumed reliable. The cost of both processes is exactly the same.

CAMEO 14-2: LUCKY STRIKE'S GREEN HAS GONE TO WAR   M

When we entered the Second World War, our government prioritied all green pigments for war production. These pigments were essential for camouflage coloring.

Lucky Strike's product managers were extremely concerned because they considered their "Lucky Strike Green" package an essential ingredient for cigarette sales. Lucky was fifth in sales at the time. Since they couldn't get the green pigment, they filled the radio airways with the advertisement, "Lucky Strike's green has gone to war. We must all do our part in saving America and we want you to know that Lucky Strike green has gone to the front lines to do its part. But, when the Axis is defeated, you'll see your beloved Lucky Strike green on your grocery shelves again. Until then, please accept our color substitute, red."

Lucky changed its package to red and saw sales soar. When the war was over, they were slightly behind Camels for first place in sales. Needless to say, Lucky Strike's green was a casualty and never returned from the war to the grocers' shelves.

Example 14-1: A Typical Market Profile   M, IS, RS, F

Assume that your company is manufacturing a medical instrument that will be used by doctors and dentists. Before you can even address your marketing discipline, you must receive from your marketing manager an industry profile. A typical medical instrument's industry profile might look like the following:

Medical Segment	Probable Sales Price	Market Size	Distribution Machinery
Single-doctor offices	$2,500	82,000	(1) Medical equipment reps (2) Factory agents (3) Catalog houses (4) Medical distributors (5) Factory direct offices
Multi-doctor clinics	$6,500	22,000	(1) thru (5) above (6) Hospital equipment reps (7) Hospital distributors
Private hospitals	$8,500	1,300	(1) thru (7) above
Government hospitals	$9,100	450	(1) thru (7) above
Universities and colleges	$8,300	690	(1) thru (7) above
Single-dentist offices	$1,250	49,500	(8) Dental equipment reps (9) Dental distributors (2), (3), and (5) above
Multi-dentist clinics	$2,300	10,350	(2), (3), (5), (8), and (9) above
Homes for the aged	$1,000	15,000	(2), (3), and (5) above

From this kind of profile, it doesn't take long to determine which market segments you will address first, or to determine your growth strategies and your milestones. Once you have decided which segments to address, your marketing plans and sales strategies fall accurately into place.

Minor Point 14-7: The Rook Theory

There is a temptation for young start-ups to attempt to immediately fill several lucrative but unrelated market gaps. Usually the simultaneous introduction of two or more unrelated products and services spreads the founders' time and efforts so thin that a poor job is done in all areas.

Imagine that there is a chess board in front of you. Along the vertical axis (Y axis) is a list of the production capabilities essential for each gap. (Example: line 1, minicomputer electronics production; line 2, Oscilloscopes; line 3, LED inspection production; etc.). Along the horizontal (X axis), list the specific sales distributions essential for market penetration. (Example: line 1, rep/distributor networks; line 2, networks for OEM component sales; line 3, sales agents for capital equipment sales to government agencies, etc.)

As a chess player knows, the rook (or castle) can move only in a straight line in either the horizontal or vertical directions. Diagonal moves (like those taken by the bishop) are illegal.

The Rook Theory states that new products should be introduced and released only as the rook moves. In other words, you should either hold your manufacturing constant while building parallel sales networks or you should hold distribution constant while you develop additional manufacturing capabilities. If you introduce new products which force you to use both new distribution and new production (a diagonal move on our imaginary chess board), you are in essence starting a completely new company and you face the full gambit of problems faced by all conglomerates.

CAMEO 14-3: THE PHYDEAUX (THAT'S FRENCH FOR FIDO) CARTOONS   M, IS, RS, F

Joan Thall is a highly respected personnel consultant and successful negotiator for management in union contract talks. This lady developed a unique wrinkle in labor negotiations that is deadly. This unique wrinkle has since developed into a highly profitable mini-profit center for her.

Briefly, when the negotiations begin, Miss Thall is usually extremely quiet while her team skirmishes with the union's negotiators. While the war of words goes on about her, she doodles cartoons of a dog's expressive face and labels him Phydeaux. She does this for however long is necessary for her to be certain that all of the union's cards are on the table and that the timing is absolutely right. Then she talks for the first time. In a very quiet and ladylike voice, she appears to be taking the union's side as she re-expresses their points in syllogistic premises. At the end of each premise, she looks sweetly at the top union negotiator and says, "Isn't that correct Mr. X?" After each premise is agreed upon by her opponents, she then draws back and reorganizes each of the verified premises so that they either develop the conclusions that her clients wanted or they are presented in such a way as to contradict each other or lead to invalid and unjust conclusions. In her quiet ladylike manner, she kills you with your own words.

There is nothing new to this technique of negotiating—several top labor negotiators on both sides use it. However, Miss Thall has added a new wrinkle, her Phydeaux cartoons. Since she is such a lady, she feels uncomfortable calling an S.O.B. an S.O.B., so she has her animated dog do it for her. Once when the Teamsters Union refused to admit that their demands were invalid, unethical, and damaging, old Phydeaux (with a horselaughing facial expression) simply said, "What's mine is mine. . . what's yours is what is up for negotiations." When Miss Thall passed this cartoon up the conference table to Mr. Dave Beck (then the president of the Teamsters Union), every negotiator laughed, including the union's people. Mr. Beck, who couldn't take being laughed at, wadded up the cartoon, threw it at Miss Thall along with a few curse words, and stormed out of the meeting. When a fair contract was finally negotiated, Miss Thall was surprised to find that her wadded-up Phydeaux cartoon had been salvaged by the president of the company, framed, and hung in his office. There are probably a hundred such tales in the construction industry about quiet Miss Thall.

Then approximately four years ago, the marketing director of an equipment manufacturer to the construction industry saw several of Miss Thall's cartoons hung in corporate offices and hit upon an excellent idea. Why not reproduce the best and give them to his sales force to give away to their best customers? Joan agreed to supply each of his salesmen 50 reproductions each month of her better Phydeaux cartoons, at $1 each. Every month, each salesman walks into his choice customer's offices with the latest Phydeaux Cartoon. The salesman will automatically walk to the frame which holds last month's cartoon and attempt to replace it and throw away the obsolete drawing. However, since most cartoons are so funny, pithy, and truthful, very few are allowed to remain in the wastebasket. Most either go into the customer's lobby or are displayed elsewhere in the company.

When someone complained to the marketing director about the charge for the cartoons (Miss Thall makes 96¢ a reproduction and about $25,000 a year from his company), he stated, "We average about $8 for each business luncheon and within two hours after the luncheon is over, the customer has probably forgotten it. That's $8 spent on something that buys little customer loyalty. For a lousy dollar, we get a framable cartoon that every customer places on his desk or hangs on his wall. This $1 gives our salesman an alibi to visit his customer each month to replace the old with the new. He looks at that $1 picture perhaps five times a day, twenty days a month, so it costs us maybe 1¢ for each time he thinks of us. Every time a visitor comes into his office, he'll look at Phydeaux, laugh, and comment on it. Therefore every visitor in essence reminds our customer of us. I suspect that a few of our customers are more "hooked' on Phydeaux than they are on us. Therefore, in all probability we get orders from people who want their Phydeaux cartoons and order from us to insure that they'll keep getting that stupid dog's sayings. Now tell me which has more value—the $8 business luncheon or the $1 cartoon? That crazy mutt makes us a lot of sales."

This cameo has a lot of messages for your consideration. They are: (1) syllogistic logic can frequently run around irrational hurdles such as labor problems, sales resistances, departmental loyalties, or in-vogue trends that aren't profitable, (2) mini-profit centers can come out of the woodwork (Miss Thall could comfortably retire on Phydeaux's incomes—she now nets over $58,000 a year from them), (3) a product's price is only a function of its value ($1 per reproduction is highway robbery for a 4¢ item but since it is worth it, that's its price), and (4) you can be extremely innovative in stretching your sales budgets to buy "customer purchasing loyalties" (a lovely phrase that too few companies consider). I've seen sales budgets spent on puppies (a gift no customer will ever forget), on excellent books (one of the best and most personal gifts you can give someone), on special school supplies for the customers' college bound children (a thoughtfulness always appreciated), and a myriad of other "purchasing loyalty" concepts. One business luncheon's expenses can do wonders. Since the IRS has no set policy on this aspect (some companies are allowed to deduct these expenses while others aren't), make certain that your controller lists them as entertainment expenses.

CAMEO 14-4: OUR OKIE MECHANIC REVISITED
PART 3   M, IS

Remember our Okie mechanic, who started an electric truckbed crane company to utilize his production facilities more efficiently while taking advantage of surplus motors and gear trains? He did everything right except his marketing homework, and for this oversight he paid dearly.

Briefly, his truckbed cranes had customer demand in four separate and unique industries—utilities and governments, the construction industry, repair services, and miscellaneous areas (tombstone monuments, fishing fleets, billboard advertisers, aerospace firms). Not one sales firm called on more than one area, yet all demanded exclusive territories. Everything sold in their territories rewarded them.

Our mechanic agreed to these exclusive demands and thereby received only one-fourth of the sales coverage that he should have received. However, since the cranes for each industry segment had to be customized to that segment's needs, he was forced to supply all of the engineering development for all segments. As an example, his Michigan rep sold only to utilities and governments. These customers required long booms for light loads (usually less than 2,000 lbs.). His Texas rep sold primarily to road contractors, who needed short booms to lift very heavy loads (such as earth movers' engines). His Florida rep sold hundreds of shrimp cranes to fishing fleets, and these boats needed lightning-fast line speeds. His Washington, D.C., rep sold cranes for every missile silo to handle delicate missile-component installations in which high accuracy was essential.

Therefore, with his typical horse sense approach to all problems, he innovatively eliminated his problem by forming four different companies under four totally different names. Each company signed exclusive reps in each territory. Each company had its own sales manager, each had its own applications engineer, and each its own stationery, post office box, and telephone number. Each crane company utilized a different color and had slightly different lines. Each of course had its own literature pointed at its own market segment.

Other than these minor differences, all cranes were manufactured on the same production lines by the same workers, all had the support groups, and all were administered by the same management team.

In the first five years, the company only competed against itself three times. At the end of this period, two of the divisions (under different company names) were the leaders of their segments, and the other two were in the top three. Since most of the "exclusive" reps never ventured out of their specific market segment, very few even knew that the other companies existed.

Though the term "market profile" would have snowed our Okie mechanic, his innovative solution to address different markets with the same product is a classic that can be followed by your company.

When the crane companies were sold several years ago, they were sold separately for prices which ranged from $900,000 to $1,300,000. It's a trick worth remembering.

15 · The Techniques of Setting Up Distribution Networks

PROLOGUE   M, IS

This chapter addresses the tasks of: (1) investigating sales firms, (2) evaluating them, (3) training them, (4) motivating them, and (5) sustaining their sales efforts.

Though the chapter is vectored towards setting up commissioned sales distribution, the principles apply to all other forms of networks. Commissioned networks demand the most professional support, so that once you master these networks, you'll find all others child's play in comparison.

We unfortunately are ignoring foreign sales machinery, however you shouldn't once you establish your U.S. operations. As a rule of thumb, most of our clients realize 65% of their sales from the U.S., 25% from Europe, and 10% from the balance of the world. With China and Russia opening up, these percentages could shift to 50% foreign and 50% U.S. in the next decade.

Please realize that any author who writes about distribution networks runs into a thorny terminology problem. Words that mean one thing in one industry mean something totally different in another. Yet the machinery of sales networks is almost the same in every industry. To get around this problem, allow me to use the terminologies of the electronics industry, define them where necessary, and then leave it up to you to apply the principles to your industry, using whatever terminologies you wish.

SECTION ONE: A BRIEF BACKGROUND OF DIRECT DISTRIBUTION NETWORKS

THE BASICS   M, IS, RS, F

The United States is divided into 25 sales territories. In each territory there are from 20 to 500 manufacturers' representatives (hereafter we'll call them reps) who specialize in each basic industry. As an example, in the San Francisco territory there are 85 reps in electronics, 67 in production capital equipment, 147 in ladies garments, 93 in men's clothing, 49 in restaurant equipment, 122 in grocery products, 35 in sex-oriented products, and equivalent numbers in almost any other industry that you can name.

Rep firms are basically professional sales organizations which range in size from the small one-man office (with answering service) to 50 direct salesmen with a staff of 20 support people. They carry from 6 to 50 principals (manufacturers like yourself) whose lines complement each other (but never compete against each other). They select complementing lines so that their sales engineers can discuss several principals at each call and can put together combinations of purchases (a resistor salesman has few problems adding capacitors, inductors, connectors, and cables to orders).

A rep's responsibilities are to sell the territory's major accounts direct; to train, motivate, and support your sales agents and distributors in their territory; to make certain that your agencies train, motivate, and support the retailers and distributors in their sub-territories; and to make certain that things flow smoothly in their territories. For this, the reps get a commission on everything shipped into their territories.

In every major metropolitan area there are sales agencies. These firms are also professional sales groups which call on the major accounts in their sub-territory (district) to make major sales; call on medium-sized customers to make mid-range sales; support the distributors in their districts and complement the rep's work; assume complete responsibilities for training, motivating, and promoting your retailers in their district; make certain that both your distributors and retailers carry ample inventories of your products; and warehouse at least two months of their district's inventory needs. This warehousing function varies from industry to industry but usually the inventories are carried on a consignment basis with the principal (you) picking up all of the insurance and handling expenses. Like the rep firm, the agency receives commissions on all shipments made into its exclusive district. The average agency carries from 10 to 50 principals who complement each other. These sales firms average from 2 to 50 direct salesmen and from 1 to 20 support people.

The next step down in the sales machinery are the authorized non-exclusive distributors. These firms inventory from three to six months of products. In almost all cases, they pay for the products when they receive them but insist upon a buy-back clause if your products do not move. The average distributor has from 5 to 50 direct salesmen and from 2 to 20 support staff. They carry from 500 to 5,000 principals and try to carry competing as well as complementing lines. Their direct salesmen rarely penetrate beyond the purchasing departments. They primarily fight for the small orders (10 to 500 units) and try to average at least 25% markup on each sale.

The lowest level is the retailer. This is strictly over-the-counter sales on a 1-to-10 unit basis. The average retailer would like to see stock movement of 52 times per year, however it's your agent's responsibility to make certain that he carries at least a two-month supply.

Now that you see the machinery, let's look at the effects of it. The average major customer receives 2 calls/month at each management level, 1 call/month at each engineering and production level, and 10 to 20 calls/ month at the purchasing levels. The average medium-sized customer receives from 4 to 6 calls/month at the purchasing level and 1 call/month at the engineering and management levels. The small accounts receive from 1 to 3 calls/month. All accounts can walk into retailers anytime they wish. In a large territory, you have from 200 to 400 trained salesmen pushing your products and you pay for their efforts (in commissions) only when they close sales.

Let's look at typical costs. The average rep firm spends from $300 to $500 per principal per salesman per month. In other words, if a rep has 20 principals and 10 salesmen, it will cost him approximately $60,000 a month to support that staff. If he averages 7.5% commissions, then his territory must produce $4,500,000 a month in gross sales. The average agency calculates that it costs them $100 to $150 per principal per salesman per month. The average distributor calculates that it costs him $50 per principal per salesman per month. Though any marketing man can shoot holes in this logic, these sales firms believe it and therefore are extremely selective in choosing their principals (you).

Both reps and agencies select principals who complement each other because they want their salesmen to be able to discuss several principals at each sales call. The truly professional salesman will discuss two to four principals in depth at each sales call and mention one to two more. The beginning salesman will attempt to discuss them all and the lazy salesman will only discuss one to two principals. Distributors and retailers are true order takers and therefore want to carry whatever the customer requests. They are good at substituting one manufacturer for another but that is about all that you can expect from them.

THE LAW OF SCHLOCK   M, IS

There are significant quantities of marginal and poor reps and agencies (approximately 65% of the pack). These firms attract the marginal and poor manufacturers and therefore present the "schlock" image to their customers.

Regardless of how good your product is and how professionally you conduct yourself, both your company and its products will present a "schlock" image to your customers if you employ "schlock" firms to sell your products. This image will transmit itself to your sales, market penetration, product's sales prices, and finally to your profits.

Therefore, since you cannot afford anything but the best firms, how do you select the best and get them to actively sell your products? Like everything else, there is an expensive and wrong way and an inexpensive and right way. Let's examine some of the techniques used by start-ups.

SECTION TWO: THE INVESTIGATION OF SALES FIRMS

DO YOUR HOMEWORK   M, IS

Contact the major customers in each territory and ask them which sales firms (reps, agencies, and distributors) serve them the best. Don't restrict these inquiries to just purchasing departments. Ask managers, engineers, manufacturing people, and administrators for contributions.

Contact the better distributors and retailers and ask them which reps and agencies support them the best.

In most industries, the better reps and agencies belong to an association which restricts their membership to ethical and professional firms. Get these associations' membership lists. Buy their registry which describes the personnel, capabilities, experience and principals of each sales firm.

Because of "the Law of Schlock," most top grade manufacturers will not tolerate anything but excellence from their distribution levels. Get a list of their sales firms. Write these manufacturers and ask them about the strengths and weaknesses of their sales firms.

Select the most promising three firms in each territory. Write their owners and describe your homework and the results. They will be flattered that you consider them one of the best and will be interested in further discussions. Send them your literature, your projected sales plans (do not disclose proprietary information), and let them know that you hope that their firm will become a candidate to represent you. After the owner has had a chance to digest this material, telephone him and arrange a mutually acceptable time for you to visit him and evaluate his capabilities first hand. You can probably evaluate three reps in a one-week visit to each territory.

FURTHER SCREENING   M, IS

When you visit each rep and agency firm, realize that the owners are probably master salesmen who have outstanding "bedside manners." Each will impress you greatly and make you want to work with his firm. However, realize that this is not the characteristic that is important. The reps' salesmen, not the owners, make the bulk of their sales calls and therefore you want to assure yourself that these salesmen are professional, ethical, enthusiastic, hungry, and capable. How well are these men received and respected by your potential customers?

Remember that both reps and agents have many other responsibilities besides just direct selling. How good is their paper flow? How long does it take an order or an inquiry to flow from the customer to your plant? What is the reliability of this paper flow? How are the firms equipped to train, motivate, and support distributors and retailers? What is the "chemistry" between these different levels? What percentage of their effective sales time can you expect if you conduct yourself professionally? How vulnerable are these firms' salesmen to your strategies of monopolizing their sales efforts? Are their salesmen just order takers or are there a few sales engineers who will push your innovative and pioneering products? Will the firm and its personnel become a real part of your company team or are they just another dead-head operation?

To get answers to these questions, most of our clients spend from one-and-a-half to two days at each firm. They make "buddy calls" with their salesmen, they talk to the support personnel, they visit the major accounts, and they nose around the warehouses.

After each screening visit, tell the rep firm that you are impressed and know that your firms will work together well if you both decide there is a fit. However, tell them that you are committed to investigating other reps and can't ethically make a decision until after you have visited each. Tell them openly who the other candidates are. If you did a good job in your homework, they will be impressed with the caliber of the other firms that you are considering.

FINAL SELECTION   M, IS

When you have completed your first visit to a territory, make precise notes of your impressions and rapidly make a decision on whether any of the candidates are good enough, and if so, which is the best.

Notify the winner by telephone as soon as you decide and then write a thank you letter to the losers. Again tell them how impressed you were and state that the only reason that you selected another rep is for the following minor point. It is important that you not burn your bridges behind you because if your selection falls down on you, you want to be able to attract a replacement firm fast.

SECTION THREE: INITIAL TRAINING OF YOUR SALES FIRMS

AXIOM FIFTEEN: SALES TRAINING IS A FOREVER THING, AN ONGOING REQUIREMENT AS LONG AS YOUR COMPANY EXISTS.

It's a fact of life that your company's sales success is directly proportional to the product knowledge and the salesmanship crafts of your sales force. A considerable percent of your marketing and sales efforts (and budgets) will be invested in training, re-training, and re-re-training your salesmen. Unless a salesman feels that he knows more about your products than his customers, he'll not sell you. Also realize that salesmen get lazy in their closing arts and must be continually overhauled.

The balance of this section will address only the initial training essential to kick your sales off, but never make the mistake of ignoring ongoing training.

Minor Point 15-1: A Technique for Initial Training of Reps   M, IS, RS

Consider sending a two-to-five-man team into each rep's territory to begin the training of reps. Each team should proceed as follows.

Remember that long sales conferences are self defeating. Instead of holding one long seminar, consider holding three short ones after normal sales hours (e.g., from 6:00 p.m. to 9:30 p.m., Monday through Wednesday).

Arrive at the rep's offices Monday afternoon, stock his bins with literature, and assemble individual sales manuals for all personnel (both sales and support people). Set up the conference room and your presentation apparatus and make certain that they work properly before the meeting.

From 5:00 to 6:00, have an open bar and plenty of snacks available. Have each member of your team mingle, including yourself, and get to know each other.

At the first seminar, lay out the agendas for all three seminars. Establish that you are a sales oriented, customer oriented, and a professional firm and make it crystal clear that not only the team but all personnel are as available to the reps as their telephones. (Most of our clients give the home telephone numbers of all founders and encourage the reps to telephone any founder collect whenever they have a problem.)

After you have established that you are a professionally run company, briefly describe your products. Give them as much information as they will need to make "buddy calls" with your team and then assure them that you will go into the products' characteristics much more deeply before you leave them at the end of the week.

Next, describe your products' sales features and the customer applications. Have plenty of enthusiasm here and give them the attitude that they are doing their customers a real favor by offering them your superior products.

After getting this far, you want to have the session develop into a brainstorming session on which of their customers has the greatest need for your products and how best to penetrate each account. Arrange your buddy call schedule for the balance of the week. Close the meeting and open the bar until 9:30.

Many of our clients have set up their agents and distributors at the same time they set up the reps. If this is the case, these meetings are open to them as well.

Hereafter, during the days, you and your team members will be busy making sales calls on the customers. Refer to Example 15-1 for the rules of these calls.

During the second session (Tuesday night) go into the technical discussions of your products. Don't teach the salesmen how to build your product. Instead teach them how to impress their customers with their knowledge and understanding.

Unless your products are extremely complex (atomic reactors, complex heat transfer equipment), you and your team should be able to explain your products in depth in a matter of 45 minutes to an hour. This leaves the balance of the time for other important topics. Have plenty of charts available which compare your products' strengths and weaknesses with competitors. Be extremely honest here. Where a competitor outperforms you, admit it openly. Never lie or attempt to cover up because salesmen will spot it a mile off and lose confidence in you.

When these comparison charts have been covered, consider going into a role-playing presentation for the balance of the meeting. First, you and your team members act out sales situations, then the rep salesmen act like buyers, then they act like salesmen. In these role-playing situations present a general scenario and have everyone ad-lib within it. Try out several sales closes in each of these situations.

In the third session, cover any ground that you may have missed in the first two sessions. Consider discussing some of your experiences that you have run into in your buddy calls. Find out about any of the concerns that anyone has. Re-sell your company's desires to work with the salesmen. When this is done, force the session to develop into a day-dreaming session. Show your projected sales curves and show the milestones in which additional rewards will come back to the salesmen. If the session goes according to plan, when the third session is complete, each salesman will feel that he understands what your products will and won't do, what your company will and won't do, and how everyone will benefit as you reach your sales milestones. You may even consider giving them a preview of coming attractions on the future products down the pike.

On Thursday and Friday, you and your team will probably want to make buddy calls with agency and distributor salesmen. You may wish to hold additional seminars at their facilities. You will probably want to visit retailers to get their coverage started.

Throughout the week keep good notes. Record whom you visited when, what promises you have made, what answers you need to find. When you return to your home office, write each person a sincere thank you letter, summarize what transpired at the visit, and either complete your promises or give them a date when they can expect the promise to be completed. Make dead certain that you meet those dates.

We've now gotten the territory off on the right foot from a training standpoint. Hereafter, every visit, every telephone call, and every letter should carry the training a little further.

SECTION FOUR: MOTIVATING YOUR DISTRIBUTION

AXIOM SIXTEEN: LIKE SALES TRAINING, MOTIVATING YOUR SALESMEN IS A FOREVER THING, AN ONGOING REQUIRE-MENT AS LONG AS YOUR COMPANY EXISTS

This is so obvious, yet so ignored. The expression, "Sell, don't tell," applies to your behavior with your salesmen. If you just give your salesmen marching orders instead of the motivators to make them want to march to your beat, then you'll only be kidding yourself and hurting your company.

SOME SHOELACE TECHNIQUES TO MOTIVATE SALESMEN   M, IS, RS, F

Remember the premise that most salesmen sell what sells easiest? Since you are a start-up, it is improbable that your products and services have the demand that your salesmen's other principals have. It is also doubtful that your young company has the cash reserves to "buy" salesmen's efforts. Therefore, you have to run that extra mile in motivating commissioned salesmen to push your product over established competition. And initially, you'll probably have to make a dime do a dollar's work in this essential requirement. Here are some techniques used by others that you may modify.

Many of our clients establish a sales corporation (held by your company) and give salesmen stock bonuses in this sales corporation with each sale. The value of the held corporation's stock gains because it acquires the holding company's stock with each cash transfer to the holding company. (That is, for every $100 in cash transferred to the holding company, $1 in holding company stock is passed back to the held company—a percentage of which the salesman receives in the form of held company's stock). Besides being an excellent motivator for your salesmen (they are building an estate which will have value when they retire), this technique also opens the door for the founders to raise additional funds by attracting investors in the held corporation.

Also be aware that this pyramiding technique is a viable tool for setting up parallel distribution for greater market penetrations. Some of our older clients have set up as many as three selling corporations which market the same products (under different names with different appearances) through three parallel distribution networks. On occasions, where two of these networks overlap, these firms find themselves bidding against themselves. It's a nice competitive situation to be in provided that you do not over-saturate and kill all networks' incentives.

Another extremely successful technique is the gambit that we'll call the college trust fund technique. Every time a salesman closes a sale, a small percentage of that sale's profits is placed in a reserve for the salesman's children's education. Each month, the status of this reserve is sent to the salesman's wife (or children) so that they can judge (and motivate you hope) Daddy's performance for your products.

With salesmen, nothing succeeds like success. There is a bandwagon effect in sales that every start-up should recognize and use. Consider letting your rep and agent salesmen know of other rep's and agent's successes. For example, "Hats off to Bill Smith of Gassner & Clark. The Magnavox Corporation in Fort Wayne has always used Texas Instruments diodes in their commercial production. Bill showed them how our model 202C would outperform TI's 8A292P (and our costs are only 3% higher!) and got them to begin a qualification test on our diode. When the testing is completed (don't worry—we'll run rings around TI's obsolete design), Magnavox will become one of our largest users. Bill is going to try to get permission to reproduce Magnavox's test results and allow us to distribute these results to you. Nice going, Bill, and thanks for a darned good sales job. This should result in at least 100,000 diodes a month." This little blurb will force every salesman to mentally think about 2% of the sale of 100,000, the salesman's take each month, and every time they see a TI Model 8A292P, they'll attempt to replace it with your model 202C.

Remember that recognition is a very real ego need in salesmen. Satisfy this need by having each of your co-founders make at least five telephone calls each month to five different salesmen to thank them for their performance and sales. When your head of R&D, QA, Production, or Administration calls a salesman to thank him, that salesman feels that yours is truly a sales oriented firm which tracks his performances. He also will get to know your "brass" on a first-name basis and will feel free to phone them when he needs help and isn't getting it.

Give every salesman your management's home telephone numbers and tell them to call collect whenever they need help.

When you utilize the free advertising of publicity releases, give your sales firms top billing. Consider this release, "ABC Manufacturers' Representatives were chosen to market XYZ diodes in the Seattle area. ABC won the right to be exclusive sales agents after a vigorous competition with the best organizations in Seattle. 'We had to select them because they are the most respected sales firm in the Northwest,' stated John Doe, president of XYZ Manufacturing. 'As an example, the Boeing Corporation told us that ABC had the best record for service, Coors stated that ABC was the most professional, and Darlington Industries stated that they always preferred to work with the best and ABC is the best. XYZ Manufacturing is the cream of the diode industry so we only select the very best to represent us and ABC wins that honor hands down.' '' What newspaper in the Seattle area wouldn't print that story with all of the name dropping that took place?

Get the word out on unique sales closes so that other salesmen might consider them. For instance, ''George Bacon of the George R. Bacon Company in Atlanta wins our Most Innovative Sales Close Award for this month. Briefly, we were up against IBM (its model 370-45) for the Atlanta Sewer Department. Now all of you know that we have sewer software programs that are far superior to IBM, but it looked like we were sure to lose the computer main frame sale because city bureaucrats like to play it safe and what is safer than buying from IBM. Then George closed the sale by taking the most innovative tactic that we have ever heard. Briefly, he compared computers to prostitutes and described our model 404CB with IBM's 370 as if they were very available women and described the ''satisfaction'' that the supervisors would get from both. George's pitch was strictly X-rated but after comparing the partial fulfillment of Ms. IBM vs. greater fulfillment by us, he had the sewer supervisor's full attention. He then described how the Charlottesville Sewer Department spent seven months in bed with IBM before they could get up and he described New York City's sewer problems in such a way that his customer was rolling in laughter. I'm not recommending that you attempt George's approach but I think that you will agree that it is the most unusual sales method that you have heard.''

Humor goes a long way in interesting and motivating salesmen. Make working with you a fun experience and come up with a few surprises. As an example, one of our clients who was still in the shoelace phase of his marketing was upstaged by a competitor who was offering vacations in the Bahamas for winning salesmen. Our boy held a contest and offered a one-day paid vacation in Milpitas (a suburb of San Jose with a questionable reputation) to the salesman who came in first. To the last place finisher, the punishment was two weeks in Milpitas.

Another client gave away shares in the Golden Gate Bridge, another gave away tapes of Nixon's humor (blank tapes), another gave away the embarrassing AEC ultra-reliability specifications (with the typo errors highlighted) and then he released the story of how the AEC was going to replace the National Bureau of Standards in standards controls. Since two of the AEC's prime standards were off (their 1 gram standard weighed 1.003 grams and their 1 volt standard was 0.999998 volts), all hell broke loose in companies which supplied both the AEC and other government agencies. The AEC dropped out of the calibration business.

The best example of a profitable use of humor in sales is another story about our Okie mechanic (Cameo 15-1). It illustrates the many facets of effectively implemented humor.

The above techniques are meant merely as examples to show you that you can go a long way in sales motivation with little front money. Most salesmen will stick with you until your company is well on its feet and can afford more expensive motivators. You'll be wise to build cash reserves so that you can implement some of the more expensive but longer lasting techniques. A few of the better techniques are:

(1) *Commission Plateaus.* Assign each salesman sales plateaus with milestone bonuses when they exceed each plateau. As an example, let's say that a specific salesman can readily sell $50,000 a year with just normal efforts and selling time. Therefore, for all sales above $50,000, he gets an additional 0.5%. For all sales above $60,000, he gets an additional 1%, $70,000 gives him 2%, 80,000 gives him 3.5%, $90,000 yields 5%, and all above $100,000 gives him 7.5%. These additional bonuses are of course paid directly to the salesman instead of the rep firm.

(2) *Vary Commissions With Profits.* Some salesmen can sell products at top dollar while others are lucky to close a sale at breakeven costs. If your commission structure rewards top dollar (and therefore top profit) sales, you'll receive more lost sales but greater profits.

Consider paying the rep firm its normal commission percentages from gross sales but splitting the additional profits directly with the salesman. We have one client (a specialty manufacturer) who can accept orders at $4 each. He applies the variable profit bonuses with his salesmen on a 50–50 basis. If a salesman sells his products for $6 each, then the $2 additional profit is divided equally between the salesman and the manufacturer.

This practice is excellent for specialty manufacturers, however it can be extremely dangerous in a repeat business industry such as industrial sales where there is a term for it, "sandbagging." The manufacturer who gets the reputation for sandbagging has a limited life expectancy.

(3) *Contests.* Contests work extremely well for manufacturers who want to move inventories in discontinued lines, however I question their validity in normal sales. Let's take the case of a product like dump truck bodies. It is an industry convention to award outstanding prizes to the first salesman to sell 10 dump bodies (say in the month of May) and give another outstanding award for the salesman who sells the most bodies in May. How does this work for the manufacturer? What usually happens is that most commissioned salesmen ask their customers to start holding off orders in March and April and place them on May 1. At midnight on April 31, the telex machines go wild with orders in quantities of 10. Frequently salesmen will then go back to their favorite customers and ask them to

place all their projected dump body sales for June and July in May so that the salesman can win his contest. Therefore, instead of increasing sales, the contest merely forces customers to lump their sales.

Contests also seem to have no effect in marginal sales territories. Can a rep selling office supplies in Billings, Montana ever hope to compete against the New York City rep?

(4) *National Sales Conferences.* Occasional nationwide sales conferences work extremely well in training all rep salesmen in your newest products. However, realize three things before you attempt to budget for too many sales conferences.

First, you are calling all of your salesmen into your home plant for three days of seminars, plant tours, and testing. Salesmen will cost you approximately $600 each in overhead expenses and they do not sell when they are sitting in your audience.

Second, the preparations for the seminars must be professional and outstanding to accomplish what you need to accomplish. Budget four man hours for every hour of formal presentation. Also, realize that your plant will lose some efficiency and productiveness while everyone is visiting.

Third, saturation is quickly reached at all-day sessions. If your salesmen absorb 25% of what is thrown at them over a three-day (10-hour day) conference, then you are doing an excellent job.

(5) *Mini-Sales Conferences.* Everytime a factory man goes into a territory, consider having him carry a three-hour seminar in his briefcase. Have him present this seminar at the rep's facilities (after prime sales hours). To make certain that he properly presented the material that you feel is essential, have him conduct a half-hour quiz after each seminar session.

The key to salesman motivation is professionalism, incentives, and fun all wrapped into a single package. Never expect to keep a sales force motivated with broken customer promises, unreliable products, poor control systems, and few visits to each region, territory, district, and sub-district.

SECTION FIVE: SUSTAINING YOUR DISTRIBUTION NETWORKS

THE THREE PRIORITIES   M, IS

If you enforce the following three operating priorities as your top three priorities, you'll have no problems in sustaining your sales networks. In order of importance to the salesmen, they are:

Priority One

Handle all quotes the same day that they are received. This includes both formal price quotations and information inquiries. If a customer inquiry cannot be handled the same day, then rush him a letter telling him when he can expect his answer and enforce that date.

This priority is so important that you should make it a rule that if your sales department's typists can't get the day's quotations out, then they should even "bump" the president's typing until the last quote is typed, proofed, sealed, and stamped.

Priority Two

Handle all customer problems on the basis of "Let's get the customer's production up fast and worry about administrative problems later."

Your quality assurance people should have the authority to do whatever is necessary to make the customer happy, even if they have to pirate top R&D and manufacturing personnel to define and cure problems.

Priority Three

Meet your delivery promises as if they were your word to God. At the end of each day, make darned certain that every shipping promise made for that day was met. If it wasn't, take corrective actions fast.

If you accept these ongoing priorities, let them be known to your salesmen. If you can then convince these men that you will enforce these priorities, they will have a greater degree of confidence in your firm than they have in the majority of their other principals.

Minor Point 15-2: The "Can't-Do-Until-Overdue" Syndrome   M, IS, RS, F

You will discover that 75% of your competition has fallen into the "Don't-do-until-due" operating syndrome. This is just one short inch from the "Can't-do-until-overdue" syndrome.

When this occurs (and it does continually), your competitors' customer bases are vulnerable to your penetrations. Utilize the "I'm in the wings as an understudy" tactic (see next chapter) and you'll penetrate your market.

Minor Point 15-3: Other Techniques for Motivating and Sustaining Sales   M, IS

A majority of our start-up clients utilize these additional techniques.

When you or your people visit a territory, always have a real reason for the trip besides "Just seeing how things are going." Rep's salesmen are extremely busy and resent drop-ins. Before arriving, schedule visits to potential customers, schedule after-hours seminars, introduce a new product, perform a market survey, introduce a new incentive program, or think up any other viable reason for each of your field visits, once every six weeks.

Mail your reps and agents journal and newspaper clippings about their customers. Though chances are that they already know the information, the ploy is excellent because it shows them that you too are tracking their customers' progresses.

Realize that the average salesman gets between 50 and 100 letters each month from his principals. The average salesman scans them all, carefully reads perhaps 20%, and studies maybe 1%. If your company gets the reputation of sending "flack mail," then expect to be a portion of that 80% that isn't digested.

If the material in your letters is important and you want it to be part of the 1% that is studied and retained, do the following.

In the first two lines of your letter, tell him that the letter is important and why it is important. This is all that is contained in the first paragraph.

Make the second paragraph a one-liner telling him that you are going to give him a chance to digest the contents and will telephone him within X days to ask him the following questions.

Paragraph three lists the questions that the salesman will have to answer in your telephone follow-up.

The balance of the letter can give him the information which you wished him to receive in the first place.

If the information is too long to get comfortably in one-and-a-half pages, then resort to the tactic that you used in your business plan and summarize the information in the body of your letter and add on addendum with the bulk of the verbiage.

Don't forget to telephone him as you promised and ask your questions.

Never be afraid of being different in your approach to sales. Realize that most principals have a "me too" outlook in marketing and you'll be a refreshing change of pace if you are innovative, professional, and fun. Never confuse the word "professional" with "me too." It doesn't make you professional to copy everyone else in the industry.

Force yourself to add two tablespoons of zest for living to every marketing receipt that you introduce. Remember that salesmen like to do what is fun first and what is essential second. If you can overlay fun with what is essential to your company, you give them an alibi to service you before they service their other principals (your real competitors).

Minor Point 15-4: Out of Sight, Out of Mind

The saying, "Out-of-sight, out-of-mind" unfortunately is very accurate in sales networks. If you don't think enough of your product, your salesmen, or your company's sales, to get out in the field and visit each territory at least once every six weeks, then why should you expect your commissioned salesmen to care? Budget your sales program so that every territory receives an in-depth visit from one of your founders at least nine times yearly.

CAMEO 15-1: THE BIG DICKS AND THE LITTLE DICKS, OUR OKIE MECHANIC PART 4   M, IS, RS, F

When our Okie mechanic found himself in the truck crane business (see Cameo 12-2), he had major problems penetrating the construction industry. Though 25% of a contractor's crane needs could be filled with his inexpensive small truck cranes, most opted for competitors' $100,000 giant cranes to do all jobs. Though it was a matter of simple economics to prove that if the contractor could save the $250 costs of transporting his enormous crane to a site and if he could save the $100 an hour to operate it, he could pay for his tiny 1,000 or 2,000 pound cranes in just three jobs. This sales approach didn't float, so our Okie mechanic drew back and took a different tack.

His construction cranes had one unique feature. They looked like a man's penis as they telescoped in and out, raised and lowered, and rotated. So the mechanic renamed his cranes "The Little Dick" and "The Big Dick" and sales soared in the construction industry. Not one contractor could forget their names and many considered his own fleet of "Dicks" a real status symbol. These names introduced another surprise bonus. No man, with any masculinity, should have a "Little Dick" when for just a few hundred more, he could have a "Big Dick." Therefore, most bought the more profitable larger crane.

These truckbed cranes initially caused a slug of complaints because they were electrical and ran off the truck batteries. Though all of the company's specifications stated that the crane operator should start the truck's engine every hour to re-charge their batteries, many didn't and therefore completely drained their truck's batteries. However, all crane operators accepted the fact that their "Dick" could fatigue when overworked, and this field complaint stopped with the new names.

The final real bonus the company realized was that nothing travels as fast as a joke. Since their small cranes were the butts of thousands of off-beat jokes, they received word-of-mouth advertising (the best advertising that you can ever hope for) that was worth a fortune. Even now, 20 years after the introduction of the new names, the company realizes the benefits of at least two fresh jokes a month.

This is the last Cameo on our Okie friend. I hope that these brief case histories trigger innovative solutions to your problems. I also hope that you found him as interesting reading as I did in researching and writing about him.

I must also be honest and say that though our friend was truly brilliant in his businesses, he was also a devastating failure in his personal life. He never did things by halfway measures, he went all the way openly for all to see and judge. His blunders sent him to jail six times from 1943 until he died. His experiments in life styles hurt his family, and because of this and their fear that old wounds will be re-opened, I promised to disguise his case and not disclose his name.

I would like to end my presentation by quoting this man's basic slogan for his management teams, "If it ain't simple, then mister, you ain't uncovered the right way of doing it." This horsesense outlook forced his people to get at the very heart of the problem and solve it the first time right.

How far would this man have gone if he hadn't been handicapped by almost no formal education and therefore been employable in the depression?

Minor Point 15-5: Sharing Expenses with Commissioned Salesmen   M, IS

It is an unwritten agreement that when you and your people visit a territory, you pay all of your own travel bills, motel bills, telephone calls, and taxi fares. The commissioned sales firms will transport you around their territory and pay automobile expenses, tolls, etc.

In the matter of entertainment, you pick up all meal bills except when one of the salesmen's customers is involved. Then the salesman picks up all bills.

If you are a swinger and go in for such things as call girls, drugs, poker, or the horses, everything should be "Dutch Treat." You'll be surprised at how little fun and games are involved in sales. It's hard to put in an effective 12-hour day after partying too much.

Example 15-1: A Checklist to Follow on Buddy Calls with Rep Salesmen   M, IS

If you and your fellow founders are to be welcomed back into a terri-tory, you must learn how to behave when working with a commissioned salesman. I recommend that before you ever call on the first customer with a salesman, you establish the following ground rules of how you'll behave with the salesman. Consider following this outlined checklist:

(1)   Before we get started, let's define how you want me to perform before the customer.
(2)   First, you are the professional salesman and you know both your territory and your customer far better than I do. Therefore, you are the captain and call the shots. I know our products better than you and therefore will support you technically.
(3)   I'll keep you from making major technical mistakes. If you make a big mistake, I'll correct it in a professional manner. If you make a minor error, I'll let it ride and tell you about it in the car after the call.

(4) The reasons that I am working with you are:
 (1) To train you on our products so that you are better equipped to sell them.
 (b) To learn and understand your customers' needs so that we can develop better products.
 (c) If we are going to work together, we need a healthy relationship. We are really nowhere until you can tell me that you don't like the cut of my jib for the following reasons. . . and vice versa.

(5) You are a commissioned salesman and I am a salaried manager. I know that if I want to make buddy calls with you hereafter, I'd better not stand in your way of making sales. Please feel free to discuss your other principals on these calls. Not only will this help you, it will give me a better insight of your sales rhythm and help us complement instead of hinder this rhythm.

(6) When you want me to keep quiet, give me the high sign and I will. The last thing I want to do is get in the way of a close.

If you establish this kind of working foundation and follow it, there isn't one salesman who will not welcome you to visit any of his key accounts with him.

Minor Point 15-6: Team Selling   M, IS, RS, F

Nothing is worse than to see a founders' team walk into a venture capitalist's office, a sales agency's headquarters, or a customer's facilities, start to make a presentation and then start working against each other and splinter before the client's eyes. In every team selling effort, you must have your horses lined up and present a solid front, or every time an experienced negotiator will force you to fragment. Consider the following techniques to assure you of a working team appearance:

(1) Establish the reasons for the team visit. After you define your objectives, everyone involved will keep their eyes on these goals.

(2) Establish a team quarterback who is in total charge of the selling attempt. This man calls the shots and orchestrates the presentation.

(3) Establish what proprietary information you will disclose and what will not be disclosed. Define the dirty laundry not to be mentioned.

(4) Assign each member a role. The team quarterback will pass all questions on to the man who is playing that role. In other words, one man will field the technical questions, another the administrative questions, another the marketing decisions, etc. If you have a team member who is a good man but makes the weak presentation assign him an assistant's role.

(5) Make certain that every role player brings with him the necessary

background work to sustain his discipline. This is so obvious, but unless it is definitely pointed out prior to the team selling effort, you can expect someone to forget to collect his materials. It happens every time.

(6) Develop a series of signals which will allow the team quarterback to orchestrate the presentation. A typical set of signals is accomplished with a pen, in this way: (a) If any team member puts a pen to his ear, he wants to be heard and expects the team quarterback to vector the presentation so that he will be called upon. (b) If the team captain scratches his eyebrow with his pen, it means that whoever is talking should swiftly and smoothly end his presentation. (c) A pen to the mouth means everyone shut up. A sales-close attempt is being used.

(7) Sales close is so important that it must be discussed further. Most non-sales types (and even many sales types) do not know a sales close when they hear one. The intent of the meeting is to accomplish something and usually the only way you get the objective accomplished is to get the person who is receiving the presentation to do something (invest in your firm, buy your product, agree to sell your products). The only way you can get him to agree to do this is to close him. A good presentation usually has from 10 to 20 sales-close attempts. When one of these attempts is underway, the last thing that you want is for a team member to destroy the attempt by opening his mouth and shifting the conversation. And a non-sales type will always feel the tension of the close attempt, become uneasy, and to relieve tension, talk at the wrong time. Therefore, whoever makes the sales close attempt has the authority to order everyone else (by pen to mouth) to shut up until the close either works or fails.

(8) Meet somewhere else before your appointment so that no team members come straggling into the presentation late, so that all team members walk into the client's office together and thus present a solid front from the start, and so that you have a few minutes to review the objectives of the meeting, the signals, the roles, and then get all team members in the right frame of mind.

(9) Prior to the meeting, determine who is going to introduce all of the team members, who is going to make the opening statements, and who is going to handle all displays. Please don't over rehearse. Rehearsals usually take the freshness out of the presentations and things never go as expected anyway. The canned approach limits your team's flexibilities.

(10) When the sale is closed, you have accomplished your objectives and therefore want to smoothly and swiftly leave. If you tarry too long, you can be almost positive that some team member is going to say something to cancel the close. The bromide, "An inexperienced man will talk himself into and then out of a sale every time," is unfortunately true too often.

(11) After the meeting, make complete notes of who promised who what and then make certain that your team carries out its promises. It never hurts to immediately write the client, put into writing the promises

made by both sides, the agreements made, and the dates these things will occur. Don't forget to include your opinion that you think the customer made a wise decision in selecting your firm and how you'll make certain he'll never regret his trust.

Minor Point 15-7: A Trick to Handling Swinger Salesmen

If you suspect that an evening on the town with a salesman might lead to trouble, invite the man's wife to join you. Though you'll have to pay for an additional dinner, it is a lot cheaper in the long run. If the swinger isn't married, then invite his boss to join you. This practice will allow you to get into bed by eleven.

Minor Point 15-8: The Method of Responding to Salesmen's Inquiries

If a salesman wires you, respond by wire. If he writes you airmail, special delivery, respond the same way, and if he telephones collect (and the reason for the telephone call isn't because of your company's foul-ups), then call him back collect. The unwritten law of sales is always respond the same way the inquiry was made unless the situation warrants a faster response.

CAMEO 15-2: "SO YOU THINK THAT YOU KNOW SALES? . . . TRY THIS ONE"

Almost every salesman considers himself a professional closer and likes to be challenged with different sales situations. We had a production furnace client who made real inroads into his training and motivation problems by publishing a series of blurbs titled, "So You Think You Know Sales? . . . Try This One." Each blurb presented a hypothetical set of circumstances and asked the salesmen how they would conduct themselves to close the order. In each case, the home team's furnace was held up to a specific competitor's furnace, and in each case, the quote was always about 10% higher than the competition's. Accurate strengths and weaknesses of each furnace were given. The salesman was asked how he would proceed. The best answers were to be published and the winners were to receive 10 shares of no par stock.

Although only 25% of the sales force ever took part in these contests, these blurbs were the best-read documents that ever hit the field. The best solutions of course were published so that other salesmen could build up their arsenal of closes. It was surprising how swiftly all salesmen learned the rather difficult and complex heat-transfer specifications of this start-up's furnace.

There was another unusual situation with this client. Production furnaces are a kind of status symbol to facility engineers, so the start-up intentionally priced its furnaces 10% higher than the market so that it would create a Tiffany image. Actually, this young start-up could have priced its furnaces lower than the market because it had extremely low overhead costs and through leveraging money, it cost only 60% as much as competition to produce the furnaces. Yet since the "So You Think. . ." blurb taught the salesmen how to sell at higher prices and made it a point of pride to beat competition on specifications, the start-up realized approximately 10% additional on sales prices which evolved into 25% higher profits. This is no bad thing.

Example 15-2: The Harvard Scholarship Fund

This sales motivating technique has been used by many of our clients with excellent results. Briefly, there isn't one salesman or one salesman's wife who doesn't believe that their children aren't Harvard quality. Therefore, these start-ups assigned 0.1 of 1% of their salesmen's sales to a special education reserve. Every month, each salesman's wife and child gets a special status report on how that child's scholarship fund is progressing. It has become kind of a report card on judging daddy's performance, and pressures brought upon daddy can be extreme.

These individual reserves can become significant. One client has several individual children's trusts built up to well over $5,000. At 0.1 of 1%, this isn't bad. The trusts of course can be applied to Aggie Tech if Junior falls short of Harvard requirements.

Minor Point 15-9: The "Admiral's Yacht" Syndrome

All start-ups which have developed an innovative solution to our government (local, state, and federal) bureaucracy problem should keep the Admiral's Yacht Syndrome in mind.

Briefly, if you try to make a bureaucracy more effective and lower its expenses, you stand a 90% chance of running into the Admiral's Yacht Syndrome. Let's say that you had the power to demand that the Navy Department cut its expenses by 5%. In all probability, instead of cutting fat, they would mothball a bit of their muscle (such as some aircraft carriers). If you persisted in trying to cut fat and lowered their budget another 5%, then more muscles would be eliminated (say, a portion of the submarine fleet). You keep cutting and they will continue to keep eliminating muscle instead of fat until finally Annapolis is closed. Finally in desperation about losing so much muscle, you'd have to reinstitute their original budgets. All through the expense squeeze, the admiral's yacht will remain operational.

One of the last things a bureaucracy wants is to solve its problems, because then there is no excuse for the bureaucracy to exist. If your start-up has products or services which will compound the bureaucracy's problems and increase its manpower loading and its budget needs, you stand an excellent chance for success. However, if your start-up goes against this syndrome, expect to join the hundreds of other start-up failures which tried to improve performance.

We had a client who developed a postal system which would significantly improve mail delivery at a fraction of the costs our postal system spends. For a full year, they couldn't even make a presentation to our postal department. Then they decided to sell their concept to Germany, Switzerland, Israel, and Japan. In the 2½ years that these countries have used the system, our post office department has spent in excess of $250,000 studying it abroad.

Another start-up had a unique solution to part of our unemployment problem. For $800 funding, they held a trial seminar in which three companies were born. (These three companies today employ well over 200 people). HUD spent $22,000 studying the seminar and its effects. Though HUD's final evaluation of the experiment was glowing, they responded to a second trial attempt by outlawing the sessions. Any unemployed person who attended these seminars would be made ineligible for collecting their unemployment insurance. The start-up periodically follows-up with HUD to determine the outcome of their decisions on whether or not they would fund future seminars. After five years, the proposal is still being evaluated. The start-up of course went on to greener pastures.

A third start-up had a revolutionary concept in eliminating duplication of services and efforts within our government. They requested as payment 1% of the money they saved. It took them only six months to realize the Admiral's Yacht Syndrome and go after greener pastures.

Minor Point 15-10: The Corporal Syndrome

This syndrome is named the "Corporal Syndrome" because in the army no man is harder to please than a new corporal. This man has been the lowest man on the command totem pole until he gets that second stripe and then suddenly he has power and authority! And does he know how to use that second stripe against those who have less rank!

Briefly, most giant corporations, utilities, and government bureaus are blessed with corporals in their lower rungs of management. If you are to penetrate these accounts to realize sales, then you must accept the corporal syndrome for what it is and make it work for you. Also be thankful that these same corporals probably have blocked your lean and hungry competition so that once you clear this hurdle, you'll discover only the old and tired competition. This is the easiest competition to defeat. But before you can compete, you must clear the corporals who block your efforts. And before you can do this, you must understand the dynamics involved.

Briefly, every large company (the only type which can afford corporals) has a definite social structure which is a very powerful thing. At the top of the pecking order are the upper echelons of management. Under them you'll find the research group, under them the design groups, under them the marketing (not sales) specialists, then production, then QA, and then finally you get down in the dregs of the social structure and discover the facility engineers, the component engineers, the buyers, the expeditors, the procurement liaison people, and the maintenance people. The logic (usually unstated but always foremost in everyone's minds) is, "If you can't make it anywhere else, we'll put you down at the bottom with these clowns because any fool can do their jobs." These people make the least money, get the fewest interesting challenges, have their decisions frequently overruled, are the least respected, and usually have offices next to the boiler room or the noisiest and dirtiest production. Needless to say, most of a company's problems are generated from these groups and these people are extremely sensitive about their status.

Now that you have the picture, stop and think about the kind of man who tolerates this caste system without quitting. Would you agree that he is probably a man who has so little respect for himself and his abilities that he doesn't think that he could improve his lot by going out and searching for a more meaningful job? Also realize that if your start-up is going to sell to this company, the entry people that you must clear are these people.

What do these unfortunate people see when they see you and your people come through their doors the first time? They see a dynamic start-up, they see a fresh approach to life, they see an innovative product or service, they see enthusiasm, and in their warped atmosphere they think that they see a man who is going to be a multi-millionaire in the next few years. You represent almost everything that the corporal wants from life and therefore you raise the worst qualities in this individual. Since you are a new start-up and haven't yet gained penetration in his company, he believes he must squash you now or forever regret his lack of action. Yet, until you get past this man, you are going nowhere in his company. He must qualify you as a company, he must qualify your products and services, he must open the right doors for you (or at least not bar them) to upper management, and he must give his appraisals of how his company will profit from purchasing your products. Too often, corporals block innovation because . . . just because.

When they do, are you going to make the same blunders that most hungry founders make? They get frustrated and do stupid things like tell the jerk what a jerk he is, contact the jerk's bosses and attempt to get them to either fire him (or at least override him), overstate their products' specifications so that the corporal's company cannot afford to not evaluate them, or a combination of equally silly and damaging activities. As you can see, these actions will not only not work, they will probably freeze you out forever.

The classical approaches are: (1) Sell downwards as well as upwards.

Force the company's top management, research groups, design groups, and marketing groups to realize that they will be placed in a poor competitive posture unless they utilize your products. (2) Give the upper echelons your product either free or on consignment so that they can actually see that your product is so superior that they will design you into their next generation of products. (3) Decide that you'll force the company to realize the error of their ways by selling to their competition and letting their competition outperform them. These classical approaches are OK in theory and I'm certain that you will use them, however they are ducking the question instead of answering it. All three classical approaches have long lead times and do nothing toward helping you receive sales (and profits) now. Therefore you might consider the following oblique approaches for penetration. You will note that in all cases you are making the corporal syndrome work for you instead of against you.

Let the corporal think that he sees the light at the end of the tunnel in his employment problem. As soon as your tiny company can grow large enough to afford the corporal's great talents, you will consider hiring him for a key slot.

Force the corporal to overcome his own roadblocks by hiring him as a technical consultant (on a moonlighting basis) to advise you on how you should service his industry (see Cameo 16-4 for this tactic).

Play on the corporal's ego by treating him as a true expert. Have him judge your literature and make significant changes on that literature which is sent to him to file. Invite him to co-author technical papers which will be presented at symposiums, etc.

Hire the jerk as an honorary consultant or advisor to your board of directors and pay great lip service to his recommendations on policy matters, on technical strategies, etc.

Make the clown feel like a major wheel by treating him with great respect, by valuing his opinions, and by lifting his badly bruised ego. Have your directors telephone him occasionally to ask advice. When you or your salesmen come to town, invite him and his wife to the swankiest resturant in town and give his utterances (made in front of his wife) major significance. When he goes to the rest room, confide in his wife your opinion that she married a very gifted man. Never laugh at this man behind his back nor vomit over his stupidity.

Ask for the privilege of being a reference for him if ever he decides to leave his present company.

Give him a sculpture for his desk (as payment for his sage advice), send him the latest texts on business management for his library, get your celebrity directors to autograph their pictures with a personal note to him, etc.

Above all, make certain that your salesmen never discuss these tactics with anyone. These tactics always make excellent stories and the stories always seem to get back to the corporal.

It is never difficult to make your visits to this man's company his high points of the year because so few people respect him. When you have completed the account's penetration, chances are that you will have developed a loyal and devoted friend and you'll discover that the scorn you originally felt will be replaced with empathy, understanding, and friendship.

CAMEO 15-3: PENETRATING A TELEPHONE PRODUCTION PLANT

Utilities are abundantly blessed with "corporal syndromed" individuals placed in strategic positions. A start-up, which had developed a unique component to replace three components used in every long-lines switching terminal, discovered that this particular utility had not qualified a new component's vendor in seven years. The primary reason for this was that this telephone company had particularly obnoxious corporals in components' approval and in purchasing. However, since this plant ordered several hundred thousand components every year, the problem had to be addressed.

In the first visit to the facility, the founders were immediately told: "We know all about your component and find it inferior to what we presently use. Also, be aware that it costs us $65,000 to qualify a new vendor's products and also be aware that we presently have five-year contracts with our present suppliers and can not order from others until after this period is over." How is that for opening roadblocks?

The founders, instead of fighting the issues, sat back and discussed everything else under the sun with the corporal. They hung on his every utterance, they treated him with great respect so that he felt that he was an extremely important person, and after an hour's conversation, they thanked him sincerely for investing such a long period of his valuable time in helping them.

Approximately two weeks after this visit, the president wrote the corporal a brief note and asked permission to have his vice president in charge of design engineering contact him for professional guidance. The corporal of course agreed and within a week got a call from the manager of engineering asking if he could send the specifications of their newest components to the corporal for his evaluation and guidance. The start-up of course knew that the corporal's plant wasn't in the market for their component but he wanted to get this man's guidance because he would be an expert and a disinterested party. The VP then mailed his specifications, and for the first time the corporal evaluated them. Since the specs were superior to competition's, the corporal wrote back and said they were adequate, however he then made some recommendations on the presentation format and the wording. The VP wrote back, thanked him for his guidance, and stated that his recommendations were excellent and would be incorporated. They were—but only in specifications sent to this one plant. The VP also stated that a small thank you gift was in the mail and sent the corporal three wheels of Dutch cheese (approximate cost, $22).

Two weeks later, the start-up's director of quality assurance wrote the corporal and asked his guidance on some test results. The director of QA sent him all of the component's qualification data (all of it was excellent except for humidity testing) and stated that he was concerned about their components failing moisture testing. What did the corporal think caused the failures? Also included were several opened components and several sealed components to help the corporal make his evaluation. The corporal spent several days studying the test results and the component's materials and construction (they were excellent). When the corporal could make no knowledgeable recommendations, the QA manager then wrote that they had defined the problem area (he explained it) and the solution (he explained it). Two weeks later he sent another set of test data in which the components passed moisture testing and said that a small thank you gift was in the mail. A gold embossed leather desk appointment booklet (approximate cost $10) soon arrived.

Three weeks later, the VP of Engineering again wrote the corporal and said that he was preparing a technical paper on the thermal properties of silicone and would like the corporal to co-author the work with him. Enclosed was the first rough draft of a paper that was to be presented at IEEE that summer. While the corporal was busy rearranging a few commas and proofing all the following drafts mailed to him, the VP of Marketing called him and said that another telephone plant was performing qualification testing and asked if his plant would be interested in saving the $65,000 expense by getting the test results directly from their sister telephone plant? The corporal turned down the offer, however several weeks later telephoned the president and stated that he had used his influence to get funds released for qualification testing. Actually, the company was re-qualifying an old vendor which had made design changes and for a few dollars more could simultaneously qualify all new sources. However, since the corporal never mentioned this, the founders never disclosed that they knew.

It took this start-up approximately five months and perhaps $100 in gifts and telephone calls to penetrate a customer who no others had penetrated in seven years. Though the start-up still isn't the prime source of supply for the components, they did exceed $150,000 in sales to this unpenetratable account.

How far do you think they would have gotten if initially they had argued with the corporal about his roadblocks, called him a liar over the $65,000 test charge, and pointed out his stupidity in not at least letting them show their wares? How far would they have gotten if they allowed the jerk to see what a big jerk they thought he was? Where would they be if they had gone to the jerk's boss, disclosed how dishonest he was, and tried to remove the roadblock by removing the jerk? These questions seem stupid but do you realize that these mistakes are made by the bulk of the start-ups?

CAMEO 15-4: THE "CONFIDENTIAL" LETTER

Dear Bill,

I was highly impressed with Don Farmington when you and I called on him last week. I've been in the facilities engineering game now for over 10 years and have seen a lot of good men, however in my opinion Don is the best I've seen. Besides really knowing his field, I was impressed by Don's attitudes in other things also. There is merit in recommending that we should invade Red China, bomb Moscow, and send all those minorities who don't seem to love America back where they came from.

Bill, as you know, ours is a brand new company which needs to attract the best men in our industry. Do you think Don would ever be interested in leaving XYZ Inc. and moving to Iowa and working with us? We can't afford to make Don an offer right now, however when we can afford him, we'd like to make him division manager of our aerospace facility group. Don is a typical $35,000-a-year man who could build this division into something of real value. What do you think, Bill? Would Don ever be interested in joining us?

Cordially,

Dave.

This letter (the names have been changed) was written by a start-up's president and sent to his San Francisco rep. The rep salesman showed the letter to Don Farmington, a corporal who was blocking the start-up's path. Needless to say, Don (a $16,000-a-year clerk), was flattered to the extent that he helped the start-up penetrate his company. The start-up has never grown large enough to start their aerospace division, but Don is still so flattered by the compliment that he is a loyal friend.

CAMEO 15-5: PRAY FOR CUSTOMER PROBLEMS   M, IS

This is probably the riskiest and most unethical true sales story that I know and shouldn't be construed as a viable marketing tactic. The only reason for passing it on to you is that it graphically illustrates the blessings that you can realize with customer problems.

Briefly, a bay area manufacturer was founded by three engineers who pioneered a family of medical instruments. Since the medical industry paid them high sales prices, these engineers never bothered with the usual cost savings systems that most manufacturers utilize.

When this firm started 15 years ago, it dealt with one set of vendors and never bothered to second-source them or get competitive bids. When the firm first opened its doors, it spent approximately $271 to manufacture an instrument that it sold for $2,500. When it first started, it bought components in small quantities, however after 15 years of continual growths, its production orders amounted to well over 100,000 components each month. Many component suppliers never bothered to lower prices as quantities increased.

All went well for the particular rep whose principals were sole-sourced for 15 years. He considered it his vest pocket account and since there were few problems, he never really bothered to work the account very hard.

Then storm clouds appeared. Our government wanted to purchase approximately 100,000 instruments and asked this company to bid on this quantity. Since the company was badly back-ordered in the civilian areas and since it only had production capabilities of 3,000 instruments a month, it had major management decisions to make. If they got the government order, they couldn't service and therefore would eventually lose their lucrative private industry penetration. Therefore, they turned in one of the strangest quotes the government probably ever received. They quoted:

1 Instrument	$2,500 each
1,000 Instruments	$2,500 each
10,000 Instruments	$2,500 each
100,000 Instruments	$2,500 each

Needless to say, the founders felt that this was equivalent to a "no bid" to the government and forgot the order. The rep was extremely pleased because he knew that our government would force its supplier to have a minimum of three sources on every part and he knew that competitive bids would illuminate the high prices that he had been charging his customer throughout the years.

As it turned out, these engineers had the most reliable instrument on the market and government doctors wanted the best and insisted that the government get the best regardless of the prices. So after a lot of haggling, a few threats, and a few games, the manufacturer got an order for 100,000 units (minimum shipments 1,000 instruments per month) for $2,500 each.

Now our rep had a significant problem. How could he convince his customer to ignore government requirements and not seek competitive bids? This problem was compounded by the small problem that the rep salesman had never really worked the account properly and with the exception of a clerk who placed monthly orders, a receiving clerk who inspected incoming shipments, and a components engineer (a brother-in-law of one of the engineer founders), the salesman had no penetration into his customer. Any competitor could walk in cold off the street and attain equal penetration within an hour. What strategy could the rep pull to immediately get penetration to the highest levels and convince everyone to not seek second sources?

The solution seemed simple. All the rep had to do was convince one of his principals to ship defective components, shut down his customer's production lines, perform very professionally in defining the problem, and appear very professional in getting the customer's production back up.

To boil a long story down, he convinced one of his principals to do just that. They shipped defective components, and within days every production line was stopped.

Now, when a customer's production lines stop, your salesman will swiftly get to meet every man of authority in a hurry. This rep did. Within hours after the first line stopped, he was called into the executive vice president's office, the general manager's office, the production vice president's office, and the quality assurance manager's office. Within minutes, his principal received a telephone call and had agreed to immediately rush out a team to define and resolve the problems. The vendor's team boarded an airplane that same day, was met at the airport by the manufacturer, and worked days and nights for three days defining the problem. There wasn't one corner of the plant that this team didn't visit to define the problems. There wasn't one design engineer, one production supervisor, or one key person in the company who wasn't met, talked with, and impressed. At the end of the third day, enough parts (with corrective action taken) were on the airplane, and the fourth day, production was back up on a limited scale. For weeks after the shut down, the rep salesman met an early morning flight, picked up his customer's day's production of parts, delivered them to the production vice president, then visited every other key employee to notify them of the delivery and discuss long-term corrective actions underway. Each day, the vendor team, now back at their own plant, telephoned each key man to give status reports of their progress. After several weeks, more parts were shipped than short-term production could use and within a month and a half, things were back to normal. However, now the rep knew everyone in the plant and he did an excellent job in maintaining his penetration.

When production orders for the government job began to be released, competitive bids were ignored. The rep and his vendors had effectively used their customer's problem to give the image of true professionalism and service and the customer wanted to retain this talent if future problems occurred.

I certainly do not recommend that you generate customer problems intentionally. If you are like every other manufacturer, you'll get your share without looking for them. However, when they do crop up, look at them as an opportunity to present your talents and your professionalism and to gain long-term penetrations.

To those of you who might think that this gambit might be an excellent tool for you to use, let's swiftly examine some of the risks that both the rep and his principal took.

The probability that competitors might learn of the "ploy" is extreme. Then it is a minor task for them to get the story out to all of your other customers (nationwide) and destroy your customer base.

It is unethical and causes extreme hardships to your customer. If your customer even suspected that he had been duped, his recourse in courts of law could be harsh. In all probability, you would end up paying all his losses plus penalties. Needless to say, the newspapers and journals would cover the case thoroughly.

Your employees are in a position to blackmail you. An employee who took part in the sham could always threaten to disclose the full case if you attempted to fire him, transfer him, or pass him in promotions.

There is a very subtle punishment that always seems to take place whether or not you get by with something unethical. For a company to operate unethically forces its employees to operate (in the company's behalf) unethically. Since you condone cheating in one way, in many minds this means that you condone cheating in many ways. Besides experiencing thefts, lies, gamesmanships, politics, and the other factors which hurt a company internally, you can expect your people to feel free to cheat with other customers, reps, and outside firms. Like the kid who starts cheating to pass an exam and soon can't take any exam without cheating, you'll find dishonesties will creep in all areas and you will have problems you never dreamed of.

To prove the point, the rep involved is still a one-man office. Though he has been in business for well over 17 years, he hasn't been able to grow in an industry that has had enormous growths.

The principal who agreed to the ploy has been in business for over 25 years. This firm has less than 2% of the market and has had red-ink income statements for the past 5 years. It's improbable that this company will exist for another 5 years.

16 · The Mechanics of Sales

PROLOGUE   M, IS, RS, F

Theoretically, this chapter shouldn't be necessary for this text. As a founder, your responsibilities should end after you have established your distribution network and installed the systems to train, motivate, and support these networks' sales efforts.

However, unless you run that extra mile and literally become involved in the sales process, I'll guarantee you that your company will not meet its fourth milestone (market penetration) within years after you should meet it. Also, I'll guarantee you that most of your operational managers will never learn to distinguish between legitimate sales obstacles (the kind that they should address and cure) and sales resistances (fictitious alibis, mirages which can eat up your budgets). The average company wastes between 6% and 10% of its total budget on sales resistance mirages.

In this chapter, let's first look at some statistics on field sales, then look at the sales process, and finally look at the basic sales closes. If you are wise, you'll assume your share of the responsibilities for closing sales and orchestrate your sales machinery.

SECTION ONE: BACKGROUND OF THE FIELD SALES DISCIPLINE AS IT EXISTS TODAY

SOME SURPRISING STATISTICS   M, IS, RS, F

Would you believe that those sales engineers whose performance in their craft is superior (approximately 2% of the pack) claim that they average five sales close attempts on each customer before they can close?

Or that the average sales engineer (75% of the pack) knows only four closes and practices only two? This means that he either must repeat the same sales close technique in each presentation (and therefore become obvious in his efforts) or quit before the close is made.

Did you know that most competent sales engineers (approximately 45% of the pack) pray for both sales objections and sales resistances? They can use these hurdles to close sales more easily. Since these sales resistances aren't rational and are therefore undefendable, a customer is in the position of searching frantically for some legitimate obstacle or alibi for not buying. Thus he is vulnerable.

The real pros observe this process and take advantage of it to close your sales. However a significant percentage of the salesmen selling your products (approximately 55%) can't distinguish between a sales resistance and a legitimate obstacle if their life depends upon it, and then two things occur. The salesman accepts the resistance (a mirage) as legitimate and forefeits the sale and he also passes the mirage as an obstacle back to your company to solve. Since most of the operational people in your company likewise can't distinguish between a fictitious obstacle and a real one, they invest your company's budgets and priorities in attempting to define and correct a mirage.

The Institute of American Business Consultants has been very active in techniques for overcoming budget wastes in the sales resistance areas. The following norms were selected from over 100 manufacturers who had active campaigns to combat sales resistances.

Department	Percent of Operational Budget Spent on Sales Resistances
R&D	8%
Manufacturing	2%
Administration	3%
Quality Assurance	6%
Marketing	18%
Sales	4%

What is interesting is that the financial impacts on manufacturers who totally ignore sales resistances usually run from two to three times as high (up to 10% of some companies' total operating budgets).

Later we'll dwell upon a few techniques of using sales resistances to work for you, however for now realize that you must accept and address the effects of sales resistances either in wasted money (and man hours) or in introducing those control systems which minimize it.

Would you believe that approximately one-third of the people who call themselves sales engineers do not even know the stages of the sales process? They therefore usually completely blow stage one and in doing so, never progress through the other stages correctly. Nothing is sadder than seeing a sales engineer attempting to work in stage five while his customer is frustratedly hung up in stage two.

Would you believe that almost one-half of the people who call themselves sales engineers do not attempt to close in any way? Many make an excellent presentation and then leave it totally up to the customer to buy or not to buy. If your company depends upon a sales effort without sales closes, expect to realize only 30% of the sales that you should realize.

Or would you believe that those companies which assume the responsibilities for sales closes and lost sales (approximately 2% of the pack) realize from two to five times as many sales closes as their competition which depends totally upon their field salesmen's efforts and abilities? Of the 98% who do not assume responsibilities, few have even thought of giving their sales force the ongoing systems which assume sales close responsibilities for those sales that their salesmen can't close. Though this oversight is unbelievable, be thankful because it gives you a wide open path to dominate commissioned salesmen's selling efforts.

AXIOM EIGHTEEN: IT IS HUMAN NATURE TO RESIST SALES. THEREFORE, OVER 70% OF THE PURCHASES MADE ARE MADE THROUGH SALES CLOSES.

SALES RESISTANCE   M, IS, RS, F

Every rational human being is filled with built-in sales resistances. If we weren't, we would all be bankrupt.

When subjected to a buy-don't-buy decision, it is human nature to resist buying. We don't want to buy because we fear that someone will challenge our buying decision, we don't know the consequences involved with a new vendor—an unknown quantity (you and your young firm), we don't want to admit that we are not current with the new advances and techniques that your product utilizes, we dislike your salesman's tie, we are jealous and resentful of your vibrant young company and its breakthroughs, and a host of other hang ups that we will never admit to (even to ourselves).

SECTION TWO: THE SALES PROCESS

THE STAGES INVOLVED IN THE SALES PROCESS
M, IS, RS, F

For ease in getting a complex subject across so that it is simple to follow, please allow me to discuss the sales process as though it is a path that each salesman and his customer must mutually walk. The operative word is "mutually," for if the salesman either leads or lags his customer on the pathway, the sale is in jeopardy.

The pathway of each sales process is identical in many ways and totally unique and different in other ways. This difference is why "canned talks" rarely work well. The path's curves and distances always vary with the customer's mental agility, flexibility, and speed; the customer's job knowledge, experience, and confidence; the customer's need for your products or services; the complexity of your products and services; and the customer's moods and attitudes at the time he walks down the pathway with your salesman. Likewise the path varies with your salesman's abilities, training, knowledge, and moods. Now that we have covered the differences, let's concentrate on the samenesses of each presentation.

Stage One: The Preamble

While the customer thinks that your salesman is trying to set a mood with small talk, amenities, and jokes, in truth the professional is swiftly determining what authorities and responsibilities his customer has, plus his abilities, confidence, flexibilities, attitudes, and moods, plus his rationality and mental speed, and finally, what strategies and techniques might work the best.

Rookie salesmen always blow this stage and therefore usually lead or lag the customer throughout the balance of the pathway.

Stage Two: Establishing the Customer's Need

There are always three needs at the beginning of this stage. The customer's needs as the salesman sees it, the customer's needs as the customer sees it, and the customer's needs as they really exist. In stage two, the salesman and the customer must mutually transpose these three images into one need.

Oddly enough, stage two is the most ignored stage. The number of sales hours wasted each year ignoring this essential stage is tremendous.

Usually, one of three errors occurs in this stage. They are:

(1)   The salesman doesn't really believe in your product or company and though he may go through the motions of a sales presentation, this lack of confidence transmits and the sale rarely comes off. Give yourself a black mark in training and take instant corrective actions.

(2)   The salesman is so enthusiastic about your products that he assumes his customers will immediately see their value. Therefore stage two is given a lick and a promise by the salesman while he rushes to stage five. Meanwhile, the customer is stitting there wondering how he could ever use your contraption. Give yourself another black mark in training.

(3)   The customer and the salesman are equally strong and set on their two different images of what the customer's needs are and these two images are never overlayed. The path therefore forks at this point and each continues down a different leg. Give your salesman a black mark for bullheadedness.

The baby will never be born unless both proceed through stage two at the same time.

Stage Three: The Modular Sales Presentations

No sophisticated person is going to buy until he feels that he thoroughly understands and needs what you are selling. To attempt to close before this need is met will insult your customer and give your salesman (and your company) the image of schlock operators. Your salesman must make a complete presentation on the points the customer wants to hear about. The operative words here are "the points the customer wants to hear about."

The true professional modularizes his sales presentations and thoroughly presents those modules which are of the greatest interest to the customer. Once he completes these first modules, he'll then jump to stages four, five, and six. If stages four or five abort, he'll then fall back into presenting another module, whet the customer's appetite, perform another interim sales close, and if they take, again attempt a final close. This process continues until the customer agrees to buy or the salesman runs out of time or modules.

If you ever observe a gifted salesman in stage three, you'll usually see him induce the customer into making objections, asking questions, or getting his concerns out on the table. His reasons for forcing the customer to make objections are that he wants the customer to feel that he is truly part of the sales process pathway. They are mutually walking it together to explore and locate the best solutions for his customer.

The professional wants the customer to transpose his sales resistances into legitimate obstacles early so that he can overcome them in the early stages instead of having them hamper his close techniques.

These questions and objections show the salesman where he and the customer are on the sales pathway. If the customer is returning to stage two, the salesman must return with him. If the customer is growing tired of stage three and is ready to progress to stages four, five, and six, the salesman doesn't want to frustrate him.

The questions and objections either reinforce or contradict the salesman's swift evaluations of stage one.

Never allow your salesmen to degrade stage three to a monolog with the salesman always talking and the customer just listening.

Stage Four: Appetite Whetting

There are hundreds of techniques which force the customer to want to buy. Even a poor salesman can name at least two dozen and any professional can outline at least a hundred. Therefore, we will not dwell on these techniques except to say that they are impossible to apply unless you do a good job in the first three stages. The key is to observe when your customer's appetite is whetted enough to proceed to stage five.

Stage Five: The Interim Close

Most professionals have several dozen interim close techniques that are so smooth that the customer never realizes that he has been subjected to a close.

The key to an interim close is that it must open the door for the final close in such a way that the customer always feels that he bought—not that he was sold. We'll cover several of the best later in this chapter, however as a factory man who will be making buddy calls with your salesmen, you must realize that this is a time when you shut up in front of the customer. Nothing blotches a sale faster than a founder who leads a customer away from a close attempt.

Stage Six: The Final Close

Once a customer accepts an interim close, the professional immediately proceeds into the final close and gets the order. If he is good, the final close will be so binding that the sale will remain closed after he leaves the customer's office.

The key to the sixth stage is to never attempt it until the interim close works and to never delay in attempting it once the interim close works. Once the final close is completed, please never go back into stage three and make the balance of your presentation modules. You have heard the saying, "He talked himself into the sale and then out of it." This happens so frequently with both rookie salesmen and factory men. To them, the sales presentation is more important than the sale.

Stage Seven: The Reinforcement Stage

Getting the sale is one thing and keeping it is another. Realize that your buyer had to overcome his personal sales resistances to allow your salesman to complete stage six, and this is a painful and frequently festering process. After your salesman leaves his office, doubts can still fester and those doubts can translate into cancellations. I have seen competitive salesmen unseat a closed order by saying something simple like, "George, I sincerely hope that your decision to buy from XYZ doesn't come back to haunt you and make you the laughing stock of the industry. People are still laughing at Bill Fredrickson of LMN Inc. and Pete Dayton of OPQ Company. For your sake, I hope things work out all right." Needless to say, when the competitive salesman left, George called both Bill and Pete and then cancelled. The last thing any man wants is to be laughed at.

This wouldn't have happened had the salesman seated e order after the close. He could have done this with a simple statement like, "George, I would like to complement you on your wise decision. One year from now, you'll be as proud of your decision as you are today." or "I sincerely want to thank you for allowing us to show you how we'll perform. I want you to know that I will never let your trust down."

Whatever words your salesman states just after the painful close will remain in the buyer's mind. Yet less than half of the field salesmen even acknowledge a need for stage seven.

Many of our clients handle stage seven themselves by sending out a short blurb to all new customers. If their salesman performed this stage, then their blurb reinforces his reinforcement. If he ignored it, then the factory performs it for him.

Stage Eight: Support the Sale

When your customer placed his order, he in essence hired your field salesman to make damned certain that his order flows smoothly and that he, the customer, is never embarrassed by your company's conduct. Approximately 90% of your salesmen accept this responsibility to varying degrees and you, as a founder, must acknowledge your salesman's responsibilities to support his customer. Suspect any salesman who doesn't fight you for your customers' sake.

SECTION THREE: SOME FACTORS WHICH FOUNDERS FREQUENTLY OVERLOOK

SALES PRESSURES VS. OBVIOUS AND INSULTING TECHNIQUES   M, IS, RS, F

Some idiot must have once observed a carnival barker's poor taste and transparent attempts and classified them as "high pressure sales," and since then we have all accepted this definition. We all make a mental promise to ourselves that we'll never be connected with any firm which depends upon high pressure tactics and we'll never be responsible for applying pressures ourselves. Therefore, when we are in a critical sales situation, we feel the pressures build as our customer wavers between buying or not buying. Since you feel the pressures, an internal flag comes up and you suddenly become concerned at using high pressure tactics and feel that you are jeopardizing your relationship with your customer. Therefore, you relieve the pressures by moving the presentation away from the sales close stage (stage six) back to stage three. This happens more times than you would care to admit.

Right now, let's eliminate the false notion that equates pressure with poor taste and obvious tactics. Pressure is as essential an ingredient to all sales techniques as are good taste, ethics, empathy, courtesy, and service.

Let's put the false notion to bed once and for all by the following logic.

(1)   Every buyer is a human being.

(2)   Every human being has built-in sales resistances.

(3)   Sales resistances are irrational or undefendable fears that rarely surface to exposure. However, until the buyer can overcome them, the sale will never be made.

(4)   To get the buyer to want to overcome them, subtle but very real pressures must be applied.

(5)   The amount of pressure needed is proportional to the buyer's sales resistances.

SALES CLOSE SMOOTHNESS   M, IS, RS, F

Realize that the average professional must make from 3 to 20 sales close attempts at each presentation. Usually, these close techniques are so smooth and so subtle that the buyer never realizes that he has been exposed to a close attempt. After the sale is consummated, the buyer usually feels that all the salesman did was to present the facts and leave the decision totally to the buyer. The buyer then made a rational decision to buy for the good of his company.

THE TIME VARIABLE   M, IS, RS, F

Recall that in the first stage the salesman invested the effort to determine his customer's mental speed and flexibilities? Every person has a different comprehension speed and the sales process must move at that speed. If the buyer is slow, then the sales pathway must be followed at a slow pace. If the salesman becomes impatient and begins to lead the buyer too fast, then he runs the probability of his mutual-path partner becoming confused, and the sales process is aborted. Equally bad is the customer with exceptional comprehension speed who must endure the salesman who explains the obvious.

Besides the customer's mental speed, realize that time is very much a variable in other aspects of the sales process. It takes time to digest and correlate the many specifications of your products, it takes time to digest that the legitimate sales objections have been adequately answered and are therefore no longer valid obstacles, it takes time to fight the inner battle against sales resistances and to gain confidence in the decision to buy, and it takes time to build the courage to go out on a limb and buy from a new and unknown vendor.

In addition, the variable time is lengthened or shortened by the complexity of your products, the complexity of your customer's company, the customer's budget, your higher (or lower) sales prices, and the degree of your customer's needs (as seen by your buyer's supervisors).

Most start-up founders become very impatient for sales and in trying to speed up the sales process, they jeopardize the close.

SALES RHYTHMS   M, IS, RS, F

We introduced the term "sales rhythms" in an earlier chapter and stressed that your company must either complement the salesman's sales rhythm or expect to be ignored. From examining the sales process above, you can get a good feel for the type of sales rhythms essential for a commissioned salesman's success. Most salesmen have from 50 to 200 sales processes in various stages in process at any one time. They all attempt to orchestrate their schedules so that they conform with the timing of each customer. If your company is in conflict with this juggling act, then the salesman will be forced to give you a minimal effort.

COVERING MORE THAN ONE PRINCIPAL AT EACH
SALES CALL   M, IS

We'll get into this again in the next chapter, however realize that the professional tries to thoroughly cover up to three principals (manufacturers) in depth at each sales call and to mention one or two others. The rookie attempts to cover them all, and the lazy salesman discusses only one or two manufacturers.

The professional usually modularizes his presentation in such a way that complementary lines are integrated into each sales process.

If you select a manufacturers' representative whose primary principals do not complement your products, then expect to be only a minor principal and receive a minimal effort.

Minor Point 16-1: "Please OK This"　　　M, IS, RS, F

People are trained to be extremely cautious of "signing" any contract (and your purchase orders are definitely contracts). Therefore you'll observe that the professional will never require the customer to sign anything. He'll use the term, "Please OK this agreement," and direct the customer to sign in your signature line.

Minor Point 16-2: Agreement Vs. Contract

Remember in an earlier chapter we recommended that you use the term "agreement" instead of "contract"? The same definitely holds with your purchase order forms. A simple heading of "Agreement" is more than enough at the top of your order form.

Please do your salesmen a favor by not making your purchase order look or read like a legal contract. Keep it in everyday English (if you don't, the buyer will always forward it to his legal department for approval, and this is a delaying obstacle that no professional salesman can overcome).

If there are complex paragraphs that your lawyer insists upon, then consider the boiler plate solution, which is simply to place all of the legal specifications on the back of the purchase order in extremely small print. These boiler plates always follow the same format. They begin with the extremely minor points (that no buyer will object to) and after six or seven minor points, inject the clauses that may raise objections.

Minor Point 16-3: The Great Boiler Plate War　　　M, IS

Most customers have grown pretty sophisticated in handling boiler plates. They rarely even pay attention to them. All that they do is sign your order form and then "confirm" this order on their own purchase order. The back of this confirmation paperwork is the customer's boiler plate which adds legal clauses to protect his company's interests.

You'll probably want to plagiarize these clauses to add to your purchase order forms.

Minor Point 16-4: The Pre-Stage-One Step in the Sales Process　　　M, IS, RS, F

Every truly professional salesman that I know practices a mental preparation before he begins Stage one. This preparation usually goes along the following lines. Approximately 20 minutes before his appointment, he reviews his manufacturers' specifications. After approximately 10 minutes, he sets everything aside and reviews what kind of image he must project. He evaluates the image that his buyer wishes to see, reinforces his own self image, and finally sets the objectives of this sales call firmly in his mind. He resolves to meet these objectives and then . . . he leaves himself and enters his customer's lobby.

Oddly enough, this mental preparation is frowned upon as amateurism by the schlock salesmen. They see this preparation as 20 minutes of prime sales time lost and blunder into the first stage totally unprepared. Too frequently, they are without direction, poorly prepared, and their quantity of sales illuminates it.

Minor Point 16-5: The Analogy of Sales to Fishing   M, IS, RS, F

Almost all people who write books on sales or give seminars seem to be ex-insurance salesmen. These one-shot salesmen have refined the business of single-shot sales down to an art form, however usually their transparent techniques are a disaster in all other forms of sales except insurance.

Unfortunately, most of these men look upon sales as a game in which the customer (the sucker) is on one side and they (the master salesmen) are on the other. Their books always seem to equate sales to sport fishing in which the customer is "played," then "hooked," and finally "landed."

Unless your industry is in the single-shot area, please never use these terms in training your salesmen. Your salesmen are in the business of repeat sales and the only way that they can get these sales is by working with (instead of playing with) their customers. As soon as you fall into the trap of using terms like "nail the trophy to the wall," "single-source the sucker," or "play the bait," expect to see your salesmen distrust your intentions and therefore be afraid of properly representing you.

SECTION FOUR: THE BASIC SALES CLOSES

There are probably thousands of variations to these basic closes and it will be up to you to determine which variations will work best for your company. These close techniques are being presented so that you can judge and alter them for your particular needs.

SALES CLOSE ONE: THE ASSUMPTIVE TECHNIQUE

This sales close involves no words. When used, the attitude, body language, and inner feelings transmit to the customer without a word being said.

The salesman assumes that his product is excellent, that its price is just, that his principal (you) is ethical and will meet all commitments, that he, the salesman, will support the customer in every way needed, and that the customer is a rational, intelligent individual who will buy once he hears all of the aspects and judges them properly. This may sound like bunk, but it works well. Customers gain confidence rapidly and then buy because it is the right thing to do. Those who believe in a sixth sense can give all kinds of reasons that the salesman's attitudes and convictions are transmitted without words.

CAMEO 16-1: THE ASSUMPTIVE TECHNIQUE

There is a very famous story of the time Fred Clarkson and a used car salesman (who published a best seller on sales techniques) sat on a panel to answer college students' questions on sales as a profession. The used car salesman disputed Fred's statements on the effectiveness of the assumptive technique to the degree that Fred challenged him to a contest. Fred stated that he would use nothing but the assumptive technique, that he would allow the used car salesman to use every trick in the books. Fred bet that he could sell more $5 bills for $10 than the car salesman could sell $10 bills for $5. The contest took place that evening in downtown Boston. Each man was allowed to make 20 attempts and the one who had the most sales was the winner.

Fred won, 6 sales to 2. In asking the 6 (who had obviously made poor purchases) why they had agreed to buy a $5 bill for $10, all 6 stated that they knew it was a poor trade but that they bought because something inside them told them it was the right thing to do. In asking the 18 who refused to pay $5 for a $10 bill, all stated that they knew it was an excellent trade but they opposed the manipulation of the used car salesman.

SALES CLOSE TWO: THE SUBORDINATE QUESTION TECHNIQUE

This is an extremely smooth close. It works by asking the customer a question pertaining to some secondary or subordinate phase and in answering it, the customer agrees to buy.

This technique is also one of the smoothest interim closes (or trial close to see if the customer is ready to buy). If the customer isn't ready, the salesman can naturally begin presenting another module of his presentation for another trial.

SALES CLOSE THREE: THE IMPENDING EVENT TECHNIQUE

This sales close is extremely tricky and must be orchestrated by the principal to keep it from becoming apparent or an obvious sales trick. It works extremely well when a principal wants to break the procrastination backlog in all territories. The basic technique is to warn the customer of some impending event, and unless he takes advantage of the salesman's offer in X days, the event will occur.

SALES CLOSE FOUR: THE INDUCEMENT TECHNIQUE

This is the reverse of the impending event technique and again is an orchestrated program designed to shake loose buyer procrastination. If the customer buys within X time, an additional bonus will be given.

SALES CLOSE FIVE: THE NARRATIVE TECHNIQUE

A significant percentage of salesmen have the ability to utilize this technique because they are such excellent joke and story tellers. If a buyer lacks job confidence, lacks job knowledge, is at either extreme of the optimist-pessimist line, or is in a mood not conducive to accepting a sales presentation, then this technique works well. Briefly, tell the customer a true story about another customer (preferably one whom he respects). Use this technique to illustrate the points which interest the customer most and also utilize it to illustrate those points the customer should (but doesn't) consider. Besides entertaining the customer, you are name-dropping references and building confidence.

SALES CLOSE SIX: THE BENJAMIN FRANKLIN TECHNIQUE

This technique works well with the extremely rational and hard-headed customer. Briefly, when Ben Franklin was an ambassador to England and later to France, he used this technique to sell these foreign governments on helping our struggling nation. It is also rumored that he used it to induce beautiful young women into going to bed with a fat, balding, near-sighted old man.

Briefly, the technique is to make a buy-don't-buy ledger sheet. Along the left hand side of the ledger, entitle the column "assets" and along the right hand side entitle the column "liabilities." Then give the customer your pen and the Franklin ledger and together you two brainstorm the reasons he should buy. The customer writes the reasons down. When you have completed the assets, the salesman sits back and lets the customer think of all the reasons that he will not buy. If the salesman is any kind of salesman at all, he can help the customer see that there are five times as many reasons for buying as not buying.

The other feature is that it forces the customer to list his objections. Any salesman worth his salt can easily close on objections.

SALES CLOSE SEVEN: THE INVERSE FRANKLIN LEDGER

This technique is similar to close six except the salesman forces the customer to say no in such a way that he is really saying yes. ''Are you considering buying an IBM main frame computer instead of our mini-computer because you have an excess capital budget and want to spend it?'' Or, ''Are you considering buying that main frame computer instead of a mini-computer because your boss considers it a status symbol and worth the excess capacity and expenses?'' Or, ''We will have our mini-computer installed by next Tuesday and the software operational by next Friday. Is this too slow?'' This process continues until the buyer sees that he must either say ''yes'' to one of your questions, must define his sales resistance into a legitimate objection, or he must agree to buy. Since the salesman can close from the first two alternatives, this technique works well when the customer is wishy-washy, offers the salesman no real reasons, and refuses to be tied down.

SALES CLOSE EIGHT: THE ASK-FOR-THE-SALE TECHNIQUE

This close works, though I don't know why it works. In fighting the sales resistance battle, we hit upon this technique to make the customer verbalize the reasons that he would not order. It worked beautifully as an interim close because the customer usually gave his objections. With something concrete to work with, the salesman could function, overcome the objections, and try to close again. The sales resistance was transcribed into more objections and the process continued until the customer ran out of resistance.

However, we discovered a surprise. About 25% of the people who refused other close attempts agreed to give their order when the salesman asked for it. We thought it was a fluke and tried it with a client who was setting up a string of water sports retail stores. By placing a display close to the cash register and having the clerk ask anyone who dwelled at the display to buy one, approximately one-fourth did buy.

SALES CLOSE NINE: THE ORDER-PAD TECHNIQUE

This is a standard close used by approximately 25% of the salesmen. When the salesman walks into the office, he pulls out his order pad and makes it obvious to the buyer. As points are made in the presentation, the salesman asks the customer if he wants that feature. If the customer says ''yes'' the salesman adds it to his order. When the presentation is complete, the order pad is completely filled out. A simple request, "Would you please OK this for us," closes the order.

SALES CLOSE TEN: THE CLARKSON CLOSE

This is one of the smoothest and most often occurring closes that less than 5% of salesmen know. The opportunity to use it occurs approximately three times during every sales call.

Briefly, when the salesman has progressed deep into stage three (the presentation stage), he induces the customer to ask any question to which he can asnwer "Yes." But instead of answering yes, he turns the customer's question into a question and when the customer answers "Yes," he proceeds into further closes. It works something like this:

"Can I get it in my company's colors?"

"Do you want it in your company's colors?"—(Clarkson Close, attempt 1)

"Yes, if there are no differences in price."

"When do you need delivery?"—(Subordinate question, attempt 1)

"As soon as possible. Can I get it in three weeks?"

"Do you want it in three weeks?"—(Clarkson close, attempt 2)

"Yes."

"How do you want it shipped, air, rail, or truck?"—(Subordinate question, attempt 2)

"By truck."

The entire time they were talking, the salesman was filling in his order form. He now simply responds, "We're going to have to move on this right now to meet your delivery needs. Would you please OK this while I use your telephone to get things rolling? I'll use my telephone credit card."—(Order pad close, attempt 1.)

Do you see how simple and smooth it was? The customer never realized that he was subjected to five distinct sales closes. The only time that there was even slight pressure was in the final close. How would things have progressed if the salesman had just answered "Yes" to the first question. The sales process would have been at an impasse.

SALES CLOSE ELEVEN: THE CLOSE-ON-AN-OBJECTION
TECHNIQUE #1

This technique is used primarily when the salesman suspects that he isn't running into real objections but is being stopped by a yet undefined sales resistance. The sales call has degraded into the buyer thinking up every possible objection that he can think of and while the salesman is busy answering the last objection, the buyer is busy trying to invent new ones. This Ping-Pong match will go on until the buyer either stumps the salesman with an objection or until the salesman grows tired and quits.

The salesman can stop this kind of stupidity by following this formula:

(1)   He hears out the objection completely. Many salesmen make the mistake of not listening to what the buyer is trying to say and therefore either insult the buyer or never respond to the real objection.

(2)   The salesman suddenly looks defeated. The buyer sees that he has won the Ping-Pong match by stumping the salesman. It is essential that the salesman look defeated.

(3)   The salesman then restates the objection as the buyer stated it. He builds upon it, he makes it important by examining all of the ramifications of the objection and he converts it into a major objection.

(4)   The salesman hesitates and now the buyer knows that his sales resistance will not be challenged any further. He has definitely won.

(5)   The salesman then asks if, with the exception of this one major objection, there are any other reasons that the buyer won't buy. Now the buyer has a choice of saying no, this is the only objection, or else coming out with the real reasons that he won't buy. If the buyer takes the latter course, then the salesman with confidence responds to the further objections and puts them to bed. Again he interrogates the buyer by asking with the exception of the one major objection, are there any further objections. This process continues until the salesman has put all but the one objection to rest.

(6)   Now, still defeated, he makes the statement that if it weren't for the one objection (and here he restates it again), his principal would get the order. "Isn't that so, Mr. Jones?" When Mr. Jones says yes, the salesman has the order.

(7)   Now, in a very humble manner, almost a brainstorming attitude, he works with the buyer to overcome that one major objection. He acts like he is plowing new ground as he and the buyer develop the solution to the major objection. Finally, in excitement, he restates the major objection and then restates the solution.

(8)   Then he repeats the agreement made in step (6) that if this objection could be solved his principal would have the order. He hands the buyer the order form for his OK.

SALES CLOSE TWELVE: THE CLOSE-ON-AN-OBJECTION TECHNIQUE #2

This technique is similar to close eleven except it is used when the objection doesn't make sense to the salesman. He can not paraphrase the objection because he can't follow it. The technique is to question the customer as to why he feels that his objection (which you can't follow) is important. Ask him to restate it for you so that you can understand it. One of three things will happen. He will restate it in another way so that you can understand it and use the Clarkson close. In restating it, he will disclose his real objection, which you may then address. In trying to restate it, it will suddenly look pretty stupid to him and he will eliminate the objection himself.

Remember that sales resistance is an emotional thing and therefore it isn't necessarily always rational.

SALES CLOSE THIRTEEN: THE CLOSE-ON-AN-OBJECTION TECHNIQUE #3

This technique is frequently called the "Lost Sales Close." When the customer refuses to buy, the salesman acts like he is leaving. He does everything he would normally do when he leaves the office except when he gets to the door, he turns and asks, "Would you do me a favor? This company is a young dynamic start-up which makes the best medical scope on the market. I know the founders and I can honestly say that they are going to turn the medical instrument industry on its ear because their instruments are so far advanced technologically. The problem isn't with the product, it's with the sales. Will you tell me what I did wrong or why you decided not to buy?"

In almost every case, the customer, who now feels secure because the salesman has stopped trying to sell him, will state the objection that he has to buying. When he states the objection the salesman will say surprisedly, "What a dummy I am, I forgot to cover that in my presentation to you." Then the salesman goes back into that module of his presentation which covers this objection, and then he closes the sale.

SALES CLOSE FOURTEEN: THE MacADOO CLOSE

We have approximately 27 start-up clients who use this technique with phenomenal success. This close is extremely powerful and successful because it takes the salesman off the hook and places all responsibilities squarely on your shoulders. In 25 of the 27 cases, these start-ups catapulted into their rep salesmen's favorite principal category because of the MacAdoo option.

Briefly, you invent a fictious name and give this name the title of general manager, executive vice president, operations vice president, or something along this line. The fictious Mr. MacAdoo must have authority and must be able to delegate responsibility to any founder. When a customer raises an objection that the salesman cannot answer, when the customer requires something special that the salesman doesn't have the authority to grant, when a salesman can't give an instant price quote, or if the salesman feels that the close is within a fraction of an inch and he cannot shake the order loose, then he asks to use the customer's telephone for a collect call to your general manager, Mr. MacAdoo. When the call comes into your switchboard, your operator knows that it is a top priority call and goes immediately to her "MacAdoo list" of founders and managers who are qualified to handle a MacAdoo call. Frequently as many as three MacAdoo calls will be running simultaneously. When the founder is notified that he has a MacAdoo call, he immediately knows what role he has to play and he knows that he has almost complete authority to make the decisions essential to get the sale. He gets a brief introduction from the salesman and then asks to speak to the customer. While he talks to the customer, the salesman begins to fill out his order form so that when the call is complete, all the customer has to do is OK the order. The founder, who is playing the role of Mr. MacAdoo, then listens to the customer, promises those features that the salesman couldn't grant, gives additional pricing for the features, commits to delivery, asks the technical questions that the salesman isn't able to ask or understand, and satisfies the customer. He then states that he'll have Mr. X, a real person, supervise the customer's needs and handle all details. The real person then rushes the customer a letter stating that Mr. MacAdoo has delegated to him the responsibility of the customer's project and hereafter he will handle all inquiries and problems. This letter is essential so that the customer will not telephone Mr. MacAdoo and run the risk of talking to a different founder.

SALES CLOSE FIFTEEN: THE PUPPY DOG CLOSE

"Mister, the last thing our pet store wants is to sell you a puppy that your children might not want. You take this pup home to your children and see if they like him and he likes them. If you don't return the pup within two weeks, we'll assume that your children like him and we will then bill you." Can you imagine the pressures that would be brought on Dad if, after that pup is seen by his children, he tried to pry him loose and return him?

The Puppy Dog close works extremely well when your product is superior and the customer has a real need for it. Several of our start-up clients give their reps a quota of consignment equipment. The salesman leaves the "demonstration model" for a few weeks and then goes back to get the order. It's cheaper to have your products tested by the customer than to allow them to gather dust in your warehouse.

Example 16-1: The Interim Close

There are hundreds of situations which make it impossible for a salesman to close a sale on the day of his major presentation. Typical situations are: (1) The person who specifies the product to be ordered (the man you closed) doesn't do the actual buying. His recommendations are forwarded to the purchasing department for actual buying. (2) The manager wants his key employees (the ones who will use your products) to be in on the decision-making process. (3) Your product or the customer's application of your product is so complex that it will take months of evaluation before he can buy (e.g., in selling to a refinery or a power plant). (4) Your product must pass qualification testing before the buyer can order it in production quantities. (5) The president isn't positive of the exact direction his company will follow and will postpone every buying decision until his board of directors defines that direction. (6) The purchase must wait for the new fiscal year when budgets are available. (7) The amount of money involved is so large that the customer will not move until he again justifies his buying decision in solitude and away from outside distractions (your salesman). And there are hundreds of other valid reasons.

Since your salesman can not make a final close, he must make an interim close to keep the order open until he has an opportunity to sell the customer when conditions are right for buying, to expedite the buying decision along the proper path, and to force the customer to think about your product and want it until he can purchase it.

The interim close unfortunately varies with each situation and therefore cannot be cataloged in a full text, much less a single chapter of a text. However, the following examples may tickle your imagination so that your people will develop their own interim closes.

Example 1: A general manager who doesn't have full decision-making authority needs to get the R&D manager, the production manager, and the marketing manager to approve a sale. The salesman simply asks the general manager the exact names and spelling of the other three and writes them down. He then asks the general manager if next Thursday afternoon at 2:00 p.m. would be convenient for the general manager. He then asks the general manager's secretary's name and rises to leave. As he goes out the door, he says he will have his secretary type up the invitations to next Thursday's meeting, and in the meantime he will make certain that a factory man will be present to answer any questions he couldn't answer.

When the salesman gets out the door, he goes to the general manager's secretary and gives her a handwritten memo, with the general manager's name for signature and asks her to send a copy to each name on the list and to send him a copy also. He then leaves, confident that next Thursday afternoon he will close the sale.

Example 2: The close is impossible because the production manager doesn't know what size conveyor system he needs. It is all contingent upon the sales forecast that is to be out next week. The salesman then fabricates several assignments that he must perform for the production manager and lists them on a sheet of paper. To this list he adds the production manager's assignment of getting his next year's production forecast and pulls the same stunt as in example 1. He has the production manager's secretary type a list of what each party was to accomplish for next Thursday's meeting and asks the secretary to type a copy for herself. He knows that she will be the one to run down the sales forecast figures for her boss and that she needs a copy if it is to get done.

Example 3: The R&D engineer agrees to design a salesman's component into the next modification and to send this design change to purchasing's buyer. The salesman thanks the engineer and then hot foots it to the proper buyer for a sales presentation. When he is through with the buyer, the buyer is certain that the component change would make a significant production savings and that he, the buyer, will get credit for this savings. He begins to expedite the company's drafting group to rush through the change in drawings with the component change so that they can start realizing savings as soon as possible. The buyer also starts phasing down purchases with the old component. Next, the salesman hot foots it to the company's purchasing expeditor to determine how many components this customer would need each day for production. Since his principal is a six-month-old start-up, he knows that they have limited production capabilities and will need all of the lead time they can get to tool up for the expected orders. Within three days, this salesman has greased the skids to such an extent that the customer never knows that his "small production orders" of 15,000 components a week quadruples a principal's sales, makes them go to three shifts a day, makes them meet their two-year milestone 15 months earlier, and is the basis of the founders getting the needed venture capitalists for their needed growth.

Minor Point 16-6: Sales Resistance That Can't Be Defeated

If you ever feel that you want to think things out before buying and the salesman's presentation makes you want to buy, there is a technique that you can use that will stop any salesman cold. When he goes into a close, compliment him on the close technique that he used. "Gee that was beautiful, John. I liked the way you worked your way into the subordinate-question close and combined it with the impending-event close. Let me see you use the Davidson close and the Ben Franklin Balance Sheet."

The salesman will laugh with you, stop his close attempts and give you all of the information on his product or service that you need fast and depart until you call him.

Minor Point 16-7: Salesmen as Buyers

Salesmen make the world's worst buyers. It is easier to sell to salesmen than to any other profession in the world. I don't know why this is true but it is. I guess it is kind of like why pitchers are usually the team's worst hitters. Show me a firm that has specialty products to sell to salesmen and I'll show you a firm that will have few sales problems.

If your sales manager has authority to make major purchases, you'll be wise to have someone else approve all purchases over X dollars to keep him down to earth.

Minor Point 16-8: The "In-The-Wings" Close

The basic concept here is that after you have lost an order to a competitor, you ask the customer if you can be an understudy to the competitor and wait in the wings, so to speak. You want to be an insurance policy in case the competitor falls down on the job or defaults in any way. It's a simple request and takes you and your salesman about three minutes to make properly. There are no hard feelings . . . just a business proposal to be an additional source if and when the primary source cannot produce.

Though the sales realized from this minor close are frequently negligible (usually between 0.5% and 2%), the real benefit is that this close puts you back on the team. Though you are warming the bench, you're still in the stadium, and even substitutes get to talk to the coach. In almost every case, the salesman can freely visit the customer's production lines, assure the managers that their insurance policy is still on the job, talk with the design engineers to make certain of any changes upstream, and penetrate the account as effectively as the primary vendor (your competitor). The next year, when you two lock horns over the purchasing contract again, you'll at least be on equal footing instead of being an outsider looking in.

CAMEO 16-2: THE INDUCEMENT TECHNIQUE AND SUBORDINATE-QUESTION CLOSE COMBINED

A production furnace start-up utilized a unique inducement in the sales of their $35,000 and up conveyor furnaces. They asked the facilities supervisor what color he would like his company's name engraved on his production furnace (gold or silver plate?). When the facilities manager was stopped by this question, the salesman would pull out some gold letters and spell out the customer's name. "We always put your name on our furnaces," was the next statement, and then, "What letter style do you prefer, Old English or Gothic Bold?"

Now facilities people are extremely proud of their equipment and this minor inducement (the average cost is only $45) makes them see the furnace as almost a monument. The inducement fitted the circumstance and the subordinate questions made the customer, by making a minor decision, make a large decision.

As an aside, the founders of this start-up had a third goal in mind also. When the furnace was delivered, the gold plated letters spelled out, "The XYZ Furnace Company's model 102B, delivered to the Hewlett-Packard Corporation on March 30, 1969." You see, the founders, all ex-furnace design engineers, had developed a unique design that was extremely forgiving to the working parts of the furnace. Where other manufacturers stress to the limits their heating elements, their ceramic manifolds, their chain conveyors, these engineers buy oversepced components and run them at half their capacity. Therefore, when other furnaces "go-down" for maintenance and repairs, this start-up's furnaces continue to stay on line. Soon, the facilities and production managers started observing that this furnace was X years old and so far had never needed a repair. "Every six months, I have to change ABC's elements, manifold, and conveyor belt but we've had XYZ's unit now well over five years, see, it was delivered in March of 1969, and would you believe that we haven't had to shut it down yet?" Since production and facility managers talk to other production and facility managers, this still-young company has the best reliability image in their industry. That reliability image nets them 10% more in sales prices and gives them a marketable difference over their older and better established competitors.

Minor Point 16-9: A Trick to Make Competition Fight on Your Terms

AXIOM NINETEEN: YOU'RE NOT AFTER ALL OF THE BUSINESS. YOU ARE AFTER ALL OF THE PROFITABLE BUSINESS THAT YOU CAN HANDLE.

Frequently, when a dynamic start-up begins making significant market penetration, the established companies panic, begin unethical sales tactics, and lower prices as far as they can to hurt the intruder. Everyone suffers when this occurs.

We usually recommend to our clients that they keep a low profile with competition until their market penetration becomes significant enough for the competitor to observe them and take corrective actions. This is easy to spot. You'll see your name appear on their cross reference sheets, you'll observe repeated tactics when the competitor suspects that you are in the running, and you'll observe all kinds of dummy companies (blind corporations) trying to find out all kinds of information. When this occurs, we recommend that you lay out the ground rules for competition through the following technique.

Write the competitor's president, controller, marketing manager, sales manager, and every salesman the following letter.

Dear Mr. X,

We see that you are concerned about our young company entering your industry. We therefore want to send you all of the pertinent information that we can so that you will not make a judgment error about our intentions.

Briefly, our young company has been in business for X years. It was founded by several design engineers who wanted to express their technical innovations and advance our industry. We would like to throw down the gauntlet and challenge your firm in the following areas:

(1) In technical excellence. Our goal is to become the lasting leader in our industry in performance and reliability.

(2) In customer satisfaction. I think that by now, you know that our instruments are well accepted and well serviced. We are depending upon customer word-of-mouth sales to become the backbone of our company's growth.

Gentlemen, our company is a profit oriented company. Since we consider ourselves superior in both product and support, we see no need to cut our prices to "buy sales." When a company must resort to price cutting, it is admitting that either its product and service are inferior (and therefore a lower sales price is essential to compensate for this inferiority) or it is admitting that its management and sales force is inferior and doesn't know how to sell. Therefore, when you see us in a competitive situation, you'll know that we are going to attempt to beat you in product performance, not prices.

It is unfortunate that Robinson-Patnum laws will not allow me to send you our price structure because you would find that we are equal or slightly higher than you. Because of Robinson-Patnum, I am not allowed and therefore will not knowingly give you our prices.[1] However, since we got your prices from mutual customers, I assume that you have done likewise with us.

To summarize, we are challenging you on performance and excellence. If you wish to compete ethically, we will both improve our industry.

Very truly yours,

This tactic has worked extremely well in holding prices. You have notified your competitors' profit managers that they shouldn't cut prices to compete and therefore, the sales manager, when he asks for lower prices to buy a sale, will not get them.

Other benefits are: (1) This tactic impresses your competitors' salesmen. They start viewing your young company as a viable and potentially excellent firm instead of just another risky start-up. This opinion transmits to their customers. (2) You have opened the doors for further communications. When a competitor's salesman utilizes unethical sales tactics against you, all that you have to do is notify the president of his actions. When this does no good and he doesn't respond within X days after the first warning, all that you have to do is follow-up with the statement that you are documenting the competitor's unethical actions and by bringing them to the attention of the president, you are assuming that he is now

---

[1] Interpretations of the Robinson-Patnum laws vary, especially in the area involving private industry with government contracts. Start-ups should obtain sound legal advice before applying this principle.

aware of them and if he doesn't take corrective action, both he and his company will be held accountable. Add a small lecture on the law and ethics and he'll consider how they will sound in court. You can then be assured that he will put a stop to further similar actions.

Minor Point 16-10: Unethical Sales Practices

There are dozens of techniques and strategies open to a marketing man to destroy a competitor's sales programs. It is beyond the scope of this text to discuss these techniques except to state that when a firm buries a competitor, it usually either buries itself also or damages its industry.

Do not turn your back on the strategies used against your firm. When they border close to panic or dishonesty, put a stop to them fast by threatening exposure and legal action.

Example 16-2: The MacAdoo System

Since the MacAdoo system is such a powerful sales tool for a start-up (or any other firm for that matter) and since so few companies have enough confidence in their people to employ it, very few people understand all of its flexibilities and capabilities. Therefore, I think that we should dwell upon it to give you a deeper insight into its strengths.

The founders agree upon a fictious name (MacAdoo) and a second-in-command title (General Manager). Whoever handles a MacAdoo call automatically assumes the power, the responsibility, the authority, and the bearing of your firm's second-to-top spot for this one transaction.

Then the founders determine which founders and managers have the ability to handle the hot seat. They list these names and give a copy of this list to the person who handles all in-coming calls. This operator is given instructions to always start at the top of the list and work down unless the call is for a specific MacAdoo. A typical MacAdoo list might read as follows:

1.	P. MacAdoo	George Patterson	President
2.	M. MacAdoo	Bill Mathews	VP, Marketing
3.	R. MacAdoo	Fred Robbins	VP, R&D
4.	A. MacAdoo	John Adams	VP, Administration & Finance
5.	T. MacAdoo	Sam Thompson	VP, Manufacturing
6.	S. MacAdoo	Al Sparks	Sales Manager

The founders should agree that there will always be a minimum of two MacAdoos in town and all MacAdoo calls are to be considered top priority. Otherwise, your field salesmen will attempt this system, work their close towards it, telephone to find no MacAdoo available, and look bad in front of their customer.

The man who plays MacAdoo is sitting in a hot seat at the end of a very long limb. He must make instant decisions from sometimes sketchy information and therefore he will make some mistakes. It is easy to get a saw and cut the limb by sniping at a man's errors, by playing office politics against him, or by torpedoing him in a dozen different ways. It is because of this tendency that the MacAdoo system may fail. If a man cannot make decisions free from sniping, then he can't role-play general manager with confidence and with feeling. He will postpone the decisions essential to close the sale and your firm will lose the sale. Therefore, all founders must agree that the MacAdoo hot seat is to be free from sniping and if an error does occur, then all must pull together to minimize the effects of that error.

When a MacAdoo call comes in (you'll get several dozen a day when you have nationwide distribution), you know that there is a sale that will be yours if MacAdoo handles himself properly. The operator must delay putting his call through until he gets back to his office, pulls out the MacAdoo role notes (reminders of closes, of authorities, of responsibilities, and any other factors), prepares the recorder (this isn't a bad tool to augment your notes), and spends a few seconds preparing himself for the role that he must play.

When he signals for the girl to put through the call, he expects to talk to the salesman first. A typical conversation might be, "Hello, Mr. MacAdoo, this is Fred Jacobs here. Mr. MacAdoo, I am calling from Mr. Adam Blake's office. Mr. Blake is purchasing agent for The Able Brakeshoe Company and he is concerned about our delivery of the model 202B. He must be positive that we can meet his production needs before he places the order. Since I am a salesman and do not know our delivery capabilities, I thought that I would put Mr. Blake on the telephone to help us work out his needs."

While Mr. Blake is on the telephone, the salesman sits down and completely fills out his order form. When the Blake-MacAdoo telephone conversation is complete, he stands a 90% chance of getting Mr. Blake's signature and a closed order.

Mr. MacAdoo completely hears out Mr. Blake without interruption. He makes darned certain that he understands Mr. Blake's concerns and needs before he opens his mouth. If he can meet Mr. Blake's needs, he jumps into the Clarkson close and closes. If he can not, then he has several options open to him. They are: (a) Convert the customer to a model that he can make delivery on. (b) Attempt a partial close (get the order for the quantities that he knows he can deliver and let a competitor have the rest). (c) Doubt that the customer's delivery desires are necessarily the same as his actual production needs (many times they aren't) and obliquely determine if that doubt is valid. If MacAdoo determines that there is a strong probability that the customer could accept X units a week for 52 weeks (instead of 52X units to be delivered in 30 days), then he might close the order and plan on renegotiating delivery after he has the signed order. (d) Several dozen other options that are always open to him.

He sells that option in a negotiating and problem solving manner. He attempts his trial closes and as soon as Mr. Blake accepts a solution and a trial close, he makes the final close by telling the customer that he will start immediately and please OK the decisions that "we have made to-day" on the salesman's order form.

Before he says goodbye, he must establish the following: (1) that his name is Paul MacAdoo (so that if the customer should think of something new and immediately telephone back, he'll talk to the same man), (2) that he is delegating complete responsibility and authority to Mr. Sam Thompson, VP, Manufacturing, and (3) that the company must get started immediately if Mr. MacAdoo is going to make good on his promises. He then asks to speak to the salesman.

He swiftly briefs the salesman on what promises are made, what action MacAdoo must make immediately, tells the salesman what additional points he must add to his order form, what prices to charge, and tells him to get the signature on the order before he leaves. If the customer balks or refuses to OK the order, then the salesman is to telephone Mr. Paul MacAdoo again from the buyer's desk and give him another shot at closing the sale again.

There are some very strong factors that you must understand about this system. They are:

You are playing prestige to the hilt. Mr. Adams, a purchasing agent, is now rubbing shoulders with the VP General Manager and with the VP of Manufacturing instead of just another lowly salesman.

Your titles and telephone attitude will give the customer the confidence that he needs from knowing that his order will be handled properly. If some problem should arise, he can go directly to the top operational people and get satisfaction.

He knows that there will be no buck passing on this order. Nowadays, many established firms make the buyer feel alone through their buck passing antics.

Not only does the buyer have communications into your company, you have communications into his. This penetration comes in handy if you want to parallel your field salesman's efforts with factory sales attempts or if you should want to terminate your field sales group for a replacement rep firm.

Probably the biggest asset that you have is that you have taken the responsibility off your salesman when he elects to capitalize on this system. He lays the groundwork, hands you the ball and you either run or fall. If everything goes well, you both look good. If everything goes wrong, you have assumed the responsibility and therefore the salesman can go back through the doorway to sell again.

You will discover that frequently (75% of the cases in industrial sales) price is not a factor. The buyer is so concened about your solutions to his primary objections, resistance, and problems that price is squeezed into a very secondary role. The buyer doesn't concern himself about prices until he OKs the order. However, do not gouge or sandbag him in pricing or your competitors will have you for lunch.

The MacAdoo system completely eliminates competitive bid situations. Frequently, the lobby will be filled with competitive salesmen who lose the order before they even have a chance to quote. If your salesmen will keep their mouths shut about the system, these competitors will never know what happened.

System security is essential to enforce. The MacAdoo system makes excellent sales stories which are real temptations for salesmen to tell. These stories have a way of getting to your competition and customers. Though there is nothing unethical or illegal about the system, the last thing that you want is for your competitors to develop a similar or a counter system.

The MacAdoo system will always make your firm a primary principal with your reps and agents until you either lose your courage and refuse to accept responsibility or until you become so back ordered that you can't accept a sale. These problems of course can be solved.

You always make MacAdoo second in command, never first. Since it is possible for MacAdoo to make a swift decision that will destroy the start-up, you need to have the escape path of the president overriding his decision and voiding the verbal agreement. To the best of my knowledge, this has happened only once and in that case, it was the president who played the role of MacAdoo and then had to override his own decision.

Though the MacAdoo system works best when the founder makes a decision and closes the sale, occasionally it is impossible to give an instant answer to a technical question. Then MacAdoo can delay the buyer's decision to place his order until the answer is researched and given. Frequently, the answer is given to the salesman so that he has an alibi to call again on the customer and he can then either close or use the MacAdoo system again.

17 · Tools for Forecasting and Controlling Sales

Until recently, sales forecasting techniques were both inaccurate and unreliable. Most companies do not utilize proforma financial projections because they have so little faith in their marketing department's sales forecasts, which are the cornerstone of all projected decision milestones or proforma accounting goals.

In the last decade, the young Turks of marketing scrapped the classical sales forecasting techniques and developed new systems which forecast sales much more accurately. There are approximately 3 new systems (with perhaps 10 refinements of each) commonly used by these young Turks. Oddly enough, if you utilize all three totally different systems, you'll discover that the end results will come out to within 5% of each other.

One of the more reliable systems and the most easily understood techniques is the R. W. Wood Sales Tables system. Not only does this system accurately forecast sales, it raises red flags when things start to go wrong. We have therefore taken excerpts from Mr. Wood's tables.

BRIEF HISTORY OF THE R. W. WOOD TABLES   M, IS

Approximately seven years ago, a group of nine marketing consultants met to brainstorm sales forecasting techniques to see whether they could develop a more reliable system. In evaluating the old classical sales probability systems, these men discovered that these classical techniques were strictly a statistical probability exercise which ignored the basic premises of sales. Most of the classical methods were developed by mathematicians and statistics specialists who had little or no knowledge of sales and therefore utilized physical science probabilities instead of the human variables involved in sales. Sales is a people-to-people discipline and therefore its probabilities are derived totally differently.

Therefore, these consultants were forced to go back to ground zero to derive the variables involved in sales, the relative weighting of each variable, and finally to develop the initial equations of forecasting direct sales. R. W. Wood, an outstanding computer specialist as well as a marketing researcher, then computerized, tested, and refined these equations with data from approximately 300 manufacturing firms. After approximately three years of refining, his tables were within 7% accuracy for the norm and within 15% accuracy for the worst case. Today his tables have an accuracy norm of 5%. Since most sales managers were content with 25% accuracies until very recently, this was a significant contribution.

Though the primary value of Wood's sales tables is accurate forecasting, it is the only system which will define problem areas and allow both your marketing manager and sales manager to take swift, corrective actions. A sales manager can swiftly determine which of your salesmen are weak and a marketing manager can swiftly determine whether your support, your products, or your distribution network needs corrections.

HOW TO USE THE R. W. WOOD SALES TABLES   M, IS

The primary premise of this technique is that if all other variables are held constant, your sales are directly proportional to the number of effective sales calls you realize each week.[1] In other words, the firm that realizes 5,000 effective sales calls each week will realize 100 times more sales orders than the firm that realizes only 50 effective sales calls each week.

The adjective "effective" is a critical feature that takes some explaining. Briefly, in any given territory and industry, almost all salesmen make the same number of sales calls each week. Let's take a hypothetical example and see how both marketing managers and sales managers can use the term "effective" to trouble-shoot problem areas.

---

[1] We are ignoring the variable of sales saturation so carefully explored by Wood. As a start-up, it will probably take you years to saturate your sales coverage. However, once you do reach saturation, you must shift to optimum (instead of maximum) sales coverage.

HYPOTHETICAL CASE ONE: SALES MANAGER'S TROUBLE-SHOOTING WORKSHEET

Let's assume that your Chicago sales rep firm has six outside salesmen and a typical week's performance for each man is as follows:

Salesman	Number of Sales Calls Made This Week:	Average Number of Principals Discussed at Each Call:	Percent of Sales Calls Considered Effective Calls	Percent of Effective Calls that Become Orders:	Sales Closes Realized This Week:
A	40	3.2	20%	25%	5
B	36	3	25%	30%	9
C	30	3	30%	50%	15
D	40	2	10%	50%	4
E	10	4	50%	50%	10
F	36	3	33.3%	10%	4

We see six salesmen with six totally different sets of problems which need six completely different solutions. Let's look at each salesman individually:

Salesman A hits all of the average levels. He needs training on almost all facets of sales. He is a hard worker with probably marginal organization, marginal knowledge of his principals and territory; and has marginal abilities to close sales. Any figures lower than these will probably mean that he could be replaced with a better man.

Salesman B is just adequate. He is on the threshold of being good in all of the facets of sales. Further work is needed.

Salesman C is an excellent salesman. He has it all together, has a sales rhythm that works right for him and is probably bordering on laziness with sales calls because he is satisfied with his income and is enjoying himself with a slackened load.

Salesman D is strong in sales closes, however he has real problems otherwise. He doesn't know his territory, he is probably disorganized, and is suspect of not knowing his principals. Though salesman D's performance is inferior to Salesman A's, in all probability he can, with minor help, equal salesman's C's performances in a short time.

Salesman E also has a completely different set of corrective actions needed. He is probably a professional salesman breaking in a new series of principals or addressing a new set of customers. It is very possible that salesman E is being misused by his principals and therefore has an extremely poor sales rhythm.

Salesman F is going to make a better-than-adequate salesman as soon as he learns to close sales. Two seminars and frequent buddy calls with an experienced closer will triple his sales closes.

HYPOTHETICAL CASE TWO: HOW YOU AS A PRINCIPAL WILL EVALUATE THIS REP FIRM'S PERFORMANCE

You, as a principal, will not have access to the individual performances described above. Remember, the rep firm feels that it is just as important to keep you sold as it is to sell to customers and the last thing that they want is for you to see the weaknesses of their salesmen. However, since you performed extensive research before you signed the rep firm and since you and your founders make frequent visits to each territory, it is probable that you have a pretty good feel for each salesman's capabilities, what turns them on and off, and how active they are in selling your products.

Let's assume that you manufacture a pioneering medical instrument which retails in the $50 range. Of the 47 orders that the rep received last week, let's assume that your firm got three orders for the following amounts: (a) one prototype order for 10 units, (b) one production order for 100 units, and (c) one stock order for 10 units. Using the R. W. Wood Tables, you'll observe that it took 6 effective calls for (a), it took 12 effective calls for (b), and it took 7 effective calls for (c). Therefore, your start-up firm probably realized around 25 effective calls from the rep firm last week. You know that this rep firm has six salesmen of varying abilities and you assume that approximately 30% of their sales calls are effective sales calls. Therefore, on 83 of their sales calls, they discussed your product. You further know that in the Chicago territory, six salesmen will average approximately 35 sales calls a week and discuss approximately three principals at each sales call. Therefore, there were $6 \times 35 \times 3 = 630$ sales presentations of which you realized 83 probable presentations (or 13%). If the rep firm has 20 principals and they covered each equally, then each principal should realize $630 \div 20 = 31$ sales presentations. Your start-up is receiving approximately 270% of this average.

Actually, in real life, each rep firm has from four to five favorite principals to which they give two-thirds of their sales efforts. Therefore, if your rep has five favorites, each will receive $^1/_5 \times ^2/_3 \times 630 = 84$ sales calls each. Your start-up is therefore one of the favorite five and now you have a very unique marketing problem. For the three sales that they realized, are you worth being considered one of the top five principals? If you are going to remain in favor, you are going to have to get your product established as an intermediate and then as a staple as fast as possible. To sustain your sales efforts, your marketing manager is going to have to swiftly establish parallel sales supports fast because it will not take the rep owners too long to realize that they aren't receiving rewards commensurate with efforts. Last week, it cost the rep firm approximately $30 per sales call (or $10 per principal mentioned) and therefore to break even, it must realize $830 in commissions. To make it worthwhile (and therefore worth favored status) they should realize $20 for every sales call and for every principal mentioned. Therefore, until they receive $1,660 a week in commissions, you are in trouble.

OTHER CONSIDERATIONS OF THE R. W. WOOD TABLES

You'll observe a spread in the number of effective sales calls per close. Actually, this is an envelope which covers almost all of the industries and almost all territories. In actual practice, Wood has varied these numbers by both territories and by industries. In the growth industries, use the lower figure, in the static industries, the upper figures. Territories like New York, Houston, and Los Angeles usually require one less effective sales call per close than San Francisco, Chicago, Denver, Boston, and Atlanta. Washington D.C., Seattle, Portland, Phoenix, Kansas City, Oklahoma City, Minneapolis, St. Paul, Ft. Smith, Indianapolis, Philadelphia, and Louisville require two additional effective sales calls per close in the high quantity figures.

MULTIPLIERS

There are obviously other variables which control your sales other than the number of effective sales calls realized each week. The following multipliers should be applied to your table values (effective sales calls ÷ sales close).

MARKETING MACHINERY COMPONENTS	MULTIPLIER ENVELOPE
I. *Quality of Training efforts*	
Product Knowledge of:	
Direct OEM Salesmen (Company, Rep, Agents)	0.85–1.30
Distributor/Jobber Salesmen	0.90–1.10
Retailers' Clerks	0.85–1.05
Product Knowledge of:	
Major Customers' Key Personnel	0.85–1.15
Minor Customers	0.95–1.05
Frequency of Training	0.90–1.10
Quality of Training Sessions	0.85–1.05
Quality of Materials, Manuals, Aids, etc.	0.95–1.20
II. *Quality of Motivation and Sustaining efforts*	
Speed and Accuracy of Handling Customer Inquiries	0.75–1.25
Speed and Accuracy of Handling Customer Quotations	0.75–1.25
Quality of Advertising	0.90–1.10
Frequency of Advertising	0.90–1.10
Quality and Frequency of Publicity Releases	0.85–1.05
Quality of Customer Public Relations	0.90–1.05

Quality of Public Relations to the Community	0.98–1.02
Your Company's Sales Empathy as Seen by Salesmen	0.90–1.10
Your Management's Understanding of Sales	0.85–1.15
Your Company's Image of Professionalism in:	
Direct OEM Salesmanship	0.80–1.10
Distributors' and Jobbers' Salesmanship	0.90–1.10
Retailer Salesmanship	0.90–1.05
In Your Major Customers' Eyes	0.75–1.25
In Your Minor Customers' Eyes	0.95–1.10
Your Company's Reputation for Shipping as Promised	0.90–1.25
Your Company's Reputation for Service, Quality and	
Reliability as Seen by:	
Direct OEM Salesmen (Company, Rep, Agents)	0.85–1.10
Distributors/Jobbers	0.85–1.10
Retailers	0.90–1.05
Major Customers	0.75–1.25
Minor Customers	0.90–1.05
Your Machinery's Support of Salesmen's Sales Rhythms	0.75–1.30
Your Machinery's Abilities to Distinguish Between Sales	
Resistances and True Sales Objections	0.95–1.25
Your Sales Forces' Hunger and Ability to Close Sales	0.60–1.25
Incentives Offered to Commissioned Sales Companies	0.95–1.05
Incentives Offered Directly to Salesmen:	
Direct OEM Salesmen (Company, Reps, Agents)	0.80–1.00
Distributor/Jobber Salesmen	0.85–1.05
Retailers' Clerks	0.90–1.10

III. *Quality of Outside Pressures and Forces*

Quality of Pressures Applied by Other Divisions and	
Principals on Your Salesmen's Prime Selling Times	0.90–1.50
Quality of Pressures Applied by Your Marketing Department and Marketing Machinery for This Prime Selling	
Time	0.50–1.25
Marketable Differences of Your Products to Competition	0.85–1.15
Ability of Your Salesmen to Capitalize on These	
Differences	0.75–1.25
Ability of Your Competition to React and "Pro-act"	0.75–1.25
Your Prime Competitions' Images as Seen by Your	
Industry	1.00–1.25
The Quality of Your Prime Competitors' Sales Networks	0.95–1.30

Discussion of R. W. Wood Sales Multipliers

I like using the R. W. Wood Sales Tables for a start-up because they lay it straight on the line. If you are going to be lazy in your marketing efforts, then use Wood's tables, determine the number of effective sales calls per close, and then use the higher numbered multipliers and watch your probable sales drop. If on the other hand you are going to have an energetic and professional sales program, your probable sales will continue to increase as your marketing team addresses each marketing requirement.

Also observe that these multipliers pretty well define where your marketing and sales budgets should go. As an example, it is extremely easy to fund major dollars for advertising. Many firms do because they don't know any better and because advertising is an ego trip. However, there are many other ways to educate the public which are just as effective and a lot less expensive. You will observe that there are many significant multipliers which do not cost you a cent.

The third reason that I like to use the R. W. Wood system is that it lays the blame directly where it belongs. If a territory is beginning to fall short of its sales quota, there is usually a very real reason for this effect. A quick evaluation of the variables involved in these multipliers will probably swiftly define the cause or causes of this effect and you can take immediate action to reverse the trend.

Did you observe that the multipliers do not always have equal reward and punishment values? As an example, if you give your sales firms greater-than-average commissions, it does nothing for your sales. If you pay them less than average, your sales closes are punished. Conversely, if you give the individual salesmen additional incentives, your sales should increase significantly. If you offer no incentives, there are minimal effects.

Wood has an extremely complex formula to derive the multipliers for the growth or decline of your industry and for the growth or decline of the national economy. To simplify them and ignore all the little wrinkles of his complex equation, let's say from the value of 1.000 subtract the increase in percentage of paper consumption[2] and add the percentage of increase in unemployment.[3] In other words, if paper consumption increases by 5% and unemployment increases by 2%, then you should use the multiplier of 0.97 times your effective sales calls per sales close $(1.000 - 0.050 + 0.020 = 0.970)$.

For growth industry considerations, your sales are directly related to the growth of your customers' industries, not the projected growth of your industry. Also, before using this multiplier, realize that you must work in numbers of units shipped by your customers, not the increase or decrease

[2] You will discover that our national paper consumption is a leading indicator (by approximately three months) of our GNP. Therefore, by plugging in the figures of the national paper consumption monthly, you are building in three months into your forecasts.

[3] All of Mr. Wood's research is in single-digit inflation rates and therefore he considers them accurate for inflation rates from 3% to 7%. In double-digit inflationary spirals, variables which used to be considered insignificant suddenly begin to play a major role. Be aware that if the inflation rate is beyond the 7% maximum, small errors are introduced when you use this simplified formula.

of profits of that industry. For the growth-industry multiplying factor, from 1.000 subtract the percentage increase of the number of units shipped by your customers' industries. As an example, if you sell a component to a television manufacturer, and in the last six months he has shipped 2% less televisions, then your multiplier should be 1.000 minus a minus 0.02. Since a minus times a minus is a plus, your multiplier to the number of effective sales calls per sales close is 1.02.[4]

LEAD/LAG FACTORS

Lead/lag factors vary greatly from industry to industry and therefore cannot be exactly stated in this book, however these general rules of thumb usually apply:

In the U.S., in technology, the western part of the country usually leads the east. In pricing, the east usually leads the west, and in production, the midwest usually leads everyone. The following tables are frequently accurate for most industries:

Technology		*Pricing*		*Production*	
Los Angeles	0 months	New York	0 months	Chicago	0 months
New York	2 months	Los Angeles	2 months	Los Angeles, New York	2 months
San Francisco, Houston, Chicago	4 months	Boston, Chicago, Philadelphia	4 months	Balance of midwest	4 months
Balance of northeast and west coast	6 months	Balance of northeast and west coast	6 months	Balance of northeast and west coast	6 months
Southwest and Rocky Mountain areas	7 months	Southwest and Rocky Mountain areas	7 months	Southwest and Rocky Mountain areas	7 months
Southeast and foreign	8 months	Southeast and foreign	8 months	Southeast and foreign	8 months

In other words, when you observe a trend in pricing in New York, you can expect to see the same trend in San Francisco in approximately 4 months. When the midwest opens up with major production orders, expect to see the same percentage increases come from New York and Los Angeles in two months. Get your loan capital lined up in case the leading trends hold.

---

[4] The simplified formula for growth rates is accurate for companies which realize between −4% and +4% changes in shipments each month. If your customers' industries exceed these limits then double the values between ±4% and ±6% and double again the values between ±6% and ±9%.

CONCLUSIONS

There is no reason that you cannot forecast properly. There is no reason that you and the other founders can't be innovative and realize sales maximization with the minimum of dollars. Good marketing is always simple (not complex) but rarely easy.

THE R. W. WOOD SALES FORECASTING TABLES

Unit Price ($)	Quantities (Units)	Type of Demand	Number of Effective Sales Calls/Close	Type of Customer
$1.00	1	Staple	1	Manufacturing
``	10	``	1	``
``	100	``	1 to 2	``
``	1000	``	3	``
``	10000	``	4 to 5	``
``	100000	``	6 to 7	``
``	1	Pioneering	2 to 4	``
``	10	``	2 to 4	``
``	100	``	4 to 5	``
``	1000	``	7 to 8	``
``	10000	``	12 to 14	``
``	100000	``	8 to 12	``
``	1	Intermediate	1 to 2	``
``	10	``	1 to 2	``
``	100	``	2 to 3	``
``	1000	``	4 to 5	``
``	10000	``	8 to 12	``
``	100000	``	8 to 12	``
``	1	Staple	1	Resale Outlets
``	10	``	1	``
``	100	``	1	``
``	1000	``	1 to 2	``
``	10000	``	1 to 2	``
``	100000	``	2 to 3	``
``	1	Pioneering	2 to 4	``
``	10	``	2 to 4	``
``	100	``	6 to 8	``
``	1000	``	12 to 20	``
``	10000	``	Undefined	``
``	100000	``	Undefined	``
``	1	Intermediate	1	``
``	10	``	1	``
``	100	``	1 to 2	``
``	1000	``	3 to 4	``

THE R. W. WOOD SALES FORECASTING TABLES
(Continued)

Unit Price ($)	Quantities (Units)	Type of Demand	Number of Effective Sales Calls/Close	Type of Customer
$1.00	10000	Intermediate	6 to 8	Resale Outlets
``	100000	``	Undefined	``
``	1	Staple	1	Service Companies
``	10	``	1	``
``	100	``	1 to 2	``
``	1000	``	3 to 6	``
``	10000	``	8 to 12	``
``	1	Pioneering	2 to 3	``
``	10	``	2 to 4	``
``	100	``	4 to 8	``
``	1000	``	6 to 14	``
``	1	Intermediate	1	``
``	10	``	1 to 2	``
``	100	``	1 to 3	``
``	1000	``	4 to 8	``
``	10000	``	10 to 16	``
$5.00	1	Staple	1	Manufacturing
``	10	``	1	``
``	100	``	1 to 2	``
``	1000	``	3 to 4	``
``	10000	``	3 to 5	``
``	100000	``	6 to 8	``
``	1	Pioneering	2 to 3	``
``	10	``	2 to 4	``
``	100	``	4 to 6	``
``	1000	``	6 to 8	``
``	10000	``	10 to 14	``
``	100000	``	8 to 12	``
``	1	Intermediate	1	``
``	10	``	1	``
``	100	``	1 to 2	``
``	1000	``	3 to 5	``
``	10000	``	6 to 8	``
``	100000	``	6 to 10	``
``	1	Staple	1	Resale Outlets
``	10	``	1	``
``	100	``	1 to 2	``
``	1000	``	2 to 3	``
``	10000	``	6 to 9	``
``	1	Pioneering	2 to 4	``
``	10	``	2 to 4	``

THE R. W. WOOD SALES FORECASTING TABLES
(Continued)

Unit Price ($)	Quantities (Units)	Type of Demand	Number of Effective Sales Calls/Close	Type of Customer
$5.00	100	Pioneering	6 to 8	Resale Outlets
``	1000 & Up	``	Undefined	``
``	1	Intermediate	1	``
``	10	``	1	``
``	100	``	1 to 2	``
``	1000	``	4 to 6	``
``	10000	``	10 to 14	``
``	100000	``	Undefined	``
``	1	Staple	1	Service Companies
``	10	``	1	``
``	100	``	1 to 2	``
``	1000	``	3 to 6	``
``	10000 & Up	``	Undefined	``
``	1	Pioneering	2 to 3	``
``	10	``	3 to 5	``
``	100	``	4 to 8	``
``	1000 & Up	``	Undefined	``
``	1	Intermediate	1	``
``	10	``	1 to 2	``
``	100	``	1 to 3	``
``	1000	``	3 to 8	``
``	10000 & Up	``	Undefined	``
$10.00	1	Staple	1	Manufacturing
``	10	``	1	``
``	100	``	2 to 3	``
``	1000	``	3 to 5	``
``	10000	``	3 to 6	``
``	100000	``	6 to 9	``
``	1	Pioneering	2 to 3	``
``	10	``	2 to 4	``
``	100	``	4 to 6	``
``	1000	``	6 to 8	``
``	10000 & Up	``	Undefined	``
``	1	Intermediate	1	``
``	10	``	1 to 2	``
``	100	``	2 to 3	``
``	1000	``	4 to 6	``
``	10000	``	10 to 14	``
``	100000	``	Undefined	``
``	1	Staple	1	Resale Outlets
``	10	``	1	``

THE R. W. WOOD SALES FORECASTING TABLES
(Continued)

Unit Price ($)	Quantities (Units)	Type of Demand	Number of Effective Sales Calls/Close	Type of Customer
$10.00	100	Staple	1 to 2	Resale Outlets
" "	1000	" "	2 to 4	" "
" "	10000	" "	8 to 14	" "
" "	1	Pioneering	3 to 4	" "
" "	10	" "	3 to 4	" "
" "	100	" "	8 to 14	" "
" "	1000 & Up	" "	Undefined	" "
" "	1	Intermediate	1	" "
" "	10	" "	2 to 3	" "
" "	100	" "	3 to 5	" "
" "	1000	" "	6 to 9	" "
" "	10000	" "	10 to 14	" "
" "	100000	" "	Undefined	" "
" "	1	Staple	1	" "
" "	10	" "	1	" "
" "	100	" "	2 to 3	" "
" "	1000	" "	4 to 6	" "
" "	10000	" "	8 to 14	" "
" "	100000	" "	Undefined	" "
" "	1	Pioneering	2 to 3	" "
" "	10	" "	3 to 5	" "
" "	100	" "	5 to 9	" "
" "	1000 & Up	" "	Undefined	" "
" "	1	Intermediate	1 to 2	" "
" "	10	" "	1 to 3	" "
" "	100	" "	2 to 5	" "
" "	1000	" "	6 to 9	" "
" "	10000 & Up	" "	Undefined	" "
$25.00	1	Staple	1	Manufacturing
" "	10	" "	1	" "
" "	100	" "	2 to 3	" "
" "	1000	" "	3 to 5	" "
" "	10000	" "	4 to 9	" "
" "	100000	" "	8 to 14	" "
" "	1	Pioneering	2 to 3	" "
" "	10	" "	3 to 5	" "
" "	100	" "	4 to 6	" "
" "	1000	" "	6 to 9	" "
" "	10000 & Up	" "	Undefined	" "
" "	1	Intermediate	1	" "
" "	10	" "	1 to 2	" "
" "	100	" "	3 to 6	" "

THE R. W. WOOD SALES FORECASTING TABLES
(Continued)

Unit Price ($)	Quantities (Units)	Type of Demand	Number of Effective Sales Calls/Close	Type of Customer
$25.00	1000	Intermediate	9 to 14	Manufacturing
``	10000 & Up	``	Undefined	``
``	1	Staple	1	Resale Outlets
``	10	``	1	``
``	100	``	1 to 2	``
``	1000	``	2 to 3	``
``	10000	``	8 to 14	``
``	100000 & Up	``	Undefined	``
``	1	Pioneering	3 to 4	``
``	10	``	4 to 6	``
``	100	``	8 to 14	``
``	1000 & Up	``	Undefined	``
``	1	Intermediate	1	``
``	10	``	2 to 3	``
``	100	``	3 to 5	``
``	1000	``	5 to 10	``
``	10000 & Up	``	Undefined	``
``	1	Staple	1	Service Companies
``	10	``	1 to 2	``
``	100	``	2 to 3	``
``	1000	``	5 to 9	``
``	10000	``	8 to 14	``
``	100000 & Up	``	Undefined	``
``	1	Pioncering	2 to 4	``
``	10	``	4 to 7	``
``	100	``	8 to 14	``
``	1000 & Up	``	Undefined	``
``	1	Intermediate	1 to 2	``
``	10	``	2 to 4	``
``	100	``	4 to 9	``
``	1000 & Up	``	Undefined	``
$50.00	1	Staple	1	Manufacturing
``	10	``	1	``
``	100	``	2 to 3	``
``	1000	``	3 to 5	``
``	10000	``	4 to 9	``
``	100000	``	8 to 14	``
``	1	Pioneering	2 to 4	``
``	10	``	4 to 6	``
``	100	``	7 to 12	``
``	1000	``	8 to 12	``
``	10000 & Up	``	8 to 12	``

THE R. W. WOOD SALES FORECASTING TABLES
(Continued)

Unit Price ($)	Quantities (Units)	Type of Demand	Number of Effective Sales Calls/Close	Type of Customer
$50.00	1	Intermediate	1	Manufacturing
``	10	``	1 to 3	``
``	100	``	3 to 6	``
``	1000	``	8 to 14	``
``	10000 & Up	``	Undefined	``
``	1	Staple	1	Resale Outlets
``	10	``	1	``
``	100	``	2 to 4	``
``	1000	``	4 to 7	``
``	10000	``	8 to 12	``
``	100000 & Up	``	Undefined	``
``	1	Pioneering	5 to 7	``
``	10	``	5 to 7	``
``	100 & Up	``	Undefined	``
``	1	Intermediate	1 to 2	``
``	10	``	2 to 3	``
``	100	``	3 to 5	``
``	1000	``	5 to 10	``
``	10000 & Up	``	Undefined	``
``	1	Staple	1	Service Companies
``	10	``	2 to 4	``
``	100	``	4 to 9	``
``	1000 & Up	``	Undefined	``
``	1	Pioneering	2 to 4	``
``	10	``	4 to 7	``
``	100	``	8 to 14	``
``	1000 & Up	``	Undefined	``
``	1	Intermediate	1 to 2	``
``	10	``	2 to 4	``
``	100	``	4 to 9	``
``	1000 & Up	``	Undefined	``
$100.00	1	Staple	1	Manufacturing
``	10	``	1	``
``	100	``	1 to 2	``
``	1000	``	2 to 4	``
``	10000	``	5 to 8	``
``	100000	``	5 to 8	``
``	1	Pioneering	1 to 4	``
``	10	``	4 to 6	``
``	100	``	8 to 12	``
``	1000 & Up	``	Undefined	``

THE R. W. WOOD SALES FORECASTING TABLES
(Continued)

Unit Price ($)	Quantities (Units)	Type of Demand	Number of Effective Sales Calls/Close	Type of Customer
$100.00	1	Intermediate	1	Manufacturing
"	10	"	2 to 4	"
"	100	"	4 to 9	"
"	1000	"	8 to 12	"
"	1000 & Up	"	Undefined	"
"	1	Staple	1	Resale Outlets
"	10	"	2 to 4	"
"	100	"	4 to 7	"
"	1000 & Up	"	Undefined	"
"	1	Pioneering	5 to 7	"
"	10	"	5 to 7	"
"	100 & Up	"	Undefined	"
"	1	Intermediate	2 to 3	"
"	10	"	4 to 7	"
"	100	"	5 to 7	"
"	1000 & Up	"	Undefined	"
"	1	Staple	1	Service Companies
"	10	"	2 to 4	"
"	100	"	4 to 7	"
"	1000 & Up	"	Undefined	"
"	1	Pioneering	2 to 4	"
"	10	"	4 to 7	"
"	100 & Up	"	Undefined	"
"	1	Intermediate	1 to 2	"
"	10	"	2 to 4	"
"	100	"	4 to 7	"
"	100 & Up	"	Undefined	"
$500.00	1	Staple	1	Manufacturing
"	10	"	1 to 3	"
"	100	"	5 to 8	"
"	1000	"	5 to 8	"
"	10000	"	5 to 8	"
"	100000	"	5 to 8	"
"	1	Pioneering	2 to 6	"
"	10	"	4 to 12	"
"	100	"	8 to 12	"
"	1000 & Up	"	Undefined	"
"	1	Intermediate	1 to 2	"
"	10	"	2 to 4	"
"	100	"	4 to 9	"
"	1000	"	8 to 12	"
"	10000 & Up	"	Undefined	"

THE R. W. WOOD SALES FORECASTING TABLES
(Continued)

Unit Price ($)	Quantities (Units)	Type of Demand	Number of Effective Sales Calls/Close	Type of Customer
$500.00	1	Staple	1	Resale Outlets
"	10	"	2 to 4	"
"	100	"	5 to 7	"
"	1000 & Up	"	Undefined	"
"	1	Pioneering	5 to 7	"
"	10 & Up	"	Undefined	"
"	1	Intermediate	2 to 3	"
"	10	"	5 to 7	"
"	100 & Up	"	Undefined	"
"	1	Staple	1	Service Companies
"	10	"	2 to 4	"
"	100	"	5 to 8	"
"	1000	"	Undefined	"
"	1	Pioneering	5 to 8	"
"	10 & Up	"	Undefined	"
"	1	Intermediate	2 to 4	"
"	10	"	3 to 8	"
"	100 & Up	"	Undefined	"
$1,000.00	1	Staple	1 to 3	Manufacturing
"	10	"	5 to 8	"
"	100	"	5 to 8	"
"	1000 & Up	"	Undefined	"
"	1	Pioneering	5 to 12	"
"	5	"	8 to 12	"
"	10 & Up	"	Undefined	"
"	1	Intermediate	3 to 8	"
"	5	"	5 to 10	"
"	10	"	8 to 12	"
"	100 & Up	"	Undefined	"
"	1	Staple	1 to 3	Resale Outlets
"	10	"	2 to 5	"
"	100	"	Undefined	"
"	1	Pioneering	5 to 7	"
"	5 & Up	"	Undefined	"
"	1	Intermediate	2 to 4	"
"	5	"	5 to 7	"
"	10 & Up	"	Undefined	"
"	1	Staple	1 to 3	Service Companies
"	5	"	1 to 5	"
"	10	"	5 to 8	"
"	100 & Up	"	Undefined	"

THE R. W. WOOD SALES FORECASTING TABLES
(Continued)

Unit Price ($)	Quantities (Units)	Type of Demand	Number of Effective Sales Calls/Close	Type of Customer
$10,000.00	1	Staple	3 to 7	Manufacturing
''	3	''	5 to 12	''
''	5	''	8 to 12	''
''	10 & Up	''	Undefined	''
''	1	Pioneering	8 to 12	''
''	3	''	8 to 12	''
''	5 & Up	''	Undefined	''
''	1	Intermediate	5 to 12	''
''	3	''	8 to 12	''
''	5	''	8 to 12	''
''	10 & Up	''	Undefined	''
''	1	Staple	5 to 7	Service Companies
''	3	''	5 to 7	''
''	5 & Up	''	Undefined	''
''	1	Pioneering	5 to 7	''
''	3 & Up	''	Undefined	''
''	1	Intermediate	5 to 7	''
''	3	''	5 to 7	''
''	5 & Up	''	Undefined	''

For products whose unit costs exceed $10,000, little data has been gathered. However, it appears that for manufacturing customers, it will take from 8 to 12 effective sales calls per sales close, and for service companies, it will take from 7 to 9 effective sales calls for every sales close.

MARKETING MACHINERY GRADING WORKSHEET

DATE _____
NAME _____

INTENT: This worksheet is designed to give you a unique insight into the priorities of your company's marketing machinery.

INSTRUCTIONS:

1. List your company's operating budget for each component in the second column.
2. List the estimated man-power loading for each component in the third column.
3. From "Marketing Worksheet One", list the grades of your marketing machinery in the fourth column. (The usual practice is to use only those grades developed by the persons who truly understand your company's marketing machinery).
4. In the fifth column, you'll observe two sets of multipliers (R.W. Wood's envelopes). If your company has a perfect score, apply the lowest multiplier. If your company completely ignores a category, then the upper multiplier is to be used. For grades in between, use straight line interpolation. Record your exact multiplier in the sixth column.
5. For every category in which the multiplier is less than 1.00, your marketing machinery decreases sales resistances and the number of effective sales calls to each sales close is lowered. The opposite is true for multipliers greater than one.
6. Evaluate the multipliers with respect to the dollars and man-hours invested in each category. Should priorities be shifted?
7. For forecasting, refer to the instructions in the R.W. Wood tables (a copy is free to all member firms).

MARKETING MACHINERY COMPONENTS	BUDGETED DOLLARS	BUDGETED MANPOWER	GRADES	MULTIPLIER ENVELOPE	INTERPOLATED MULTIPLIER
I. QUALITY OF TRAINING EFFORTS					
Product Knowledge of:					
. Direct OEM Salesmen (Company, Rep, Agents)	___	___	___	0.85-1.30	___
. Distributor/Jobber Salesmen	___	___	___	0.90-1.10	___
. Retailers' Clerks	___	___	___	0.85-1.05	___
Product Knowledge of:					
. Major Customers' Key Personnel	___	___	___	0.85-1.15	___
. Minor Customers	___	___	___	0.95-1.05	___
Frequency of Training	___	___	___	0.90-1.10	___
Quality of Training Sessions	___	___	___	0.85-1.05	___
Quality of Materials, Manuals, Aids, etc.	___	___	___	0.95-1.20	___
II. QUALITY OF MOTIVATION & SUSTAINING EFFORTS					
Speed & Accuracy of Handling Customer Inquiries	___	___	___	0.75-1.25	___
Speed & Accuracy of Handling Customer Quotations	___	___	___	0.75-1.25	___
Quality of Advertising	___	___	___	0.90-1.10	___
Frequency of Advertising	___	___	___	0.90-1.10	___
Quality & Frequency of Publicity Releases	___	___	___	0.85-1.05	___
Quality of Customer Public Relations	___	___	___	0.90-1.05	___
Quality of Public Relations to the Community	___	___	___	0.98-1.02	___
Your Company's Sales Empathy as Seen by Salesmen	___	___	___	0.90-1.10	___
Your Management's Understanding of Sales	___	___	___	0.85-1.15	___
Your Company's Image of Professionalism in:					
. Direct OEM Salesmanship	___	___	___	0.80-1.10	___
. Distributors' & Jobbers' Salesmanship	___	___	___	0.90-1.10	___
. Retailer Salesmanship	___	___	___	0.90-1.05	___
. In Your Major Customers' Eyes	___	___	___	0.75-1.25	___
. In Your Minor Customers' Eyes	___	___	___	0.95-1.10	___
Your Company's Reputation for Shipping as Promised	___	___	___	0.90-1.25	___
Your Company's Reputation for Service, Quality, & Reliability as Seen by:					
. Direct OEM Salesmen (Company, Rep, Agents)	___	___	___	0.85-1.10	___
. Distributors/Jobbers	___	___	___	0.85-1.10	___
. Retailers	___	___	___	0.90-1.05	___
. Major Customers	___	___	___	0.75-1.25	___
. Minor Customers	___	___	___	0.90-1.05	___
Your Machinery's Support of Salesmen's Sales Rhythms	___	___	___	0.75-1.30	___
Your Machinery's Abilities to Distinguish Between Sales Resistances & True Sales Objections	___	___	___	0.95-1.25	___
Your Sales Forces' Hunger & Ability to Close Sales	___	___	___	0.60-1.25	___
Incentives Offered to Commissioned Sales Companies	___	___	___	0.95-1.05	___
Incentives Offered Directly to Salesmen:					
. Direct OEM Salesmen (Company, Reps, Agents)	___	___	___	0.80-1.00	___
. Distributor/Jobber Salesmen	___	___	___	0.85-1.05	___
. Retailers' Clerks	___	___	___	0.90-1.10	___
III. QUALITY OF OUTSIDE PRESSURES & FORCES					
Quality of Pressures Applied by Other Divisions & Principals on your Salesmen's Prime Selling Times	___	___	___	0.90-1.50	___
Quality of Pressures Applied by your Marketing Department & Marketing Machinery for this Prime Selling Time	___	___	___	0.50-1.25	___
Marketable Differences of Your Products to Competition	___	___	___	0.85-1.15	___
Ability of your Salesmen to Capitalize on These Differences	___	___	___	0.75-1.25	___
Ability of your Competition to React & "Pro-act"	___	___	___	0.75-1.25	___
Your Prime Competitions' Images as seen by Your Industry	___	___	___	1.00-1.25	___
The Quality of your Prime Competitors' Sales Networks	___	___	___	0.95-1.30	___

76513V -- **Association of Marketing Professionals**

DISTRICT SALES MANAGERS' OVERVIEW WORKSHEET: NUMBER ONE
(For Industrial Sales Only and for Company Employed District Salesmen Only)

DATE _____
NAME _____

INTENT:

This worksheet will give you an insight into each salesman's utilization of sales disciplines. It is the intent of this overview worksheet to flag problem areas that may be missed by other techniques of evaluating salesmen's performances.

INSTRUCTIONS:

This worksheet must be used in conjunction with The R.W. Wood Sales Controls & Sales Forecasting Tables (a copy is offered free to member firms). The following procedure should be followed:

1. Establish the average number of sales calls each salesman should make each month.
2. From last month's data, determine the quantity of orders each salesman received from his industrial accounts.
3. Using the R.W. Wood Tables, determine the number of effective sales calls that it should take to close each of these orders. Total these effective sales calls.
4. Compare the calculated number of effective sales calls to the average number of sales calls in (1) above.
5. If the effective sales calls: a.   exceeds 50%, the salesman's selling disciplines are excellent.
   b.   exceeds 40%, the salesman is a professional who needs minor corrections.
   c.   exceeds 30%, the salesman is average only and needs significant corrections.
   d.   is lower than 30%, major sales discipline problems are flagged.

SALESMAN	AVERAGE NUMBER OF SALES CALLS EACH MONTH	QUANTITY OF INDUSTRIAL ORDERS LAST MONTH	CALCULATED NUMBER OF EFFECTIVE SALES CALLS	PERCENTAGE OF SALES CALLS THAT WERE EFFECTIVE	COMMENTS

76834V—The Association of Marketing Professionals

332

INTENT:

This worksheet is designed to have you grade the various components which make up our marketing machinery. Your grades will reflect how each of these components is working in your territory with our customers and we hope flag problem areas which need corrective actions.

INSTRUCTIONS:

Grade each of the following components on a scale from 0 to 10. A zero grade indicates extremely poor performance and a ten grade indicates true excellence. A grade of five is average.

MARKETING MACHINERY COMPONENTS	SCALE	NOTES
	0 . 1 . 2 . 3 . 4 . 5 . 6 . 7 . 8 . 9 . 10	

I. QUALITY OF TRAINING EFFORTS

Product Knowledge of:
. Direct OEM Salesmen (Company, Reps, Agents)
. Distributor/Jobber Salesmen
. Retailers' Clerks
Product Knowledge of:
. Major Customers' Key Personnel
. Minor Customers
Frequency of Training
Quality of Training Sessions
Quality of Materials, Manuals, Aids, etc.

II. QUALITY OF MOTIVATION & SUSTAINING EFFORTS

Speed & Accuracy of Handling Customer Inquiries
Speed & Accuracy of Handling Customer Quotations
Quality of Advertising
Frequency of Advertising
Quality & Frequency of Publicity Releases
Quality of Customer Public Relations
Quality of Public Relations to the Community
Your Company's Sales Empathy as Seen by Salesmen
Your Management's understanding of Sales
Your Company's Image of Professionalism in:
. Direct OEM Salesmanship
. Distributors' & Jobbers' Salesmanship
. Retailer Salesmanship
. In Your Major Customers' Eyes
. In Your Minor Customers' Eyes

Your Company's Reputation for Shipping As Promised
Your Company's Reputation for Service, Quality, &
        Reliability as Seen by:
. Direct OEM Salesmen (Company, Reps, Agents)
. Distributors/Jobbers
. Retailers
. Major Customers
. Minor Customers
Your Machinery's Support of Salesmen's Sales Rhythms
Your Machinery's Abilities to Distinguish Between Sales
        Resistances & True Sales Objections
Your Sales Forces' Hunger & Ability To Close Sales
Incentives Offered To Commissioned Sales Companies
Incentives Offered Directly to Salesmen:
. Direct OEM Salesmen (Company, Reps, Agents)
. Distributor/Jobber Salesmen
. Retailers' Clerks

III. QUALITY OF OUTSIDE PRESSURES & FORCES

Quality of Pressures Applied by Other Divisions &
        Principals on your Salesmen's Prime Selling Times
Quality of Pressures Applied by your Marketing Department &
        Marketing Machinery for this Prime Selling Time
Marketable Differences of Your Products to Competition
Ability of your Salesmen to Capitalize on These Differences
Ability of your Competition to React and "Pro-act"
Your Prime Competitions' Images as Seen by Your Industry
The Quality of Your Prime Competitors' Sales Networks

ADDITIONAL COMMENTS: _____
_____
_____
_____
_____

DISTRICT SALES MANAGERS' OVERVIEW WORKSHEET: NUMBER TWO
(For Industrial Sales Only and for Commissioned Sales Networks [Reps, Agents, Distributors, etc.])

DATE _____
NAME _____

INTENT:

This worksheet is intended to give you evaluation tools that are different from those frequently used in evaluating sales firms which sell your products on a commissioned basis. It is assumed that these same firms sell for other principals and the significant marketing task is to make certain that your firm realizes its fair share of their marketing sales efforts.

INSTRUCTIONS:

This overview worksheet is to be used in conjunction with The R.W. Wood Sales Control & Sales Forecasting Tables (a copy is offered free to member firms). The following procedure should be followed:

1. Determine the number of direct salesmen that each sales firm has.
2. Determine the average number of sales calls that each salesman should make each month and multiply it by the number of salesmen.
3. Estimate the average number of principals that each salesman should present in each sales call (the norm is between three and four). Multiply this with (2) above.
4. Determine the number of sales closes (quantity) made last month.
5. Using the R.W. Wood Tables, determine the number of effective sales calls necessary to make closes in (4) above.
6. Compare the calculated number of effective sales calls to the sales presentations of (3) above.
7. From (3) and (6) above, determine the percentages of time the commissioned sales firm invested on your product line.

COMMENT:

For those firms which hire direct salesmen to sell many divisions' different products, this worksheet is effective if you feel that the

primary hurdle is the battle for each salesman's prime sales times.

Sales Organizations	Number of Salesmen	Number of Presentations (Average each Sales Call)	Number of Sales Calls Each Month	Quantity of Industrial Orders Last Month	Calculated No. Of Effective Sales Calls	Percentage of Effective Calls To (4) Above	Comments

18 · Other Techniques of Insuring Sales Success

MY CONFLICT OF INTERESTS   M, IS

I must walk a tightrope in this chapter because it forces me into a conflict of interests. As you know, whenever you are placed into a dilemma situation of conflict of interest, the only way out is to lay your cards face up for all to see.

As the earlier chapters illustrated, the largest sales hurdle your young company must face is to realize your fair share of each commissioned salesman's selling efforts. It's a never-ending battle. Though we have discussed some techniques for fighting this continuing war against your salesmen's other principals (your true competition for selling efforts), let's face it—your young company is still at a disadvantage. The more established principals will use their advantages to attempt to monopolize your salesmen's selling time. Therefore, this workbook would not be complete if it didn't give you the tools to shift the advantages your way.

Realize that I have fought this battle all of my consulting life. It is therefore natural that I am a co-founder, a major stock holder, and a board member of U.S. Sales Applications Inc., the firm that monopolizes services in this area. Therefore, I am pirating this company's control systems to give you these tools.

SALES CONTROL SYSTEMS   M, IS

As a profession, sales badly lags behind most other disciplines in controls. Technologies and systems which are commonplace in manufacturing, marketing, administration, and almost all other disciplines are still considered new and innovative in sales. It is the intent of this chapter to show you a few "advanced" techniques. These will significantly increase your salesmen's effective sales calls in your product or service lines. They'll keep your salesmen always organized in your product or service lines. They'll greatly improve the quality and quantity of your salesmen's communications, reports, and planning in your product or service lines. And they'll improve your salesmen's image for professionalism in front of their customers in your product line. Finally, you'll be able to convert each salesman from being just another salesman into being a true sales manager of his own territory as it relates to your product line.

Please observe that the real intent of this chapter is to give you the tools which will force the salesman to give your start-up better service than the salesman gives his other principals (your real selling competitors). If you are wise, you will not attempt to upgrade your sales firms so that they do a better job in selling all of their principals. All that we are looking for is an unfair advantage in commanding the salesman's selling efforts. Once this unfair advantage is in effect, you, not your salesmen, have complete control over your sales destiny.

MAKE COMMUNICATIONS EASY AND NATURAL   M, IS

As you know, most salesmen hate to "ride a desk" and write. Since they dislike it so much, at best they turn out marginal work. Yet since their forecasts, call reports, trend reports, expense reports, expediting demands, etc., are essential, most principals must demand that the salesman write them reports. Consider the following:

Cassette Communications

Supply each salesman with a compact and reliable tape recorder. This will allow your salesman to dictate his messages and requests while he is driving from one customer to the next. At the end of each day, he stops by a post office box and mails his cassette magazine to you. You of course, supply him with the magazines, self-addressed stamped boxes to hold the magazines, and fresh batteries to keep the recorders operative.[1]

---

[1] If you decide to use this option, the following additional information is necessary. Keep the ownership of the cassettes in your firm's name and insure them. The break-in and theft rate of these cassettes is very high (approximately 2.5% per month). Between the salesman's insurance and your insurance, this large theft rate can be compensated for. Also, the life of the machines is relatively short. Since most salesmen carry them in their briefcases, they receive excessive bumps, shock, and vibrations. Most of our clients amortize them over a 12-month period.

Utilize Tape Cassettes for Training as Well as Communications

Every client who utilizes this system uses frequent mini-seminars on the tapes sent to the field as replacements. The salesman can then receive short courses while he drives through his territory. Most start-ups even ask questions after the training session so that the salesman can, in his own words, give you back the meat of the mini-session.

Another excellent training program is to give simulated sales presentations over the tapes so that the salesman can hear different variations while he is driving down the road. Of course, in these presentations, you practice the sales closes that he should remember. At the end of the presentation, you summarize the presentation and closes so that he is aware of the mechanics that you followed.

Another effective tool is the monthly ''confidential newsletter'' put on tapes. In this letter, you summarize what competition is doing, the tactics they are attempting, techniques to end run these tactics, the marketable differences between your product line and your competitions' new products to be released, and news on what has and is happening back at the plant. It is not a bad practice to have each founder talk briefly on each tape so that the salesman feels that he knows each founder.

Personalized ''Form'' Sales Letters

There is no reason for your salesman not to utilize duplicate sales paths in lining up prospective buyers. As an additional incentive, most of our clients give each salesman a monthly budget of sales letters to be typed by the principal. Briefly, the system works as follows:

The salesman is given a catalog of sales paragraphs (approximately 800 paragraphs exist in each letter catalog). The salesman may then construct a very unique and personal letter by simply calling out the application paragraph number.

At the end of each paragraph, there is a spot in which he may add any comments which would make his letter even more personalized.

If your salesman refers to his customer's purchase order number, quotation number, or inquiry number, then the specific details of these pending transactions, which are stored in a computer's memory bank, can be integrated into the sales letter. This allows the salesman to further customize his letter without having to take the time to dictate the specifics of the pending transaction.

All letters are typed, the same day received, on an automatic word processor and rushed to the salesman for his signature. Since the word processor is a carbon-ribbon impact typewriter, no customer can distinguish between it and a standard letter typed by a secretary. Since the word processor will type 30 characters a second without error, the average machine will produce up to 200 customized letters a day.

The average salesman will send approximately 50 letters a month on your product line if you will supply him with these capabilities. The average cost is less than $1 per letter.

Telephone Solicitors

We have all been irritated by firms which misuse telephone solicitors in high pressure and transparent promotions to the extent where we decide that telephone soliciting is an extremely poor tool. Actually, it is an excellent tool if used properly. The customer will not even know that he has talked to a solicitor.

Call it a different name than telephone soliciting so that no salesman will fear using it. Many of our clients have used the term "bird dogging campaign" with excellent salesman acceptance.

Like the customized letters, give each salesman an allotment of monthly calls. Since most of our clients install WATS lines (Wide Area Telephone Service), the only expense is the solicitor's time.

Since almost all pool type telephone solicitors utilize poorly paid women callers, use a man to do the calling.

The caller must have a great deal of information about each person whom he is calling and have a plausible alibi for calling. This is easily received from each salesman.

A typical soliciting call might be, "Hello, Mr. Davidson, this is John Smith here. Mr. Davidson, Bill Williamson asked me to telephone you and apologize for not visiting you this week. Bill had to fly to Los Angeles this week for a seminar (this had better be the truth) and he asked me to call to make certain that you got those 3,000 model 202C's that you ordered. . . . You did. . . . Good. We really expedited that order because we knew that you needed them fast.

"Mr. Davidson, Bill is quite concerned about getting you the proper quantities on time for next month's production. How many units will you need?

"Four thousand? . . . that's great. I'll get on the TWX machine right now and start pushing so that you'll get them on time. How do you want them shipped this time? Air Express like last time?

"I agree, that is expensive. Tell you what, let's tell the factory to ship them the cheapest way and still assure us that you'll get them on the 15th of next month. Is this OK?

"Fine, will do. Should we use the same purchase order that you used last time or do you want to assign a new number?

"Fine, will do. We'll get started on it right now. Oh, before I hang up, Bill told me to tell you that he has finally gotten rid of that wicked slice and he wants to get revenge for the pasting you gave him last month."

Do you see what this soliciting system bought for both you and your salesman? While your man was at a sales seminar, you made certain that his territory was being worked in your product line in a manner that very few principals even consider. A combination of personalized form letters and telephone soliciting, when combined with a salesman's active follow-up, can greatly increase his effective sales calls in your product lines.

SALESMAN CONTROL SYSTEMS   M, IS

So far, all that we have discussed is what you are giving the salesman. You have given him the tools to communicate easily and accurately and you have given him two extremely effective parallel sales avenues to increase his sales in your product lines. Now, it is time for him to give you something. All you request in return is that he becomes almost a complete slave in helping you sell your product. He'll be a willing slave because you are increasing his income with increased sales and meaningful incentives, however as soon as he accepts and uses these systems, he is almost totally controlled by your management.

Consider the following steps:

(1)   Require every salesman to mail you his day's tapes at the end of each day. If he sends you a blank tape, you know that he hasn't worked you that day.

(2)   Have a default letter always go to the customer. When the salesman gives you an input of a customer inquiry, have an automatic letter typed and sent to that customer. It might say, "Bill Williamson, our representative, called and stated that he had discussed the model 202C's reliability with you yesterday. I am therefore taking this opportunity to send you the test data run by NASA on this model. We are also proud that the AEC, DESC, and almost every blue chip manufacturer of high performance electronic equipment has used the model 202C and had excellent results. If you would like to talk to some of these customers, please tell Bill and we'll get you their names and numbers."

(3)   Enter all orders, quotations, and inquiries into your computer's memory bank for continual follow-up. If the field salesman must take actions, assign tickle dates so that if that action is still pending, you can follow-up with the salesman and assure yourself that those actions will be done properly and on time.

(4)   To (3) above, assign flags to the actions that you must take. When a flag flies, you must take corrective actions to make certain that you do not drop the ball.

(5)   Massage all of the information that you have received to give the salesman, his boss, the rep and agency owners, and all of your people the information needed to evaluate performances and make corrections. Send

these monthly reports to the salesman and ask him to add any items which weren't entered into these reports.

(6) When the salesman has added new information, re-rake all of the information into final forecasts, final back orders, final expense reports, final lost sales reports, etc. From these reports you generate commissions, incentive payments, evaluations on strengths and weaknesses, short-term production scheduling, proforma financial reports, cash flow projections, and future sales strategies.

Since these are relatively important areas, typical reports are shown below.

Example 18-1: The Salesman's Memory Tickler System   M, IS

To develop and maintain a smooth sales rhythm the salesman must be extremely organized in your product line. The memory tickler system allows him to forget completely about a transaction until the timing is right. Then, the tickler system kicks out a reminder of the pending action, completely restates all of the information that is needed, so that the salesman won't have to maintain files in his automobile, and asks the salesman if he wants to dictate a letter.

If you evaluate the following ticklers, you'll observe that they are programming the salesman to follow-up in your product line. Memory ticklers are given on a day-to-day basis and if the salesman doesn't take action, your sales manager is alerted for swift corrective actions.

Example 18-2: The Customized Form Letter   M, IS

The letter on page 342 was dictated onto a tape recorder while the salesman drove from one customer to the next. It took the salesman approximately three minutes to dictate this letter. All that he did was state, "Paragraphs 112, 209, and 903 please. To paragraph 209, please add . . . ."

If you received this letter, would you suspect that it was a form letter?

Example 18-3: The Lost Sales Report   M, IS

In the evolution of your orders, a pending transaction will pass through many stages before the order is placed. As soon as the first inquiry is received, the pending order is placed in your memory banks and stays there until the sale is closed and shipped or until the order is lost. You will have constant follow-up until either of these two events occurs.

PAGE 1

U.S. SALES CORPORATION
1961 THE ALAMEDA
SAN JOSE CA 95126
(408) 247-3983

ATTENTION: MR DAN SCHWADRON
SALES ENGINEER
THE SAMPLE MANUFACTURING CORPORATION
1492 NORTH ATLANTIC AVENUE
PALO ALTO   CA   94301

YOUR MEMORY TICKLERS - AUG. 31, 1976

DALMO VICTOR INC.   PO.: 766426-3MN:8-2423

| YOUR REQUESTED MEMORY TICKLE DATE: 8-31 | ACTUAL DUE DATE: | REQUIRED SHIP DATE: 8-31 | CONFIDENCE LEVEL = 100% |

	QUANTITY:	UNITS:	DESCRIPTION:	PROBABLE DELIVERY DATE:	ESTIMATED UNIT PRICE:	ESTIMATED TOTAL: ($)	PRINCIPALS OR DIVISIONS:	NOTES OR COMMENTS:
1	1,000	PCS.	RTR22C2P203	8-31-76	1.4500	1,450	IRC	SLIPPED 2 WKS
2	500	PCS.	RTR22C2P103	8-31-76	1.4500	725	IRC	
3	1,000	PCS.	RTR22C2P502	8-31-76	1.4500	1,450	IRC	
3A	1,000	PCS.	"	9-30-76	1.4500	1,450	IRC	
3B	1,000	PCS.	"	10-31-76	1.4500	1,450	IRC	
3C	500	PCS.	"	11-30-76	1.4500	725	IRC	
4	10,000	PCS.	RT24C2W103	9-31-76	.8750	8,750	IRC	SLIPPED 1 WK.
5	25,000	PCS.	RT26C2X103	10-31-76	1.1500	11,500	IRC	

HEWLETT-PACKARD ASSOCIATES   RFQ 10783-18M

| YOUR REQUESTED MEMORY TICKLE DATE: 11-1 | ACTUAL DUE DATE: 9-7 | REQUIRED SHIP DATE: 11-1 | CONFIDENCE LEVEL = 65% |

	QUANTITY:	UNITS:	DESCRIPTION:	PROBABLE DELIVERY DATE:	ESTIMATED UNIT PRICE:	ESTIMATED TOTAL: ($)	PRINCIPALS OR DIVISIONS:	NOTES OR COMMENTS:
1	100,000	PCS.	RJ12CP103	11-1-76	.9350	9,350	IRC	BEST DEL'VY 10,000 WK. STARTING 11-22-76
2	250,000	PCS.	RJ12CP104	11-1-76	.9350	23,375	IRC	20,000 STOCK 10,000 WK. STARTING 11-22-76

FLAG...... DAN, CALL CARL HELLER ON ESTIMATED PRICING, YOU'RE HIGH
FLAG...... DAN, CALL GUY SOULES CONCERNING DELIVERIES, CAN DO BETTER IF ESSENTIAL
FLAG...... FORMAL QUOTATION ON HOLD PENDING THESE TELEPHONE CONCLUSIONS

LOCKHEED, SUNNYVALE   ENGINEERING INQUIRY: DON FAVORITO

| YOUR REQUESTED MEMORY TICKLE DATE: 8-31 | ACTUAL DUE DATE: 8-31 | REQUIRED SHIP DATE: | CONFIDENCE LEVEL = 10% |

1   SPECIAL GANGED PRECISION, 3 LEVELS, SINE, TANGENT, AND COSINE (CONFORMITY 0.05%), ASSIGNED PART NUMBER 3500L-943-202/103/103

FLAG...... QUOTATION STILL IN ENGINEERING, 2 WEEKS SLIPPAGE, CALL ED SWARTZER IF THIS IS NOT ACCEPTABLE
FLAG...... WHO IS COMPETITION? CAN WE QUOTE $1,135.00 PER INSTRUMENT? LOWEST PRICE IS $1,050.00. IF CONFORMATIVE SPEC. CAN BE LOOSENED TO 0.25%, PRICE DROPS TO $450.00 PER INSTRUMENT ADVISE DAVE OF LOCKHEED'S DECISIONS.
FLAG...... DAN, QUOTTING THIS JOB HAS COST US OVER $200 TO DATE IN DESIGN ENGINEERING TIME. YOUR 10% CONFIDENCE LEVEL MAKES THIS A BAD RISK. IS LOCKHEED GOLD PLATTING, IS THERE A CONTRACT, & DO YOU FEEL THERE WILL BE FOLLOW-ON ORDERS? ADVISE. B.M.

The Sample Manufacturers' Rep. Co.
1481 North Atlantic Avenue
Palo Alto, California 94301
November 18, 1976

Mr. Jim Sullivan
Senior Buyer
Applied Technology Inc.
3412 Hillview Avenue
Palo Alto, California 94303

Reference: Your P.O. 8274729 JS 402

Dear Mr. Sullivan:

I just learned about your purchase order and want to drop
you a brief note to say "Thank You". I am personally going
to follow this order's progress to make certain that you get
the service that you expect and require.

Mr. Sullivan, we can meet and exceed all of the specifications
called out in your control documents with the exception of
the following:

    A.T.I. Specification 811741, Paragraph 209

    The model 224P-1-104 utilizes resistance wire whose
    diameter is less than the 0.5 mil minimum your
    specification requires.

I'll be telephoning you shortly after you receive this letter
to see if we can set-up an appointment to discuss these details
in greater depth.

If this information should generate any questions or if there
is any service that we can perfqrm, please let us know.

                        Very truly yours,

                        Bill Moorehouse

                        William T. Moorehouse
                        Sales Engineer

WTM/bs

A lost sale is a flag for corrective actions that you must take. Yet you cannot take them until you have a system to report them to you. The following detailed report is sent to the field salesman involved for his verification and comments. When he makes these comments, you have an extremely effective tool to swiftly define the causes of the failures and remove the obstacle so that the failure mode will not be repeated.

PAGE 4

U.S. SALES CORPORATION
1961 THE ALAMEDA
SAN JOSE, CA 95126
(408) 247-3883

LOST SALES REPORT - AUGUST 1976

THE SAMPLE MANUFACTURERS' REPRESENTATIVE CORP.
1431 NORTH ATLANTIC AVENUE
PALO ALTO   CA   94301

PRINCIPAL: THE IRC DIVISION OF TRW

LOCKHEED   RFQ 137660629-JRM-42A

			UNIT $	TOTAL $	REASON FOR LOST SALE:
1.	827	PCS. RT12C2L253M	1.2500	1,033.75	LATE DELIVERY DATES.
2.	1,450	PCS. RT12C2P103	1.2500	1,812.50	ORDER PLACED WITH BOURNS
3.	1,825	PCS. RT22C2X203	1.2500	2,281.50	AT SAME PRICE.
4.	650	PCS. RT22C2X503	1.5000	975.00	

				6,102.75	

APPLIED TECHNOLOGY   RFQ 282937

		UNIT $	TOTAL $	REASON FOR LOST SALE:
1	1976-77 TRIMMER PURCHASE AGREEMENT		82,500.00	1. QUOTATION ARRIVED TWO WEEKS LATE.
				2. QUOTATION INCOMPLETE
				3. EVALUATION SAMPLES FAILED TESTING
				ORDERS PLACED WITH:
				BOURNS $44,500
				SPECTROL $38,000

HEWLETT-PACKARD   P.O. 76-10014-JM

			UNIT $	TOTAL $	REASON FOR LOST SALE:
1.	250	PCS. RT24C2W203	2.0000	500.00	H-P REDESIGNED. NEW
2.	100	PCS. RT24C2W103	2.0000	200.00	INSTRUMENT USES RT22

				700.00	

TOTAL LOST SALES IN THE MONTH OF AUGUST $99,302.75

CUMMULATIVE LOST SALES FOR YEAR OF 1976 $132,289.20

Example 18-4: The Pending Shipment Report (Or Back-Orders Report)   M, IS

This monthly report has real value because it shows your controller the cash-in flows that he can expect in the next few months, and it gives you an excellent territory profile showing which customers use what. Your marketing manager can compare buying profiles of like customers in different territories and determine what strengths and weaknesses your salesmen have. Also, this summary report is an excellent communicator to the rep involved. It tells him in a glance what his men have accomplished in the past. This report, when coupled with the Pending Orders Report (Example 18-5) gives everyone an in-depth insight into a territory's performance.

Example 18-5: Detailed Pending Order (Inquiries and Quotations) Report   M, IS

This report ignores the salesmen's confidence levels that inquiries and quotations will develop into sales. The report's primary value is that it shows, in detail, the work being handled by the salesmen. This report should correlate closely with the pending shipment report (Example 19-4) in customer usages by model numbers or else you have a problem in repeat orders.

Since this report ignores confidence levels, it isn't too valuable a document from which to forecast cash flows, production scheduling, and purchasing needs. Sales forecasts (Example 19-6) are far better inputs for these needs.

Example 18-6: Sales Forecasts   M, IS

The forecasting report on page 347 gives you approximately all that you need for each territory. Observe that no forecasted sales with confidence levels lower than 50% are shown. Also observe that the salesman forecasts the 90%, 70%, and 50% levels every time he enters a specific request for quotation, inquiry, or whatever. When this raw material is put in the computer memory banks on a day-by-day basis, all that you have to do is rake this bank to give him what he has forecasted on a daily basis.

We don't recommend that you give the salesmen the R. W. Wood forecasts because it alerts them that they are spending too much time on your product line. Instead, we recommend that you use the R. W. Wood tables, add the lead/lag and indicator variables, and call it a modified Rho system (a legitimate name). The modified Rho should be bracketed by the salesman's forecasts or something is wrong.

PAGE 18

THE SAMPLE MANUFACTURING CORPORATION
ATTENTION: BOB SHARMAN, APPLICATIONS SALES
1492 NORTH ATLANIC AVENUE
PALO ALTO   CA   94301

PENDING SHIPMENT REPORT - AUG. 31, 1976
TERRITORY 18 - SAN FRANCISCO REGION

U.S. SALES CORPORATION
1961 THE ALAMEDA
SAN JOSE, CA 95126
(408) 247-3883

CUSTOMER:	TOTAL VALUE ($)	MODEL 3250 & RT 22	MODEL 3290 & RT 24	MODEL 3260 & RT 26	MODEL 224 & RT 12	MODEL 270 SERIES	MODEL 200 SERIES	CUSTOM SALES
APPLIED TECHNOLOGY	10,084	336	0	0	1,426	0	0	8,320
BECHTEL CORPORATION	7,363	0	0	682	0	4,295	1,168	518
BERKELEY SCIENTICFIC	1,551	375	0	0	1,031	0	145	0
CAELUS MEMORIES DIV.	5,441	3,187	262	0	0	582	1,380	0
CONTROL DATA	2,431	795	1,418	0	0	0	0	218
DALMO VICTOR	9,431	8,993	285	65	0	0	0	0
DATA PATHING	1,828	0	0	0	0	1,828	0	0
ELMAR ELECTRONICS	5,154	1,482	650	1,128	641	835	418	0
FAIRCHILD INSTRUMENTS	12,895	382	0	0	492	0	10,380	641
HAMILTON - AVNET	5,109	851	1,920	318	850	418	752	0
HEWLETT-PACKARD ASSOCIATION	11,020	9,175	0	0	0	0	0	1,845
INTEL	3,599	0	1,425	0	0	1,685	0	439
LOCKHEED, SUNNYVALE DIV.	14,026	22,670	845	1,782	786	0	0	1,033
MEASUREX	2,620	0	0	0	0	2,620	0	0
MEMOREX	1,630	0	0	0	0	0	1,385	245
NOVAT - GTE	2,820	(5,175)	7,995	0	0	0	0	0
PHILCO-FORD, PALO ALTO	13,205	4,938	1,816	4,940	185	427	282	607
SYLVANIA - GTE	7,235	1,260	695	1,314	4,817	35	0	114
U.T.C.	4,238	0	0	0	0	3,518	0	720
VERSATEC	718	414	0	0	0	0	85	219
WYLIE LABORATORIES	2,588	336	941	85	318	35	614	159
TOTALS	139,338	50,419	13,077	10,324	10,548	16,578	18,309	15,168

TERRITORY 18 GRAND TOTAL = 139,338

PENDING ORDER REPORT -- AUGUST 31, 1976

THE SAMPLE MANUFACTURERS' REPRESENTATIVES CORP.
1481 NORTH ATLANTIC AVENUE
PALO ALTO   CA   94301
297361

U.S. SALES CORPORATION
1961 THE ALAMEDA
SAN JOSE CA 95126
(408) 247-3883
PAGE 1

CUSTOMER:	TOTAL VALUE ($)	SPRAGUE & SON ELECTRIC	AIRBORNE INSTRUMTS INC.	FAIRCHILD SEMICOND DIVISION	ALPHA WIRE & CABLE	CANNON CONNECTOR	BENDIX TUBE DIVISION	BENDIX MICROWAVE DIVISION	TRW IRC DIVISION
ANDERSON JACOBSON	27,274	4,280	18	14,492	0	8,204	0	0	280
ALPHA NUMERICS, INC.	1,803	0	0	1,128	0	675	0	0	0
ATI	33,028	17,318	11,420	0	0	0	0	0	4,290
BECKMAN INSTRUMENTS	3,296	1,420	0	1,876	0	0	0	0	0
DALMO VICTOR	61,698	0	0	0	2,180	17,200	0	42,318	0
ELMAR ELECTRONICS	22,035	22,035	0	0	0	0	0	0	0
FAIRCHILD INSTRUMENTS	9,300	0	0	0	0	0	1,100	8,200	0
HEWLETT PACKARD ASSOCIATES	12,205	8,197	0	0	0	0	4,273	0	0
HEWLETT PACKARD CUPERTINO	31,512	14,138	0	0	0	11,352	1,749	0	4,273
HEWLETT PACKARD LABS DIV.	2,427	0	620	0	0	0	675	1,132	0
ISS	24,213	1,496	235	11,450	0	3,842	1,113	0	6,842
ITEK	966	731	0	235	0	0	0	0	0
LOCKHEED, PALO ALTO	8,431	0	8,431	0	0	0	0	0	0
LOCKHEED, SUNNYVALE	36,511	23,827	0	6,293	0	3,487	0	1,167	1,737
LINK DIVISION OF SINGER	18	18	0	0	0	0	0	0	0
OREGON TECHNICAL PRODUCTS	281	0	281	0	0	0	0	0	0
OPTICS TECHNOLOGY INC.	421	0	0	0	421	0	0	0	0
PHILCO FORD	7,056	1,387	0	2,915	0	2,327	0	427	0
QUANTIMETRICS INC.	1,088	473	0	615	0	0	0	0	0
RESALAB INC.	1,354	735	0	619	0	0	0	0	0
SYLVANIA, MTN VIEW	17,100	1,372	13,800	0	0	1,928	0	0	0
TOTALS: GRAND TOTAL:	302,772	95,427	34,805	39,613	2,601	50,750	8,910	53,244	17,422

THE SAMPLE MANUFACTURING CORPORATION
1492 NORTH ATLANTIC AVENUE
PALO ALTO   CA   94301
031708

SALES FORECAST - SEPTEMBER, OCTOBER & NOVEMBER 1976
AUGUST 31, 1976

U.S. SALES CORPORATION
1961 THE ALAMEDA
SAN JOSE   CA   95126
(408) 247-3883

PAGE   1

PRODUCT LINE	SEPTEMBER CONFIDENCE LEVELS 90%	70%	50%	MODIFIED RHO SYSTEM	OCTOBER CONFIDENCE LEVELS 90%	70%	50%	MODIFIED RHO SYSTEM
3250 FAMILY	13,600	17,200	22,000	16,100	4,200	16,000	22,500	19,200
3290 FAMILY	4,200	5,800	7,500	8,200	3,100	3,750	11,800	10,000
3260 FAMILY	8,400	8,600	9,100	1,600	3,600	4,340	7,900	2,000
224 FAMILY	14,500	19,300	22,000	21,300	4,150	9,200	18,500	14,000
200 FAMILY	1,450	2,100	8,200	7,500	1,820	2,300	4,700	8,300
270 FAMILY	1,775	3,500	3,700	1,850	650	1,750	1,100	2,100
HIGH REL MODELS	750	750	750	4,200	750	1,750	750	4,400
CUSTOM SPECIALS	5,150	7,300	8,500	7,800	4,260	6,950	9,250	800
3070	0	200	200	0	0	200	0	100
3500 FAMILY	8,330	22,800	25,400	11,200	3,840	4,100	4,750	10,100
3600 FAMILY	550	1,800	1,500	2,600	0	2,200	3,100	2,800
SPECIAL PRECISIONS	7,360	8,400	8,600	14,800	9,275	15,250	15,250	13,900
THIN LINE SERIES	2,280	3,950	5,150	850	1,100	2,150	2,750	1,100
TOTALS	67,845	101,700	113,400	99,000	38,745	68,290	102,550	96,800

PRODUCT LINE	NOVEMBER CONFIDENCE LEVELS 90%	70%	50%	MODIFIED RHO SYSTEM	QUARTERLY TOTALS CONFIDENCE LEVELS 90%	70%	50%	MODIFIED RHO SYSTEM
3250 FAMILY	2,500	11,000	24,000	17,500	20,500	44,200	68,500	52,800
3290 FAMILY	1,400	2,950	5,825	9,300	8,700	12,500	25,525	27,500
3260 FAMILY	4,800	4,800	8,150	1,400	16,800	17,740	25,150	5,000
224 FAMILY	450	1,350	18,000	18,200	19,100	29,850	55,500	53,500
200 FAMILY	1,100	1,425	3,100	8,200	3,370	5,825	15,000	23,900
270 FAMILY	200	1,450	1,750	1,950	2,825	6,050	6,550	5,900
HIGH REL MODELS	750	750	1,750	3,700	2,250	2,250	6,250	12,300
CUSTOM SPECIALS	1,375	2,850	4,125	8,000	10,785	17,100	16,875	23,900
3070	0	200	200	0	0	600	600	2,900
3500 FAMILY	2,200	3,650	4,475	13,300	14,370	34,550	34,625	34,600
3600 FAMILY	550	1,100	1,700	2,400	550	5,100	6,700	7,800
SPECIAL PRECISIONS	4,125	13,750	19,500	14,200	20,760	37,400	41,350	42,900
THIN LINE SERIES	750	1,650	2,450	1,500	4,130	7,750	10,350	3,450
TOTALS	19,650	46,925	93,825	101,650	124,140	241,215	308,925	303,450

If production and purchasing see that the Rho system is complemented by the salesman's forecasts, they should be relatively confident (to within 15%) that they can purchase and schedule production from this forecast. Also, your controller can be 85% confident that he'll have cash flows as these forecasts predict.

### CAMEO 18-1: THE COMPUTER TERMINAL START-UP	M, IS

This tiny start-up opted to sell its terminals through the direct sales offices of a main frame computer manufacturer. To both parties, it seemed like an ideal marriage. The computer manufacturer needed a reliable terminal to sell and this start-up even agreed to put the selling party's name on its terminals. The computer manufacturer's sales manager estimated that the additional profit center would take only 2% of his salesmen's time and bring in major dollars.

For the start-up, it appeared ideal also. They inherited a nationwide sales force which knew the computer industry and had all of the technical knowledge essential to sell terminals. Also, they inherited a recognized name that had market acceptance. The primary problem was to get enough sales coverage to sell.

For a year, things appeared to be working extremely well. Terminal sales were approximately 20 times higher than the computer manufacturer expected, however they were right on forecast for the start-up. Then the explosion hit and the computer manufacturer pulled out of the agreement.

What had happened was the start-up realized that to grow, it had to command the salesmen's selling time. Its little marketing group of three men used every technique in the books to make the salesmen want to sell them. At the end of the year's time, the computer manufacturing marketing group (a sophisticated group of over 250 employees) realized that the tiny start-up was commanding over 60% of their salesmen's efforts. Salesmen were going into accounts to sell terminals first and computers second. A three-man marketing group had outperformed a highly paid 250-man group to such an extent that it was embarrassing. Therefore, they broke relations.

Since the little start-up (now not too small) had expected to someday have the relationship broken, they had used the system so that their customer penetration could be passed on to another sales force. They therefore, with a minimum of down time, had signed up the best reps, given them the spade work performed by the computer manufacturer (key accounts with key individuals within each account. . . the pending work to be done with each), and they saw their sales continue to expand.

The unbelievable part of this cameo was the computer manufacturer's reaction. Their total sales force was indoctrinated with sales controls which any marketing group would envy. The reliability of these controls had been proven by the fact that three men had outperformed 250 men. Yet, instead of incorporating these controls and using them to sell computers, they ignored them and blamed their being outclassed to the start-up's management's ability to make rapid decisions and the start-up's ability to offer incentives which they couldn't offer.

THE EVOLUTION OF ORDERS CONTROL   M, IS

Do you see the evolution control that you exercise? When a pending order is in the embryo stage, the salesman reports it to you on his tape cassette. It usually starts with an inquiry for information. Besides storing this inquiry in your sales memory bank with ticklers for pendig action, you can have the system initiate food for the embryo such as sales letters, literature, or telephone follow-up, to make certain that it grows into a quotation. When the inquiry passes into the quotation stage, you now have specifics which, if filled professionally, will assure you of the order. The memory bank continues to track the pending transaction and tickle everyone involved when further action is required. The next stage is when the quotation evolves into an order. Again the memory bank tracks the event to make certain that shipments are made on time and invoices are typed properly. Finally, the order is shipped and the transaction is erased from the memory bank except to flag you of possible follow-on orders. The only other way that a transaction can be cleaned from the memory is in the form of lost sales. One of three possibilities exists here. They are: (1) The customer didn't need your product (a marketing and R&D flag to force you to evaluate what the customer did want so that you can consider developing it for him). (2) The sale was lost due to legitimate product objections (again a flag for you to consider overcoming the objections). (3) The sale was lost due to sales resistance (a flag to your marketing and sales management that they have a training task on their hands).

When the evolution process begins, the system keeps pressure on you and your salesmen to handle each stage of the order process promptly and properly. When someone drops the ball and defaults the order, the finger (or buck) stops at the proper person. After each salesman has the finger pointed at him twice, he'll never again let it point at him. When the finger stops at you or your people, you can take corrective actions.

The finger makes each man (salesman and your people) a slave to the system. Everyone will have to do what is necessary to get the orders and your start-up will have sales success.

THE COSTS TO BUDGET IN YOUR BUSINESS PLAN
M, IS

According to U.S. Sales Applications, the average client pays between $750 a month and 0.5% of gross sales (whichever is higher) for the sales control system. A few clients wanted to run the system themselves (instead of having U.S. Sales run it for them) and paid $25,000 for the computer programs and $15,000 a month for computer and word processing equipment leasing. The costs of the WATS lines and cassettes are not included in these figures.

COMPETITION PROGRAM   M, IS

Consider starting a simple competition program. Maintain a library on all of your competitor's equipment and progress. Periodically evaluate each competitor's strengths and weaknesses and review your strategies when you are in against them. There isn't a competitor alive who cannot be eliminated from a buy situation provided that your sales presentation and closes are calibrated for that competitor. So many of our clients eliminate competitors from even quoting because their presentations make the competitor eliminate himself. Keep your salesmen informed on what competition is doing, their strengths, their weaknesses, and what works in end-running them.

Now that you have accomplished this, reduce competition to its rightful place in your objectives. Is your goal to make profits or is your goal to eliminate competition? The two goals are rarely compatible.

Wrap-Up

We have traveled a significant distance together. In 18 short chapters, we have covered as much ground as you would cover in obtaining an MBA degree (in fact, successfully completing a company start-up is equivalent to an MBA degree anyday).

I hope that you realize that one reading will not allow you to retain all of the thousands of essential points and therefore you will use this book as it is intended, a workbook to be continuously used until your company passes its fourth significant milestone (market penetration).

Besides giving you the techniques and systems to assure you of meeting your goals, I think that we should cover a few other points so that they will not surprise you when they occur. It is the intent of this wrap-up to briefly touch upon them.

A SHIFT IN YOUR VALUES   M, IS, RS, F

Entrepreneurship is extremely heady stuff. It can hook you more strongly than alcohol, gambling, or drugs. When men, who have experienced the minor fulfillments of being an employee, taste its wines, they can never again be satisfied as someone else's hireling.

Once you become an entrepreneur, you'll realize rewards that you never knew were possible. The frustrations, the prostituting of your inner self, the pettiness, the lack of meaningful challenges, the limited growth opportunities, the restrictions which limit your innovation, the cash and time limitations upon your life style. . . all prices that you must pay so that others may realize their dreams. . . seem to well-up and explode inside you so that you can never again return to your old life. The dream of being master of your own fate and in total control of your own finances and time so overpowers you that the security of being an employee seems a small reward. You'll refuse to compromise yourself and your goals any longer.

Your perspective on what life is all about will mature and you'll become determined to pursue only those goals that you find meaningful. Your priorities will change and you'll refuse to deny your inner needs. You'll march to a different drumbeat and in doing so, leave the mainstream of our employee population. You'll begin to appear in others' eyes as a unique or odd individual. But being different won't bother you. You're far too absorbed in attaining your dreams.

There are other consequences of this maturing process. Old friends may suddenly seem shallow; you may forfeit months of television and never miss it; you'll become unconcerned about things which happen that are beyond your control; and you'll become a vector force as it were, a person with direction, instead of a scaler quantity, a person with potential but little direction. You'll discover things about yourself that you never knew. You'll try to live life to its fullest and care less about what others think.

By the time that you reach your fourth milestone, your values and you will have changed considerably.

THE SURPRISE   M, IS, RS, F

Most successful entrepreneurs are extremely goal-directed people. The goal of all is either the fifth milestone (leadership of your industry) or the sixth milestone (the sale of your company so that you can be free to pursue life and living). Though this book ends at the fourth milestone (market penetration), it would be unfair not to warn you of the surprise that almost all find when they reach their final goal.

The fun is in the trip and not the arrival. The responsibilities of wealth and authority usually become extremely heavy and the freedoms that you dream about do not exist. If you are a shallow person when you arrive, you'll probably be a very unhappy person after you're there.

THE ROADWAY   M, IS, RS, F

Realize that thousands of earlier pioneers have traveled the same roadway that we have followed in these 18 chapters. These earlier people have cleared the way, eliminated many barriers, built bridges, and made your trip much smoother. You have an obligation to those that will follow you to be a success, to knock down a hurdle or two, and make the roadway a little straighter and a little smoother. If you get halfway and decide to quit, then quit like a man and meet your commitments and obligations so that the roadway is not damaged for others.

You'll find that the roadway isn't a lonely one (unless you want to make it lonely). There are plenty of helping hands and plenty of encouragement by those who have passed that way before you. Entrepreneurism is a true frontier (perhaps the last frontier to open to those who want the most from life) and you and your fellow travelers are true pioneers. Have the frontier spirit and help and be helped by other pioneers.

If you are like others, you'll find an outstretched hand when the going gets tough or you lose confidence in yourself. When you arrive, you have an obligation to hold out your hand to those who follow you. Then they will follow your example and help later pilgrims. Don't break the cycle.

Enjoy your trip. It's an experience of a lifetime.

Venture Capital Groups

**TABLE OF VENTURE CAPITAL GROUPS WHICH
INVEST IN START-UPS**

State	Number	State	Number
Alaska	2	Michigan	6
Arizona	3	Minnesota	3
Arkansas	1	Missouri	1
California	54	Montana	1
Colorado	5	New Hampshire	1
Connecticut	13	New Jersey	11
Delaware	1	New York	43
District of Columbia	3	North Carolina	1
Florida	8	Ohio	7
Georgia	4	Oklahoma	1
Hawaii	1	Oregon	1
Idaho	1	Pennsylvania	6
Illinois	13	Rhode Island	1
Indiana	2	South Carolina	1
Iowa	1	Tennessee	2
Kentucky	1	Texas	7
Louisiana	2	Virginia	3
Maine	1	Washington	2
Maryland	3	Wisconsin	5
Massachusetts	28	Total	250

ESTIMATED PERCENTAGES OF DOLLARS INVESTED IN START-UPS		ESTIMATED PERCENTAGES OF START-UPS FUNDED BY VENTURE CAPITALISTS	
State	*Percentage*	*State*	*Percentage*
New York	29	California	18
California	17	New York	16
Massachusetts	12	Massachusetts	11
Texas	9	Texas	8
Connecticut	6	Connecticut	6
New Jersey	5	New Jersey	6
Florida	4	Florida	4
Pennsylvania	3	Illinois	4
Georgia	2	Arizona	3
Illinois	2	Ohio	3
Ohio	2	Georgia	2
Arizona	1	Maryland	2
Maryland	1	Pennsylvania	2
Michigan	1	Wisconsin	2
Wisconsin	1	Colorado	1
Balance	5	Michigan	1
		Minnesota	1
		Virginia	1
		Washington	1
		Balance	8

These tables were developed by Business Solutions from questionaires sent to venture capitalists. Only about one-third will even consider investing in start-ups and first round companies. These tables' only value is to illustrate to you "where the action is" so that regardless of where you decide to locate your company, you'll go nationwide for your capitalists.

INSTRUCTIONS FOR USING THE FOLLOWING LISTS OF VENTURE CAPITALISTS

The following tables of venture capitalists give you the names, addresses, people to contact, telephone numbers, the type of firm, the geographical areas in which they are interested in investing, the industries which interest them, the minimum and preferred investment levels, their fees, and their affiliations.

Those firms which are promoters, finders, consultants, or are known marketing research shells have been omitted. Though many of these firms are ethical, unfortunately many are proposal mills whose primary intent is to extract fees, commissions, and expenses from founders. Many marketing research firms utilize a venture capital company (or corporate) shell to keep them abreast of industry trends.

Likewise, those bonafide investment firms which have no interests in financing start-ups and young companies have been omitted. The majority of firms which define themselves as "venture capital firms" aren't interested in anything before second round investments.

Please be aware that most sophisticated venture capital companies are extremely flexible and far sighted. Therefore, most freely break their rules as to minimum and preferred investment levels, industry preferences, and geographical limitations. Also, be aware that terminology varies from firm to firm. Some companies consider the "start-up" round of financing as "seed money," others define it as "feasibility money," while others define it as "first round money." Also, be aware of the "bandwagon" effect of growth and glamour industries. As you read through the industries preferred, you'll observe the "me to-ism" of the growth industries. Therefore, when the "smart money" starts being invested in a new industry, you'll discover that many other firms leap on the bandwagon without understanding the technologies involved. To illustrate this point, at the time of this writing both mini-computers and microprocessors are growth industries. Half of the firms which listed mini-computers confused them with microprocessors.

The last major point is that though we tried to give you an insight into the affiliations of as many companies as we could, there is no way that we can really determine their money pipelines. Most cash rich companies, foundations, and groups funnel their funds into several venture capital firms for investments. At the time of this writing, one oil company's surplus funds have been funneled into seven venture capitalists that I know about. Foreign countries jump in and out with great frequency. This variable shouldn't affect you unless a heavy plunger gets into a cash bind and tries to force liquidation or defaults on commitments (a rare occurrence).

ALASKA

Alaska Business Investment Corporation
P.O. Box 600, Anchorage, AK 99501
D. L. Mellish, 907-279-6913

This SBIC prefers latter rounds of investments however will consider all rounds. Though it has no industry preference, it will consider Alaska based firms only.

Minimum investment = $100,000
Preferred investment = $250–500,000
Affiliation: National Bank of Alaska

Alyeska Investment Company
1815 S. Bragaw St., Anchorage, AK 99504
R. L. Miller, 907-279-9584

This MESBIC will invest in Alaskan firms only. Prefer Eskimoe founders. This firm is very active in all phases of investments and has no industry preference.

Minimum investment = Under $100,000
Preferred investment = Under $100,000
Affiliation: Alyeska Pipeline Company

ARIZONA

First Southwest SBIC
1611 E. Camelback, Phoenix, AZ 85016
W. Howard O'Brien, 602-274-3623

This SBIC prefers investments in the Southwest and in Japan. Industry preferences are: crime prevention, telephone products, nursing homes, forestry, franchised foods, and advertising.

Minimum investment = $100,000
Preferred investment = no preferences
Affiliation: None
Fees: legal, points, closing costs.

La Raza Investment Corporation
3001 W. Indian School Rd., Phoenix 85017
Fausto Miranda 602-263-9506

This MESBIC is interested in all rounds of financing in the Southwest. It has no industry preferences.

Minimum & Preferred investments = Under $100,000
Affiliations: None
Fees: legal, points, closing costs.

Motorola New Venture Development
8201 E. McDowell Rd., Scottsdale 95235
Robert M. Handy, 602-949-3243

This privately owned subsidiary is interested in all rounds of financing. Primary interests are in high technology industries: computers, word processing, automated equipment, chemicals, crime prevention, drugs & medicines, CATV, and instrumentation.

Minimum investment = $100,000
Preferred investment = $250–500,000
Affiliation: Motorola Inc.

357

ARKANSAS

MESBIC of Arkansas
212 Center, Rm. 302, Little Rock 72203
C. E. Sims, 501-374-9977

This MESBIC is interested in all rounds of financing of all companies within 2 hours of Little Rock. Primary industries are: plastics, numerical controlled equipment, leisure time operations, and electronics.

Minimum & Preferred investments = Under $100,000
Affiliations: First Pyramid Life Ins. Company
Six Little Rock banks
Fees: legal, points, and closing costs

CALIFORNIA

American Express Investment Management Co.
550 Laurel, San Francisco 94022
James P. Norris, 415-563-7900

This affiliate is interested in all rounds of financing in high technology firms. Primarily interested in San Franciscan firms in: lasers, integrated circuits, optics, pollution controls, computers, crime prevention, plastics, drugs, medical instruments, & publishing.

Minimum investment = $100,000
Preferred investment = $250–500,000
Affiliations: American Express

Asset Management Company
1411 Edgewood Dr., Palo Alto 94301
Brook Byers, 415-321-3131

This privately owned company is interested in early rounds of financing in high technology industries: integrated circuits, lasers, microfilm, optics, and medical instruments.

Minimum investment = $100,000
Preferred investment = $250–500,000
Fees: legal, points, closing costs.

Bamerica International Finance Corporation
555 California, Rm 2271,
San Francisco 94104
C. A. MacIlvaine, 415-622-5015

This international affiliate is interested only in foreign investments. The industry preferences are primarily all high technology industries or new ventures which have real value to the specific country in which the firm is based.

Minimum investment = $600,000
Preferred investment = $1,000,000 & up
Affiliations: Bank of America

Small Business Enterprises Company
555 California, San Francisco 94104
Steven L. Merrill, 415-622-2582

This extremely active affiliate (an SBIC) is interested in all rounds of financing in all areas of the US. Though it prefers high technology firms (like its sister company above), it is active in every industry.

Minimum investment = no minimum
Preferred investment = $250–500,000 & up
Affiliations: Bank of America

Bancal Capital Company
550 S. Flower, Rm 919, Los Angeles 90017
J. Gorham Arend, 213-627-4874

This SBIC is interested in Southwestern and Southern Californian firms. Industry preferences are: motion pictures, computer products, manufacturing, crime prevention, plastics, sporting goods, all facets of the medical industry, drugs, hospital management, TV, publishing, and natural resources.

Minimum investment = $100,000
Preferred investment = $250–500,000
Affiliations: Ban Cal Tri-State Corp.

Bay Equities Incorporated
555 California, Rm 5000,
San Francisco 94104
B. Jack Brooks, 415-398-1006

This affiliate has no geographical preferences and is a privately owned venture capital group. Industries preferred are: microfilm, lasers, optics, pollution controls, all phases of computers, and automated equipment. Firm prefers early rounds of financing only.

Minimum investments = $100,000
Preferred investments = $250–500,000
Affiliations: First National Bank of Chicago

Beckman Instruments Incorporated
2500 Harbor Blvd., Fullerton 92634
Bob B. Brown, 714-871-4848

Though this firm is primarily in the electronics manufacturing industry, it frequently becomes involved in all phases of financing in the growth segments of the electronics industry.

Minimum investments = no minimums
Preferred investments = no preferences

Benbow Research Corporation
601 California, Rm 605,
San Francisco 94108
J. Benbow Bullock, 415-981-2516

This private venture capital and consulting firm is primarily interested in West Coast high technology firms and Southwestern resources. Primary interests are electronics, computers, medical services, banks, leasing.

Minimum investments = $100,000
Preferred investments = $250–500,000

Bixby Associates Incorporated
11661 San Vicente Blvd.,
Los Angeles 90049
Roy Sug Robins, 213-820-5625

This affiliate is primarily interested in early rounds of financing for West Coast firms. No industry preferences.

Minimum investments = $250,000
Preferred investments = $250–500,000
Affiliations: The Bixby Ranch Company
Fees: Legal, points, & closing costs.

CALIFORNIA (Continued):

Blalack, Loop, & Townsend Incorporated
199 N. Lake Ave., Pasadena 91101
Charles M. Blalack, 213-684-2311

This private venture capital group prefers investments within 2 hours drive of Pasadena and has no industry preference.

Minimum investment = $100,000
Preferred investment = $1,000,000 & up
Fees: legal, points, and closing costs.

Bruce A. Blinn
One Embarcadero, Rm 3901,
San Francisco 94111
Bruce A. Blinn, 415-981-3666

This privately owned venture capital firm is interested in all rounds of financing for West Coast firms only. Mr Blinn has no industry preferences.

Minimum investment = $100,000
Preferred investments = $100–250,000

Blyth, Eastman, Dillon & Co. Incorporated
555 California, San Francisco 94104
Bill K. Bowes, 415-382-8000

This affiliate is interested in all industries and in all rounds of financing. The firm must be within 4 hours drive of any major airport in the US.

Minimum investment = no minimum
Preferred investment = $1,000,000 & up
Affiliations: INA Insurance Corporation
Fees: Professional fee whether or not the deal is closed.

Baentwood Associates
11661 San Vicente Blvd.,
Los Angeles 90049
B. K. Hagopian, 213-826-6581

This private company is interested in all high technology firms and in all phases of financing. It is interested in opportunities in the US.

Minimum investment = $100,000
Preferred investment = $250–750,000
Fees: legal, points, and closing costs.

Bryan & Edwards Company and Edvestco Incorporated
235 Montgomery, Rm 2220,
San Francisco 94104
John Bryan, 415-421-9990

These two SBIC's are owned and operated by the same management team. They are interested in all rounds of financing, in all growth industries, for firms located on the West Coast.

Minimum investment = no minimums
Preferred investment = $100–250,000

Citicorp Venture Capital Limited
44 Montgomery, San Francisco 94104
David G. Arscott, 415-788-6016

This affiliate is interested in all rounds of financing, in all industries, and in all US areas.

Minimum investment = no minimums
Preferred investment = no preferences
Affiliations: Citicorp of New York

City of Commerce Investment Corp.
1117 S. Goodrich Blvd.,
Los Angeles 90022
John Robert Flour, 213-724-6141

This MESBIC is interested in first and second rounds of financing in all West Coast areas. No industry preference.

Minimum & preferred investments = Under $100,000

360

Clark, Dodge, & Company Incorporated
730 Welch Rd., Palo Alto 94304
John Maurer, 415-321-1500

This affiliate is interested in all rounds of financing on the West Coast. No industry preference.

Minimum investment = no minimums
Preferred investment = no preferences
Affiliations: Investment Bank of New York

Continental Capital Corporation
555 California, Rm 2690,
San Francisco 94104
Frank G. Chambers, 415-989-2020

This publicly held SBIC is interested in all rounds of financing in the Southwest and West Coast. Primary industries are high technology industries: computers, microfilm, optics, pollution controls, telephone products, automation, crime prevention, medical industry, and graphic arts.

Minimum investment = $100,000
Preferred investment = $250-500,000
Fees: Legal, points, and closing costs.

James S. Crane
25655 Fernhill Dr., Los Altos 94022
James S. Crane, 415-948-5112

This gentleman is interested only in start-ups in microfilm, data communications, forests, and electronics. He invests in the Midwest, Southwest, and West Coast.

Minimum investments = Under $100,000
Preferred investment = $100,000

Crocker Capital Corporation
2 Palo Alto Square, Palo Alto 94304
Bill Dawson, 415-493-4521

This SBIC is interested in all rounds of financing on the West Coast. Its primary interests are: drugs, hospital management, integrated circuits, optics, pollution controls, and telephone related products.

Minimum investment = Under $100,000
Preferred investment = $100-250,000
Affiliations: Crocker-Citizens Bank

Delta Investment Co. Incorporated
555 Capital Mall, #640,
Sacramento 95814
John L. Dowdell, 916-444-0494

The affiliate is interested in early rounds of financing for West Coast firms. Primary interests are in: drugs, lasers, optics, sporting goods, clinical laboratories, medicines, and forestry products.

Minimum investments = Under $100,000
Preferred investments = $100-250,000
Affiliations: Delta Investment Research Corp.
Fees: Legal, points, and closing costs.

Developers Equity Capital Corporation
9348 Santa Monica Blvd, Rm 307
Beverly Hills 90210
K. M. Dolan, 213-878-2533

Though this firm is primarily interested in any real estate development or contracting company anywhere in the US, it is also interested in food and medical products for Los Angeles based firms.

Minimum investment = Under $100,000
Preferred investment = $100-250,000
Fees: Legal, points, and closing costs.

361

CALIFORNIA (Continued):

Eldridge Investment Company
167 Isabella Ave., Atherton 94025
Donald F. Eldridge, 415-325-6070

This venture capital firm is interested only in start-ups in Northern California. Primary interests are: motion pictures, TV programming, integrated circuits, microfilm, lasers, optics, pollution, computers, and telephone related products.

Minimum investment = Under $100,000
Preferred investment = $100–250,000

Richard D. Farrer
2742 Brant Ave., San Diego 92103
Richard D. Farrer, 714-297-4489

This gentleman is interested in first and second round investments in computers, medical, and high technology companies.

Minimum investment = no minimums
Preferred investments = no preferences

First California Financial
555 California, Rm 2900,
San Francisco 94104
Jack H. Canvin, 415-622-7788

This combination of private venture capital firm and investment banker is interested in all rounds of financing in all industries, and in all areas within the US.

Minimum investment = $100,000
Preferred investment = $250–500,000
Fees: Legal, points, and closing costs.

The FMC Corporation
P.O. Box 1201, San Jose 95108
N. A. Weil, 408-289-2236

This conglomerate has in excess of 3 billion dollars in sales and is continually searching for new ventures which complement FMC operations.

Minimum investment = no minimums
Preferred investments = $250–750,000

Foothill Venture Corporation
8383 Wilshire Blvd, Beverly Hills 90211
Russell B. Faucett, 213-655-5620

This SBIC affiliate is interested in all rounds of financing, all industries, for West Coast firms.

Minimum investment = Under $100,000
Preferred investment = $250–750,000
Affiliate: The Foothill Group Inc.
Financial Management and Services

Formations
2827 Prince, Berkeley 94705
Thomas Schwartzberg, 415-653-5215

This private company specializes in start-up financing for West Coast based firms. It prefers: optics, pollution controls, graphic arts, automated equipment, crime prevention, chemicals, drugs, medicines, and medical instruments.

Minimum & preferred investments = Under $100,000

Goodman & Mautner, Limited
5250 W. Century Blvd, Rm 444
L.A. 90045
David Goodman, 213-776-4011

This private company prefers the first three rounds of financing for firms within major metropolitan areas (for easy commuting by air). Its primary industries are: electronics,

Minimum investments = $100,000
Preferred investments = $100–250,000

362

optics, telephone products, computers, medical, chemicals, plastics, automated equipment, and proprietary patents.

Growth SBIC, Incorporated
1500 Orange Ave, Coronado 92118
James W. Howard

This SBIC affiliate is interested in all rounds of financing in Midwestern and West Coast firms. Primary industries of investments are: recreational companies, publishing, and land development.

Minimum & preferred investments = Under $100,000
Affiliates: Growth Capital Inc., Holding Company
Fees: legal, points, and closing costs.

Hambrecht & Quist
235 Montgomery, San Francisco 94104
George Quist, 415-433-1720

This combination venture capital company and investment banker is interested in all rounds of financing in both the Southwest and West Coast. They are interested in all growth industries.

Minimum investment = no minimums
Preferred investment = $100–500,000
Fees: Placement fees only

Hoebich Venture Management
860 Hamilton Ave, Palo Alto 94301
Christian E. Hoebich, 415-326-5590

This consulting firm is interested in early rounds of investment in high technology industries in Northern California.

Minimum investment = Under $100,000
Preferred investment = $250–500,000
Fees: Professional fees whether or not deal is closed.

Idanta Partners
Bank of California Plaza, Rm 1680
San Diego 92101
David J. Dunn, 714-236-0036

This branch office is operated on a part time basis for all rounds of financing. It claims no limitations or preferences in either industry or geography.

Minimum investment = $100,000
Preferred investment = $500–1,000,000
Affiliates: Idanta of New York

Kleiner & Perkins
3000 Sand Hill Rd. Bldg. 11,104
Menlo Park 94025
Eugene Kleiner, 415-854-1055

This private firm is interested in all rounds of financing in both the Southwest and West Coast. Principal industries are: computers, automated equipment, crime prevention, sporting goods, all phases of medicine, specialty natural resources, gold, silver, CATV, and mail order.

Minimum investments = $100,000
Preferred investments = $250–750,000

CALIFORNIA (Continued):

The Mayfield Fund
2200 Sand Hill Rd., Rm 201,
Menlo Park 94025
Tom or Wallace Davis, 415-854-5560

This private company is interested in only the first two rounds of investment for West Coast based firms. Principal industries are: electronics, lasers, optics, pollution controls, telephone products, computers, automated equipment, food products, sporting goods, drugs, medicines, and medical instruments.

Minimum investment = $100,000
Preferred investments = $100–250,000

McMorgan & Company
1000 Welsh Rd., Palo Alto 94304
John Glynn Jr. 415-328-2443

This private firm is interested in all rounds of financing for West Coast firms. Principal industries are all high technology growth industries and drugs.

Minimum investment = $100,000
Preferred investment = $100–250,000

Northrup Technology
 Development Inc.
1800 Century Park East,
Century City 90067
Ted A. McCabe, 213-553-1818

This affiliate is interested in the first three rounds of financing in all high technology growth industries. It has no geographical preferences.

Minimum investment = $200,000
Preferred investment = $400–750,000
Affiliates: The Northrup Corporation

Oak Grove Ventures
2200 Sand Hill Rd. Rm 110,
Menlo Park 94025
Paul Cook, 415-854-1415

This private firm invests anywhere in the US provided there is "suitable management". Primary financial investments in only start-up and first rounds. Preferred industries are: Microfilm, lasers, optics, pollution, telephone products, specialty chemicals, computers, word processing, drugs, medicines, medical instruments, and tomorrow's growth areas.

Minimum investment = $100,000
Preferred investments = $250–750,000

Palo Alto Investment Company
233 3rd St., Rm A, Los Altos 94022
Burton J. McMurty, 415-941-4363

This firm is an investment advising company for selected clients in start-ups and first round financing. Primary industries

Minimum investment = any amount
Preferred investments = $250–500,000

364

are: pollution, computers, word processing, medical instruments, and proprietary patents.

Wayne L. Prim
650 California, Rm 2950,
San Francisco 94108
Wayne L. Prim, 415-434-1600

This gentleman is interested in investing in all rounds of financing for West Coast firms. No industry preferences. Prefers passive role.

Minimum investments = $150,000
Preferred investments = $300–750,000

Robertson, Coleman, Siebel, & Weisel
235 Montgomery St, San Francisco 94104
Tom J. Cable, 415-981-3921

This investment banking firm prefers first thru third rounds of financing in primarily manufacturing, computers, and medical industries. It works with Southwestern and West Coast firms.

Minimum investment = $500,000
Preferred investments = $1,000,000 & up
Fees: Placement fees

Arthur Rock & Associates
Russ Bldg, 235 Montgomery, Suite 1636
San Francisco 94104
Arthur Rock, 415-981-3921

This private firm is interested primarily in start-up thru second round financing in high technology, medical, computer related products, oil & gas, specialty retailers, publishing and CATV industries. Firms must be within two hours of the home office.

Minimum investment = $100,000
Preferred investment = $750,000 & up

Rodal Corporation
2 Palo Alto Square, Rm 1034,
Palo Alto 94304
Bob Sackman, 415-493-0141

This affiliate is interested in start-up thru second round financing in any major metropolitan area in the US. Major areas of interest are: medical industry, electronics, computers, and automated equipment.

Minimum investment = $100,000
Preferred investments = $250–750,000
Affiliates: Agathos Investments S.A. (Panama)

San Francisco Venture Capital
350 Pacific, San Francisco 94111
Tony Manlove, 415-986-1844

This private firm is interested primarily in San Francisco based firms needing start-up or first round financing. Primary areas of interest are: pollution controls, crime prevention, medical instruments, and automated controls.

Minimum & preferred investments = under $100,000

The San Francisco Group
235 Montgomery St.,
San Francisco 94104
Dobbs Dalton, No phone

This foundation invests small amounts to San Francisco start-ups which enhance the beauty and culture of San Francisco.

Minimum investment = $500
Maximum investment = $1,500

Space Age SBIC
1368 Lincoln Ave., Rm 111,
San Rafael 94901
Bob Boyden, 415-454-9600

This SBIC is interested in first rounds of financing for West Coast firms. No industry preferences.

Minimum investment = $100,000
Preferred investments = $100–250,000
Fees: legal, points, and closing costs.

Stanford University Endowment Fund
Encina Hall, Stanford University 94305
Rod Adams, 415-321-2300

Stanford invests percentages of its endowment funds in early rounds of financing for firms addressing major growth industries.

Minimum investment = no minimums
Preferred investments = $100–500,000
Affiliations: Stanford University

Sutro & Company Incorporated
460 Montgomery St.,
San Francisco 94104
John Blumlein Sr., 415-392-0900

This investment banking firm specializes in first four rounds of financing for firms in Southwest, West Coast, Canada, and Japan. It is interested in all growth areas.

Minimum investment = $100,000
Preferred investments = $750,000 & up
Fees: Contingent upon equity

Sutter Hill Ventures
Two Palo Alto Square, Rm 700
Palo Alto 94304
Bill Draper, 415-493-5600

This affiliate is interested in start-up and first round financing throughout the US. No industry preferences.

Minimum investment = $100,000
Preferred investment = $250–500,000
Affiliations: The Genstar Corporation

Technology Resources Inc.
P.O. Box 3517, Orange 92665
Dr. J. C. Chu, 714-639-4941

This MESBIC is interested in all rounds of financing throughout the US. No specific industries are preferred.

Minimum investment = $100,000
Preferred investments = $250–500,000
Fees: legal, points, closing costs, equity, and professional fees whether deal closes or not.

Transamerica Computer Company
Box 7994, San Francisco 94957
J. W. Rush, 415-983-5000

This affiliate is interested only in computer related products throughout the US.

Minimum investment = no minimums
Preferred investments = no preferences
Affiliates: TransAmerica
             Insurance Corporation

Ungersmith Securities Company
555 California, San Francisco 94104
Joseph Chulick, 415-421-2850

This branch office invests in start-ups through second round financing throughout the US. It's interested in all growth industries.

Minimum investment = $100,000
Preferred investment = $250–750,000
Affiliates: Ungersmith of New York City

UnionAmerica Capital Corporation
445 S. Figueroa, Los Angeles 90017
Brent Rider, 213-687-5587

This SBIC invests in all rounds to all areas in the US. It is interested in: electronics, microfilm, optics, pollution controls, telephone products, computers, computer related products, word processing, all manufacturing, drugs, medical instruments, hospital and clinic management, CATV, and publishing.

Minimum investment = $100,000
Preferred investments = $250–750,000
Affiliates: Union Bank

Wells Fargo Investment Company
475 Sansome, San Francisco 94111
Daniel D. Tompkins, 415-396-3292

This SBIC is interested in all rounds to all areas in the US. Primary industries are: electronics, lasers, optics, pollution controls, telephone products, all computer areas, automated equipment, materials handling, drugs, diagnostic centers, medical instruments, hospital management, and leisure products.

Minimum investment = $100,000
Preferred investments = $250–750,000
Affiliates: Wells Fargo Bank

367

COLORADO

Bosworth, Sullivan & Company
660 17th St., Denver 80202
Bruce B. Bee, 303-534-1177

This investment banking firm is interested in all rounds of financing in the Rocky Mountains, Southwest, and West Coast. No industry preferences.

Minimum investment = $100,000
Preferred investments = $250–500,000
Fees: Contingent upon equity

Cambridge Banking Partners
1711 Security Life Bldg, Denver 80202
Bruce B. Paul, 303-222-5727

This private firm is interested in first thru third round financing in all growth industries throughout the US.

Minimum investment = $100,000
Preferred investment = $250–500,000

COLORADO (Continued):

Colorado Investment Securities Inc.
1660 Lincoln St. Rm 1900, Denver 80203
Dick Emmons, 303-892-5559

This private company invests in all phases of financing throughout the US. Preferred industries are: optics, pollution controls, telephone products, data communications, automated equipment, patented proprietary products, and medical instruments.

Minimum investment = under $100,000
Preferred investments = $250–750,000
Fees: legal, points, and closing costs.

Henry Goldman III
3450 Rainbow Lane, Colo. Springs 80908
Henry Goldman III, 303-495-2589

This gentleman invests in the first three rounds of financing throughout the US. Primary industries are: electronics, telephone products, all manufacturing, drugs, clinical laboratories, minerals, oil, gas, coal, mail order, discount stores, publishing, and banks.

Minimum investment = under $100,000
Preferred investments = $100–150,000

Investment Securities of Colorado, Inc.
First National Bank Bldg, Rm 2540
Denver 80202
Vern Korneisen, 303-893-0011

This banker invests in start-ups and first round financing in high technology industries, all manufacturing, drugs, medicines, banks, and leasing companies.

Minimum investment = no minimums
Preferred investment = $100,000
Fee: contingent upon equity

CONNECTICUT

Aetna Life & Casualty Company
151 Farmington Ave., Hartford 06115
Ronald Clark, 203-273-0123

This publicly held insurance company invests portions of its pension funds, profit sharing funds, and endowment funds in first thru fourth rounds of financing. It has no industry preference and invests nationwide.

Minimum investment = $100,000
Preferred investment = $250–500,000

All State Venture Capital Corporation
855 Main St. Rm 860,
Bridgeport 06604
Tom H. Brown Jr., 203-368-0092

Though this SBIC prefers later rounds of financing, it will consider start-ups and first rounds for excellent firms and concepts. It has no industry preference however limits itself to East Coast firms.

Minimum investment = $100,000
Preferred investment = $250–500,000
Fees: legal, points, and closing costs.

368

Anderson Investment Company
49 Locust, New Canaan 06840
Harlan Anderson, 203-966-5684

This privately owned firm invests its own money in start-ups and first rounds in East Coast firms only. Industry preferences are: graphic arts, telephone related products, computer related products, time sharing, and automated equipment.

Minimum investment = under $100,000
Preferred investment = $100,000

Ciminvest of Hartford Incorporated
18 Asylum St., Hartford 06103
Vernan R. Mendez, 203-246-7259

This MESBIC invests in first and second rounds of financing for East Coast firms. It claims no industry preferences.

Minimum & preferred investments = under $100,000
Fees: legal, points, and closing costs.

Dewey Investment Corporation
101 Middle Turnpike West,
Manchester 06040
George Mrosek, 203-643-5110

This SBIC invests only in Connecticut firms. Primary interests are in young growth industries.

Minimum & preferred investments = under $100,000
Fees: legal, points, and closing costs.

Euclid Financial Corporation
35 Mason St., Greenwich 06830
King Cayce, 203-661-2782

This privately owned firm invests its own money in East Coast and Southeastern firms. Primary industries of interest are: manufacturing of proprietary products, drugs, clinical laboratories, diagnostic centers, medical instruments, oil, gas, electronics, and retail sales.

Minimum & preferred investments = under $100,000

369

GTE New Ventures Corporation
One Stamford Forum, Stamford 06904
Craig Huston

This affiliate is interested in the first three rounds of financing in any US based firm. Principal areas of interest are: high technology manufacturing, computers, hospital management, drugs, clinical laboratories, diagnostic centers, oil, and gas.

Minimum investment = $100,000
Preferred investments = $500,000 & up
Affiliates: General Telephone & Electronics Corp.

Hartford Community Capital Corporation
70 Farmington Ave, Hartford 06106
Mrs Jan-Gee W. McCollum, 203-547-2684

This MESBIC is interested in all early rounds of financing for Connecticut based firms.

Minimum & preferred investments = under $100,000
Affiliations: Hartford National Bank & Trust Co.

CONNECTICUT (Continued):

Marwit Capital Corporation
111 Prospect St., Stamford 06901
Martin Witte, 203-324-5793

This SBIC is interested in all rounds of financing in motion pictures, TV programming, publishing, CATV, chemicals, and pollution controls.

Minimum investment = under $100,000
Preferred investment = $250–500,000
Fees: Contingent upon equity.

Nationwide Funding Corporation
10A Ambassador Dr., Manchester 06040
Dick Ketler, 203-649-5361

This SBIC is interested only in start-ups in the US. It has no industry preferences.

Minimum & preferred investments = under $100,000
Fees: legal, points, and closing costs.

Nutmeg Capital Corporation
35 Elm St., Suite 4, New Haven 06510
Leigh Raymond, 203-776-0643

This SBIC is interested primarily in start-up and first round funding for Connecticut based firms. Principal industries are: franchised food, pollution controls, and automated equipment.

Minimum & preferred investments = under $100,000
Fees: legal, points, and closing costs.

The Prospect Company
One Tower Square, Hartford 06115
Richard B. Park, 203-277-3435

This affiliate is interested in all rounds of investments nationwide. No industry preferences.

Minimum investment = $100,000
Preferred investments = $250–500,000
Affiliates: Travelers Insurance Company

The Xerox Corporation
High Park Ridge, Stamford 06904
J. F. Lyons, 203-329-8711

This company is interested in start-ups, first, and second rounds of financing nationwide. Primary interests are: electronics, microfilm, lasers, optics, graphic arts, telephone related products, computers, proprietary product manufacturing, medical instruments, and publishing.

Minimum investment = $100,000
Preferred investments = $250–500,000

DELAWARE

Hercules Incorporated
910 Market St., Wilmington 19899
Dr. E. D. Crittenden Jr., 302-656-9811

This division of the Hercules Corporation is interested in the first three rounds of funding for firms nationwide. Primary industries are: data communications, recreational and leisure products, medical instruments, and manufacturing.

Minimum investment = no minimums
Preferred investments = $750,000 & up.

DISTRICT OF COLUMBIA

Greater Washington Investors, Inc.
1015 18th St. NW, Rm. 300,
Wash. DC 20036
Don Christensen, 202-466-2210

This publicly held venture capital corporation is interested in funding the first three rounds of firms nationwide. Areas of interest are: electronics, microfilm, optics, pollution controls, telephone products, all phases of computers, manufacturing, and medical instruments.

Minimum investment = $100,000
Preferred investments = $250–750,000
Fees: legal, points, and closing costs.

Rollinson, Stein, & Halpert
1019 19th St. NW, Suite 1300,
Wash. DC 20006
Mark Rollinson, 202-785-4200

This law firm invests client and partners' funds in all rounds of financing nationwide.

Minimum investment = $100,000
Preferred investments = $750,000 & up
Fees: Professional fees whether deal closes or not.

Wachtel & Company Inc.
1000 Vermont Ave. NW, Wash. DC 20005
Sidney Wachtel, 202-347-9588

This investment banking firm is interested in all rounds of financing in the Washington D.C. area. Primary industries are: telephone products, mail order, and retail.

Minimum investment = under $100,000
Preferred investments = $250–500,000
Fees: contingent upon equity.

FLORIDA

Burger King MESBIC Incorporated
P.O. Box 338, Kendell Branch,
Miami 33156
Zane Leshner 305-274-7656

This MESBIC is interested primarily in start-ups in franchise food.

Minimum investment = under $100,000
Preferred investment = no preferences
Affiliates: The Burger King Corporation

Electro-Science Management Corporation
2170 S.E. 17th St., Rm 303,
Ft. Lauderdale 33316
John Boone 305-523-3411

This private firm is interested in first and second rounds of financing anywhere in the US. Its industry preferences are in optics, pollution controls, all phases of computers, automated equipment, plastics, wool processing, and medical instruments.

Minimum investment = under $100,000
Preferred investments = $100–250,000
Fees: legal, points, and closing costs.

Florida Crown MESBIC
604 Hogan St., Jacksonville 32202
Tom Bolden Jr. 904-353-6161

This MESBIC is primarily interested only in start-ups in the franchise food area for Florida based firms.

Minimum & Preferred investments = under $100,000
Fees: legal, points, and closing costs.

FLORIDA (Continued):

Market Capital Corporation
1102 N. 28th St., Tampa 33605
E. E. Eads 813-247-1357

This SBIC is interested in start-ups and first round financing in Florida based firms specializing in franchised food businesses.

Minimum & preferred investments = under $100,000

North American Company
111 E. Las Olas Blvd.,
Ft. Lauderdale 33301
Charles Palmer 305-525-0681

This privately owned firm is interested in first and second rounds of financing in firms based in the Southeast, Southwest, Midwest, and East Coast. Principal areas of interest are: banking, leasing, publishing, drugs, and medical instruments.

Minimum investment = $100,000
Preferred investments = $750,000 & up
Fees: legal, points, and closing costs.

Small Business Assistance Corporation
6704 W. Highway 98, Panama City 32401
John Laslie 904-234-3359

This SBIC is interested in Southeastern firms for start-up, first, and second round financing. Primary interests are in: hotels, motels, and real estate developments.

Minimum investment = under $100,000
Preferred investments = $250–750,000
Affiliations: West Florida Bank Holding Co.
Fees: legal, points, and closing costs.

Southeast SBIC, Incorporated
100 S. Biscayne Blvd., Miami 33131
J. S. Higgins 305-577-3528

This SBIC is interested in all rounds of financing for firms throughout the US. No industry preferences.

Minimum investment = $100,000
Preferred investment = $250–500,000
Affiliations: Southeast Banking Corporation
Fees: legal, points, and closing costs.

Urban Ventures Inc.
Tower Three, 825 S. Bayshore,
Miami 33131
Bill Wynn Jr. 305-373-4691

This MESBIC is interested in early rounds of financing in the Southeast. Principal areas of interest are: crime prevention, narcotics control, discount stores, banks, CATV, leasing, sporting goods, and pollution.

Minimum & preferred investments = under $100,000
Fees: legal, points, closing costs, and professional fees whether deal is closed or not.
Affiliation: United Way of America

GEORGIA

CSRA Capital Corporation
699 Broad St., Rm. 914, Augusta 30902
Allen Caldwell 404-722-7505

This SBIC is interested in all rounds of financing for real estate proposals throughout the US.

Minimum investment = $100,000
Preferred investment = $250–500,000
Fees: legal, points, and closing costs.

Fidelity Capital Corporation
300 Fidelity North, Atlanta 30339
Wayne Haskins 404-432-3211

This SBIC is interested in start-ups in real estate in the Southeast and Southwest.

Minimum investment = $100,000
Preferred investment = $250–500,000
Affiliate: Fidelity Enterprises Inc.
Fees: legal, points, and closing costs.

First American Investment Corporation
300 Interstate North, Rm. 290, Atlanta 30339
Joe Chastain 404-432-3211

This SBIC is interested in start-ups in real estate developments in the Southeast and Southwest.

Minimum investment = $100,000
Preferred investment = $250–500,000
Fees: legal, points, and closing costs.

The Robinson-Humphrey Company, Inc.
2 Peachtree St. NW, Atlanta 30303
Jerome Sands Jr. 404-658-1100

This investment banker is interested in all rounds of financing for firms based in the Southeast. It has no industry preferences.

Minimum investment = $100,000
Preferred investment = $750,000 & up.
Fee: Placement fees.

HAWAII

SBIC of Hawaii Incorporated
1575 S. Beretania St., Honolulu 96814
James W. Y. Wong 808-949-3677

This SBIC is interested in all rounds of investments in Hawaii based firms. Primary areas of interest are: hotels, motels, restaurants, real estate development, and retail outlets.

Minimum investment = $100,000
Preferred investment = $100–250,000
Fees: legal, points, and closing costs.

IDAHO

Industrial Investment Corporation
413 W. Idaho St., Rm. 200, Boise 83702
J. Robert Tullis 208-543-6491

This SBIC is interested in early rounds of financing for West Coast firms. No industry preference.

Minimum investment = under $100,000
Preferred investment = $100–150,000
Fees: legal, points, and closing costs.

ILLINOIS

Allstate Insurance Company
Allstate Plaza, Northbrook 60062
Dennis Repp 312-291-5000

This insurance company is interested in all rounds of financing in all areas of the US. No industry preferences.

Minimum investment = $100,000
Preferred investments = $1,000,000 & up.
Affiliate: Sears & Roebuck Inc.

AMOCO Venture Capital Company
200 E. Randolph Dr., Chicago 60601
Robert Anderson 312-856-6523

This MESBIC is interested in all early rounds of financing in Midwestern companies. No industry preferences.

Minimum investment = under $100,000
Preferred investments = $100–150,000
Affiliate: Standard Oil of Indiana

ILLINOIS (continued):

Combined Opportunities Incorporated
5050 N. Broadway, Chicago 60640
Frank Brooks 312-275-3871

This MESBIC is interested in nursing homes, franchise foods, medical instruments, and manufacturing for Chicago based firms.

Minimum & preferred investments = under $100,000

Continental Illinois Venture Corporation
231 S. LaSalle St., Chicago 60604
John Hines 312-828-8023

This affiliate is interested in all rounds of financing in optics, word processing, automated equipment, tools, chemicals, food products, plastics, drugs, medicines, medical instruments, franchise foods, and mail order.

Minimum investment = $100,000
Preferred investment = $250–750,000
Affiliates: Continental Illinois Nat'l. Bank, Universal Oil Co., Illinois Central Industries.

Equity Planning Corporation
7366 N. Lincoln Ave.,
Lincolnwood 60646
Bob Geras 312-677-1240

This private firm is interested in first round financing throughout the U.S. Its primary industries are: crime prevention, plastics, drugs, medical instruments, oil, gas, and banks.

Minimum & preferred investments = under $100,000
Fees: legal, points, and closing costs.

First Capital Corporation
One First National Plaza, Suite 2628
Chicago 60670
Stanley Golder 312-732-8068

This SBIC is interested in first round financing in all industries and in all areas of the US.

Minimum investment = $100,000
Preferred investment = $250–750,000
Affiliates: First National Bank of Chicago
First Chicago Corporation (bank)

First Chicago Investment Corporation
One First National Plaza, Suite 2628
Chicago 60670
Stanley Golder 312-732-8068

This SBIC is operated by the same management team as above, has the same affiliates, and the same offices. However, the difference lies in the amounts invested.

Minimum investment = $750,000
Preferred investments = $1,000,000 & up.

Greenbaum & Associates
135 S. LaSalle St., Rm. 713
Chicago 60603
Edgar Greenbaum 312-346-2137

This private firm is interested in all rounds of financing. The firms must be based in a major metropolitan area. Industries of interest are: lasers, electronics, optics, microfilm, telephone products, motion pictures, TV programming, and CATV.

Minimum investment = under $100,000
Preferred investment = $250–500,000

374

Heizer Corporation
20 N. Wacker Dr., Chicago 60606
Ned Heizer Jr. 312-641-2200

This is both a privately owned venture capital firm and a wholly owned SBIC which has three groups investing in technical, non-technical, and special proposals in almost all industries in the US and Canada.

Minimum investment = no minimums
Preferred investments = $750,000 & up
Fees: Closing fees only

High Technology II, Incorporated
Two First National Plaza, Chicago 60670
Joseph M. Cvengros 312-236-4492

This private firm is interested in all rounds of financing for US firms. Primary industries are: light energy, diagnostic equipment, data communication, special raw materials, and solid waste recycling.

Minimum investment = $100,000
Preferred investments = $750,000 & up
Affiliates: McCormick & Company

Motorola New Venture Development
3034 Malmo Dr., Arlington Heights 60005
Robert M. Handy 312-593-2151

Please refer to this company's write-up listed in Arizona.

375

Sucsy, Fisher, & Company
230 W. Monroe St. Rm. 2144
Chicago 60606
Lawrence Sucsy 312-346-0750

This investment banker is interested in all rounds of financing for firms throughout the US. Preferred industries are: lasers, optics, pollution controls, manufacturing, all phases of medical, forestry, electronics, banks, and CATV.

Minimum investment = $100,000
Preferred investments = $100–250,000
Fees: Contingent upon equity

Vanguard Capital Corporation
120 S. LaSalle St., Rm. 1720
Chicago 60603
Kenneth M. Arenberg 312-346-1211

This private firm is interested in early rounds of financing for firms throughout the US. Industry preferences are: lasers, pollution controls, computer peripherals, automated equipment, chemicals, food products, drugs, medicines, medical equipment, banks, leasing, and publishing.

Minimum investment = $100,000
Preferred investments = $100–250,000

INDIANA

Indiana Capital Corporation
927 S. Harrison St., Ft. Wayne 46802
Samual Rea 219-422-7852

This privately owned firm is interested in financing Midwestern based firms. Its primary industries are: all phases of medical industry, banking, and leasing.

Minimum investment = $100,000
Preferred investments = $250–500,000

Inland International Incorporated
120 E. Market St., Indianapolis 46206
R. W. Haldi

This affiliate is interested in early rounds of financing to Midwestern firms. Primary interests are in high technology firms and raw materials.

Minimum investment = $100,000
Preferred investments = $250–750,000
Affiliates: Inland Container Corporation

IOWA

North America Capital Corporation
200 American Blvd., Cedar Rapids 52401
Bob Allsop 319-363-0261

This SBIC is interested in Midwestern firms only. Primary industries are: graphic arts, pollution controls, data communications, nursing homes, diagnostic centers, funeral homes, and skating rinks.

Minimum investment = $100,000
Preferred investments = $250–500,000
Affiliate: North American Finance Corp.

KENTUCKY

Equal Opportunity Finance Corporation
224 E. Broadway, Louisville 40201
Clyde Webb 502-583-0601

This MESBIC is interested in early rounds of financing for Kentucky and bordering states. It has no industry preferences.

Minimum investment = $100,000
Preferred investments = $100–250,000
Affiliate: Ashland Oil Company

LOUISIANA

First Southern Capital Corporation
821 Gravier St., Rm. 1206
New Orleans 70112
Dennis Cross 504-529-3177

This SBIC is interested in early rounds of financing for Southeastern and Southwestern firms. It's interested in all industries.

Minimum investment = under $100,000
Preferred investments = $100–250,000
Affiliate: 1st Nat'l Bank of Commerce of New Orleans

Royal Street Investment Corporation
521 Royal St., New Orleans 70130
Bill Hunphries 504-588-9271

This SBIC is interested in all rounds of financing in all areas within the US. No industry preferences.

Minimum investment = $100,000
Preferred investment = $250–750,000

376

MAINE

IRV-New England
157 High St., Portland 04101
Walter Corley 207-772-7429

This privately owned firm is interested in East Coast investments in data communications, medical instruments, and manufacturing.

Minimum investment = $100,000
Preferred investment = $100–250,000

MARYLAND

Commercial Credit Corporation
301 N. Charles St., Baltimore 21201
John Pfouts 301-685-1400

This affiliate is interested in early rounds of financing nationwide. Primary interests are: electronics, optics, computers, hospital management, diagnostic centers, banks, leasing, CATV, and education.

Minimum investment = $100,000
Preferred investments = $250–750,000
Affiliations: Control Data Corporation
Commercial Credit Corporation

Dorsets Associates
135 E. Baltimore St., Baltimore 21202
Frank Bonsal Jr. 301-727-1700

This private venture capital firm is interested in all phases of investments, nationwide. Primary industries are: microfilm, optics, lasers, pollution controls, telephone related products, computers, chemicals, clinical laboratories, oil, gas, and CATV.

Minimum investment = under $100,000
Preferred investments = $100–150,000

T. Rowe Price and Associates
One Charles Center, Baltimore 21201
Charles Newhall III

This privately owned company is interested in early rounds of investments nationwide. No industry preference.

Minimum investment = under $100,000
Preferred investment = $.00–250,000

MASSACHUSETTS

Advent Company
31 State St., Boston 02109
Peter Brooke 617-523-2000

This privately owned firm is interested in all rounds of financing in the US and Europe. Primary industries are: electronics, optics, microfilm, telephone products, mini-computers, microprocessors, chemicals, automated equipment, plastics, machine tools, drugs, clinical laboratories, medical instruments, mail order, CATV, and publishing.

Minimum investment = $100,000
Preferred investments = $250–500,000
Affiliates: Tucker, Anthory, & R. L. Day Investment Bankers.

377

MASSACHUSETTS (Continued):

American Research & Development Company
1 Beacon St., Rm. 1540, Boston 02108
Charles Coulter 617-523-6411

This affiliate is interested in early rounds of financing nationwide. It has no industry preferences.

Minimum investment = under $100,000
Preferred investments = $250–750,000
Affiliations: Textron Inc.

Atlas Capital Corporation
55 Court St., Rm. 200, Boston 02108
Herbert Drucker 617-482-1218

This SBIC is interested in Massachusetts based firms. It has no industry preferences.

Minimum investment = $100,000
Preferred investment = $250,000 and up
Affiliates: The Atlantic Corporation

Bolt, Beranek, & Newman Incorporated
50 Moulton St., Cambridge 02138
617-491-1850

This private company is interested in the early rounds of investments in Boston and East Coast firms. Primary industries are: medical instruments, hospital management, oil, gas, electronics, publishing, CATV, specialty consulting, automated equipment, and manufacturing.

Minimum investment = $100,000
Preferred investments = $250–750,000

Breck, McBeish, Nagel, & De Lorey, Inc.
Three Center Plaza, Rm. 510
Boston 02108
Edward De Lorey 617-742-5757

This investment banking firm concentrates on Boston and East Coast firms. Primary industries are: All phases of computers, hospital management, medical instruments, and diagnostic centers.

Minimum investment = $500,000
Preferred investments = $1,000,000 & up

Burley, Harkins, & Funk, Inc.
1 Boston Pl., Rm. 3615, Boston 02108
David Funk 617-723-6930

This investment banker is interested only in early rounds of funding nationwide. Principal industries are: microfilm, pollution controls, optics, hydraulics, computer peripherals, data communications, crime prevention, food, plastics, sporting goods, clinical laboratories, drugs, hospital management, banks, leasing, courier, CATV, motion pictures, and TV.

Minimum investment = $100,000
Preferred investments = $250–750,000
Affiliations: Massachusetts Capital Corp. (SBIC)

378

Cabot Corporation
125 High St., Boston 02110
Ralph Seferian 617-423-6000

This operating and venture capital firm is interested in all rounds of investments, nationwide. Primary industries are: pollution controls, chemicals, food products, and natural resources.

Minimum investment = no minimums
Preferred investments = $250–1,000,000

The Charles River Partnership
575 Technology Square, Cambridge 02139
John Carter 617-868-0530

This privately owned firm is interested only in first stage investments. No geographical preferences. Industries of interest are: electronics, pollution, telephone, graphic arts, data communications, chemicals, plastics, automated equipment, clinical laboratories, and drugs.

Minimum investment = under $100,000
Preferred investments = $200–300,000

Federal Street Capital Corporation
75 Federal St., Rm. 914, Boston 02110
W. L. Welling 617-542-1380

This SBIC is owned and operated by 26 banks in the Boston area and prefers East Coast investments. Its primary industries are: optics, graphic arts, computer peripherals, data communications, plastics, crime prevention, & CATV.

Minimum investment = $100,000
Preferred investments = $250–750,000

First Capital Corporation of Boston
100 Federal St., Boston 02110
Philip W. Crutchfield 617-434-2440

This SBIC is interested only in first stage projects in Boston and on the East Coast. No industry preference.

Minimum investment = under $100,000
Preferred investments = $250–750,000
Affiliations: 1st Nat'l Bank of Boston

Goldman, Del Rossi, & Company, Inc.
100 Charles River Plaza, Boston 02116
Maynard Goldman 617-732-2176

This affiliate is interested in start-ups and has no industry or geographical preferences.

Minimum investment = $100,000
Preferred investments = none
Fees: Consulting, legal, points, and closing costs.

Greater Springfield Investment Corporation
121 Chestnut St., Rm. 208
Springfield 01103
William Matthews 413-781-7130

This MESBIC is interested primarily in Springfield investments for all rounds of financing.

Minimum investment = under $100,000
Preferred investments = $250–500,000

379

Groco Incorporated
1295 State St., Springfield 01101
John Lippincott 413-788-8411

This private firm is interested in all rounds of funding in high technology industries.

Minimum investment = $100,000
Preferred investments = $250–500,000
Affiliates: Mass. Mutual Life Insurance Co.

Hogan-Harry Company, Incorporated
125 Water St., Boston 02100
Bill Hogan Jr. 617-482-2490

This privately owned venture capital firm and investment banking firm has no preferences as to geographical areas or industries. It specializes in first through third round financing.

Minimum investment = $100,000
Preferred investments = $250–750,000
Fees: legal, points, and closing costs.

Kendall Square Associates
238 Main St., Rm. 408, Cambridge 02142
Walter Winshall 617-864-5450

This privately owned firm invests its own money in all rounds of financing in East Coast firms. No industry preferences.

Minimum investments = no minimums
Preferred investments = none

Koch Venture Capital
45 Hancock St., Cambridge 02139
Bill Koch 617-868-0480

This private firm joins in all rounds of investments throughout the US. Preferred industries are: electronics, optics, pollution, graphic arts, chemicals, all phases of computers, food products, plastics, drugs, medicines, natural resources, oil distribution, importing, exporting, and transportation.

Minimum investments = under $100,000
Preferred investments = $250–750,000
Fees: Contingent upon equities.
Affiliations: Koch Development Corp.

Memorial Drive Trust
20 Acorn Park, Cambridge 02178
W. B. Martin 617-864-5770

This private firm is interested in first round fundings in: lasers, optics, pollution controls, data communications, automated equipment, chemicals, machine tools, oil, gas, banks, and CATV.

Minimum investment = $100,000
Preferred investments = $250–500,000

Millcap Corporation
Ashby Rd., Bedford 01730
John Bush 617-275-9200

This subsidiary of its operating company is interested in all early round financing. No geographical or industry preferences.

Minimum investment = $100,000
Preferred investment = $250–500,000
Affiliations: Millpore Corporation

380

F. S. Moseley, Estabrook, Inc.
50 Congress St., Boston 02109
John Dutton 617-482-1300

This investment banking firm is interested in all rounds of investments. It has no geographical or industry preferences. See New York for branch office.

Minimum investment = $750,000
Preferred investment = $1,000,000 & up
Fees: contingent upon equity.

New Enterprise System, Inc.
850 Boylston St., Chestnut Hill 02167
Carl Novotny 617-738-6712

This is a combination private venture capital firm and consulting firm interested in all rounds of investments for East Coast & Southwestern companies. No industry preferences.

Minimum investment = no minimum
Preferred investments = $250–500,000
Fees: Professional, legal, points, and closing.

Paine Venture Fund
100 Federal St., Boston 02101
Walter Aikman 617-423-8000

This affiliate is interested in all rounds of financing for firms near major metropolitan areas. Primary interests are in all growth industries.

Minimum investment = under $100,000
Preferred investments = $100–250,000
Affiliations: Payne, Webber, Jackson, & Curtis Inc. (investment bankers)

The Palmer Organization
183 Essex St., Boston 02111
John Shane 617-423-4355

This private venture capital firm invests its own capital in early rounds of financing. No geographical or industry preferences.

Minimum investment = under $100,000
Preferred investments = none
Fees: legal, points, and closing costs.

Pilgrim Capital Corporation
842A Beacon St., Boston 02215
Stev O'Donnall 617-566-5212

This SBIC is interested in first round investing in East Coast firms. Primary industries are: automated equipment, food products, sporting goods, drugs, medicines, hospital management, nursing homes, and leisure products and services.

Minimum & preferred investments = under $100,000

State Street Bank & Trust Company
225 Franklin St., Boston 02101
J. A. Geishecker 617-786-3774

This division of the bank provides evaluation and analysis on firms and arranges private fundings for all rounds of financing for East Coast, Midwestern, and Southwestern firms. No industry preferences.

Minimum investment = $250,000
Preferred investments = $750,000 & up
Fees: Contingent upon equity.

MASSACHUSETTS (Continued):

The Top Company
470 Atlantic Ave., Rm. 700, Boston 02210
J. A. Aldridge 617-482-4430

This private venture capital firm concentrates on first round financing for East Coast firms. Industry preferences are: pollution controls, clinical laboratories, diagnostic centers, medical instruments, hospital management, services to the health industry, mail order, special retail concepts, and leisure industry.

Minimum investment = under $100,000
Preferred investments = $100–250,000

Venture Founders Corporation
400 Totten Pond Rd., Waltham 02154
Brian Haslett 617-890-4888

The privately owned venture capital firm invests its own funds in East Coast firms. Its primary interest is in start-ups and first round financing. No industry preferences.

Minimum investment = under $100,000
Preferred investments = $100–250,000

WCCI Capital Corporation
791 Main St., Worcester 01610
Dick Sullivan 617-791-3259

This MESBIC is interested in all rounds of financing for Worcester based firms.

Minimum & preferred investments = under $100,000

Worcester Capital Corporation
446 Main St., Worcester 01608
William A. Gregg 617-853-7000

This SBIC is interested in all early rounds of financing for New England companies. It has no industry preferences.

Minimum & preferred investments = under $100,000
Affiliations: Worcester County Nat'l Bank

MICHIGAN

Bank of the Commonwealth
719 Griswald, Detroit 48231
Arthur F. Snyder 313-965-8800

This SBIC is interested in early rounds of financing in Midwestern companies. Industries of interest are: electronics, telephone products, computer peripherals, data communications, crime prevention, medical instruments, and CATV.

No minimum or preferred investments.
Affiliations: Bank of the Commonwealth

Doan Associates
110 E. Grove St., Midland 48640
Ted Doan 517-631-2471

This private venture capital firm is interested in all early rounds of fundings for Midwestern based companies. Principle

Minimum investment = $100,000
Preferred investments = $250–500,000

industries are: electronics, pollution, graphic arts, all phases of computers, chemicals, foods, drugs, medicines, diagnostic centers, and CATV.

Dow Chemical Investment & Finance Corporation
2020 Dow Center, Midland 48640
R. McFedries 517-636-0787

This subsidiary is interested in early rounds of financing nationwide in the following industries: lasers, optics, pollution controls, chemicals, plastics, patented proprietary products, automated equipment, and medical instruments.

Minimum investments = $100,000
Preferred investments = $250–500,000
Affiliations: The Dow Chemical Corporation

Michigan Capital & Service Company
202 E. Washington, Rms. 408–410,
Ann Arbor 48108
Neil Staebler 313-663-0702

This SBIC is interested in early rounds of financing in Michigan based firms. It's interested in all industries.

Minimum & preferred investments =
under $100,000
Affiliations: Michigan National Bank
Fees: legal, points, and closing costs.

Motor Enterprises, Inc.
3044 W. Grand Blvd., Rm. 7-166,
Detroit 48202
Herbert Lorenz 313-556-4273

This MESBIC is interested in all early rounds of financing in all cities in which General Motors has plant facilities. No industry preferences.

Minimum & preferred investments =
under $100,000
Affiliations: General Motors Corporation

Prime Inc.
2990 W. Grand Blvd., Suite M-15
Detroit 48202
Frank Mullen 313-963-6700

This MESBIC is interested in early rounds of fundings for firms in major metropolitan areas. No industry preferences.

Minimum & preferred investments =
under $100,000
Fees: legal, points, and closing costs.

MINNESOTA

Community Investment Enterprises, Inc.
7515 Wayzata Blvd., Minneapolis 55426
Don Soukup 612-544-2754

This private venture capital firm is interested in all rounds of financing in Minneapolis. It has no industry preferences.

Minimum investment = under $100,000
Preferred investments = $100–250,000

Northland Capital Corporation
402 W. First St. Duluth 55802
George Barnum Jr. 218-722-0545

This SBIC is interested in first round financing in Deluth and the Midwest. It has no industry preferences.

Minimum & preferred investments =
under $100,000
Fees: legal, points, and closing costs.

MINNESOTA (Continued):
Westland Capital Corporation
2021 E. Hennepin Ave.
Rm. 115, Minneapolis
Minneapolis 55413
Ron Barnes 612-331-9210

This SBIC is interested in start-up rounds of financing and low risk third rounds. Primary interest is in Minneapolis and Midwestern companies in: microfilm, computers, food products, hospital management, medical instruments, forestry, banks, leasing, and CATV

Minimum & preferred investments = under $100,000
Fees: legal, points, and closing costs.

MISSOURI
Techno-Ventures Incorporated
8100 W. Florissant Ave., St. Louis 63301
W. C. Nusbaum 314-553-2337

This affiliate is interested in all rounds of financing nationwide. Primary industries: electronics, lasers, optics, pollution controls, crime prevention, plastics, automated controls, materials handling, and patented proprietary products.

No minimum or preferred investment levels.
Affiliations: Emerson Electric Company

MONTANA
Capital Investors Corporation
Capital Bldg., Missoula 59801
Allen Bradley 406-7888

This SBIC is primarily interested in second and third round financing for the Pacific Northwest. No industry preferences.

Minimum investments = under $100,000
Preferred investments = $100–250,000
Fees: legal, points, and closing costs.

NEW HAMPSHIRE
Sci-Tronics Fund Incorporated
6 Manchester St., Nashua 03060
George Cartier 603-882-2282

This SBIC is primarily interested in second and third round financing for the Northeast. Industries of interest are: medical instruments, medical products, construction and development.

Minimum & preferred investments = under $100,000
Fees: legal, points, and closing costs.

Broad Arrow Investment Corporation
40 Whippany Rd., Morristown 07960
Charles Bellon 201-267-4414

This MESBIC is interested in East Coast start-ups. No industry preferences.

Minimum and preferred investments = under $100,000
Fees: legal, points, and closing costs.

Data Science Ventures Incorporated
221 Nassau St., Princeton 08540
Morton Collins 609-924-6420

This private venture firm is interested in all rounds of financing, nationwide. Primary industries are: the complete computer industry, electronics, microfilm, lasers, optics, pollution, hospital management, medical instruments, and laimos technology.

Minimum investment = $100,000
Preferred investments = $250–500,000

Eagle Investment Company
35 Essex St., Hackensack 07601
Murray Handel 201-489-3583

This SBIC is interested in all rounds of investments in East Coast firms. No industry preferences.

Minimum investment = under $100,000
Preferred investments = $100–250,000
Fees: legal, points, and closing costs.

Globe Capital Corporation
2 Forest Rd., Tenafly 07670
Samuel Silverman 212-757-4980

This SBIC is interested in all rounds of investments in New Jersey and New York City areas. Of interest are: diagnostic centers, nursing homes, hospital management, private schools, homes for the aged, restaurants, bakeries, and small operative contractors.

Minimum & preferred investments = under $100,000
Fees: legal, points, and closing costs.

Inno Ven Capital Corporation
Park 80 Plaza West, Saddle Brook 07662
Gerald Lodge 201-845-4900

This private firm is interested in all rounds of investments, nationwide. Principle industries are: electronics, optics, graphic arts, pollution controls, telephone products, computer peripherals, data communications, chemicals, plastics, crime prevention, food products, medical products, and mail order.

Minimum investment = $100,000
Preferred investments = $250–750,000
Affiliations: Emerson Electric, Monsanto Chemicals

NEW JERSEY (Continued):

Johnson & Johnson Development Company
501 George St., New Brunswick 08903
David Baxendale 201-524-6298

This subsidiary is interested in early rounds of financing nationwide. Primary industries are: optics, pollution controls, ethical nutrition, hospital disposables, and all phases of medical and health industries.

Minimum investment = under $100,000
Preferred investments = $250–750,000
Affiliations: Johnson & Johnson Corp.

Main Capital Investment Company
818 Main St., New Brunswick 08903
Sam Klotz 201-489-2080

This SBIC is interested in all rounds of financing nationwide. Principle industries are: lasers, optics, pollution controls, telephone products, graphic arts, banks, financing companies, motion pictures, and TV programming.

Minimum investment = $750,000
Preferred investments = $1,000,000 and up

Prudential Insurance Company
Prudential Plaza, Newark 07101
Richard R. Hume 201-336-4567

This insurance company is interested in all rounds of financing nationwide. No industry preferences.

Minimum investment = $100,000
Preferred investments = $750,000 and up

Rutgers Minority Enterprise Inc.
18 Washington Pl., Newark 07102
Russell Mass 201-747-5557

This MESBIC is interested in all early rounds of financing on the East Coast. No industry preferences.

Minimum & preferred investments = under $100,000

Venture Science Association
291 River Rd. Clifton 07014
Don Pierson 212-371-8035

This private firm invests its own funds in early rounds of financing in East Coast and West Coast firms. Preferred industries are: heat pipe technology, mini-computers, microprocessors, computer peripherals, data communications, computer applications, crime prevention, motion pictures, and TV programming.

Minimum & preferred investments = under $100,000

Wall Street Venture Capital Corporation
2 Esterbrook Ln., Cherry Hill 08034
Robert Sinn 609-424-4732

This private venture firm is interested in early rounds of funding in the East Coast and Southeast. Industries of interest are: electronics, optics, chemicals, food products, drugs, medicines, narcotics control, banks, and tax shelters.

Minimum investment = under $100,000
Preferred investments = $250–500,000

Frederick R. Adler
One Chase Manhattan Plaza
New York 10005
Frederick Adler 212-269-7600

This private firm is interested in early rounds of financing in the US and Europe. Industries are: lasers, optics, pollution, telephone products, computer peripherals, data communications, plastics, materials handling, automated equipment, and medical products.

Minimum investment = under $100,000
Preferred investments = $250–500,000

Bancap Corporation
420 Lexington Ave. Rm. 2352
New York 10017
William Whitely 212-684-6460

This MESBIC is interested in all rounds of financing for New York City and surrounding counties. No industry preferences.

Minimum & preferred investments = under $100,000
Fees: legal, points, and closing costs.

Bardco Incorporated
30 E. 68th St. Rm. A. New York 10021
Arthur Crawford 212-628-3830

This private venture firm is interested in early rounds of funding in US, Canada, Australia, Europe, and Japan. Principal industries are: pollution controls, plastics, forestry products, minerals, oil, gas, and patented proprietary products.

Minimum investment = under $100,000
Preferred investments = $250–500,000
Fees: legal, points, and closing costs.

Becker Technological Associates
55 Water St., New York 10041
Grant Inman 212-747-4463

This affiliate is primarily interested in early rounds of investments nationwide. Principal industries are: lasers, optics, pollution controls, telephone products, graphic arts, computer peripherals, data communications, automated equipment, crime prevention, machine tools, materials handling, proprietary products, medical instruments, energy efficient engines, purification of fuels, novel recreational concepts, and medical diagnostic aids.

Minimum investment = $250,000
Preferred investments = $250–750,000
Affiliations: A. G. Becker & Company, Investment Bankers

Bessemer Securities Corporation
245 Park Ave., New York 10017
Robert Buescher 212-986-6900

This private venture capital firm invests its own funds in the first three rounds of financing nationwide. It has no industry preferences.

Minimum investment = $250,000
Preferred investments = $500,000 and up

Biomed Patents Incorporated
Box 748, FDR Station, New York 10022
Victor Krasan 212-289-8004

This private venture firm invests its own capital in the first two rounds of financing, nationwide. It is interested only in the medical industry. Specific areas of interest are: clinical laboratories, diagnostic centers, drugs, medicines, medical instruments, hospital management, bio-medical patents, and hospital equipment.

Minimum & preferred investments = under $100,000
Fees: professional, legal, points, and closing costs contingent upon equity.

Milton D. Blauner & Company, Inc.
115 Broadway, New York 10006
Milton or Jon Blauner 212-227-7626

This investment banking firm is interested in the first three rounds of financing of New York City, East Coast, and Midwest firms. Industries are: pollution, telephone products, data communications, word processing, plastics, sporting goods, diagnostic centers, hospital management, drugs, medicines, medical instruments, and leasing.

Minimum investment = $100,000
Preferred investments = $750,000 and up
Fees: professional, legal, points, and closing costs contingent upon equity.

Blyth, Eastman, Dillon, & Company, Inc.
1 Chase Manhattan Plaza
New York 10005
John Kelsey 212-770-8000

This investment banking firm is interested in all rounds of financing nationwide. It has no industry preferences.

Minimum investment = $750,000
Preferred investments = over $1,000,000
Fees: professional, legal, points, and closing costs contingent upon equity.

Business Development Services, Inc.
570 Lexington Ave., Suite 1601
N.Y. 10022
Walton Storm 212-750-3527

This subsidiary is interested in the first three rounds of financing, nationwide. Primary industries: electronics, lasers, optics, pollution, telephone products, data

Minimum investment = $100,000
Preferred investments = $250–750,000
Fees: legal, points, and closing costs.
Affiliations: Subsidiary of General Electric

388

...communications, automated equipment, and medical instruments.

Canaveral Capital Corporation
635 Madison Ave., New York 10022
Joseph Levine 212-759-8060

This SBIC is interested only in start-ups nationwide. No industry preferences.

Minimum & preferred investments = under $100,000

EMW Ventures Incorporated
277 Park Ave., New York 10017
Herbert Adler 212-593-0300

This private venture firm is interested in early rounds of financing, nationwide. No industrial preferences.

Minimum investment = $250,000
Preferred investments = $500,000–$10,000,000
Affiliations: E. M. Warburg, Pincus, & Co. Investment Bankers.

Euclid Partners
50 Rockefeller Plaza, Rm. 840
N.Y. 10020
Milton Pappas 212-489-1770

This private venture company is interested in early rounds of financing, nationwide. No industrial preferences.

Minimum investment = $100,000
Preferred investments = $250–500,000

Exxon Enterprises Incorporated
1251 Ave. of Americas, New York 10020
George Kokkinakis 212-974-2569

This subsidiary is interested in early rounds of financing, nationwide. Industries of interest are: pollution, telephone products, energy storage, energy conversion, remote spectral sensing, computer peripherals, data communications, word processing, patented products, diagnostic centers, drugs, medicines, medical instruments, CATV, Educational services, oil and gas.

Minimum investment = $100,000
Preferred investments = $250–750,000
Affiliates: The Exxon Corporation

15 Broad Street Resources Corporation
15 Broad St., New York 10015
David Savage 212-483-2983

This SBIC is interested in the early rounds of financing in the US, Canada, and Europe. Principal industries are: Computers (all phases), Manufacturing (proprietary products), Medical, and CATV.

Minimum investment = $100,000
Preferred investments = $250–500,000
Affiliates: J. P. Morgan & Company

NEW YORK (Continued):

First Century Partnership
345 Ave. of Americas, New York 10019
John Dulaney 212-333-5790

This company is both a private venture capital group and an investment banker which is interested in all rounds of financing in the East Coast, Midwest, and Southeast. Primary industries are: electronics, optics, microfilm, pollution, minicomputers, microprocessors, peripherals, word processing, chemicals, food products, drugs, medicines, mail order, and banks.

Minimum investment = $750,000
Preferred investments = over $750,000
Affiliates: Smith, Barney, & Co., Inc. Investment Bankers

General Electric Company
R & D Center, Schenectady 12301
David Ben Daniels 518-346-8771

This division of G.E. is primarily interested in spinning off General Electric technologies, developments, and products into independent businesses. Refer to Business Development Services (New York) for non-GE initiations.

Minimum & preferred investments = not applicable.

Globus Incorporated
1345 Ave. of Americas, New York 10019
Morton Globus 212-582-5200

This subsidiary is interested in first stage projects in computers, medical, and growth industries, nationwide.

Minimum investment = $100,000
Preferred investments = $250–500,000
Affiliations: T. H. Lehman & Company Investment Bankers

R. E. Hart & Co., Inc.
380 Madison Ave., New York 10017
Richard Hart 212-986-8700

This venture capital group and investment banker is interested in early rounds of financing for East Coast firms. Interested in all industries.

Minimum investment = $100,000
Preferred investments = $750,000 and up
Fees: legal, points, and closing costs.

CEDC MESBIC, Incorporated
106 Main St., Hempstead 11550
Arthur Choice 516-292-9710

This MESBIC funds all rounds of financing in the Hempstead, New York area. No industry preferences.

Minimum & preferred investments = under $100,000
Affiliations: CEDC Inc., a community development corporation.

Charter New York Corporation
1 Wall St., New York 10006
Allen Freedman 212-487-6101

This is the venture capital division of the bank and is interested in all rounds of financing in US and European companies. It is interested in all industries.

Minimum investment = $100,000
Preferred investments = $250–750,000
Affiliations: Charter New York and The Irving Trust Company

Chase Manhattan Capital Corporation
One Chase Manhattan Plaza
New York 10005
Robert Hubbard 212-552-6811

This SBIC is interested in all rounds of financing nationwide. Interested in all industries.

Minimum investment = $100,000
Preferred investments = $250–750,000
Affiliations: Chase Manhattan Bank

Citicorp Venture Capital Ltd.
399 Park Ave., New York 10022
Patrick J. Walsh 212-559-5011

This is both a private venture capital company and an SBIC which is interested in all rounds of financing worldwide. Interested in all industries.

Minimum investment = $250,000
Preferred investments = $500,000 and up
Affiliations: First Nat'l City Bank

Clarion Capital Corporation
99 Park Avenue, New York 10016
M. D. Stewart 212-986-5595

This SBIC is interested in all rounds of financing in Midwestern companies only. It's interested in all industries.

Minimum investment = $100,000
Preferred investments = $250–750,000
Affiliations: Union Commerce Bank of Cleveland, Provident National Bank of Philadelphia

Contemporary Enterprises Incorporated
60 E. 42nd. St., New York 10017
Theodore J. Robertson 212-972-9527

This private venture capital firm is interested in start-ups in New York City and the East Coast. It has no industry preferences.

Minimum investment = $100,000
Preferred investments = $250–500,000
Fees: Contingent upon equity.

Diebold Venture Capital Corporation
430 Park Ave., New York 10022
George Pratt 212-755-9510

This affiliate is interested in the first three rounds of financing nationwide. Principal industries are: electronics, optics, telephone products, mini-computers, microprocessors, computer peripherals, data communications, crime prevention, automated equipment, life sciences, medical instruments, and microbiology.

Minimum investment = $100,000
Preferred investments = $250–500,000
Affiliations: John Diebold & Company

Diversified Technologies Incorporated
30 Rockefeller Center, New York 10020
Gilbert Kennedy 212-581-4800

This affiliate is interested in all rounds of financing, all industries, nationwide.

Minimum investment = $100,000
Preferred investments = $250–750,000
Affiliations: The Singer Company

Drexel Burnham & Company
60 Broad St., New York 10004
Robert Linton 212-344-1400

This investment banking firm is interested in all rounds of financing, all industries, nationwide.

Minimum investment = $100,000
Preferred investments = $750,000 and up
Fees: Contingent upon equity.

F. Eberstadt & Co., Incorporated
61 Broadway, New York 10006
Walter Lubanko 212-944-8787

This investment banker is interested in all rounds of financing, all industries, nationwide.

Minimum investment = $750,000
Preferred investments = $1,000,000 and up
Affiliations: Chemical Fund Inc.,
Eberstadt Fund Inc., various mutual funds.

Eli S. Jacobs
One Wall St., New York 10005
Eli S. Jacobs 212-425-2470

This gentleman is interested in early rounds of financing in the following areas: microfilm, optics, food products, plastics, medicines, medical instruments, forestry products, minerals, oil, gas, educational services, motion pictures, and TV programming.

Minimum investment = under $100,000
Preferred investments = over $600,000

Killion, Barney, & Oettinger Inc.
500 Fifth Ave., Rm. 1102
New York 10036
Jack Killion 212-354-1758

This private venture capital firm is interested in early rounds of financing in: electronics, pollution, crime prevention, plastics, sporting goods, hospital management, medical instruments, mail order, advertising, and publishing.

Minimum investment = $100,000
Preferred investments = $250–500,000
Fees: Professional contingent upon equity.

Lehman Brothers
42 Wall St., New York 10005
Joseph J. Gal 212-269-3702

This investment banker is interested in all rounds of financing, nationwide. No industry preferences.

Minimum investment = $100,000
Preferred investments = $1,000,000 and up
Fees: Contingent upon equity.

Loeb, Rhodes, & Company
42 Wall St., New York 10005
Paul J. Mejean 212-530-4000

This investment banking firm is interested in all early rounds of financing, nationwide. It has no industry preferences.

Minimum investment = $100,000
Preferred investments = $1,000,000 and up
Fees: Contingent upon equity.

Midland Capital Corporation
110 William St., New York 10038
H. Wayne Williams 212-732-6580

This publicly owned SBIC is interested in start-ups in the US and Virgin Islands. It is primarily interested in new products and services in growth industries or unique products and services in an established field.

Minimum investment = $100,000
Preferred investments = $250,000 and up
Fees: legal, points, and closing costs.

New York Plaza Association
One New York Plaza, New York 10024
Kenneth Rind 212-825-4000

This affiliate is interested in all rounds of financing and in all industries in the US, Europe, and Japan.

Minimum investment = under $100,000
Preferred investments = $250–750,000
Affiliates: Oppenheimer & Company

New York Securities Co., Inc.
1 New York Plaza, New York 10024
F. Kenneth Melis 212-425-2800

This investment banker is interested in all rounds of financing nationwide. No industry preferences.

Minimum investment = $100,000
Preferred investments = $250–500,000
Fees: Contingent upon equity.

Payne, Webber, Jackson, & Curtis
140 Broadway, New York 10005
Orest Bliss 212-437-2121

This investment banking firm is interested in all rounds of investments, all industries, nationwide.

Minimum investment = $300,000
Preferred investments = $750,000 and up

Pioneer Capital Corporation
1440 Broadway, New York 10018
Gerald Taber 212-594-4860

This SBIC and MESBIC is interested in start-ups and first round fundings in all industries, nationwide.

Minimum investment = under $100,000
Preferred investments = $250–500,000

Printers Capital Corporation
One World Trade Center, Rm. 1927
N.Y. 10048
Herbert Brandon 212-432-0750

This SBIC is interested in early rounds of financing nationwide. Principal industries are: graphic arts, advertising, publishing, plastics, and sporting goods.

Minimum investment = $100,000
Preferred investments = $100–250,000
Fees: legal, points, and closing costs.

Salomon Brothers
1 New York Plaza, New York 10024
James McKay 212-747-7000

This investment banker is interested in all phases of finances in all industries nationwide.

Minimum investment = $250,000
Preferred investments = $750,000 and up
Fees: Contingent upon equity.

NEW YORK (Continued):

Steven Seeberg
Main Place Tower, Buffalo 14202
Steven Seeberg 716-852-2821

This private venture firm invests in start-ups and first stage financing in: lasers, microfilm, optics, pollution controls, tele-phone products, word processing, diagnostic centers, medical instruments, and automated equipment.

Minimum investment = under $25,000
Preferred investments = $50–100,000

Sperry & Hutchinson Company
330 Madison Ave., New York 10022
Fred Collins 212-983-2000

This subsidiary is interested in all rounds of financing nationwide. Industry preferences are: plastics, sporting goods, interior furnishings, dental supply, dental laboratories, and mail order.

Minimum investment = $100,000
Preferred investments = $250–500,000
Affiliates: Sperry & Hutchinson Co.

Ungersmith Securities Company
One Battery Park Plaza, N.Y. 10004
William Hack 212-747-5400

This private venture capital firm is inter-ested in early rounds of financing nation-wide. No industry preferences.

Minimum investment = $100,000
Preferred investments = $250–500,000

Venrock Associates
30 Rockefeller Plaza, New York 10020
T. H. McCcurtney 212-247-3700

This private venture capital firm invests its own funds in start-up through third round financing..

Minimum & preferred investments = none
Affiliates: The Rockefeller Family & Associates

NORTH CAROLINA

Forsyth County Investment Corporation
Pepper Bldg., Rm. 305
Winston-Salem 27101
James Hansley 919-724-3676

This MESBIC is interested in start-ups in Forsyth County.

Minimum & preferred investments = under $100,000
Affiliations: Forsyth County Economic Development Corporation.

OHIO

Diamond Shamrock Corporation
1100 Superior Ave., Cleveland 44114
Allan Tomlinson 216-694-5624

This venture capital firm invests in start-ups nationwide. Areas of interest are: pollution controls, chemicals, plastics, clinical laboratories, diagnostic centers, drugs, medicines, medical instruments, oil, and gas.

Minimum investment = $750,000
Preferred investments = $750,000 and up

394

Eaton Venture Capital Corporation
100 Erie View Plaza, Cleveland 44114
Richard Stoddart

This affiliate is interested in all rounds of financing nationwide. No industry preferences.

Minimum investment = $100,000
Preferred investments = Varies with clients
Affiliates: The Eaton Corporation

Gries Investment Company
Terminal Tower, Rm. 2310
Cleveland 44113
Bob Gries 216-861-1146

This private venture capital firm and SBIC is interested in all rounds of financing in the Midwest, East Coast, and West Coast. No industry preferences.

Minimum investment = $100,000
Preferred investments = $100–200,000
Fees: legal, points, and closing costs.

The Kanter Corporation
650 Northland Road, Cincinnati 45240
Branch Office, Miami, Fl. 305-751-0843
R. E. Wildermuth 513-851-6000

This private venture capital firm is interested in all rounds of financing, nationwide. It is also interested in all industries.

Minimum investment = $100,000
Preferred investments = $750,000 and up

Morgenthaler Associates
National City Bank Bldg., Rm. 1034
Cleveland 44114
Robert Pavev 216-687-6740

This private venture firm is interested in all rounds of financing, in all industries, nationwide.

Minimum investment = $100,000
Preferred investments = $100–250,000

Scientific Advances Incorporated
4041 Roberts Rd., Columbus 43228
Tom Harvey 614-876-2461

This private venture firm is interested in start-ups nationwide. No industry preferences.

Minimum investment = $100,000
Preferred investments = $250–500,000
Affiliations: Battelle Memorial Institute

Winston-Walker Enterprises
3491 Ingleside Rd., Shaker Heights 44122
Dale Winston 216-491-8555

This private firm is interested in start-ups nationwide. No industry preferences.

Minimum & preferred investments = under $100,000
Affiliations: Capital Consultants
Fees: Contingent upon equity.

OKLAHOMA

American Indian Investment Opportunities Inc.
555 Constitution, Norman 73069
A. C. Block 405-329-8110

This MESBIC is interested in Indian owned businesses across the nation, all rounds of financing. Primary industry interests are: computers and franchised businesses.

Minimum & preferred investments = under $100,000
Affiliations: Oklahomans for Indian Opportunity

OREGON

Cascade Capital Corporation
421 SW Sixth Ave., Portland 97204
Jack Flowers 503-225-4281

This SBIC is interested in all rounds of financing in the Pacific Northwest. Primary industries are: Forestry products, optics, pollution, telephone products, graphic arts, chemicals, crime prevention, clinical laboratories, medical instruments, publishing, mail order, and patented products.

Minimum investment = $100,000
Preferred investments = $250–500,000

PENNSYLVANIA

Capital Corporation of America
1521 Walnut St., Philadelphia 19102
Barton Banks 215-564-2843

This publicly held SBIC is interested in all rounds of financing for firms based in Philadelphia, the East Coast, Midwest, and Southeast. Principal industries are: chemicals, automated equipment, crime prevention, food products, machine tools, drugs, medicines, nursing homes, rental medical supplies, construction, second home developments, condominiums, and apartments.

Minimum investment = no minimums
Preferred investments = $100–250,000

Delaware Valley SBIC
Wolf Bldg., Chester 19103
Bill Wolf 215-876-2669
Branch: 1604 Walnut St.,
Philadelphia 19103

This SBIC is interested in all rounds of financing in Philadelphia and the East Coast. Primary industries are: food products, machine tools, materials handling, sporting goods, discount stores, department stores, mail order, CATV, and publishing.

Minimum investment = under $100,000
Preferred investments = $250–500,000
Fees: legal, points, and closing costs.

Greater Philadelphia Venture
Capital Corp.
225 S. 15th. Rm. 920, Philadelphia 19102
Guyon Turner 215-732-3415

This MESBIC is interested in all rounds of financing in the Philadelphia area. It has no industry preferences.

Minimum & preferred investments = under $100,000
Affiliates: This MESBIC is owned by 13 Philadelphia banks and commercial firms.

396

Osher Capital Corporation
Wyncote House, Rm. 101
Washington Lane
Wyncote 19095
L. Canton 215-624-4800

This SBIC is interested in the early stages of start-ups in the Wyncote area. Industries of interest are: drugs, medicines, medical instruments, diagnostic centers, sporting goods, advertising, leasing, and specialty consulting.

Minimum investment = under $100,000
Preferred investments = $250–500,000

Pennsylvania Growth Investment Corp.
Gateway Two, Suite 301, Pittsburg 15222
Bill Mosenson 412-281-1403

This SBIC is interested in all rounds of financing in the Pittsburg area in: lasers, optics, automated equipment, machine tools, materials handling, hospital management, nursing homes, and CATV.

Minimum investment = $100,000
Preferred investments = $100–250,000
Affiliations: Philadelphia Financial Development Corporation
Fees: legal, points, and closing costs.

Suplee-Mosley, Incorporated
1700 Market St., Rm. 1632
Philadelphia 19103
John Moran 215-665-8000

This investment banking firm is interested in all rounds of financing in the East Coast, Midwest, and Southeast. No industry preferences.

No minimums or preferred investments
Fees: Contingent upon equity.

RHODE ISLAND

Concorse, Incorporated
121 Dyer St., Providence 02903
Robert E. Radican 401-751-6900

Though this private venture capital firm prefers investing in firms after the start-up and first rounds of financing, it occasionally makes exceptions. Primary industries are: graphic arts, computer software, word processing, chemicals, crime prevention, machine tools, plastics, and materials handling.

Minimum investment = $100,000
Preferred investments = $750,000 and up

SOUTH CAROLINA

Charleston Capital Corporation
134 Meeting St., Charleston 29402
Henry Yaschik 803-723-6464

This SBIC prefers later rounds of investments in Southeastern firms however they like to consider start-ups occasionally. No industry preferences.

Minimum investment = $100,000
Preferred investments = $100–250,000
Fees: legal, points, and closing costs.

TENNESSEE

C & C Capital Corporation
2643 Kingston Pike, Knoxville 37919
C. E. Quimby 615-637-1363

This SBIC prefers first and second rounds of investments in the Knoxville area. No industry preferences.

Minimum & preferred investments = under $100,000
Fees: legal, points, and closing costs.

New South Investment Company
One Commerce Square, Memphis 38103
A. Richard Wilson 901-526-8463

This private venture capital firm is interested in all rounds of financing in the Memphis and Mid-South area. No industry preferences.

Minimum investment = $100,000
Preferred investments = $250–500,000
Fees: legal, points, and closing costs.

TEXAS

Brittany Capital Corporation
Republic Bank Tower, Rm. 4325
Dallas 75201
M. H. Earp 214-741-3571

This SBIC is interested in early rounds of financing in the Southwest for the following industries: optics, telephone products, graphic arts, computer software, data communications, hospital management, and specialty raw materials.

Minimum investment = under $100,000
Preferred investments = $100–250,000
Fees: legal, points, and closing costs.

Capital Southwest Corporation
Mercantile Dallas Bldg., Rm. 1800
Dallas 75201
Clifford Osborn 214-747-5117

This privately held venture capital firm invests its own funds nationwide in the following industries: Mini-computers, microprocessors, main frames, peripherals, data communications, word processing, drugs, medicines, hospital management, and CATV.

Minimum investment = $100,000
Preferred investments = $250–500,000
Fees: legal, points, and closing costs.

Eagle Management & Trust Company
1206 River Oaks Bank Tower
Houston 77019
Homer Luther

This private trust investment corporation is interested in start-ups nationwide. No industry preferences.

Minimum investment = under $100,000
Preferred investments = $100–250,000
Fees: legal, points, and closing costs.

Gulf Investment Corporation
115 E. Van Buren, Harlingen 78550
Rollins M. Koppel 512-423-7761

This SBIC is interested in early rounds of investments in the South Texas area. Primary industries are: food products,

No minimum or preferred investment levels.

franchised food businesses, other franchised proposals, discount stores, and leasing companies.

MESBIC Financial Corporation of Dallas
7220 Stemmons Expressway, Rm. 630
Dallas 75222
Walter W. Durham 214-637-0445

Minimum & preferred investments = under $100,000
Fees: legal, points, and closing costs.

This MESBIC is interested in all early rounds of funding in the Dallas and Texas areas. No industry preferences.

Midland Investment Company
Milam Bldg., Suite 341
San Antonio 78205
H. K. Foster 512-225-3053

Minimum & preferred investments = under $100,000
Fees: legal, points, and closing costs.

This holding company is interested in all rounds of financing, nationwide. No industry preferences.

New Business Resources
4300 Sigma Rd., Dallas 75240
214-239-1378

Minimum investment = $250,000
Preferred investments = $750,000 and up
Fees: legal, points, and closing costs.

This private venture capital firm specializes only in start-ups in the following industries: electronics, optics, telephone products, mini-computers, microprocessors, data communications, chemicals, patented proprietary products, diagnostic centers, and hospital management.

Author's Note: There is another unique feature, a different venture capital avenue, that exists in many Texas cities and towns that might interest you. The town fathers take a lot of pride in their cities and frequently raise money to attract vigorous and attractive start-ups to their cities. This pride of hometown is a driving factor to make these city fathers want firms and people of value as neighbors. We have had seven clients begin under these circumstances to the mutual benefit of all parties. Texas is the only state that operates like this.

VIRGINIA

Equity Investment Funds, Incorporated
213 E. Main St., Norfolk 23510
John Cubilla 804-627-2386

Minimum & preferred investments = under $100,000
Fees: legal, points, and closing costs.

This SBIC is interested in all early rounds of financing for Norfolk and East Coast companies. No industry preferences.

VIRGINIA (Continued):

Inverness Capital Corporation
417 N. Washington St., Alexandria 22314
Harry Fleming 703-584-1700

This branch of the New York SBIC is interested in early rounds of financing in the Alexandria and Southeast areas. Principal industries are: graphic arts, crime prevention, electronics, CATV, and publishing.

Minimum investment = $100,000
Preferred investments = $250–500,000
Affiliations: Inverness Capital (New York).

Wheat, First Securities, Inc.
801 E. Main St., Richmond 23219
John McElroy Jr. 804-649-2311

This investment banking firm is interested in all rounds of financing in the Southeast, East Coast, and Midwest. Industries of interest are: clinical laboratories, diagnostic centers, medical instruments, and sporting goods.

Minimum investment = $100,000
Preferred investments = $750,000 and up
Fees: Contingent upon equity.

WASHINGTON

MESBIC of Washington, Inc.
3300 Rainier Ave. South, Seattle 98144
James Stone 206-732-0550

This MESBIC is interested in early rounds of financing in the Seattle and West Coast areas. Industries are: microfilm, pollution, computer software, data communications, chemicals, food products, machine tools, clinical laboratories, nursing homes, franchised foods, other franchises, discount stores, department stores, and CATV.

Minimum & preferred investments = under $100,000
Fees: legal, points, and closing costs.
Affiliations: Model Capital Corporation (MESBIC)

Trail Capital Corporation
1200 Westlake Ave. North, Seattle 98109
Richard Vertlieb 206-285-0618

This private venture firm is interested in all rounds of financing on the West & East Coasts.

400

Trail Capital Corporation
1200 Westlake Ave., North, Seattle 98109
Richard Vertlieb 206-285-0618

This private venture firm invests its own money in early rounds of financing in West & East Coast firms. Primary industries are: microfilm, data retrieval, lasers, telephone products, data communications, food products, sporting goods, banks, finance companies, leasing companies, motion pictures, and TV programming.

Minimum investment = $100,000
Preferred investments = $250–500,000

WISCONSIN

Commerce Capital Corporation
6001 N. 91st. St., Milwaukee 53225
Edward Machulak 414-462-5310
Branches:
126 Grand Ave., Wausau 54401
9 S. Main St., Fond du Lac 54935
106 W. 2nd, Ashland 54806

This SBIC is interested in all rounds of financing nationwide. Principal areas of interest are: lasers, optics, pollution controls, mini-computers, microprocessors, peripherals, data communications, automated equipment, machine tools, drugs, medicines, nursing homes, minerals, oil, gas, electronics, department stores, banks, finance companies, leasing companies, and CATV.

Minimum investment = $100,000
Preferred investments = $250–500,000
Fees: Closing fees.
Affiliations: Commerce Group Corporation

401

WISCONSIN (Continued):

Employers Insurance of Wausau
2000 Westwood Dr., Wausau 54401
James T. Lundberg 715-845-5211

This insurance company is interested in all rounds of financing in all industries throughout the US.

Minimum investment = $100,000
Preferred investments = $250–500,000

Entrepreneurial Assistance Group
3326 Robinsdale, La Crosse 54601
Charles Swayne 608-788-7484

This private venture capital firm is interested in start-ups, nationwide. Primary industries are: mini-computers, microprocessors, computer software, data communications, crime prevention, patented proprietary products, sporting goods, electronics, franchised foods, other franchises, and all new growth industries.

Minimum investment = $100,000
Preferred investments = $250–500,000
Fees: legal, points, and closing costs.

The Sentry Corporation
Stevens Point 54481
Dennis Goff 715-344-2345

This subsidiary is interested in all early rounds of financing, nationwide. It is interested in all industries.

No minimum or preferred investment levels.

Acknowledgments

Whenever I come across lists of books as references, I always feel that the author is doing little more than carrying bones from one graveyard to another. So instead of boring you with several hundred texts, I'd like to list my not-so-silent "silent co-authors" who shot torpedoes at me when I strayed off course. In alphabetical order, they are:

George Allen   a successful founder of two major companies, an ex-venture capitalist, a consultant of the first magnitude, and a man who claims to be semi-retired at age 47 and yet carries a workload that would kill an ox. George has approximately three dozen mini-profit centers that give him a not-so-mini tax problem, sits on the board of directors of 15 companies, and averages 11 start-up clients in the evenings. He is a master at getting his clients to turn cash swiftly and get into the black before they negotiate with venture capitalists. George's primary contributions to this book can be seen in the venture capitalist chapters.

Robert Anderson   a cool and thorough manufacturing specialist who has that gift of reducing complex production problems into simple and obvious solutions. When Bob finishes with you, you wonder why you had thought that there were problems in the first place. You'll see Bob's professional hand in this book's production control sections.

Cap Carpenter   an innovative, no-nonsense advertising man who can make a start-up look like a Fortune 500 company to its customers. His shoe lace approach to advertising has probably made him the most unpopular man in the advertising industry. You can see Cap's thrifty hand throughout the sections on images and advertising.

John Christenson   known as "Ivan the Terrible" in manufacturing circles. If your production costs exceed 10% of your sales price in the start-up phase, expect to see one 6-foot, 4-inch red-headed Ivan camped on your doorstep with his costs axe. John's primary contributions can be seen in the operations money-leveraging portions of this book.

Keith Elliott   an extremely quiet and soft-spoken researcher who has the ability to ferret information where others fail. Keith says perhaps two sentences a week but when he talks, turn up your amplifier and listen. He kept us all honest in our statistics, Cameo research, and examples.

Earl Erickson   a government specialist, Earl is extremely experienced at getting even the youngest company accepted for government contracts. He is a past master at discovering research funds and helping start-ups through SBA and EDA waters. Earl's advice can be seen in many of this book's sections on government, however he wishes his name disassociated from all derogatory sections on government bias.

Dick Evans   an ex-manager of a venture capital group, Dick is a practical financial consultant. Dick first made a name for himself by his techniques of funneling foundations' funds into higher risk/higher profits start-ups. You'll see Dick's hand in the business plan and capital raising sections of this book.

Paul Feeley   another practical financial man who hasn't let his Harvard education get into his way in innovation. Paul made a name for himself in profit center controls and fathered the system which forced accounting groups to change their ledger controls into understandable operations' ledgers. There isn't an old-school cost accountant who wouldn't like Paul's red scalp for his ledger baby. You'll see Paul's contributions to the book in profit center controls and many incentive controls (management-by-motivations).

Sid Goldstein   the only QA (quality assurance) consultant in our group who made his voice heard in almost every matter in this book. Sid is one of those few profit maximizers in the QA game and won considerable fame for his incentive system which turned every production worker into an in-process inspector. He also fathered the Hi-Lo system which allows the same quality system to be used for both low reliable commercial production and high reliable AEC/NASA/Military production. To the best of my knowledge, there isn't a portion of this book that Sid hasn't contributed to.

Dick Martin   a marketing consultant who is a master mechanic in setting up parallel distribution machineries. Though Dick's primary interest area is consumer sales, he fathered the MacAdoo Close System which is primarily an industrial sales close operation. Dick's hand can be seen in this book's areas on sales closes.

Eaton Peterson   "Sir Anthony" is another top grade marketing man. A successful founder of three marketing companies, two sales companies, and a government research foundation (he's still board chairman of all six), Eaton rarely does things by half measures. He is perhaps the most respected marketing man in western venture capital groups and a top grade consultant. Eaton's subtle hand is seen in the marketing testing sections of this book.

Jack Price   "Old Darbs" is the counterpart of "Sir Anthony" in the voice modulation area. "Why talk when you can shout" is his motto when he puts his nose two inches from you and stresses his point with a voice that could shatter glass. This "sell. . . don't tell" marketing man always reduces marketing to its simplest components before he builds his reliable networks. His aid in "Making Marketing Make Sense" shows you his depth.

John Robertson   An ex-venture capital researcher, a founder of two service companies, and a top grade consultant, John specializes in high technology service companies. An ex-scientist, ex-racer, ex-Ranger, ex-stunt man, and an exparachutist, John approaches problems in the most colorful way of the group. His "Why be like everybody else when by being you is the best way" approach to everything has triggered the most innovative solutions that I have seen. John helped make this book's cameos fun to read and his "inputs" on sex kept me in stitches.

Dennis Shields An ex-venture capital administrator, an ex-entrepreneur, and a top financial consultant. Mr. Shields, with his "why not" attitude, has been responsible for numerous success stories. His flexibility and innovation in financial control systems have put him in such demand that he has two years of clients waiting for him to personally help them. You can see Dennis's work in all of the purchasing, administrative, marketing, and production controls in this book.

Ted Smith a practical R&D consultant, Ted fathered two concepts that are presented in this book. They are: (a) have your inventor hand carry his design into all offices (a system that I think saved several dozen of our clients), and (b) never allot your stock rewards to a design engineer until his design is producible, practical, and marketable. Ted's very quiet voice can be heard in the milestone segments of this book.

Joan Thall a top flight labor negotiator, an innovative personnel consultant, and the most unique and talented lady that I have ever known. Miss Thall fathered the six-step interactive testing technique along with perhaps three dozen systems for training, motivating, and sustaining her single-team concepts. Her experienced hand can be seen in the personnel sections of this book.

Ron Wood a computer and marketing specialist, Mr. Wood was one of the first to develop a reliable sales forecasting system. Ron's tables and multipliers carry his name in this book. He also pioneered several of the reliable sales control systems. Mr. Wood is also president of his own computer services company, is an active marketing consultant, and sits on the boards of perhaps a dozen healthy firms. His attitude of, "If it doesn't improve your bottom right hand line (profits), then it isn't a top priority project," has helped many start-ups to make it big.

Hunter Woodward a pioneer in management-by-motivations control systems, Mr. Woodward has concentrated on adapting these systems to firms' existing controls. In addition to consulting, Mr. Woodward owns a motion picture service firm, a manufacturing firm, and sits on six boards. His contributions were primarily in management-by-motivations systems.

Sean Younger started his big operations while he was a freshman in college. He built his "students' services" operations into a $5,000 per month business just before his first expulsion. Three colleges later he graduated with a 3.9 average, engineering and MBA degrees, and $65,000 in the bank. He has parlayed this modest beginning into four successful companies. Sean is an artist at end-running problems and his fresh approach to leveraging shoe lace money into significant dollars can be seen throughout this book.

Others How do you give credit to those thousands of talented and dedicated individuals who influenced your outlooks and your life's directions without boring the hell out of everyone else? Let me end this section by saying to:

—those college professors (those whose goal was to teach instead of just publish),

—those text authors (those who had something to say instead of just re-hashing the same old garbage),

—those fellow consultants (those who cared for their clients instead of just caring for their clients next commissions),

—those progressive clients (those who weren't afraid of a fresh concept or approach and who had the courage to pioneer new territories),

—a loving (and loved) wife who takes great interest in all facets of living and life,

—a father who was a success in business and a success as a man,

—a government (far from perfect—even far from good) which allows characters like me to challenge its inefficiencies without jailing me.

To these I want to give full credit and say, "Thanks."

Subject Index

Page numbers followed by *t* indicate information found in tables; page numbers followed by *n* indicate information in notes.

Cameo Index